'Lovelock's place as an inventor and scie
autobiography... Almost anyone with a
this book'
Nature

'Lovelock is among the most important contributors to the Western scientific tradition in the last hundred years ... this is a great read if you want to understand the man and the genesis of his work'
The Ecologist

'there are few men, if any, who have had a greater influence on our view of the environment and of the nature of the earth as a whole. His life is atypical of scientists and all the more fascinating for that.'
Lewis Wolpert, *Literary Review*

'not only full of fascinating science but details an intriguing life, and it offers a compassionate (as well as a passionate) view of the relationship between science and society'
John Gribbin, *Books of the Year, The Independent*

'a warm personal testimony of this radical world-class scientist who has provided vital inspiration for the entire Green movement. It offers a stimulating and fascinating insight into Dr Lovelock's life as an independent scientist—a threatened species in these days of the corporate commissioning of science.'
Positive News

'This book is a jaunty and insightful journey into the mind of an extraordinary man ... Highly recommended'
Living Lightly

'If science is replacing religion, then Lovelock is a modern day prophet'
Dazed

'He is to science what Gandhi was to politics. And his central notion, that the planet behaves as a living organism, is as radical, profound, and far-reaching in its impact as any of Gandhi's ideas'
Fred Pearce, *New Scientist*

'His "Gaia hypothesis" is certainly heroic, with all the illusion-busting potential of Galileo's or Einstein's theories.'
Jonathan Porritt, *The Independent*

'a richly rewarding autobiography... *Homage to Gaia* is both a valuable companion to Lovelock's enduring Gaia books and a book that anyone interested in science must read'
The Times Higher

'The book crackles with the creative energy of the man'
The Times

'There is much more than science in this book ... This is ultimately an uplifting book about the way life ought to be, both at a personal and global level, and a strong contender for science book of the year'
The Sunday Times

'an entertaining and inspirational book'
The Scotsman

'His new book is a hymn to science, and to Gaia and to the other makers of his great idea, and to the forces that made him choose to swim upstream, to stay independent, to be free to follow his nose.'
Tim Radford, *The Guardian*

'His memoirs combine fascinating recollections of what science was like in its mid-20th century heyday with a life's worth of practical and moral lessons on how a scientist should think and act.'
The Economist

Homage to Gaia

James Lovelock is an independent scientist, inventor, author, and has been an Honorary Visiting Fellow of Green College, University of Oxford, since 1994. He was elected a Fellow of the Royal Society in 1974 and in 1975 received the Tswett Medal for Chromatography. In 1988 he was a recipient of the Norbert Gerbier Prize of the World Meteorological Organization, and in 1990 was awarded the first Amsterdam Prize for the Environment by the Royal Netherlands Academy of Arts and Sciences. Further awards include the Nonino Prize and the Volvo Environment Prize in 1996, and Japan's Blue Planet Prize in 1997. He was awarded a CBE in 1990 by Her Majesty the Queen. He lives in Devon with his second wife, Sandy, and his son John.

Homage to Gaia

The Life of an Independent Scientist

James Lovelock

OXFORD
UNIVERSITY PRESS

OXFORD

UNIVERSITY PRESS

Great Clarendon Street, Oxford OX2 6DP

Oxford University Press is a department of the University of Oxford.
It furthers the University's objective of excellence in research, scholarship,
and education by publishing worldwide in

Oxford New York

Athens Auckland Bangkok Bogotá Buenos Aires Cape Town
Chennai Dar es Salaam Delhi Florence Hong Kong Istanbul
Karachi Kolkata Kuala Lumpur Madrid Melbourne Mexico City Mumbai
Nairobi Paris São Paulo Singapore Taipei Tokyo Toronto Warsaw
with associated companies in Berlin Ibadan

Oxford is a registered trade mark of Oxford University Press
in the UK and in certain other countries

Published in the United States
by Oxford University Press Inc., New York

British Library Cataloguing in Publication Data
Data available

Library of Congress Cataloging in Publication Data
Data available

ISBN 019–860429–7

1 3 5 7 9 10 8 6 4 2

Typeset in Kolam Information Services Pvt. Ltd., Pondicherry, India
Printed in Great Britain by
Cox & Wyman Ltd, Reading, Berks

I dedicate this book to my beloved wife Sandy

Contents

Preface and Acknowledgements   xi

List of Plates and Figure   xxi

List of Abbreviations   xxiii

Introduction   1

1.	Childhood	7
2.	The Long Apprenticeship	39
3.	Twenty Years of Medical Research	69
	The Voyage on *HMS Vengeance* in 1949	91
4.	The Mill Hill Institute	105
	The Year in Boston	116
	My Last Years at the Mill Hill Institute	125
5.	The First Steps to Independence at Houston, Texas	147
6.	The Independent Practice of Science	155
	Shell	161
	The Security Services	169
	Hewlett Packard	180
	Inventions	186
7.	The ECD	191
8.	The Ozone War	203
	The Voyage of the *Shackleton* in 1971–2	208
	The Voyage of the *Meteor* in 1973	229
9.	The Quest for Gaia	241

CONTENTS

10.	The Practical Side of Independent Science	281
	Computers	291
	The Royal Society	295
	The Marine Biological Association	298
	Living in Ireland	303
	Coombe Mill	314
11.	Building Your Own Bypass	327
12.	Three Score Years and Ten and then the Fun Begins	371
13.	Epilogue	409
Index		421

Preface and Acknowledgements

The story of Gaia is an unfolding drama, and my acknowledgements to those who participated in it are like a cast of characters at the beginning of a play. There were many actors in this thirty-five-year show, heroes and villains, and I have listed them in the order of their appearance. I thank them for their proper criticism, support, and encouragement during the many rehearsals of the Gaia story as it went from a mere notion about detecting life on other planets to its debut as a theory in science.

Carl Sagan, Dian Hitchcock, and Louis Kaplan—all then at JPL (the Jet Propulsion Laboratory)—were the first to listen and seem interested in my idea that somehow life at the Earth's surface regulated the chemistry of the atmosphere. I am so grateful that they did not pour scorn on my ideas. Peter Fellgett was the first scientist in the UK to hear me, and he responded with agreement tempered by thoughtful criticism. Over the years, he and his family became close friends, and he has been a staunch supporter throughout the long period when Gaia was unpopular with scientists. Norman Horowitz, Professor of Biology at the California Institute of Technology, disagreed with me over Gaia but was a friend and his criticism was fair. I owe a special debt to my neighbour in Bowerchalke, the novelist William Golding. What luck to have my theory named in 1967 by so competent a wordsmith and Nobel Laureate.

Most of all I acknowledge my friend Lynn Margulis, who joined me in the development of Gaia in 1971. She put biological flesh on the bare bones of my physical chemistry. She has courageously supported Gaia in spite of hostility from parts of the United States scientific community—that sometimes threatened her own standing as a biologist.

From 1967 onwards, James Lodge has given me wholehearted support and encouragement. I acknowledge especially the introduction he gave me to the scientists of NCAR (National Centre for Atmospheric Research) and the opportunity to discuss with them Gaian aspects of the atmosphere. This was crucial in the learning phases.

The worst thing that can happen to a new theory is for it to be ignored. I therefore acknowledge the robust, even scathing, criticisms from Ford Doolittle, the microbiologist from Halifax, Nova Scotia, and from Richard Dawkins of Oxford. They hurt at the time—1979 to 1982—but they made me think and tighten what had been a loose hypothesis into a firm theory. Much friendlier was the constructive but firm criticism from the eminent geochemist Professor HD Holland of Harvard University. We have sustained a warm respect for each other and he was an outstanding presence at our meetings in Oxford. In no way do I cast these critics as villains; they are open in their dislike of Gaia.

Professors Christian Jünge and Bert Bolin were influential in Gaia's development by inviting me to present the first paper on Gaia at an open scientific meeting in Mainz, Germany. Bert Bolin, through his connections with the Swedish journal, *Tellus*, invited me to submit the first joint paper with Lynn Margulis for publication. It appeared in *Tellus* in 1973 and I acknowledge the splendid open-mindedness of that journal, which continued to publish Gaia papers throughout the time it was unacceptable in most mainstream science journals.

Professor Peter Liss, of the University of East Anglia, was the first to recognize the significance of my measurements of dimethyl sulphide (DMS) and other gases in the Atlantic Ocean: his paper on the flux of DMS was one of the key papers in Gaian research. Professor Andrew Watson, now of the University of East Anglia, joined me as a Ph.D. student in 1976 and did the first experiments that showed the relationship between atmospheric oxygen abundance and the probability of fire. This was an essential step in the understanding of the regulation of atmospheric oxygen. Andrew has become a friend and a critical supporter of Gaia.

Professor Robert Garrels of St Petersburg University in Florida was the first of the geological community to give wholehearted support to Gaian ideas, and continued to do so until, sadly, he died in 1988. He and his wife Cynthia were warm friends. Lord Rothschild was one of the few biologists to accept Gaia in the early days of the 1960s and 1970s, and he gave from his position as co-ordinator at Shell Research Limited, tangible support. Sidney Epton, also of Shell Research, wrote with me a landmark paper in 1975 in *New Scientist*, entitled 'The Quest for Gaia'. It was this paper that stirred publishers to invite the writing of my first book.

Another scientist who gave moral as well as practical support was Lester Machta, Head of the Air Resources Laboratory of NOAA (National Oceanic and Atmospheric Administration), and to him and his wife Phyllis I shall always be grateful. Tony Broderick, who became the Administrator of the Federal Aviation Administration, FAA, was another senior figure who warmed to my ideas about the Earth during the 1970s and 1980s.

From its introduction in 1968, a small group of scientists, distributed around the world, found time, but not money, to develop Gaia theory. Among them were Greg Hinkle, one of Lynn Margulis's students, Andrew Watson, Peter Liss, and Mike Whitfield. Although not about the Earth as a system, Eugene Odum's writing and research on ecosystems took the same top-down view and suffered the same misunderstanding by conventionally minded biologists. I salute him as our closest predecessor.

Professors Robert Charlson and Ann Henderson-Sellers argued that Gaia was a valid topic of science, against the strong tide of contrary opinion. Bob Charlson was the lead figure of the famous *Nature* article of 1987, linking algae, dimethyl sulphide, clouds, and climate. He, Andi Andreae, and Stephen Warren did much to make Gaia respectable, and Bob has remained a staunch supporter ever since. Professor Chris Rapley, during his presidency of the International Geosphere Biosphere Programme, and directorship of the British Antarctic Survey, has done much to make Gaia visible. The climatologists Peter Cox and Richard Betts, of the Hadley Centre, have lent their support, as have Professor Brian Hoskins and Paul Valdes and Bruce Sellwood, all of Reading University. The Open University was wonderfully supportive when Gaia was unpopular in science. I am especially grateful to Professor Robert Spicer for his paleobotany that did much to make environments of the geological past come alive. Professors Dee Edwards and David Williams and Peter Francis of the Open University gave unstinted support.

In the USA the seeds of Gaia found a harsher climate. For many years, Lynn Margulis, Bob Garrels, and Robert Charlson were alone in writing and working on Gaia. It was not until 1989 that David Schwartzman and Tyler Volk wrote their important paper on rock weathering and confirmed it as a Gaian mechanism. Lee Kump and Lee Klinger, in the last ten years or so, have established a presence in Gaian research, but it has not been easy for them against the disapproval of their scientific community. The same was true for Tyler Volk as is shown by the guarded Gaian support in his book *Gaia's Body*. I acknowledge their staunch support and welcome the book *The Earth System* by Lee Kump, James Kasting, and Robert Crane. Connie Barlow's books *From Gaia to the Selfish Gene* and *Green Space, Green Time* provide, through different eyes from mine, a historical account of Gaia's evolution. Larry Joseph's warm-hearted book *Gaia: The Growth of an Idea* tells the history of Gaia and the personalities of the actors.

The first scientists to establish a fully funded programme of Gaia research were John Schellnhuber and his colleagues at the Potsdam Institute in Germany. They have constructed the most detailed and impressive models of a Gaian world and confirmed its inherent robustness. Their book, *Earth System Analysis*, is the first professional application of Gaia theory.

Stephen Schneider and Penelope Boston, although critical, felt that Gaia should be treated as a scientific topic, and organized the meeting at San Diego in March 1988. Professor Peter Westbroek, of the University of Leiden, hosted the meeting on the Island of Walcheren where the first Daisyworld paper was presented. Peter has kept the idea alive on continental Europe ever since. In Catalonia Professor Ricardo Guerrero has worked and written on Gaian topics and is a friend.

Japan has done much to encourage the development of Gaia. Walter Shearer of the United Nations University (UNU) in Tokyo first invited me there in 1982. That unusual university supported work and meetings on Gaia in the bad years of the 1980s, and we tried, sadly without success, to build a generation of affordable scientific instruments for the developing world. Through Fred Myers of the UNU, we first met Hideo Itokawa and his wife Ann in September 1992, and so established a bond of friendship with Japan. Hideo was a staunch supporter and translated my third Gaia book *The Practical Science of Planetary Medicine* into Japanese. The Japanese scientist

Shigeru Moriyama introduced Gaian science to Japan, and is a familiar figure at our Oxford meetings. Since April 1993 Yumi Akimoto, President of Mitsubishi Materials Corporation, has continued to support the idea of Gaia. He and his wife Sadako have become our friends. A more complete account of our experiences in Japan is given in Chapter 12.

The greater part of Gaian research, and all of it before 1982, was unfunded. The first monetary support came from the Leverhulme Foundation. On the advice of Sir Eric Denton, then Director of the Marine Biological Association's laboratory in Plymouth, they generously funded my Gaia research during 1982, when I was too ill to fund myself. During the eight years until the 1990s, the only funds for research came from my own pocket, excepting only the aid given by the Commonwealth Fund towards the writing of my second book, *The Ages of Gaia*, and I am most grateful. The Schweisfurth-Stiftung, through their representative Franz-Theo Gottwald, supported the writing of my third book *The Practical Science of Planetary Medicine*.

The concept of Gaia is protean and attracts interest among philosophers, theologians, and political leaders, as well as scientists. Along with the interest first shown by William Golding in the early days of the 1960s, I acknowledge the friendship and encouragement I received from Stewart Brand, editor of *Co-Evolution Quarterly*. The historian William Thompson did me great honour by inviting me to become a member of that select society, the Lindisfarne Fellowship. To him and to the Fellowship, now led by the physicist, Arthur Zajonc, I give my thanks. More recently the distinguished English philosopher, Mary Midgley, has argued for Gaia in the clear and concise way that only the best philosophers can.

I have never been wholly on the side of environmentalism, feeling that its concern was almost always about people and not about the Earth. Environmentalists seemed to me blind to the fact that if we fail to care for the Earth, people and civilization will be among the first to suffer. But the environmentalists Jonathon Porritt and Teddy Goldsmith have my deep respect and friendship, and we agree on much more than we differ.

If it should turn out that Gaia is truly important in our lives and our relationship with the Earth then future historians will see Sir Crispin Tickell as a figure like his predecessor TH Huxley, someone who established a new way of thought in the minds of the elite. They will also see that the powerful figure of Hideo Itokawa in Japan fulfilled the same service there. Senior politicians of all parties have been interested in Gaia, none perhaps so positively as Margaret Thatcher during her premiership. I acknowledge the interest and encouragement I have received from the powerful.

I expected in the beginning that theologians and the churches would be hostile, but have been happily surprised to have their curiosity. I would like especially to acknowledge the long and fulfilling friendship of Hugh Montefiore, who was, when we first met, Bishop of Birmingham. He has been, since 1989, President of the Gaia charity. I have found theologians wonderfully open in their discussion on Gaia, especially Anne Primavesi and Laurent Leduc.

I would like to thank the journalists, TV and radio interviewers, and producers—all of who gave Gaia a fair hearing at a time when the scientific establishment was disdainful. Among them, I acknowledge especially John Groom for his *Horizon* programme on BBC in 1985, and Sue Lawley for the BBC programme, *Desert Island Discs*. The Australian producer, Julian Russell's programme *The Man who named the World* and David Jackson's joint BBC Open University programme on Daisyworld were splendid. Among the articles written on Gaia, none have been so thoughtful and balanced as those by Oliver Morton in *The Economist* in 1990 and in *Discover* in 1999. For the warmth of their appreciation, I am most grateful to Fred Pearce's articles in *New Scientist* and the understanding of Gaia expressed in the books and articles by Robert Matthews, John Gribbin, and Jonathan Weiner.

The strongest objection to Gaia came from neo-Darwinist scientists, and I was moved when Stephan Harding, an Oxford biologist, joined me in Gaia research in 1994; he is now a close friend. I had always felt that Gaia needed approval from eminent neo-Darwinists before it would be taken seriously. I am therefore deeply grateful to John Maynard Smith and William Hamilton for having the courage and generosity to discuss Gaia seriously as a scientific topic.

The Gaia story is a long-running show and provides an opportunity for new leading actors. The most prominent of these today is Tim Lenton, whose quiet competence makes his recent appearance from behind the props so welcome. Tim, as my principal successor, will have to write the plot as well as act the science.

The Gaia meetings in Oxford in 1994 and 1996 were supported by the Department of the Environment through Mr. Derek Osborn, by the Ecological Foundation through Mr. Teddy Goldsmith and by Shell Research Limited through Mr. Frank Briffa. The larger part of the funding came from a Norwegian gentleman, Knut Kloster. Soon after we met him in 1991, he gave Gaia a major opportunity for decent development as a unifying theory. Therefore, my acknowledgement to him is a story in itself but it concludes my cast of characters.

As we were preparing to return home from a visit to New York, the World City Corporation, a shipping company whose chairman was Knut Kloster, invited me to travel to Port Canaveral in Florida to give a short speech to send off a Viking ship called *Gaia*. The ship had already sailed the Atlantic from Norway, following the route taken by Eric the Red, the Norseman who had pioneered Atlantic travel when they settled Greenland, and perhaps North America. *Gaia* was a traditional Viking ship with a single square sail. The ship's name and voyage had the blessing of two Scandinavian leaders: the President of Iceland, Vigdis Finnbogadottir, and the Prime Minister of Norway, Gro Brundtland.

The ship was en route to Rio de Janeiro for the United Nations environmental conference of 1991. The World City Corporation did us proud. Sandy and I were booked into a hotel in Orlando, where we renewed acquaintance with John Rogers and Stephanie Gallagher of the Corporation. We were given time to recover from our journey and we arranged to meet for breakfast. Here, to our delight, we met the astronaut Jim Lovell and his wife. We were to be the two speakers at the launch. At Port Canaveral we wandered over to the quay where *Gaia* was berthed, went aboard, and talked with the crew. It was a small ship and, knowing how rough is the North Atlantic, I marvelled at her seaworthiness. The captain told us how easy it was to use the single, large square sail. How apposite it was to speak for this small ship *Gaia* on its journey from Cape Canaveral. Across the marshes from the port, the huge launch towers of the space vehicles were visible. A proud nostalgia filled my mind as I prepared to speak. Sixteen years back, those towers had held the giant launch vehicles which lifted the Viking mission to Mars. That mission confirmed the Gaian prediction—made long before the journey—that Mars was lifeless. The spacecraft of that mission carried the two Viking landers to Mars and left them there on the corrosive regolith of that most inhospitable planet. In the landers were essential components. These I had designed when working at the Jet Propulsion Labs.

My speech, and that of my companion on the platform, Jim Lovell, was brief, and then we watched the small vessel set sail for Rio, taking with it its message of a living Earth. Afterwards, it was fulfilling to talk with Jim Lovell about his almost ill-fated expedition, Apollo 13, the spacecraft that suffered a fuel-cell explosion on its way to the moon, a disaster that left them with barely enough power to bring it home. They had no heating, so that the interior temperature sunk at times to $-40°$ C. Their ordeal was the subject of a recent film, but no film could have equalled Jim Lovell's personal account. He confirmed that he and other astronauts shared a common feeling about the Earth. Their view of it from space led them to see the planet itself as their home. Home was not the nation, or the town, or the street, or their house. Home was the whole planet. He expressed it graphically by holding out his thumb at arm's length and saying, 'That small area of my thumbnail covered the Earth completely when we were in the moon's orbit; I knew then that home was that small blue ball.' I felt a deep sense of gratitude to Knut Kloster for having brought us here to this historic place and for this important event.

Next morning we had breakfast with him. He was what my mental model of a Viking told me he should be. He thanked me for my part and said, 'Now what can I do for you?' I have never been much good at fund-raising and, although we run a charity, Gaia, much of the money that goes into it we put in from our own pockets. Whenever I meet a wealthy organization or person there never seems to be a proper moment during which to broach the topic of support, but here, unexpectedly, Knut asked 'What can I do for you?' I said, 'We have a charity, Gaia.' Knut broke in at once and said, 'To me, charity is a dirty word. What can I do for *you*?' I replied, 'Give me a contract to work to make Gaia scientifically acceptable. I can't promise success but I would guess that a three-year contract at £25,000 per year would go far to achieve this objective.' And he did.

We might have taken Knut's gift as a grant of funds for salaries and equipment to do research on Gaia full time. However, it did not work out that way. Somehow, when the first cheque arrived we realized that it was like the gift of talents described in the New Testament. The vineyard owner gives to his servants varying numbers of talents and then comes back a year later to see what they have made of them. It seemed quite inappropriate to use Knut's gift in the same way as a grant. We were accountable for our use of it, and somehow we must use it to make the concept of Gaia grow. Sandy and I decided that the best way to achieve his, and our, objective of achieving scientific credibility for Gaia was to organize and then hold one or more special kinds of scientific meeting in a recognized scientific venue. And this is how we spent his gift.

I am indebted to Sir John Cornforth and Mr John Lane for their thoughtful criticisms of the first edition of this book.

List of Plates and Figure

1 James Lovelock in 1924

2 My father, Tom Lovelock, in 1893

3 The wedding of Tom Lovelock and Nell March, 1914

4 The March family at Deal, Kent, 1913

5 The National Institute for Medical Research, Holly Hill, Hampstead

6 James Lovelock, Owen Lidwell, and R. B. Bourdillon, 1943

7 A bullock with radio telemetering

8 *HMS Vengeance* in Arctic waters

9 Audrey Smith, James Lovelock, and Leo McKern at the rehearsals of *The Critical Point* by Lorna Frazer

10 The experimental biology lab at the Mill Hill Institute

11 The apparatus for CFC measurements aboard the *RV Shackleton*

12 The *RV Shackleton*

13 The Electron Capture Detector

14 Helen Lovelock at Bowerchalke, 1968

15 Andrew Lovelock at Bowerchalke, 1968

16 Christine and Jane Lovelock at Harvard Hospital, 1947

17 John Lovelock at Bowerchalke, 1960

18 The Bowerchalke laboratory, 1972

19 The Coombe Mill laboratory, 1985

20 James Lovelock, Lynn Margulis, and Ricardo Guerrero

21 Robert Charlson, Jim Lovelock, Andi Andreae, and Steve Warren

22 James Lovelock and Hideo Itokawa

23 James Lovelock and Tim Lenton

24 Robert Garrels and James Lovelock at Coombe Mill

25 Jim and Sandy at Portland Road, 1988

26 Sandy at Altarnun, 1999

Fig. 1 A chromatogram to illustrate the sensitivity of the ECD

List of Abbreviations

ALE	Atmospheric Long-range Experiments
CFC	chlorofluorocarbon
CMS	Chemical Manufacturers' Association
CO	carbon monoxide/conscientious objector
CCN	cloud condensation nuclei
DMS	dimethyl sulphide
ECD	Electron Capture Detector
ECG	Electrocardiogram
FAA	Federal Aviation Authority
GC	gas chromatograph
HP	Hewlett Packard
IMER	Institute for Marine Environmental Research
JPL	Jet Propulsion Laboratory
MBA	Marine Biological Association
MRC	Medical Research Council
NASA	National Aeronautical and Space Administration
NCAR	National Centre for Atmospheric Research
NERC	Natural Environment Research Council
NIH	National Institute for Health (US)
NIMR	National Institute for Medical Research
NOAA	National Oceanic and Atmospheric Administration
PCB	polychlorinated biphenyl
UNU	United Nations University

Introduction

We were enjoying our tea break in a warm cedar-panelled room with a view down the valley to the next village, Broadchalke. Suddenly and rudely as ever, the telephone rang its strident, insistent call. No one expected Helen, my first wife, to answer it—multiple sclerosis had already disabled her. I hate telephones and always wait for someone else to pick them up. Peggy Coombs—the lady from the village who helped Helen, and who came from the Welsh valleys where they are properly outspoken—burst out, 'Does no one in this house answer the phone?' and dashed to still its clamour. 'Hello. What do you want?' asked Peggy informatively. 'I want to speak to Dr Lovelock,' said the disembodied voice. Peggy replied disdainfully, 'He's not a proper doctor but I'll get him for you.' The caller was a professor from a distant university who wanted me to lecture on the possibility of life on Mars. For once, thanks to Peggy, I had had time to prepare my mind and say no.

Peggy was right. I am not a proper doctor. To her and to most of us, a proper doctor is one qualified in medicine. Someone who treats the sick and who she regards with the respect earlier generations gave to the priest. A DSc was not enough to justify the title 'Doctor'. More than this, my solitary practice in Bowerchalke spread across the sciences ranging from Astronomy to Zoology. How could anyone so divided be a proper doctor of science? For a moment, my self-doubting nature made me think of other impostor doctors like the Vicar of Unworthy in Devon, the Reverend Fiddle, DD.

When I set my heart towards independent science, I had no intention whatever of becoming a professional chemist and consultant.

That is a good and proper way of life but it was not for me. Science was and is my passion and I wanted to be free to do it unfettered by direction from anyone, not even by the mild constraints of a university department or an institute of science. Any artist or novelist would understand—some of us do not produce their best when directed. We expect the artist, the novelist and the composer to lead solitary lives, often working at home. While a few of these creative individuals exist in institutions or universities, the idea of a majority of established novelists or painters working at the 'National Institute for Painting and Fine Art' or a university 'Department of Creative Composition' seems mildly amusing. By contrast, alarm greets the idea of a creative scientist working at home. A lone scientist is as unusual as a solitary termite and regarded as irresponsible or worse.

In the early 1970s, *New Scientist* published a review of a book on Darwin's life. The reviewer claimed the book confirmed his view that our most distinguished biologist was insane. He argued that anyone with Darwin's reputation who chose to bury himself in a country village instead of enjoying the intellectual stimulation Cambridge offered must be mad. As I see it, the reviewer, not Darwin, was the lunatic.

I want to tell you in this book why I 'buried myself' in the country village of Bowerchalke. I worked happily there until 1977, when sadly the agribusiness revolution socially cleansed the village. My escape was to West Devon and to a house surrounded by trees and almost a mile from its nearest neighbour. I want to show that the solitary practice of science in a country village, or even a remote house, is both pleasant and productive.

Soon after starting work in Bowerchalke, chance favoured me with a view of the Earth from space and I saw it as the stunningly beautiful anomaly of the solar system—a planet that was palpably different from its dead and deserted siblings, Mars and Venus. I saw Earth as much more than just a ball of rock moistened by the oceans, or a spaceship put there by a beneficent God just for the use of humankind. I saw it as a planet that has always, since its origins nearly four billion years ago, kept itself a fit home for the life that happened upon it and I thought that it did so by homeostasis, the wisdom of the body, just as you and I keep our temperature and chemistry constant. In this view the spontaneous evolution of life did more than make Darwin's world: it started a joint project with the evolving Earth itself. Life does more than adapt to the earth; it changes it, and evolution is a tight-coupled dance with life and the material environment as part-ners, and from the dance emerges the entity Gaia. This book is as much about Gaia as it is about me. That part which is about me is to set the scene for the birth of what is still a revolutionary theory. I doubt if the scientific establishment would have allowed a proper doctor to work on so unfashionable a topic and one with a name that many scientists regard as politically incorrect.

The naming of things is important. Our deepest thoughts are unconscious and we need metaphors and similes to translate them into something that we, as well as the rest of humankind, can under-stand. For reasons that I never understood, many scientists dislike Gaia as a name; prominent among them is the eminent biologist, John Maynard Smith. He made clear when he said of Gaia, 'What an awful name to call a theory', that it was the name, the metaphor, more than the science that caused his disapproval. He was, like most scientists, well aware of the power of metaphor. William Hamilton's metaphors of selfish and spiteful genes have served wonderfully to make his science comprehensible, but let us never forget that the powerful metaphor of Gaia was the gift of a great novelist. I would remind those who criticize the name Gaia that they are doing battle with William Golding, who first coined it. We should not lightly turn aside from the name Gaia because of pedantic objection. Why do scientists, who now accept Gaia as a theory that they can try to falsify, continue to object to the name itself? Surely, it cannot be metaphor envy. Perhaps it is something deeper, a rejection by reductionist scientists of anything that smells of holism, anything that implies that the whole may be more than the sum of its parts. I see the battle between Gaia and the selfish gene as part of an outdated and pointless war between holists and reductionists. In a sensible world, we need them both.

I gladly accepted William Golding's choice of the name Gaia for my theory of the Earth and I have devoted all my working life, since completing my apprenticeship, to the furtherance of Gaia theory. It has been an exciting but bruising battle and this book tells both the story of Gaia and tries to explain how my life as a scientist led me to it. I take comfort in the fact that Gaia theory is now widely accepted by scientists in disciplines ranging from astrophysics to microbiology, they only reject the name Gaia, not the theory itself. Unfortunately, science is divided into a myriad of facets like the multi-lensed eye of a fly and through each separate lens peers a professor who thinks that his view alone is true. The danger now is that each of these fragmented faculties who once spurned Gaia will now claim the theory as their own. We must not stand aside and let these specialists highjack the unifying concept of Gaia.

Gaia and environmentalism have never had an easy relationship. I seem to view environmental politics much as George Orwell did the socialism of his time. My heart is with the environmentalists but I see their good intentions thwarted by their failure to see that human rights alone are not enough. If, in caring for people, we fail to care for other forms of life on Earth then our civilization and we will suffer. I wonder if in the 21st century, when the grim effects of global warming become apparent, we will regret the humanist bias that led us to continue to burn fossil fuel and plunder the natural world for food. Is our distrust of nuclear power and genetically modified food soundly based? I share Patrick Moore's disenchantment with environmentalism. He was a founder of Greenpeace, but like me has an Orwellian view of the environment lobbies as they are today.

Some who read this book might think it old fashioned, and if they do, I ask them to note that I was born in 1919, when English society was still conditioned by the code of the gentleman, a culture which valued good manners, playing by the rules, admiring the good loser and above all taking full responsibility for mistakes. In certain ways, it resembled the Samurai code of another island nation. I grew up believing in it and still do but recognize now when a young woman offers me her seat on the Underground that I am no longer with it. I acknowledge the debt I owe to the United States of America for launching me on my quest for Gaia and for sustaining me throughout my independence. Now with Sandy, my American wife, to accompany me, I no longer feel, when in the United States, a mere visiting alien. If at times in this book, I am critical of American institutions, it does not come from the spite or envy of an outsider but is the concern of one member of an American family. I am critical also of academia and share the author Robert Conquest's view, expressed in his book *Reflections on a Ravaged Century*, that a surprising number of midlife academics seem selected for dogma. He was thinking of politics, but I think it applies to science also.

Few are privately wealthy enough to develop a new theory of science and support a family from their own resources. When we started in Bowerchalke, my first wife Helen and I were less than rich; we had our parents to support as well as our children. Like most young families, we were heavily mortgaged and, like an intending artist, I knew that to make a start would not be easy. No matter how good was my science, no one would sponsor it until the science critics had approved. Like art critics, their first reactions are often cautious or negative.

The answer was to do what the artist does: expect no sale for my masterpieces but live by selling 'potboilers'. My potboilers were small research contracts and consultancies. These provided an ample income without needing more than a small proportion of my time. I had hoped that the sale of inventions would pay my bills but these turned out to be an unreliable source of income.

Strangely, wealth threatens the would-be independent as much as poverty. It would have been easy for me at several stages in my independence to have built and marketed a successful product. In the 1960s, I built a prototype leak detector that was cheaper, simpler, and over a thousand times more sensitive than those that were then on the market. I could have joined with an engineer and a marketeer to form a company to make and sell it. I do not regret parting with that chance of wealth. Becoming an entrepreneur is a full-time job. Building, testing and selling a well-made product is a right and proper way of life. It provides employment, brings wealth to our country, and is a source of pride, but it was not what I wanted. How could I devote my time to science if I was concerned about the future and the welfare of my employees and my company?

As a scientist, I have been an explorer looking for new worlds, not a harvester from safe and productive fields, and life at the frontier has shown me that there are no certainties and that dogma is usually wrong. I now recognize that with each discovery the extent of the unknown grows larger, not smaller. The discoveries I have made came mostly from doubting conventional wisdom, and I would advise any young scientist looking for a new and fresh topic to research to seek the flaw in anything claimed by the orthodox to be certain. There are several examples of the use of this approach in this book. The most important was to challenge the biological dogma that organisms simply adapt to their environment. It turned out that just as we cannot observe an atom without changing its state, so neither can we, or any living thing, evolve without changing the state of the Earth. This is the essence of Gaia.

I hope that I can convince you that the independent scientist has a wonderfully interesting and rewarding life—every bit as good as that of the artist or composer, and may even be as worthwhile. I doubt if the discovery of CFCs in the atmosphere, or the extraordinary link between the microscopic algae of the oceans and the clouds above them and, most of all, the idea that the Earth regulates its climate and composition—the Gaia theory—would have come as quickly had I stayed in employment or become an entrepreneur. Gaia has been my inspiration since it first came into my mind in September 1965. Theories in science are valued by the success of investigations and experiments they inspire; by this measure, Gaia has been fruitful. Thousands of scientists owe their employment and their grant funds to my work as an independent scientist and I include among them those who spend their time trying to disprove Gaia theory.

The four chapters that follow are about my childhood and my experiences as an apprentice practitioner of science. Then, in Chapters 5 and 6 I explain how I became an independent scientist, how I do it, and about the customers who provide support. In Chapters 7 to 9 I try to show how serious science can be done from a home laboratory and paid for from the profits of the practice. Chapter 9 is about the quest for Gaia from its start in the 1960s until the writing of this book. In Chapter 10 I explain the practical details of a life spent as an independent scientist. My more recent personal history follows in Chapters 11 and 12, and in the Epilogue, I offer Gaia as a way of life for agnostics.

Let me start by telling you about my childhood and the events that shaped my evolution as an independent scientist.

1

Childhood

The March family, that is to say, my mother's relatives, grew up in east London, north of the Thames. My grandmother was a Chatterton and, according to the family, she was a descendant of the notable Victorian, Daniel Chatterton; how true is this claim I do not know, only that a photograph of him was in the family collection, now sadly gone. I loved my grandmother dearly and she was, for all emotional and practical purposes, the mother figure of my childhood. My true mother was as confused by women's issues and their struggle for recognition as are many women today. I think that I was an unwanted child, an accident of the celebration of armistice night on 11 November, 1918. My mother then had a responsible and fulfilling job as personal secretary to what we would now call the CEO of Middlesex County Council. It stretched her very capable mind and gave her status far beyond the working-class expectations of her childhood. She had a powerful intellect, but with little chance to reach her potential, she was bitter and resentful. As the eldest of a large family, she had, when a child, to take full responsibility for her younger siblings. The bitterest blow for her came when she won a rare scholarship from her primary school in Islington to a grammar school. She could not take it because the family needed her earning power at thirteen to survive. Instead of an enlightened education that was, she thought, her due, she spent her days in a pickle factory sticking labels on the jars. She graduated to another menial job in the Middlesex County Council, but her intelligence liberated her for a brief period in the First World War, when the male employees went to feed that vast human mincing machine of the trenches.

Grandfather March was a skilled craftsman, a bookbinder, so skilled indeed that Winchester Cathedral chose to exhibit one of the books he bound. The family came from somewhere near Dagenham in Essex. I often wondered if they were Jewish: my great-grandmother's name was King and March could have once been Marx. They had many Jewish characteristics, including a love of music and an unnatural skill at card games. Great-grandfather March was a sergeant in the mounted police, hardly a Jewish occupation, but maybe things were different then. The family fortunes improved when my grandfather took a job with the Cockerel Press at Ewell in Surrey. The village of Ewell was then at the borders of the London conurbation and effectively in the countryside. Here my mother, who commuted to work by train, met my father, who travelled on the same train to the South Metropolitan Gasworks at Vauxhall. They fell into a long, intense, but unrequited love. My mother told how they walked and sat in Nonsuch Park at Ewell and held hands; that was the limit of their physical contact. My father was then in his mid-30s but married and with two children. His wife had been committed to a lunatic asylum after the birth of their second child when she developed a malign post-partum depression. In the early 20th century, extra marital liaisons met with stern disapproval, even among the rich. In the lower classes, there was an overwhelming sanctimonious righteousness about adultery, whatever the circumstances; it was a sin, and sins were worse than crimes. The cruel dogma of those times kept my father celibate but he was fortunate to have my Grandmother March's approval and the unfulfilled relationship between my mother and father continued until 1914, when his first wife died and they were able to marry.

My father was too old by then, about his mid-40s, either to be a volunteer or later a conscript for the war and with both of them working and living in a flat in Mandalay Road, Clapham, they had a happy start to their marriage. My father had a natural appreciation of the beauty of artefacts, as well as of natural things, and he developed an intense feeling for paintings. My mother had a passion for classical music. Their life during the First World War in London must have been idyllic, for they were in love and fulfilled by all that that great city had to offer. There was negligible bombing in the first war so that life in London went on more or less as usual, except for food and material shortages. I have no idea what method of contraception they used. They never talked on such intimate subjects, not even years later. I only know that whatever it was, it failed in November 1918. The last thing my mother wanted then was a child. I was born close to 2 pm in the afternoon of July 26, 1919, during a thunderstorm and at my grandmother's house in Letchworth Garden City, which is about 30 miles north of London. Pregnancy and the return of men from the war put an end to my mother's employment with the Middlesex County Council.

My mother and father then chose to take on a risky venture. They rented a shop on Brixton Hill and opened it as the Brixton Hill Galleries. Between the two wars, Brixton retained remnants of the wealthy suburb that it once was, and they hoped and believed that it would stay wealthy enough to sustain a demand for paintings and other works of art, and that this would give them a start in the life of their choice. The shop was, in fact, in a flawed position for such an upmarket enterprise. On the right-hand side was a small post office and beyond that a huge junk shop. The owner, Mr Callaby, had an extensive collection of second-hand iron goods stretching right out across the wide pavement in front of the shop—tin baths, mangles with an iron frame and wooden rollers and boxes full of oddments. On the left of our shop was an engineering workshop, Venners, and next to this a vast Victorian pub, the Telegraph. Beyond the Telegraph was a noisome alley, dark and narrow, running between tall buildings and with one courtyard leading from it. Here families lived in one-room cold-water flats, under conditions of Victorian poverty. As a small boy, I often visited the Voysey family who lived in one of these flats. The son was my friend and the mother a cheerful kindly young woman. They seemed to have no possessions, no furniture apart from boxes, and they appeared to live on bread and dripping. What little they had they shared generously, and the mother was always curious about my doings and what I thought and how we lived. The alleyway led from Brixton Hill to New Park Road—a typical London street. There were small industrial premises, among them paint shops smelling strongly of organic solvents. Across the street were rows of once agricultural cottages with long gardens in front of them. Branching off were new streets of semi-detached suburban houses that developers had built. There was little or no traffic and it was a playground for the children and the street gangs of those times. By a curious coincidence, the shop was to be, in a few years, the home of the Liss family. I first met my friend Peter Liss, now a distinguished scientist and professor, at the University of East Anglia in the 1970s.

He was the first to realize the significance of my measurements taken aboard the *Shackleton* during its voyage to Antarctica in 1971.

To make a living selling paintings in such a neighbourhood was a heroic enterprise, and my mother's and father's entire energies went into it. My father wisely kept his job with the Gas Company, now as a collector of coins from gas meters. It says something of those days that Tom Lovelock, in spite of carrying a heavy leather bag full of coins through one of the rougher areas of London, was never mugged. He was not particularly burly, 5'9" tall, slim and bespectacled. Even so, would-be assailants would have had a tough time, for he was both brave and skilled as an amateur boxer. My parents had no time to care for a baby and were glad to leave me in the willing arms of my grandmother, Alice Emily March.

Grandmother March was a small plump cockney woman endowed with a surfeit of love. My great fortune was to have spent the first five important years in her care. Her children were by then all adults and astonishingly well married for a family of working-class girls. One of them, Kit, was married into the famous Leakey family, to Hugo, a cousin of Louis Leakey of Kenya fame. Her other daughter, Ann, was married to a New Zealand tobacco company executive, Howard Mason. Florrie was married to John Leete, who owned a prosperous tailor's shop in Hitchin, the nearby market town. Their only son, Frank, was away at a job in London.

William Golding once said to me that the education of a child requires above all things, love. So long as there is love, either given or obviously around, the child will grow in knowledge. He was then talking to me about the education of my youngest boy, John. Sadly, he was born with a mental handicap and Bill had suggested that we send him to a Rudolph Steiner school on just those grounds. Looking back on my own childhood, I now know how much I personally owe to those heavenly years of loving at Norton Croft.

Grandfather March must have done well in the latter part of his life, to judge by the house that we lived in at Letchworth. Norton Croft was a detached four-bedroom villa in the characteristic Letchworth Garden City architecture—echoes of William Morris. There was a large well-kept garden at the back and across the quiet road was an open piece of wood and heathland, Letchworth Common. The road itself, Icknield Way, was tree-lined with grass verges and ran along the route of an ancient trackway that linked the communities of Neolithic south-eastern England. For me as a child, the place and the house were a perfect habitat. Grandmother March—Nana—as we called her, bustled, cooked, hugged, laughed, and was the ideal mother. My real mother, Nell, her eldest daughter, was away in London trying, like the good feminist that she was, to prove herself in a man's world. It was a good bargain. Grandma was brimming with maternal love and here at last was the first grandchild on whom she could lavish it.

The six years I lived at Letchworth formed my life. They were the years of warmth, safety and health. They were years where, unfettered by schooling, I could let my curiosity run free. Without doubt, I was a spoilt child, and sometimes dangerously mischievous. When I was about four or five years old, Grandmother March enrolled me in a small nearby school. It did not last long. One unwise teacher showed the class the various poisonous plants that grew on the Common. She had bunches of hemlock, dog's mercury, and deadly nightshade. I was fascinated and curious to know what would happen if any of these were eaten. During the break, I seized a bunch of black deadly nightshade berries and tried to persuade the girls in another class that they were good to eat. Fortunately, a teacher came in and stopped my apprenticeship to the Borgias from going any further. They sent me home in disgrace, but I can remember no punishment. Perhaps Alice could not believe that her Jimmy was responsible for such a dastardly deed. My father and grandfather had reinforced my interest in elementary pharmacy by pointing out the harmful plants during walks. Perhaps the first years of childhood are not the best time for this kind of teaching.

The real and the fantasy worlds had yet to separate. Once I stood outside the tobacco and sweet shop on the corner of Letchworth Parade. I asked passers-by for a penny, two halfpennies, or four farthings because my father was out of work, and I needed the money to repair my electric train. This unusual pitch worked and a seemingly endless flow of coins came my way. I could have added to the family income but, undisciplined as I was, I ran in with each gift to the shop and bought sweets. It was not long before the shopkeeper grew suspicious and soon they took me home again in disgrace. Our neighbour, Mrs Stallybrass, was a retired schoolteacher and she took me in hand as a part-time pupil. I spent happy afternoons in her sitting room or in her garden learning simple arithmetic and general knowledge, but she never taught me reading or writing.

Apart from these childhood crimes, they were years full of happiness and sunshine. Perhaps I should have spent more time with other children and not conversed entirely with adults, but that is how it was. Memories of childhood at Norton Croft are particularly vivid in my mind and some are accurately dated. I recall my Aunt Kit's return from Singapore. It was a great event for Alice and Kit brought with her a trunk full of presents. It was just like Christmas all over again. She had a strangely elegant pushchair for my cousin Felix, who was between one and two years old at the time. I can still see my father's mother in the kitchen before Christmas 1922, and the ambulance that stopped outside the house early in 1923 to take her away on her last journey. My Aunt Flo lived in Hitchin, a few miles away, and we would go there by bus and have tea with her in her house in Nun's Close. This house fascinated me because it had electric light and a telephone, something we did not have at Letchworth. I cannot remember how the house was lit but guess it must have been by gaslight. The most important event of my days at Norton Croft was Christmas 1923. My father gave me as a present a wooden box filled with electrical odds and ends. A bell, a flash-light bulb, wires, batteries and other items I have forgotten. Such collections now come in kit form, but not then. It was the best of all the Christmas gifts. The experiments I did with it led me to ask the family and even the postman: why do I need two wires to carry electricity? Why will one not do as with gas or water? No one could answer my simple questions and it was this, I believe, that led me to a life of science. I realized that I would have to find the answers myself.

The happy childhood at Letchworth ended when Grandfather March retired in 1925. They sold Norton Croft to provide a pension and moved to rooms above the shop. The move to Brixton was by train from Letchworth to the terminus at King's Cross, and what an excitement that was. In the 1920s, boys were, as now, interested by the engineering achievements of the time. England was still a super-power with the railways a proud part of it, but travel by train was painful as well as exciting. The engines blew off steam from their safety valves when stopped at a station, and to my young ears, the noise was intense and agonizing. I discovered from tests when I was a student at Manchester that the upper range of my hearing was above 20 kHz and more acute than most. The hiss of high pressure steam escaping is rich in ultrasonics and I heard it as an appalling noise. The journey by Tube from King's Cross to Stockwell was just as unpleasantly noisy, but the Tube system was little different from today. The trains were those familiar streamlined worms that rushed from their small tunnel into the tiny stations. We took the tram from Stockwell to Brixton Hill and the shop. The living conditions were primitive compared with Norton Croft. Behind the shop were two large rooms: one for living in and the other a bedroom where my mother and father slept in a large double bed. A door from the living room led to a tiny scullery with a WC and sink basin just beyond; for most of the time they cooked on a gas ring in this scullery. A door led on to a yard, an area of paved ground with a high wooden fence around it with a gate leading on to New Park Road. Opposite the door was a disused chapel, a storehouse for theatrical props. A large wooden shed stood in the yard, which held a gas oven used to cook the Sunday lunch, and a galvanized iron hipbath where we all bathed. Bathing was infrequent in the winter, because it was so cold in the draughty shed. My mother, in spite of these difficult surroundings, made a fighting effort to keep me clean. She gave me daily baths in front of a large gas fire in the living room. It must have been a frustrating task, for a layer of soot from the ubiquitous coal-burning fires of London coated all surfaces outside.

The customers were people living nearby who wanted photographs framed or, if they were less wealthy, put behind a sheet of glass and held by a sticky coloured tape called *passé partout*. A few middle-class customers bought framed pictures or prints. My father worked in the evenings restoring paintings in an underground basement below the shop. They employed as a shop assistant a Mr Weatherby who was a First World War veteran. He was a thin, pale, tallish man with a limp from a wound gained in the First World War and I saw him, in the thoughtless cruelty of a child, as a miserable man. No matter how much I pressed him he would never talk of the war but, like many ex-service-men, he forever grieved over the injustice of his plight. He had been called to be a hero, and was promised much, but received little. In the first years that I was at the shop, business was good. My mother and father were able to take a two weeks' holiday in Europe each year visiting centres of culture. It was usually a tour organized by Thomas Cook, and among the cities they visited were Rome, Madrid and Paris. They were also fond of Chamonix and Interlaken in Switzer-land. These holidays seemed to be what sustained them and made their life of drudgery worthwhile. They did not take me on these journeys and it never occurred to me that this was a matter of importance. My mother's thirst for music and culture was slaked by concerts every week or so. An old bachelor—Mr Wright, who seemed to find comfort away from a lonely existence in a Streatham house—accompanied her. My father never seemed to mind my mother's outings with Mr Wright, and I'm sure that he had no cause for concern.

My own excursions were with my grandparents. 'Let's go to Margate on the steamer,' they said. It was a lovely sunny Sunday morning in May and Brixton's charms were somewhat worn. We finished breakfast at the shop and the three of us—Will, my grandpa, Alice and I—took the tram to Westminster where the *Royal Sovereign* was berthed and waiting to take us down the river to the sea. Such spontaneous journeys illuminated my life as a child and left me feeling that ships were transports to heaven. The *Royal Sovereign* was a paddle steamer with two huge paddle wheels, like those of a water mill, on either side amidships. She was a coal burner and had a high funnel, but even this did not prevent the grit and soot and sulphur fumes from falling on the unwary who sat downwind. Will and Alice were old hands and they took seats near the bow. Strangely, I never remember the ship being overcrowded. There was competition from other steamers and there always seemed space to spare. In those days of course, London was not the tourist destination it is now.

Those paddle steamers that plied the Thames were in a way museums of Victoriana and Victorian engineering. The engine room had giant gleaming pistons proudly displayed to anyone who wanted to walk along the open catwalk above it. Paddle wheels turned relatively slowly so that we could watch the dignified mechanical motion of the engines and wonder about it. It was not like the fussy urgent noisiness of the internal combustion engine. Only once have I seen a comparable slow and steady internal combustion engine, and that was on an experimental farm where there was a huge single-cylinder caterpillar tractor. This strange machine had one enormous cylinder and firing a shotgun cartridge into it started the slowly moving piston.

London's river was full of ships in those days. The docks carried the cargoes of the world and the passengers who now travel to and from Heathrow. The whole journey fascinated and I needed nothing other than the prospect that was slowly moving before my eyes to keep me happily entertained. We passed the stately buildings of the Greenwich Naval Hospital set in the green of their park surroundings, and the grim satanic-looking Becton gasworks, so large it seemed to take an age to pass. Then we sailed on to Tilbury, where passenger liners left for South America, China, and anywhere in the world. How I longed to be setting off on one of them.

On the *Royal Sovereign* it was truly better to travel than to arrive; our destination was an anticlimax. The pier, where the ship arrived at Margate, led to a dirty beach and a tacky promenade with an overpowering smell of fish frying in rancid fat, and waiting to be sprinkled with malt vinegar. Malt vinegar and paraffin—kerosene to those outside these islands—were smells that I loathed as a child and still dislike. Wisely, Alice and Will did not venture into the town itself. There was in any case only an hour before the return journey to Westminster. The sheer joy of these trips left in my young mind a love of ships and the sea.

At the age of six I was sent to a private primary school at the junction of Elm Park Road and Brixton Hill. My first teacher was an embittered Irishwoman, Miss Tierney. She soon took an intense dislike to the precocious boy put in her charge and used the cane frequently on my hands and fingers. In the way of small children, I said nothing of this to my family and suffered until I could endure it no longer. Then I decided to leave home as usual in the morning and instead of going to school, play in the long untidy gardens full of shrubs that ran down to Brixton Hill. This lasted for a few days, but somehow my truancy was discovered. There was an inquest and they moved me to the next teacher, Miss Plumridge, a plump motherly woman who referred to me always as 'The brand plucked from the burning'. An accurate description, as I had tasted hell, and her disciplined effective teaching was heaven by comparison. Under her tuition, I learnt fast and soon was reading science fiction from the Brixton Library. My last teacher at this primary school was Miss Beavan, a wonderful Welsh woman, who in spite of a huge class had the capacity to make us feel that she gave each of us her full attention. I shall never forget her enthusiasm and encouragement when I painted a rose well enough to be a true likeness.

I believe that primary schooling is by far the most important part of education. We need to acquire literacy and numeracy early in childhood, so that they become automatic activities needing no more effort than that used to keep our balance while riding a bicycle. These things can be learnt later but never with the same fluency. In the same way, no language learnt later in life can be as fluent as one's first language.

My mother was full of working-class good intentions and she had an unquestioning belief in education. She was determined that

I should go to a grammar school and as soon as possible. She had been denied the chance of a 'good education' and she did not intend that I should suffer from a lack of it. I now realize that my mother blamed her lack of good schooling for her failure to realize her potential. She did not see that the 'better' schools did not so much educate as indoctrinate the customs of the middle and upper-middle classes. In her days, an incompetent with good manners and speech could easily find the employment denied a working-class applicant, no matter how able. My mother was an intelligent woman but she really believed that 'a good education' could turn any girl into Florence Nightingale or a Jane Austen and any boy into a Darwin or an Orwell. This powerful attribute of education is still widely believed. So pervasive is the idea that we can make silk purses from sows' ears that the phrase 'He never had a proper education' is the inevitable cliché that decorates an account of a misspent life. Looking back, I wish I could have stayed on until puberty at that primary school. Apart from the bad first year it provided an environment in which I was unfolding fast. In the spring of 1929, aged nine, she wrenched me from this childhood paradise and enrolled me at the Strand School about a quarter of a mile further down Elm Park Road. As grammar schools went, it was not bad, but for me it proved to be the wrong place to go.

I walked to my new school from my Uncle Fred's house near King's Road. The route took me past Brixton Prison. It was a grim place, especially in the dark years of the 1930s depression. As I walked beside the high long walls and past its vast closed door I could not help wondering what it was like inside. My father had done time as a boy in Reading gaol but he would never talk of it except to say that he had done wrong and had been punished, and that was all there was to it. Like most pre-pubescent boys, I was full of fantasies and fears, and the prospect of imprisonment was high on my mind's agenda.

At the end of the prison approach road was the main road, Brixton Hill. Directly across was Elm Park Road, a street of terraced Victorian houses that led to Strand School, my destination. The school was a London County Grammar school. By the standards of today, it was a good school, but I hated it. I saw it as a place where, unjustly, I did time for the offence of being too young to work. I did not learn much science there, but it certainly formed my views on science. Let me explain. One morning in a moment of purposeless destruction, I started to carve my initials with my penknife in the wooden bench of the biology lab. I was sitting before it listening to the natural history lesson delivered by Sidney Dark who taught biology to the senior boys and the soft subject of natural history to the young. I liked listening to him and contentedly carved away as he spoke—what made me carve I do not know. Suddenly there was a hush. The teacher stopped in mid-sentence and glared at me with eyes enlarged by thick magnifying spectacles. 'Wretched boy, what are you doing?' 'Nothing,' I replied, too startled for anything more accurate or reasonable. 'You are destroying school property and not paying attention. You will be punished. Go and fetch the book and cane.' I was astonished; Sidney Dark had never caned anyone. There were masters in the school who thoroughly enjoyed the swish and thwack of the cane as they beat a young boy's bottom, but Mr Dark was not among them. The book was used to record the punishment and I think to curb excessive beating. Reluctantly I left the lab and made my way down to the Masters' Common Room, where I knocked on the door and asked for the book and cane. In those times and earlier the process of punishment was invested with ritual so that it could entertain the innocent as well as be seen properly to punish the guilty. The ritual of the book and cane was, I know, an effective part of the punishment through its capacity to humiliate as well as hurt.

I was not too worried as I took this punishment kit back to the biology lab, for I felt sure that Sidney Dark was much too kind and decent a man to use it. I did wonder, though, what I could say that would tip the balance in my favour. So vivid is my memory of this small event that I can easily picture the corridor flanked by the chemistry and physics labs. I can still smell the tang of hydrogen sulphide mixed with that of carbolic disinfectant. I went on to the biology lab and gave the book and cane to my teacher as was required by the ritual. He immediately put it down on his desk and began his harangue. This I knew was a good sign and I put on my air of utmost contrition. The sadists among the schoolmasters never wasted time on talk but went straight into the act itself. He had hardly warmed over his voice when the clamour of the fire bell drowned it and, as if automatons, boys and master immediately started the well-rehearsed fire drill, and prepared to move to the positions allocated to them outside the school. I turned to go, relieved at my escape by the bell, for I was sure that the fire drill would cool the teacher's indignation. Suddenly, a punishment much more subtle than mere corporal came into his mind and as he turned to pick up the book and cane, he said, 'Lovelock, you take care of this,' and handed it to me. 'We cannot leave it here to be burnt.' I was obliged to rescue the cane from the mock fire in front of the whole school that found the episode hilariously funny. Ever after, they called me the boy who had saved the cane. It also was the start of my lifelong love–hate relationship with biology and biologists.

You will by now have gathered that I was neither a perfect pupil nor happy to be at school. In fact, I hated it so much that every day was a kind of ordeal. If, as often happened in the winter, the filthy coal smoke that polluted the Brixton air made me ill, it was a vast relief. I could stay at home in bed with my beloved books, freed by bronchitis or pneumonia from the tyranny of school. Because of illness, I was a weedy child and should have been the target of bullies, the more usual reason to dislike school. I was blessed by having a wonderful group of fellow sufferers as my schoolmates. To them, I was the 'mad scientist', good when needed for a wheeze that would confound our common enemy, the masters.

Let me tell you briefly of one small battle in our long war. A master, who taught French so badly that I could recall hardly a word of it, had the nickname 'Sappho'. This was not because he was inclined, like others among the staff, to a feeble fumbling of young boys that aimed at, but never reached, its target of pederasty. No, we called him 'Sappho' because it was in his hour that pubescent boys explored their bodies in an orgy of mutual masturbation. Much is made of the troubled minds of young girls of those repressed times, of their panic when they reached the menarche and first experienced bleeding from their vaginas. I cannot recall ever having heard any public comment on the similar puzzlement of boys when masturbation produced a sticky liquid product. For most of them, the 1930s were still a time when masturbation was a mortal sin, not something to mention to parents or indeed any adult. It was not so surprising that in the warm community of their peers they explored their bodies and discussed such things. As far as I know, little of this intimacy led to homosexuality; those of that inclination seemed to pair up early on and avoid the general scrimmage in Sappho's room. We had nothing against Sappho: he rarely punished and was so short-sighted that we could get away with anything. Perversely, and exhibiting the bad side of the group, we used him as an easy target and once played a cruel joke on him. In December, just before term ended, the classroom was decorated with tinsel, paper bells, and the paraphernalia of Christmas; and above the master's desk were two balloons. One of us had the idea of adding ink to one of these balloons, arranging a small leak in it, and replacing it over the desk just before Sappho entered the room. He swept in like an elderly bat, trailing his black academic gown like a pair of crumpled wings. He must have thought the class unusually quiet as he walked to his desk, sat down, and opened his notes for the day's lesson in French verbs. After a minute or so, his hand moved to his bald head as he felt something impinge on it. He gazed dimly at the class but all seemed well. Then his hand rose again, and he felt the wetness of the ink, and rubbed it around first his head and then his face. There was an explosion of laughter from the boys; we could contain ourselves no longer. We laughed so much that it hurt. Sappho tried in his way to keep order, but kept wiping more and more ink onto his face, growing ever more like a badly made-up minstrel. Aroused by the noise the headmaster entered and brought order; I cannot remember the sequel and the punishments we received, except that they were collective, and the boys responsible were not betrayed.

Although a loner by nature, I realized in adolescence and earlier the importance of my peer group. What is rarely discussed is how much good comes from it. In the grimly custodial environment of the school, the warmth and companionship of my friends went far to make life tolerable. Much more than this, a large part of the knowledge I gained in school years came from interaction with my peers. In spite of its location in Brixton, the pupils of the Strand School were an elitist bunch. They were almost all of them selected by examination, which in those days let through no more than a few per cent. I well recall four of us discussing, at about age thirteen, particle accelerators. We were, like most boys, fascinated by speed and power, and the idea of accelerating charged atoms to near the speed of light was, at the time, exciting. We knew about Cockcroft and Walton's famous experiment with an early linear accelerator—we had seen the apparatus in the Science Museum. It occurred to us that the particles would go faster if they went round a racetrack and were given a push on each rotation. In the course of an hour's discussion, we arrived at a rough design for a powerful accelerator driven by radio frequency energy. We knew nothing then of the Californian physicist Lawrence's now famous invention, the cyclotron. Of course, our invention, although independently made, was a bare skeleton of an idea and we had no means to make it in real life. Nevertheless, the recollection illustrates the power of children in a small group to learn heuristically.

I do believe that a good school or university is one blessed with good students. The teachers are less important. At the best universities, the students rarely see their professors because, by the time a professor takes a Chair at an elite university, his time is often committed for years ahead in the committee rooms of public service and the university administration. It does not matter because the students themselves set the pace and directly, or indirectly, teach each other; where the tutorial system is used, the meeting between student and tutor can be like that between apprentice and master.

The idea that there is no diversity among human minds is absurd. We vary in many ways and each of us needs teaching in a way that allows our potential to develop. The notion that all should be taught together since we are born equal is as foolish as decreeing that we can make do with only one size of clothing. It is patronizing to assume that those who fail in academic subjects are less able than the skilled passers of examinations. I suspect that many graduates with excellent degrees are barely able to do anything other than pass examinations. The sculptor Eric Gill often quoted Ananda Coomaraswamy: 'the artist is not a special sort of man but that every man is a special sort of artist'. If we expand this thought to include women and other creative professions, we see that every child has a potential. It could provide a better prescription for our children's upbringing.

The myth that egalitarian schools will break class barriers is dear to liberal humanists, but humans vary widely in their capacity and ability and it is unkind to treat them as if they were all the same. I think that the breaking of class barriers is less important than giving children the chance to develop their innate capacity. If we teach all children equally, we lessen this chance, whatever it may be. Each of us was once an egg in which the genes of our parents merged. Before and after conception our genetic composition is shuffled so that we are different from our parents. We are each of us at birth dealt a new hand and most assuredly, we are not born equal. Some are born with a hand full of aces and kings and others nothing but deuces. Rightly, we admire most the player who can win or can make a good defence from a poor hand. We admire him much more than the one who merely cashes in the gifts that the dealer dealt.

In spite of hating school, I was determined to become a scientist, whatever it took. The prospect of six more years at the Brixton school, followed perhaps by several at university, was too awful to contemplate at twelve years old, so I lived each day as it came. I knew that

I would have to soldier on for years until I possessed that small piece of paper listing me as a Bachelor of Science. Without it, I could never hope to be in charge of an experiment in a laboratory. To make this time of imprisonment bearable I decided that while society required me to submit daily to school it had no rights over my evenings and weekends. This meant refusing to do homework or to attend Saturday sports—a rebellion that I sustained throughout all my years at school.

None of this endeared me to my masters. The possession of a retentive memory and an ability to listen enabled me to do well in examinations in spite of never doing homework. This did not work with mathematics or languages where mere memory is not enough but I was too young then to realize what a loss this would be. They punished me repeatedly by caning or by making me write one hundred or more times some banal sentence. When they saw that punishment would not work, they left me alone, and things were not so bad from about fourteen years old onwards.

I learnt most of my science from books borrowed from the Brixton Library and from discussing their contents with my friends. My first visit there was at about eight years old and I went with my mother, to whom books were at least half of life. On fine days, we walked from our shop on Brixton Hill the mile to the library in the centre of Brixton, and when wet we took the tram. At first, I took home novels, mostly science fiction, by authors like Jules Verne, Olaf Stapledon and H. G. Wells, but soon I found my way to the basement where the science textbooks were stored. I can vividly recall first reading Wade's *Organic Chemistry*. In those days, long before the Health and Safety bureaucracy had forbidden the handling of chemicals, chemistry had soul. The old chemists wrote poetically about mobile refractile liquids and compared them to diamonds in motion. If ever you have held a small round flask half-full of diodomethane and shaken it in the light, you will understand. Organic chemistry, as it then was, fascinated me with the elegance of its blown glass apparatus and the powerful odours of the compounds distilling within them. There were substances with strange yet evocative odours, such as anisole (methoxybenzene), or awful but curious odours, like pyridine. I wonder if students and schoolchildren now even see sealed bottles of these wonderful substances; such is the unreasoning fear of chemicals. We chemists do occasionally die because of our love of chemicals, but on average, according to the statistics of the Royal Society of Chemistry, we live longer than most other professionals do. Is it right to deny children the real pleasure of hands-on experience because of some remote and trivial risk?

I learnt physics, like chemistry, from the books of the Brixton Library. Among them, Jeans's *Astronomy and Cosmology* and Soddy's *The Interpretation of Radium*. On Christmas 1928 I received a 'hobbies annual' and in it were the plans and instructions for building a simple short-wave radio receiver. The author claimed it was sensitive enough to receive broadcasts from Australia. My aunt Kit had married into the Leakey family and we spent some of Christmas 1928 at the house of Papa Leakey, the grandfather of my cousin Felix. The old man was famous as an early Fabian socialist and was a regular user of the airlines in his travels around Europe to promote the use of Esperanto. I was amazed to receive his full attention when I told him about this radio receiver. I suppose he saw it as a means for making the world speak one language, Esperanto. His encouragement lingered, and several years later I sold my stamp collection and used the proceeds, about ten shillings, to buy the components for this radio. I made it and was entranced to hear on first try an American station in Pittsburgh. Soon I heard Moscow, which even then seemed to be shouting, with megawatts of power, its communist faith from the highest tower of the Kremlin. There were few electronic components on sale in those days and I had to make much of the radio from raw materials. I wound the coils by hand on jam jars and the chokes, that separated the sound from the radio frequencies, on pencils. This experience with electronics was to serve me well later when I came to make my own instruments.

The physics taught in school was, by comparison, unrelievedly dull, almost as if intended to repel. I remember one exercise in physics that typified the school's inability to inspire even receptive minds. It was the reading of the Fortin Barometer. Most of us just tap the glass of an aneroid barometer to see if the pressure is increasing for fine weather or decreasing as heralds rain and wind, but to read a proper physicist's barometer is much more complicated. The Fortin Barometer measures air pressures in the classical way—by observing the height of a column of mercury when the pressure of the atmosphere balances it. It is a vertical glass tube, closed at the top and filled with liquid mercury, and the bottom rests in a cup of mercury, open to the air. The height of the tube is about eighty centimetres and chosen to be longer than seventy-six centimetres of mercury, the weight of a normal atmospheric column. This corresponds to an air pressure of about fifteen pounds per square inch, or two kilograms per square cm for the metricated. The upper part of the glass tube above the mercury column is a vacuum but for the small amount of mercury vapour. As the air pressure changes, so the mercury column rises or falls. When it rises, it is often for fine weather, and when it falls for foul. We use mercury as the liquid to fill the barometer because it is so dense. You could make a water barometer but you would need a thirty-foot tube, which is not so convenient.

The physics so far could have been interesting to a receptive twelve-year-old but not in the way it was taught. Academic scientists who drew up the school syllabus had long forgotten their childhood and wanted physics taught as an exact science. They wanted us to understand the errors inherent in the barometer that would prevent us from measuring the true pressure. We had to allow for the fact that the density of mercury changes with temperature, and that the length of the metal scale used to measure the height of the column also changes with temperature and in a different way from the mercury itself. We also had to allow for the pressure of mercury vapour above the liquid mercury, and take into account the possible error that came from the fact that the top and bottom of a column of mercury is round, not flat. We made these corrections to the observed height of the mercury column laboriously by pen-and-paper arithmetic. Now this would be fine stuff for an apprentice physicist who really needed to know the air pressure when he made a crucial and interesting experiment. To a twelve-year-old it seemed remote and absurd, especially since it took an hour to calculate the pressure, during which time it would have changed.

I never did biology at school after natural history teaching ceased at about age twelve. Those opting for science had a limited choice of subjects and mine were physics, chemistry, and pure and applied mathematics. Biology in those days was for those intending to become dentists or physicians. It included a fair amount of dissection, even of live frogs, the thought of which I found revolting.

I learnt my biology from reading, especially books by JBS Haldane. None of the other scientists' books I read had his personal and hands-on approach. He became my hero when I read of his use of himself as a 'guinea pig' in physiological experiments, such as when he swallowed grams of ammonium chloride to increase the acidity of his blood. Practical biology came from walks in the country with my father, who had a lively sense of wonder and a way of passing it on. On weekends during the warmer seasons, I would leave home with my mother and father early on Sunday morning, take the tram to Streatham Common, and there take an electric train to Dorking. At Dorking, we changed onto a small steam train that pushed and pulled its way to Horsham. Half-way was the station of Holmbury St Mary where we alighted. We then began a walk across glorious meadows to the woods on the flanks of Leith Hill. From there, we walked on to Coldharbour village, where we stopped for lunch or tea. I think my father had been an apprentice to a poacher when he was a boy and before the game-keepers caught him. He had a strong sense of ecology, knew the habitats, could see the trails of all the common mammals, and knew where the birds nested and their names. I learnt from him the common names of nearly all the wild plants, and such useful wisdom as that it is safe to enjoy the sweet crimson berries of the yew tree so long as the deadly pips are spat out. Leith Hill was a wonderland. I learnt to catch trout by hand from the small streams and gorged on blue-berries, or hurts, as the locals called them.

As a child, my parents fed and bathed me but otherwise left me to my own devices. When not at school I roamed the Brixton streets and played with the children there. Coal smoke pollution fouled the air in wintertime and, when there was a still night, the loss of heat from the ground to the dark sky lowered the surface temperature, resulting in a pool of cold air a few hundred feet deep, which filled the London basin. The United Kingdom was a superpower before the Second World War but it did nothing to relieve the harm of smog. In certain ways, the plight of the Los Angelenos, beset by smog from their cars, matches the helplessness felt by Londoners. When I was a child, London had worse smogs than other British cities because the combination of geography and meteorology made it easy for the air to form an invisible but tightly closed lid above the city. This lid, or inversion as the meteorologists call it, lies between a hundred and a few thousand feet above the ground, and under it everything emitted in the city accumulates, sometimes to lethal levels. The air in this cold pool was stable and it did not mix with the warmer atmosphere above, so that the fumes built up to make the infamous pea-soup fog. It could be so bad that I could see no further than a few yards in front of me and sometimes even one's feet seemed to be vanishing in a foul haze that smelt acrid and was choking to breathe. A clean shirt became black after a short walk as the filthy air impinged upon it, and a film of greasy black soot soon covered all exposed surfaces—it took days of rain to wash away a night's accumulation.

Dr Wise, our GP, was a wonderfully kind and cool young man, and would often call in on his bicycle during the winter. My father was never ill but my mother suffered chest infections every year, exacerbated by the foul air and by her habit of smoking, and I was often ill. It seemed that only those with a resistance to the coal smoke survived long in the London basin. We were lucky to have had the 1930s Depression, which closed the shop, for after a few more years of Brixton air I might not be writing now. It was extraordinary that we tolerated this poisonous environment, and that nearly everyone regarded the smog as a weather phenomenon, something natural and about which we could do nothing. In the 13th century, King Edward I banned the burning of coal in London and warned that hanging would be the punishment for those who disobeyed. It was not until the mephitic smog of 1952 killed more than 4000 Londoners that they reinstated the ban.

Those were times when coal dominated our lives. The open grates in our homes burnt the dirty fuel that fouled the air but gave no proper warmth. The hot smoke of its combustion rushed up the chimneys into the over-laden air and cold air flowed in through the cracks along the sides of ill-fitting windows and doors. In the evenings the family huddled round the fire trying to keep warm and retired later to bedrooms so cold that water on their bedside tables would often freeze. The English had hot water bottles not because they were under-sexed, but because they really needed them to keep warm in the wintertime. The fire demanded continual feeding with black lumps of coal, and in the morning someone had to clear the grate of its accumulation of ash and dust. To keep her home clean in those days was a heroic and strenuous task, but nearly all women in Brixton seemed to do it, and clothes and houses were clean despite the endless rain of dirt. It was a Kafkaesque scene. Working people endured a cruel regime where they must stay clean in a world where black soot falls endlessly from the smoke-filled sky. The wealthy suffered less. Many had central heating from a single, coal-fired water heater. We were lucky to have the shop heated by gas; at least there was no ash and dust to contend with. It was astonishing after the Second World War to visit government buildings in London's Whitehall where every office had its open fire, whose incessant demands were fed by minions scurrying around all day with their coal buckets.

To add to the self-inflicted harm of winter in London, smoking was a normal part of life and all the adults I knew, except my father, smoked pipes or cigarettes. Tobacconists' shops were as common as pharmacists, and deemed equally essential. No wonder the life expectation was only a year or so over sixty. It was an awful environment in which to raise children. There were other poisons more deadly and more hidden. Everything was painted with lead paint that when old, would flake into dust. Children playing would take in a daily dose of lead that could harm their developing brains and stunt their growth. The lead compounds had a sweet taste and this would attract some children to chew pieces of wood that had been lead painted, adding to the problem. Mercury was also ubiquitous. A favourite indoor firework set off regularly at children's parties was Pharaoh's Serpent. It was a little pyramid package of tinfoil containing ammonium dichromate and a pellet of mercury thiocyanate. When lit, it gently spurted forth a green powder, while a long twisting black snake arose from this green pseudo grass. Anyone unwise enough to breathe the smoke coming from this clever pyrotechnic display would breathe in a dose of mercury vapour, a potent brain poison. Toy puzzles had beads of mercury quicksilver in them. I remember when a class of thirty boys at my grammar school was given test tubes containing a few grams of red mercury oxide. The schoolmaster instructed us to heat them over our Bunsen burners until the red oxide decomposed into oxygen and metallic mercury and when we did this the vapour of the mercury condensed on the sides of the tube as a bright silvery mirror. To show the oxygen produced, we inserted a glowing wooden splint into the test tube and saw it burst into flame in the oxygen-rich gas. It scares me to think how much deadly mercury vapour that group of selected children breathed in. They were the cream of their generation, the one per cent who had passed their 11+ examinations. I suspect that the same thing took place in schools around the country and may have set a whole generation of children at risk of brain damage. Then of course there was calomel, mercurous chloride. This was a favourite laxative, given to babies when they teethed. In addition, if this were not enough, dentists thrust mercury silver amalgam into the cavities of our teeth. I have often wondered if a sudden loss of the ability to play chess, and a growing awareness of dyslexia when I was aged about eleven had something to do with the mercury in my environment. But we are a tough species—despite these insults that 1920s London imposed upon us—and my mother and father lived to their 90s and

80s, respectively. These were gross pollutions and I view with wry amusement the hypochondria of the many who now agonize over trivial levels of chemicals in the food they eat.

Sodom and Gomorrah had their attractions for their inhabitants, no doubt, and so it was with Brixton. Despite its winter miasma, or maybe because of it, Brixton seemed to be an entertainment centre for London. There were theatres and cinemas, dancehalls and skating rinks, and there were public parks and commons a short walk away and, above all, there was easy access by tram and tube to all else that London had to offer, and even to get out of it if you wanted. My grandmother and grandfather had come to live in the flat above the shop and they would take me with them on walks or to the theatre, or on voyages down the Thames. My lonely wanderings around the Brixton streets lessened, and at every school holiday—three weeks at Christmas, four weeks at Easter and six in the summer—I went away into the country. This was partly to ease the burden on my parents, whose working day was already full and partly because the well-named Dr Wise, our GP, recognized that the Brixton smog caused my frequent winter illness. Sometimes I would go to stay with my aunts, but at other times they sent me to remote farms in East Anglia, that were prepared to take children. Some of these, like the chicken farm at Baldock, where a kindly family cared for me with love and affection were heavenly. It was at the Baldock farm that I learned to ride a bicycle. Others were brutal in their cruelty. I dreaded the strongly Nonconformist religious farms in East Anglia. Here, every Sunday was a punishment. I would have to dress in a suit and go to chapel three times during the day. To me the services were intolerably boring. When not at chapel they made me sit on a stiff chair and wait for the next meal or next service. To go outside to walk, except to chapel, was forbidden, and so was reading anything other than the Bible. Any infringement of these rules led to a beating. That kind of mainly working-class religion was of course self-defeating, and no child of spirit subjected to it could do anything other than rebel.

My happiest times in this period were those spent with Miss Saunders and her brother at the village of Coldharbour near Dorking. The village was in the heart of what seemed to me endless heath and woodland on the slopes of Leith Hill. I enjoyed new explorations every day, discovered snakes and lizards, and caught trout in the sparkling water of its streams. It was what I mean by real countryside.

Miss Saunders was a countrywoman and she ate simply but not well by finicky middle-class standards. She would give me tinned peas or baked beans for lunch, and I loved them. They did not eat the fresh vegetables that her brother grew in the garden. I do not know where they went: probably they gave them away. Children and those living in the countryside often have a perverse taste for junk food, and as a child I was no exception.

The Depression of the 1930s hit us hard. There was one year when only one customer entered the shop. At the end of that year, with sorrow and with much discussion, my mother and father had no option but to dismiss our shop assistant, Mr Weatherby. The family savings were flowing away and, after much agonized talk, they finally decided to tell him that he must go because they could no longer afford to keep him on. The shop was rented, and the rent and tax were high. They sought in vain for someone to take it over until suddenly, in 1932, an art enthusiast appeared and took it on from them. They were then able, from their remaining savings, to buy a small house at Orpington in Kent, in Hillview Road, just near the station. The move to Orpington did little to change my personal life. I continued at the Strand School and travelled by train to Brixton. The journey, which involved a mile walk from Brixton Station, took over an hour, which meant early rising and a late return from school. I saw little of Orpington and made no friends there.

Although only ten to twelve during this period, I was deeply aware of their unhappiness, which resonated with my own miserable school-days. In the way of children, I was ashamed to be a shopkeeper's child. The middle-class peer group of the Strand School included children whose parents were minor civil servants, dentists, solicitors, and so on. To them, shopkeepers and small business were 'Trade' and, in the snobbery of the time, they disdained them. The sign, outside the villas of the bourgeoisie, 'Tradesman's Entrance' pointed to a dark alley leading to the scullery door. I suppose this tribal scorn against trades folk of any kind arose from envy of imagined wealth. It had trickled down from Victorian times when the aristocracy had been offended by the wealth and success of entrepreneurs. It is easy to forget how, in the 19th and early 20th centuries, their antecedents judged people. Breeding alone was thought to bring forth the good qualities. It was widely held that no newly rich person could ever be a gentleman or a gentlewoman and what the aristocracy thought yesterday the bourgeoisie thinks today. The collective contumely of the petty bourgeois was for its victims little different from racial hatred. What is odd is that the intellectual middle class, whose members would be deeply distressed to be called racist, still stigmatizes 'Trade' as if those connected with commercial activity were of a different race.

One day in December 1931, my school announced that boys could sit for the Supplementary Junior County Scholarship. I realized that this would relieve the burden of school fees from my mother and father and I asked the schoolmaster who made the announcement how I should apply. He laughed and said, 'Don't waste your time, you haven't an earthly chance.' Even so, I went to the school secretary, Miss Borer, a plump and friendly woman who had a spacious office at the front of the school, and she readily gave me a form and helped me complete it in her office. I went home and soon forgot all about it and never mentioned it, but in February 1933 a letter arrived summoning me to another school in Streatham to sit the examination itself. I was incubating pneumonia at the time and was feverish; perhaps because of this I could think more quickly. Anyway, the exam was not difficult. One requirement was an essay. There was a choice of subjects and one of these was 'Iron and Steel'. I had recently read a book from the Brixton Library about the steel industry, mostly technical, and had found it fascinating. I had a good memory and was able to write at length about iron smelting, Bessemer converters, and the production of the various alloy steels. I knew little in real terms about these metals but phrases like molybdenum steel, or chrome vanadium steel, all were filed away in my mind, along with their remarkable properties. I staggered home from the examination and was ill for six weeks. There were no antibiotics then, and infections just had to take their course. They sent me to the Saunders family at Coldharbour near Dorking to convalesce, and it was here that the good news of my award of the scholarship came. I feel sure it was the essay that did it, and I remember Miss Saunders coming to my bedroom early one spring morning with the good news that astounded as well as pleased me: just for once, something right had happened.

The school, like many today, had little trust in tests or examinations, and preferred teachers' assessments of a pupil's abilities. They ignored my scholarship success and punished me for my cheek by making me repeat the previous year's work, and in the lowest stream. The seventy-five boys of each year were divided into three streams: Upper, A, and B. Lovelock, the freak, was placed in the B stream. My life might have been a dismal one if, like today, my future had

depended on teachers' assessments alone. Examinations taken anonymously gave me my chance.

There were a few wonderful teachers like Ginger Warren, a bearded
man with ginger hair, who looked like George Bernard Shaw, and was
stern. He was strong, just, and taught so well that in one term under
his tuition I learnt more French than in three years under the flabby,
sadistic Froggy Adair. There was also Harold Toms, the chemistry
teacher, and the only one at the school with a PhD. His lessons were
my refuge. He taught so well that the Strand School excelled itself in
Firsts in the external examinations in chemistry. The masters at the
Strand School included too many incompetents and these misguided
men tried hard to diminish me. A favourite trick was to make me stand
before the class while they, like prosecuting lawyers, harangued me on
my pacifism or socialism, as if these were crimes and I were a felon. If
they expected that the boys, my peers, would then visit me with their
own bigotry, they were wrong. Their pettiness merely enhanced my
reputation as the mad scientist, who had eccentric views as well. What
matters to boys, pre- and post-adolescent, is courage. An ability to
fight back without too much fuss was all that I needed to have their
support.

In addition to air pollution, Brixton offered another pollution:
its local accent. Playing with the local children may have made me
street-wise but at the cost of a voice that would have condemned
me to a working-class life in those intensely class-conscious times. My
Pygmalion was Uncle Hugo Leakey, and when I first stayed with Kit
and Hugo at their Welwyn Garden City home, Hugo decided to
eliminate from my speech the glottal stop, the dropped h, and the
whining cockney vowels. Every morning, immediately on waking,
I had to practise vowel sounds or sentences like 'It's not the hunting
that hurts the horses' hoofs but the hammer hammer hammer on the
hard high road', and then repeat them at breakfast. He was a professional and kept this training going until I had an accent that, although
still not upper-middle-class would fool many listeners. Things change
and in England now a down-market accent is sought after, but I am
deeply grateful to my uncle for his unstinting effort to change mine.
They would never have chosen me in 1941 for the post of junior
scientist at the National Institute for Medical Research had I spoken
as a native South Londoner.

The Leakeys expanded my horizons in other important ways. They
gave me the speech and mannerisms of the avant-garde political far-

Left, which was so popular at that time. Something very different from my mother's old Labour views and antithetical to my father's natural Toryism. I soon imbibed the Marxist jargon and was, in a way, dialectically materialized. The evangelical communists, with their yellow book bibles from Gollancz's Left Book Club, were all around me, and they were as certain in their beliefs as were the Catholics I was soon to meet at university. Everyone of the Leakey crowd was sure that they were right. Soon the intense tribal conflict of the Spanish Civil War was to engulf them all: many as participants on the Republican side; many like me, supporters too young to join in. Strangely, the intensity of feeling among the Left over the civil war in Spain far exceeded their passions for the fight against Nazism during the Second World War. The Spanish war was an affair of the heart as well as the mind, and a political commitment. The Second World War seemed more to be a necessary but unfortunate act, more for principle than for passionate conviction. Also, of course, the Second World War was, in a way, an English war, and the Left, as part of their internationalism, were not enthused by England as such, or even the United Kingdom.

I have often wondered if there is a second awakening like that of puberty. At thirteen years, gender suddenly becomes invested with meaning. At somewhere around fifteen, in a similar way, politics and tribal matters suddenly reveal their colours. That is how it was for me. I would avidly absorb the *News Chronicle*, the liberal Left paper that the family favoured at Orpington. The Old Labour paper that they might have bought, the *Daily Herald*, was so dull that we all found it much too stodgy. Republican success in Spain lit up my day, and their frequent reverses depressed me. The hopelessness of the Republican cause did nothing for my adolescent angst.

The Leakeys were not merely political, they were also vegetarian and sexually enlightened, or at least in that prudish era they seemed so. The March girls, my mother included, were all first-rate cooks. Kit's vegetarian food was quite delicious, something very rare in my experience. I always looked forward to my next visit to Welwyn and drooled over the thought of her mock steak-and-kidney pie. The Leakey's art deco house had an upper storey like a ship, with a wide wall enclosing a balcony surrounding the main bedrooms. Above that, there was a flat roof for sunbathing. Here the whole family, any guests, and me included, sunbathed naked. It rapidly cured me of any prudery about my body. Nakedness in the warm sunny air became a joy and a freedom. Oddly, in spite of being over-sexed, as are most adolescent boys, naked girls were not arousing just to look at. This was not true of the act of undressing, and I remember trying to hide my erect and over-eager phallus by turning to the wall when I had watched a thoughtless striptease. This was a rare event: it was a rule that only bodies unclothed could use the sunbathing terrace. I feel sorry for the many whose acts of love have been marred by fears about their bodies. The Leakeys' ad hoc finishing school was the best of my educations.

Hugo had an amazing brother, Basil, who lived in three houses in a wood near Stevenage. One house had bedrooms on the second floor, the ground floor being a barn for gardening tools. Another house had the kitchen, and a third, the living quarters, and paved paths connected all these houses. Basil was a professional magician, part of the company called Maskelyne and Devant. I often wondered later if JBS Haldane's book, *My Friend, Mr Leakey*, which was about a magician, had Basil as its exemplar.

Felix was Kit and Hugo's only child, and was for me like a younger brother. We would spend hours together exploring the fine countryside of those days around Welwyn Garden City on our bicycles. We even made a trip together to Cornwall in 1935, travelling down the West Coast from Port Isaac to St Agnes and on round by St Ives to Land's End. We returned past the Lizard to Plymouth, Dartmoor, and home by train from Exeter.

When younger, Kit and Hugo were away in Argentina, where they had a bee and apple farm at Bahia Blanca. During their absence I would go, for school breaks, to Aunt Florrie at Hitchin. John Leete, her husband, was a handsome man who resembled the actor, Wilfrid Hyde-White. He had a firm and gentle disposition. He, together with his brother, Claude, owned Hitchin's main tailor's shop. It was a comfortable middle-class Tory home, a complete contrast to the Leakeys and to the shop in Brixton. John and Flo's great passion in life was golf. They were both quite good at it and had, at one time or another, been county champions. Life for them seemed to revolve around bridge tournaments and playing at the Letchworth Golf Club. Their friends were mainly other businessmen and their wives from Hitchin. In many ways, it represented the world my mother hated and envied most passionately. She keenly felt the injustice of her and Tom's endless struggle to keep a sinking shop afloat. The affluence of Uncle John's shop, where money flowed in apparently effortlessly was, she felt, so unfair. All that was tempered by a strong devotion and loyalty to her sister, and the recognition that John and Flo were kind and generous. In the convoluted class hierarchy of England, being in trade, and therefore people of little consequence, damned us both. Strangely, the picture shop occupied a slightly higher place in that category of snobbery than did the wealthier tailor's. Somehow, the association with art and artists made it less bourgeois. I was in grave danger, exposed to so many worlds ranging from my father's working-class friends to the upper-middle-class Leakeys, of evolving into a feeble and flabby liberal—someone without passion, who could see every point of view and yet was unable to decide what was right or wrong, someone like Judas, who betrayed from lack of commitment, not from wilful error. Fortunately, my commitment to science and the unshakeable quest to become a practising scientist kept me from this kind of indecision.

The Leetes had one daughter, Margaret, a few years younger than me. It was good to have a young girl as a cousin. It helped offset the isolation of our one-child families. A special attraction of my Hitchin visits was the Vincent family. Mr Vincent was the manager of Hitchin's only department store, and a friend of John's. Margaret and I were invited to a children's party at the Vincents when about twelve or thirteen. The Vincents had two daughters, Jean and Mary, and two sons. I must have behaved well at the party for they invited me on many occasions afterwards. They lived in a fine detached villa, two blocks from Nun's Close. One spring day in 1932 Mrs Vincent, a handsome woman whose affectionate nature reminded me of my grandmother, took her children and me on an expedition to Pirton Woods to pick primroses. I remember a heavenly sunny day and larking about with the girls—they were both older than I was—and we played games that involved plenty of contact. Suddenly they were no longer just children, and gender ceased from then on to be an abstract concept. Jean was a striking girl, with red hair and a pale freckled skin, and she was the one who enlivened my incoherent fantasies for at least a year, and then it was the more mature Mary, plainer but somehow more feminine, who became the girl of my dreams. Apart from these fantasies over Jean and Mary, I was celibate until a student at Manchester University. It seems incredible now, but celibacy was almost normal among adolescents in the 1930s. It was not, as thought by those who do not understand the English, from lack of lust, for I had that in abundance. It was a consequence of a solitary existence as a lone child, and low self-esteem. As schoolboys we wore short trousers and were in uniform up to nearly sixteen years, and we were hardly attractive. I could not believe that any female would have me, and thinking back to the child I was then, I was probably right. Unconsciously I dressed to fulfil this prophecy—round spectacles shielding myopic eyes, scuffed shoes, and knee-length shorts. Perhaps the sheer frustration of life in those times fuelled my fantasies about life as a scientist, and perhaps it was just as well, because when that friendly city, Manchester, gave me my first taste of real love, I was transported and, for a few years, science took second place.

To modern adolescents, this tame distant kind of relationship will seem quaint but in those days, the restraints of custom were so strong that our urges to explore each other's bodies stayed firmly theoretical. Practical sex was definitely out of bounds, and just as well, for other than hard-to-get French letters, there was nothing to prevent pregnancy. Any suggestion that we were timid or undersexed at that time is wrong. Our instincts are constant and do not vary; only custom changes. What a different adolescence I might have had if the Pill had been around in those days like now.

Those wonderful aunts of mine are long dead and I miss them. I was to see another one of them for the first time in 1975, Aunt Ann, who had married a New Zealander, Howard Mason, and went there with him after the First World War. She died in 1998 aged 101. I spent a week in Wellington visiting her in 1975. She was of the same stock as the other aunts and I realized how good it would have been to go there as a child. My New Zealand cousins were a lively three. Bruce, the eldest, distinguished himself as a playwright, so much so that over ten years after his death, his face looked out at me from the air-mail stamp from New Zealand. It was on a letter from his widow Diana. Lorna was the youngest cousin and still lives in New Zealand. Tim, the middle one, had moved to South Africa. I never saw him before he died. I saw little of my uncle Frank until we moved to Kent in the mid 1930s; he was away in Argentina with the Leakeys for some of the time and working in London for the rest of it.

Grandma March was right to be proud of the successes of her daughters. Sadly, they and their husbands did not much welcome long visits from Alice or Ephraim March. The two old outspoken cockneys did not fit well with the precious academic environment of the Leakeys or the cosy bourgeois atmosphere of Hitchin. In a way, the disdain of the Hitchin bourgeoisie was easier to accept, for they had never pretended otherwise. To them, the working classes were below in the natural order, and that was that. Neither the Leakeys nor the Leetes were ever unkind to my grandmother and grandfather. They did not have to be for them to see that they were unwelcome. I remember some tearful sessions with Alice March after she had returned from brief visits to her daughters. My mother and father were the ones who gave my grandparents a home and let them stay with them throughout the illnesses that ended their lives. We never understood at the time that we were a part of a vast transition in customs. In the Victorian nuclear family, the old had rights divinely instituted, of residence in the family home of their children.

Many years later, I was to face the same problem in my own home, where her daughter-in-law, Helen, rejected my mother, and I could well understand my mother's sense of injustice. She had paid her dues willingly to her parents, yet was now unwanted and unwelcome. I could see Helen's despair at having to cope with a strong-willed woman who interfered, with the best of intentions, in the running of her home. So abrading were the quarrels that the misery of it loomed like a dark cloud over the years between my father's death in 1956 and my mother's death in 1980.

Part of the problem was the dramatic intensity of her arguments. I was never sure how much of it came from conviction and how much she was acting a part. Nell had enjoyed amateur acting and had polished her histrionic talents to a fine degree, but she was a good and principled woman and unselfishly cared for me when I was a child. She and my father had a loving relationship and one that endured, so that the Brixton shop, for all its drawbacks, was a warm and safe refuge for me as a child. But in later life, after my father's death, Nell was wretchedly lonely and so strongly did she radiate her misery that no one could stand her company for long. Her fierce intensity, whether of love or hate, overwhelmed and burnt. Like the archetypal Jewish mother, she had the capacity to reduce me to a babbling child. Her widowhood was a twenty-four year torment for all of us, including her. By leaving me as a baby to be raised by my grandmother, she had unknowingly forfeited instinctive love and bonding. In later life, in her time of need, in place of a loving son, she had only a man who saw her as a relative in distress. My grandmother was to me my true mother, and her death in 1943 was a hard grief to bear.

From age fifteen onwards I spent part of the summer holidays bicycling or walking around England and Wales. The first of these expeditions was a journey from my home in Kent to Devonshire and back. I travelled sixty or so miles a day and stayed each night at a Youth Hostel. I well remember the road up the Chalke Valley in Wiltshire; it seemed endless as I pedalled my one-gear bicycle that hot July afternoon in 1934. I was thirsty and kept looking for the sign 'Teas'—one that was on cottages everywhere in southern England except, that is, in the Chalke Valley. Here, through Coombe Bissett, Stratford Tony, Bishopstone, and Broadchalke, I saw none. In Broadchalke, in desperation, I asked a man working in his garden, was there anywhere that supplied lemonade, tea, or anything to drink? 'Not here in Broadchalke,' he said. 'You are welcome to come in and have a glass of water but there is nowhere here that sells teas. We get so few visitors or folk travelling that it is just not worthwhile. Wait a minute, though, Mrs Hardiman in Bowerchalke, the next village, does do teas for walkers. You could try there. It's only a couple of miles further on.' Bowerchalke was on my route and I cycled up the slope beside the watercress beds and up the hill into the village itself. Sure enough, a few houses past the pub, The Bell Inn, Mrs Hardiman had a sign saying, 'Teas'. She made me a full pot and supplied some bread, jam, and scones. For those interested, such a meal cost about six old pence. Mrs Hardiman told me that I was the first to call for a month and she was thinking of taking down the sign. I realized that Bowerchalke was truly remote and began to look at it more closely.

Refreshed after tea, and knowing it was only about ten more miles to my final destination, the youth hostel at Iwerne Minster in Dorset, I explored the village. At the back of the church was a meadow and beyond it the steep green hill of Marleycombe. Chalk downs walled the village and seemed to intensify its feeling of privacy. To me, at sixteen, it was the perfect village and I decided that, if ever the chance arose, this was where I would live.

In 1937, I chose Wales for my summer break. On the second day, I left the youth hostel at the small Welsh village of Dolwyddelan and made my way up the stony track that led to Moel Siabod. It was just before my seventeenth birthday and this was my first Welsh mountain. All through the spring and early summer I had planned my solo expedition to North Wales. The Ordnance Survey maps had been companions, together with George Borrow's book, *Wild Wales*. These filled my mind so that the path and the climb almost had a sense of *déjà-vu*. I reached the lake below the glacial Cwm of the mountain in time for my sandwich lunch and a swim. Soon a thin sheet of cumulus clouds spread across the sky and reminded me of my objective, the peak itself. The climb was easy, never more in fact than a hill walk, and the enthralling sight of the other peaks emerging above a wide sea of clouds, was a fine reward. There in front of me was Snowdon and on either side the Glyders, and the Carneddau. It was like an archipelago of black rocks rising from a white sea. This was my first sight of clouds from above, even though Moel Siabod was a bare 3000 feet high, and I was moved. Mountains, like cathedrals and deep mature forests, are places with a transcendental ambience.

I started down through the clouds and soon I could see the Ogwen valley spread out before me. I had come out of the cloud onto a short run of scree. Scree is loose rocks and boulders piled against the mountain slope and only just stable. I had heard about scree running, the poor man's version of skiing, and decided to have a try at it. I ran onto the rock pile and to my joy the mass beneath me began to move. It was easier to run with, and slightly ahead of, the mass of moving rock than to stand still and let it move you on. In no time, I had reached the bottom and jumped off sideways as the rocks behind me continued their downward course. I was lucky to have chosen a fairly safe and short run for my first try. A few years later, I saw the thousand-feet-long scree run above Wast Water in the Lake District. It beckoned to me, but here were boulders as large as cars. I never tried it, but thoughts of it have lingered in my mind and thirty years later sustained me during the long downhill run of the quest for Gaia.

The two last years of my schooldays were tolerable. I was by then in the sixth form and treated more like a student than a child. I had passed the Matriculation examination and was now preparing to take the 'Higher School Certificate' that is now known in the UK as 'A' levels. There was little teaching and we spent most of our time in private study, which in practice meant private conversation among friends. My schooldays ended in 1938 with an interview for a job as a laboratory assistant. This job was to prove a crucial step in learning to become a scientist.

2

The Long
Apprenticeship

The tram to Victoria swayed as it clanked and ground and squealed its way round the corner into Stockwell Road. The view of the red-brick Brixton Odeon Cinema was enlivening this Tuesday morning in March 1938. I was at the front and top of the tram so that I could see everything that was going on, and I was on my way from my school in Brixton to an exciting job interview. More an inspection than an interview, for I had already been offered the job whilst still at school by a member of the firm I was to visit. In 1938 the streets of Brixton and Stockwell were poor but clean, and uncluttered by cars and throwaway bags from fast-food shops. The fast-food of those days was fish and chips and the newspaper that wrapped it was swept away by the street cleaners at dawn, their work unhindered by parked cars. Half an hour later, the Victoria clock tower came in view marking the terminus of the line; I ran down the helical staircase of the tram and leapt off. Across the road were the underground station and the train to South Kensington, and I was as happy and as excited as if it were a tryst I was approaching, not a job, but a life doing science. The long, long hated years of school were over. I knew it was still years before I would be a qualified scientist but for now, I was thrilled to be an apprentice to a master scientist.

The firm of consultants who were hiring me occupied the premises of a shop. It was on the corner of a small road leading into Fulham Road just west of Brompton Hospital and about half a mile from South Kensington underground station. The shop windows were dark and the entrance door closed. I pressed the bell, waited, and a young receptionist came and took me into the labs of Murray, Bull, and Spencer Ltd. She led me upstairs to see the proprietor, Humphrey Desmond Murray, a well-fed gentleman. He sat comfortably behind his desk like a modern Mr Pickwick and he had the upper-class speech and air so well portrayed by the actor, George Sanders. He had been a lecturer at Imperial College of Science and Technology, also in South Kensington, but he and his colleague, Spencer, had chosen to start their own business. Bull, I think, was a solicitor. They formed an independent firm of consultants who specialized in all aspects of the chemistry of photography. This included everything from the gelatine used to make the films, the chemicals of the photosensitive layers, the developers, and so on. They also were happy to take on odd jobs, such as making powders for Scotland Yard who used them to mark bank notes invisibly. They also sold dyes and stains for microscopy under the name Revector.

The labs were on the ground floor, in the cellars, and outbuildings of the shop and the offices were on the first floor. I never saw above this level and guessed that the upper floors were storerooms or empty. The labs were well-equipped by any standards. Even in 1938, they had electronic pH meters to measure acidity and alkalinity using glass electrodes, spectrometers and a wonderful suite of blown glass organic chemical pieces. To me it was the fulfilment of a dream that they wanted me to work in such a place. Humphrey Murray was firm and straight. He told me my hours: 9–5.30 with an hour for lunch and Saturday mornings 9–12.30. He insisted that in September of that year I enrol as a student in Birkbeck College of London University and go there in the evenings. He warned me that there was no future here at his firm. As soon as I graduated in chemistry I must leave and find a job elsewhere. He was quite open about this, but redeemed what would now seem a heartless attitude, by paying the fees of his apprentices to attend London University as evening-class students. More important for me than the formal education was the personal training and his insistence that the analyses I did were serious, not student experiments to emphasize a point of teaching. Because of this, unlike a full-time university student, I grew to regard accuracy in measurement as almost sacred. It took me a long while to reach this state of grace. As Humphrey was always saying, people's lives and jobs could depend on the right answer and the cheating and fudging of results—so normal in the university—became for me an abomination. My starting wage, at age eighteen, was about average for a working man in those days, £2 10s per week, and it rose shortly afterwards to £3 a week, equivalent to about £10,000 a year now.

My first task was to evaluate, under Humphrey Murray's guidance, a new analytical method called 'spot tests'. A German chemist, Fritz Feigel, had developed it, and Murray handed me a copy of his book and told me to read it. He must have known that I was the sort of boy who would take it home and read it in my own time. But this was not exploitative. Soon I was applying these novel methods of analysis, using just one drop of solution, not several millilitres in a test tube, to practical problems. I made the tests either on filter paper or in depressions spread in parallel rows across a slab of white porcelain. After a while, I grew unimpressed by these spot tests. They were fine for finding traces of things, like blood or sulphur, where they should not be, but they were hardly accurate or quantitative. The greatest surprise came when I had my first and only serious explosion in a lifetime as a chemist. It was a surprise because small-scale chemistry involving drops of reagent, not flasks full, is inherently safe. The quantities of chemicals used are so small that even violent reactions can do little harm. I had made a series of spot-test analyses for sulphur in photographic gelatine using a solution of sodium azide and iodine as a reagent. The presence of mere traces of sulphide makes this reagent fizz and lose its colour. When I completed my tests, I tipped the tray of solutions into a beaker, which happened to contain the residues of another earlier test using mercuric chloride. I was surprised to see that inside this beaker of mixed waste solutions, long delicate needle-shaped crystals had grown that glinted in the light. Elegance from dross, I thought, and I picked up the beaker, held it before me to the light, and shook it to watch the crystals move. As I shook it, there was a thunderous bang, which brought everyone rushing to my cellar. They found me unharmed, but dazed and slightly deafened. I was still holding the top of the beaker but there was no trace of the bottom of it or its contents. I learnt later that long crystals of the heavy metal azides, such as mercuric azide, are amongst the most sensitive of the primary explosives. Humphrey Murray was concerned and quite fatherly. He did not blame me. He apologized for not warning me that azides were notorious for making dangerously explosive compounds. He had just not thought that the quantities in each of the spot tests were large enough to represent a hazard, but clearly the combination of fifty or more tests certainly was. It was a valuable lesson, and one that now might not be learnt. So concerned are we today about safety that I would never have had the chance to work with such a mixture.

A tall dark young man oversaw the lab at Murray, Bull, and Spencer. He was a graduate chemist and his name was Tyrrell. He also had been at the Strand School, only several years earlier than I had. He was a kindly mentor and advisor, and on several occasions covered for me when I made stupid mistakes. One of these happened one Saturday morning, when I washed up the accumulation of glassware in a vast sink fed by a gas-heated boiler. This laboratory scullery was in an outbuilding in what had once been the garden. It was long before the days of dishwashers and automatic devices, and we did washing up by hand. Fortunate is the woman who marries a practical chemist, for not only can he provide in times of scarcity most of the familiar toilet and domestic products, from lipstick to detergent, but he can also wash up and enjoy doing it. Few things are more difficult or challenging to wash as delicate, expensive chemical glassware. Often evil-smelling toxic tars coated the flasks and resisted all attempts to clean them. These tarry flasks I cleaned by filling them with a mixture of chromic and sulphuric acids, and leaving the mess to digest. After learning to cope with these horrors, washing up at home is simple.

On that Saturday morning, I was cheerfully humming a tune as I went through my weekly chore. I picked up a flask, which appeared to contain water, and poured it into the sink. It was not water, it was ether, and on contact with the hot water, it boiled instantly. Its boiling point, if you did not know, is blood heat, $36°$ C. The vapour rose in a cloud. Ether has a powerful and almost pleasant smell so I realized my mistake, but not fast enough. The vapour ignited as it reached the pilot flame of the gas boiler. There was an enormous whoosh and I felt my eyebrows and front hair singe, but amazingly the sheet of flame vanished almost as fast as it had begun, and without burning any-thing, not even me. Tyrell came running in from the house, saw that no harm had been done, and with quick thinking called back to Humphrey, 'Nothing serious, just the boiler backfiring.' It is good when young to have such friends.

Another person who worked for the firm was R Riley Ratcliffe, a young technician who was on the permanent staff. He was a typical Londoner, pert and street conscious. He was not fond of me and used to like to irritate by calling me 'Alfie'. He probably thought me bumptious and, almost certainly, I was. There was another apprentice, my long-time friend and companion of school days, Edward Newton. He was a talented artist and mathematician and had looks I envied. Rightly, he had been head boy of the Strand School. What on earth was he doing here as a mere technician, I wondered? He could easily have gained a place at Oxford or Cambridge.

By modern standards, it was a hard life. The alarm clock woke me at 6.30 am and I caught the 7.45 train to Victoria from Orpington. After work ended at 5.30 I travelled by Tube to Birkbeck and spent the hour before lectures began either in the Students Union or having supper at the canteen there. Lectures and practical work occupied the time from 7 until 9. I arrived home usually about 11 and was rarely in bed before midnight. Sundays were for walking in what was then the perfect English countryside. I set out after breakfast and walked as far south as Ide Hill and as far east as Wrotham. Favourite places on my route were the Pilgrim's Way and Magpie Bottom. The latter was one of those dry green valleys that one finds in the chalk country. In those days, it was 'unimproved' and wildflowers studded the turf, including numerous species of orchid. I usually called to have tea at a cottage in the village of Shoreham. An old lady of the village ran it and it faced the River Darrent. After tea, usually sandwiches and cake, I ran the six miles back to Orpington up the downs and across the two valleys that lay between. A typical Sunday's walk and run would be about twenty miles. The most I ever walked in a weekend was forty-two miles, but this meant starting out on Saturday night and walking all night as well as all Sunday.

One of the firm's customers made gelatine of photographic quality for Kodak. One day they were in serious trouble, for the photographic emulsion made with their gelatine was only weakly sensitive to light. Humphrey suspected a lack of sulphide in the gelatine and sent me, together with Riley Ratcliffe, the more experienced technician, to have a look at the process and find out what had gone wrong. It was my first look at the industrial world; I had never realized that gelatine came from the indigestible leftovers of the meat industry. Hoofs and skin were boiled in vast vats to make the thick soup that was allowed to gel and then dried as sheets of gelatine. We asked the foreman if he could think of anything that had changed in the process during the past few weeks. He replied that nothing had changed; everything was exactly as before. My colleague noticed an empty, rusty bucket next to one of the vats and asked what it was. The foreman replied, 'That is the old bucket from which we add the hydrogen peroxide to clear the gelatine at the final stage of cooking. As you can see it rusted away, so we bought a new one last week. Here it is.' Light began to dawn. We knew that the lack of sulphide could have come from an excess of oxidant and here the new bucket was visibly larger than the old one. We soon solved the firm's problem when we found that the new bucket was twice the volume of the old one. This small experience made real for me the academic fact that volume increases as the cube of the linear dimensions. The foreman buying the new bucket thought that an increase of one-quarter in diameter and depth was of small consequence. Universities can rarely supply golden experiences such as this.

My most vivid memory of apprenticeship days was the preparation of several hundred grams of the dye pigment carmine. The recipe was hand-written in an exercise book emblazoned with stains of the dyer's craft. Take one hundred-weight of dried cochineal beetles, it said. Boil them in the copper with five gallons of ten-per-cent acetic acid. There was the 112-pound sack of beetles and the jars of acetic acid and in front of me was the copper. It looked just like the pictures I had seen of equipment in an alchemist's laboratory. A semicircular stone parapet supported the large copper vat. A large wooden lid closed the top of the vat and heat came from a gas burner beneath it. The instructions said to bring the acid to a boil and then adjust the gas so that it slowly simmered. This I did, and then began to ladle in the beetles until they were all in the copper. The beetles cooked for four hours while a strange vinegary and musty odour filled the outhouse. I decanted the dark red-brown liquor from the beetle stew through a strainer into a set of jars. The next step was to add alum solution. Then, while stirring the mixture, to add ammonia. I watched the carmine lake precipitate. The last and most rewarding step was to filter the suspension of lake through a foot diameter filter paper held in a large porcelain funnel. I washed the powder several times and then put it in a vacuum desiccator to dry. At this final stage, it was a pure red colour so intense that it seemed to draw the sense of colour out through my eyes from my brain. What a joy to participate in the transmutation of dried beetles into immaculate carmine. I felt more like the sorcerer's apprentice than merely Humphrey Murray's junior technician.

A more down-to-earth business experience was the discovery that the firm profited by buying kilogram cartons of dye from ICI and packaging it in one-gram bottles. They then sold this back to their customers, which included other ICI departments, for as much as the kilogram cost. I stayed with the firm until July 1939. Humphrey Murray was by then, I think, fed up with my unbridled curiosity and chose to transfer me to work with one of their customers, the blue-print manufacturers, Norton and Gregory. I had an extraordinary sense of fulfilment as I worked out my apprenticeship as a scientist. I am full of gratitude to Humphrey Murray and to Tyrell, and my friends of that extraordinary firm.

In the spring of 1939, the students at Birkbeck and other evening-class colleges in London received a rude shock. The government announced its intention to conscript all fit young men for military service. Full-time students would be exempt but not part-time students like those at evening classes. My fellow students at Birkbeck shared my view that this was monstrously unfair. Here were we working both in the daytime and at night, the most diligent of students. How dare they penalize us? The political blood in my veins began to boil and I drew up a petition that the Student Union then circulated for signing. We addressed it to the vice-chancellor of London University. My first draft petition was a cry from the heart and not too well expressed. Before it had gone too far, a copy fell into the hands of the Principal of the John Cass College, another evening-class college in London. The Principal's name was E de Barry Barnett. He asked if I would come to see him and he received me, a young student, most courteously. He asked if I would mind reading his revision of my text. He said he agreed with the general tone of what I was saying and that it was a most unfair and insensitive action by the government, but he wanted to be sure that we presented the best possible case. His revision was three pages of carefully drafted wisdom. He converted my two paragraphs into a plea that would stop a charging lawyer. I welcomed gladly his intervention, but not his request that I left him out of it. I was not happy to pretend that I had composed his wise words. We finally agreed that I would say that I had taken advice before drafting the second version of the petition. The Student Union at Birkbeck was delighted with it. The President at that time was Lena Chivers, now Lady Jeger, a Labour Peer. She gave her unstinted support and sent copies to all of the evening-class colleges of London.

Many of the students signed, and the large bundle made its way to the Vice-Chancellor. Soon afterwards, he invited me to see him. It is not usual for a vice-chancellor to invite a part-time first-year student to have sherry with him and I was nervous, but he soon put me at ease and listened. He agreed to present our case to the government. But this was by now August 1939 and, whatever was his intention, the invasion of Poland took the matter from our hands. The intense activity of this piece of politics did not seem to affect my studies at Birkbeck and luckily for me, as it happened, the end-of-term summer examinations produced a far better result than I had expected. Soon after the declaration of war, the government announced that all London colleges, evening and daytime, would close and the students would be evacuated to other universities. This of course was not an option for evening-class students. It was clear to me that my efforts for part-time students, although appropriate in peacetime, would not succeed now that we were at war.

During my childhood in Brixton, I attended Quaker meetings and they led me to let my conscience dictate my actions. Or, as the Quakers put it, 'Listen to the still small voice within.' A wonderful family named Street ran the Brixton Friends Meeting House. The men among them had been conscientious objectors to national service in the 1914 war, and their transparent honesty and decency made their pacifism honourable. Their example made me believe that it was right and proper to register as a conscientious objector. I was prepared for unpleasantness and shame. In the First World War, conscientious objectors had had a tough ride, and I expected that something similar would happen during the coming war. To those who find it difficult to understand how I could hold pacifist and warlike views—such as my feelings about the Spanish Civil War—in my mind simultaneously, I can only say it often seems to happen in wartime. We are by nature tribal carnivores, and at such times it is difficult to be rational. At the same time, I knew it would be at least one, if not more, years before my time of testing began, so I applied to enrol as a full-time student at a university outside London. I chose Manchester solely because I had fallen for a girl I met when staying at a youth hostel in the Lake District in July 1939. She was taking a degree in chemistry at Manchester University and was one year ahead of me. Even before I arrived in Manchester to enrol I had discovered that she had no interest in me whatsoever. But at that time I was young enough to hope that perhaps she would change her mind. Meanwhile, on the strength of my Birkbeck examination results I was able to persuade Kent County Council, the county in which I lived, to provide me with a student loan of £60 a year. Lodgings, food, clothes, and tuition fees cost more than this, but with the help of one of my mother's friends, a Miss Cameron, I was able to get a small grant of £15 a year from a private charitable trust. With £75 a year, I could manage, even though it was less than half of my wage from Murray, Bull, and Spencer.

I took the train from Euston to Manchester carrying all my possessions in my rucksack and having with me a raglan overcoat and umbrella to protect me against the well-known rain. All southerners in England believe that it rains every day in Manchester. It was a scary moment arriving at Manchester's Victoria Station. I had no idea where to stay and knew I had to find somewhere that was inexpensive. I asked the taxi driver at the station if he could take me to a cheap but decent hotel nearby. Luck was with me. He was a kind man and when he knew that I was a student took me the few hundred yards to a commercial hotel where, for a minute sum, they provided bed and breakfast. In those days, students were uncommon, particularly in the north of England, and people regarded us with touching respect. They thought that by going to college a young man could escape the traps of working-class poverty, and everyone cheered you on.

Next morning I walked through the centre of Manchester to the Oxford Road and down to the university. I joined the group of would-be students waiting to enrol. When my turn came, I told the secretary I had to start as a second-year student since I was from a London college now closed. This was not part of her programme and I was ushered into Professor AR Todd's room to explain myself. He was a tough, gruff young Scotsman. I showed him the letter of recommendation from Birkbeck and the results of my first year's examination. He harrumphed and said, 'This is very irregular, you know, to ask to start in the second year. You won't have been doing the same things there as we do here in the first year.' He paused, looked me in the eye, and said, 'I can see your problems, and so what I would like you to do is write an essay saying why you've chosen to come to Manchester and why you want to start in the second year.' This I did, not mentioning the girl who had attracted me to Manchester, or that Birkbeck was an evening-class college of London University. I did include the fact that I could only afford two years, and this seemed to impress him. He signed the forms for my enrolment and sent me back to his secretary. Soon she gave me my pack of papers, membership of the Student Union, and the address of landladies approved by the university. Most lived in a rather pleasant set of semi-detached suburban villas, about a mile from the university and close to the Manchester Royal Infirmary. I soon settled in comfortably, sharing accommodation with a history student, and was looked after by a kindly landlady.

At the end of my first month as a student, Professor Todd summoned me to his office and when I got there, he was angry. 'Lovelock,' he said, 'you've let me down; you have cheated.' I was dumbfounded and searched my mind for anything that would explain his accusation. 'How have I cheated?' 'You know full well,' he said. 'Students never get the exact result for their gravimetric analyses and certainly not twice running. You are not only a cheat, you are stupid. If you had thought of putting down something close to the right answer, you might have got away with it. No, you just looked at the demonstrator's book and copied down the composition of the solution you were supposed to be analysing.' What he was on about was a student exercise in analytical chemistry, the gravimetric analysis of the strength of a solution of potassium bromide. I did it by precipitating the bromide ion with silver nitrate solution, filtering the suspension of silver bromide, drying it and weighing it, and then calculating the amount of bromide in the solution. As a technician in London, I had done many such analyses. I could almost do them while sleepwalking. I was a professional and was expected and trusted to get the right answer. It took me twenty minutes to deflect Todd's anger with this explanation, and I do not think that he believed me even then. He was not convinced until he came a few days later to see me do the very much more difficult gravimetric analysis of the sulphate ion. Both of us then realized how inadequate is the training of university students. They often leave, qualified with a degree, but unskilled in the craft of chemistry. It made me thankful once more for Humphrey Murray's patient and unstinted tuition and his insistence on excellence; more than this, I give thanks that Murray taught me to be a professional. Having once learnt the dedication and discipline needed to do something well, professional behaviour in other fields is easier to acquire.

In the first year at Manchester I joined the Mountaineering Club. This student society had a club hut at a place called Tal-y-Braich in the Ogwen valley in North Wales. Thanks to the fact that medical students and young physicians were over-represented in the club, somebody nearly always legitimately had a car and could drive to Wales for a weekend of climbing from the Mountaineering Club's hut. Here I learned some of the tougher aspects of mountains and in the company of experienced climbers and hill walkers. I remember one day we left the converted farm cottage at Tal-y-Braich to satisfy an older member's wish to complete his list of Welsh 25s. A 25 is a mountain higher than 2500 feet. There is a curious obsession amongst mountain walkers to climb every mountain that high in some given area. The peak we were making for was Drum, one of the Carneddau—a mountain mass of mostly smooth moss and grass punctuated by small crags, rather like Dartmoor, only higher. The Carneddau ran to the east of the Ogwen valley, and we set out one day in a full gale from the northwest with snowflakes descending from a cold grey sky. It was over ten miles to Drum and we passed over Carnedd Dafydd, Carnedd Llewylen, and two prominent peaks on the way. By the time we reached the 3000-foot coll that links these two mountains the wind was storm force and the snow whipped into a horizontal sand-blast abrading our exposed faces. Was this the stuff of Antarctic exploration, I wondered? Suddenly, the dangers we faced became real when one of us crested the sharp rise between the mountains and a gust lifted him into the air. He fell in the snow on the slope just beside me and did not fall further. But our leader pressed on like the Bellman in 'The Hunting of the Snark'. His desire to collect the last of his 25s overcame common sense. In all, we walked about twenty to twenty-five miles. It would have been nothing on a fine day, but in the blizzard it was memorable.

In the years between puberty and the mid-twenties, young males are strangely impulsive. They do fear danger, but they suspend their fear while they meet some self-imposed challenge. For some, it is driving faster and furiously; for others, a gang fight; for me, it was the mountains. I would have scorned any suggestion that my choice was the most dangerous of them all, more dangerous than riding a motorbike. I should have known from the fate of other students that it is indeed the most dangerous of activities. Mountains then claimed a high proportion of the lives of those who climbed them. More than ten climbers and hill walkers I knew personally died in the years that I was a student, and mostly from exposure, although a few did fall.

After the day of the storm, the Welsh hills were covered with a snow blanket, and beneath a clear and sparkling blue sky, it was an exhilaration to look at it and to feel it. We rewarded ourselves with a quieter walk over the Glyders. We felt so good as we stood on that high mountain range in the snow, gazed down through the clear air, and enjoyed the exhilaration of the endorphins raised by the effort of climbing. Dangerous it may be but few other sports can offer such a reward.

My companion at the student digs was a history student who came from Redcar in Yorkshire, and I think his family was closely associated with the Navy. He was a civilized and companionable man but I think my pacifist views appalled him. We were well fed and warm, but for me as a young male it was a lonely existence.

Towards the end of my first term I met two young men in the Student Union and made friends with them. Kevin Cave and Frank Johnston were both Catholics and arts graduates. Kevin was tall, bespectacled, and had the air of a natural editor. Frank was a post-graduate student in the history department and so much an academic that no gown was needed to mark his credentials. They were also members of the university's Ambrose Barlow Catholic Society. Our friendship reached a point where they asked me if I would be inter-ested in joining. At first I said, 'Well, no. I'm far from being a Catholic. I am about to become a Quaker.' They seemed to think that this did not matter, so I joined and it was fortunate that I did. The university's Socialist Society, part of which was in the pocket of the Communist Party, was recruiting many students like me. Had I joined this, it could have led to many difficulties in my scientific career, including travel to America in later life. In those days, it was not seen to be subversive to join a society run by Irish Catholics.

The society was like most student societies—radical. It would have fitted well with the liberation theology of present-day South America. The stuffy Catholic hierarchy, represented by the Bishop of Salford, referred to the society in a letter sent to parish priests as a place where the young would be 'in the proximate occasion of mortal sin'. He used these strong words because he felt righteous anger over the society's intention to host a university debate on the subject 'God or Stalin'. They had asked the Socialist Society to provide a champion for Stalin. They proposed a debate on traditional moral theology lines and the Marxists were delighted with the chance to perform on so intellectual a stage. To add to the Bishop's concern, his informant must have mentioned my presence as an active member of the Cath-olic society. This led him to warn of the dangers of mixed marriages. I found all this fuss a refreshing change from university socialism, which by then had become indistinguishable from the dull and cheerless faith of Marxism. There were also fringe benefits. The society held dancing classes for its members in the crypt of the Holy Name church close to the University. Here I met a wonderful group of attractive and intelligent Irish girls. The girl who particularly caught my fancy was Mary Delahunty. She had been a secretary in the Architecture Department and had become a member of the Ambrose Barlow Society. Her clear-minded maturity and her good looks attracted me.

Manchester and, indeed, most northern industrial towns were deep in poverty in the 1930s. George Orwell's book, *The Road to Wigan Pier*, captures the all-pervasive squalor under which so much of northern England then lived. In the north in those days women usually worked outside the home. Many were descended from those who immigrated to England to escape the famine in Ireland at the failure of the potato crop. There was little tradition of cooking among them, and consequently malnutrition exacerbated the effects of poverty. Wandering as a student around the streets of Manchester I was amazed to find no shops or street markets selling fruit and vegetables. This was something so common in London that one expected it everywhere and, indeed, this was true in most southern cities. I did manage to find two greengrocers in greater Manchester: one was near the town centre and another in Didsbury, an affluent suburb. In most parts, the corner shops stocked only potatoes. We were well fed in my digs in terms of calories and tastiness, but the fruit and green vegetables so common in the south were lacking. I experienced the poverty of Manchester briefly when there was a severe snowstorm in January 1940—so severe that it isolated Manchester from the rest of the country for at least a week. I remember living on baked beans and nothing else. At the end of this period, they admitted me to the Manchester Royal Infirmary for the treatment of scurvy, a Vitamin C deficiency. My professor, Alexander Todd, had elucidated the chemical structure of at least one vitamin and was shocked to find vitamin deficiency in one of his students. It was to be the turning point in my days as a student at Manchester. Todd became quite concerned when he learned how I was trying to survive, and he became convinced that I was far poorer than in fact I was. He excused my poor attendance and examination results and saw me, I think, as a student struggling against adversity.

The chemistry taught at Manchester specialized in what one might call high organic chemistry, the chemistry that was to make Todd a Nobel Laureate. His award was for the discovery of the structures of the nucleoside bases, which led in its turn to perhaps the most important discovery of the 20th century—that of the structure of DNA. Perversely, I found this science, no matter how important it was, uninteresting, even boring. I would spend time that I should have spent at chemistry lectures attending lectures on history, economics, and indeed anything that seemed interesting. In some ways, this was using the university properly, but it was not part of the approved life of a student. My favourite subjects of my own syllabus were bacteriology and physics. I must admit that I chose chemistry as the main subject for my degree because it contained, in those days, relatively little mathematics. Physics was so mathematical that I feared failure if I took it. It was not that I found mathematics or its principles difficult to understand; quite the reverse. Mathematical problems still fascinate me, but I was slow in the execution of the arithmetic steps of those problems, and my slowness prevented me from answering the necessary number of set questions. Some time in the Lent term of 1940, I moved to new digs in Fallowfield, along with two other students, Malcolm Woodbine and William Griffiths. We moved partly for companionship and partly because it was considerably cheaper than the digs in town. It was much further out from the university—too far to walk, but an easy tram ride. The new digs were quite comfortable and the food was healthier and included vegetables.

At the end of my first term in physics I was singled out with two other students and warned that, if I did not improve my performance by the spring term examinations, I would be thrown out of the university. My slowness at mathematics had struck again and let me down. Therefore, from January until March 1940, I worked hard. This was the only time I did so at Manchester. I practised endless examples of physics and physical chemistry until at last I was proficient in the handling of the arithmetic background of physical principles. As the great mathematician Euler said, and the desktop computer in front of me proves, all operations in mathematics are no more than simple addition. I remember looking with distaste at the textbook proofs of electromagnetic theory and finding them all based on trigonometrical functions like sines and cosines, arranged in a near pathological prolixity. I knew that by using the Heaviside operator based on that wonderful, outrageous, impossible number, the square root of -1, the same proofs reduced from several pages of trigonometry to a few lines of equations. I knew that in the 1940s mathematical purists still regarded a proof using this operator as no more than a sleight of a hand. I gambled that my physics examiners would consider the use of these operational functions as quite appropriate and see that, as a good scientist should, I was using a simple device to achieve an end. I hoped that they would not see me merely as taking a short cut through what seemed to be an unnecessarily meandering path of trigonometrical equations. It worked, and after the spring examinations, they even praised me for my diligence in finding another way to solve the problem. This made me realize that Manchester in those days was a good university and one that rewarded enterprise. I was intrigued to read in *Nature* of September 1999 that Otto Frisch and Rudolf Peierls were on the staff of the Physics Department in 1940, and there calculated the size of the critical mass of uranium-235 needed for an atom bomb. They found it was astonishingly small, and that therefore the bomb was feasible.

Teaching labs and lecture rooms at Manchester were all but unheated in that bitter winter of 1940. I recall one Monday morning entering the physical chemistry teaching laboratory. It was a large room with benches arrayed in parallel rows with wooden stools in front of them. At my place, on the bench, was set out an experiment to measure electrode potentials. Polished wooden potentiometers, galvanometers, and a large battery, and pieces of wire, beakers, etc. were all there. My task was to find the potential as measured against a calomel electrode of various solutions of sodium chloride. There was also on the bench a wash bottle half filled with distilled water. When I picked it up a wonderful change occurred. The clear water suddenly filled with lace-like crystals of ice. So cold was the laboratory that the water was well below its freezing point, but as a super-cooled liquid. The moment I disturbed the water by lifting the wash bottle it froze. Although clothed only in trousers, shirt, vest and jacket, I cannot remember feeling cold myself at that time, nor did I feel cold when sitting for a one-hour lecture shortly afterwards on the same morning. Feeling cold is a penalty of ageing.

I registered as a conscientious objector at the Labour Exchange in Manchester. It was an uneasy experience, waiting in the queue of men enlisting and having to say, 'I want to register as a conscientious objector.' I half expected shouts of scorn or accusations of cowardice from the men around me. It did not happen. The clerk merely said, 'Go to counter No. 10 and they will deal with you.' I went to counter No. 10 and was asked courteously to take a seat while they took down what were in those days called one's particulars: age, qualifications, schooling, and so on. The clerk said, 'You know, do you, that as a registered full-time student in the sciences you do not have to register here.' I did know, but I wanted to go through with it. I wanted to feel committed; I had come too far to duck out now. When I explained this the clerk said: 'Very well, you will receive a summons to appear before a tribunal within a few months.' The Society of Friends ran a school for conscientious objectors, which trained them to cope with the problems raised by our odd status in wartime England. They held mock tribunals at which we faced questions from a panel of senior Quakers acting as judges. The questions were those actually asked at the real tribunal.

My summons came early in 1940. I was to appear before the tribunal, consisting of three judges, in March, but first I must make a written statement of about a thousand words on why I was a CO. This I had to post to the tribunal and read it to them when I appeared there. All that I can recall of this statement is the start, which went: 'A lifelong association with the Society of Friends has led me to believe that war is evil.' The Chairman of the tribunal asked me why I was not a Quaker. I replied, 'I intend to become one after the tribunal, whatever its conclusion.' It seemed to me improper to present myself before them as a Friend, since Quakers were often exempted as a matter of course. They asked me other questions, mainly, it seemed, to discover how long I had held pacifist beliefs. When it became clear that they were longstanding, and that I had not joined the Cadet Corps at my school on conscientious grounds, they conferred amongst themselves and the senior judge looked straight at me and said, 'We have decided to grant you an unconditional exemption from military service. We feel that we can rely on you to follow your conscience and do what is right.' Oddly, he added finally, 'We think you should make some kind of gesture, such as volunteering as a blood donor, but this we do not ask as a condition of your exemption. We leave it to you.' I was much moved and thankful. Their conclusion placed me in deep debt to my country. It was then truly civilized. They had shown trust in me in the most remarkable way. I went to the Royal Infirmary to enrol as a blood donor, but after tests, the young doctor came back to tell me that I had a blood group not suitable for donation.

Soon after my public appearance before the tribunal, I asked the quarterly meeting of the Quakers in Manchester if they would accept me as a Friend. They gave me the two *Books of Discipline* to read, which recount the experiences of the Quakers since their formation in the 17th century. A month or so passed and two Manchester Friends asked me to come to the Meeting House for, as they put it, a talk. They were young northerners of that quiet respectable kind that is common in north Lancashire. They first asked me if I had ever had a religious experience. I answered no, thinking probably rightly in their context, that they meant something transcendental such as that so well described by Bishop Montefiore in his autobiography, *Oh God, What Next?* Here he movingly tells how, as a schoolboy at Rugby, he saw in his room an appearance of Jesus who said 'Follow me'. This overwhelming event changed and coloured his life from then on. For me, life had always been firmly grounded and most solid in its reality. Looking back, though, I wonder, in my own context, if the whole of life is in certain ways a religious experience. The world of good human relationships can be so delightful that the concept of Heaven seems to imply a sensory overload. Sunlight dappling the fallen leaves of a wood or glinting on the pebbles of a stream is beautiful, but to look at the sun itself is blinding.

The two Friends did not seem put out by my saying no to their enquiry about a religious experience. They asked me about my philosophy, which was that of a Fabian socialist. They then moved on to what was their principal concern: was I merely asking to become a Friend because of my conscientious objection? Again, I replied no, thinking of my childhood and the benign influence of the Street family in Brixton. They then told me what I had known but had never fully understood: that each Friend was in truth a minister of religion, and that this was both a distinction and a burden. Was I ready to take it on? I asked if this meant that I should now become evangelical on behalf of the Society of Friends. Oh no, they said, not unless that is your calling. What you must do is always to obey your conscience, that still small voice within. I then realized that the God of the Quakers was part of the model Universe that exists in our minds. This was something that at that time did not clash with my true vocation as a scientist. Sometime later, they accepted me as a Friend.

My inquisitors were right to be concerned about the pressures of wartime England on my mind. I doubt, if peace had continued, that I would have taken so serious a step as to become a Quaker. Only those who lived through those years of the Second World War in England can understand how intense, how certain, and how fulfilling was the tribal acceptance that we were one nation and engaged in a just war. We knew that it was not a war of conquest in any sense, but one for justice. There was something in such a *Weltanschauung* that left no place for conscientious objectors. All I had left was a youthful fantasy of becoming a Quaker martyr. I had for years schooled myself to cope with the thought of the cruelties, the ignominy experienced by COs in the First World War, and I was certain it would be repeated. At the very least, I would be imprisoned or have to serve as a stretcher-bearer under battle conditions. It was wholly unnerving at age twenty to receive respect, especially from old soldiers, as someone of principle. It was hard to be reminded daily that everything, from the food I ate, to my clothes and books, were dearly bought with the lives of brave sailors and merchant seamen. It was impossible not to share the pride of the nation in the brave young pilots of the Battle of Britain.

As June 1940 approached, and with it the end of my first year as a student of Manchester University, I found that I was broke. I had spent the entire loan from Kent County Council and the smaller donation from the charity. I did not intend to return home to Orpington to be a charge on my parents for the three summer months before the next term started. I wanted to take a temporary job as a merchant seaman, but soon found that if I did I would probably find myself at some distant place abroad when term was due to start in October. My Quaker friends suggested I try for farm work and recommended a Quaker farm at the village of Nether Kellet near Carnforth, about fifty miles north of Manchester.

Dale Barns was a large farm even by present-day standards. There were about 150 acres around the farmhouse and vast amounts of grazing land along the seashore at Bolton le Sands, a nearby village. There was also hill grazing at another farm site near Ingleborough in the Pennines. In peacetime, the sheep grazed the mountains in the summer and the shore in the winter, and the middle farm was kept mainly for cattle and dairy farming. Wartime law obliged farmers to use up to forty per cent of their land for the growing of cereal crops and similar foodstuffs. Of the many things I learned from those months at the farm was how many skills were needed, and how often improvisation and invention were required. I had, I am ashamed to say, previously regarded the farm-worker as some dim unintelligent fellow whose mind worked as slowly as his crops rotated. I also learnt that farming life was not for me. It is an unremitting occupation. Keeping animals demands seven days a week of attention and we had to milk the cows twice a day; Sunday cannot be an exception. We could not leave the sheep to graze unattended because the weather happened to be foul with the rain driving in horizontally. The thing that most put me off farm work was the healthy euphoria of every evening, which made me so contented that there was no desire for reading or thinking. The work was so hard during the day that by evening time I just fell asleep the moment I lay down on my bed.

After a week or so I grew used to the daily round of work. I never managed milking by hand without pain and I admired Peggy, the farmer's daughter, for her facility when occasionally she would help us out. The haymaking strengthened my arms so much that by August I could lift two fifty-six-pound weights, one in each hand, above my head. The Whittaker boys and Gilbert, the Irishman who worked on the farm with us but lived in the village, were fine companions. They were forever teasing me about my love for Mary Delahunty back in Manchester. It was the daily sending and arrival of letters that stirred their interest. To them, writing was as hard a chore as milking was for me. To them, a love that inspired such a flood of correspondence must be profound indeed. Their celibacy puzzled me. The two young men never ventured far from the farm except to the Friends Meeting House on Sundays. There were plenty of eligible local girls around from other farming families, including Quakers, for this was one of the few Quaker communities in England. Perhaps even for them, the sheer drudgery of wartime farming with its shortage of labour drained them of energy and desire.

The boys' father, old Mr Whittaker, was a widower, and lived at the farm on the shore at Bolton le Sands. He was a tough, stern character and feared by the family. I found him critical and difficult to deal with at first. He had no patience with my learning phases and seemed to expect me to be as strong and as skilled as his own sons, but there was one thing I did that brought me his approval. He was obsessed about thistles and would nag endlessly about their growth in the meadows and ask why someone didn't do something about it. I found that I could use Father Time's reaper, the scythe, efficiently, and I took on voluntarily the job of mowing down the thistles from the meadows, a job the boys detested. So on days when the weather or some other event prevented haymaking and turnip-weeding, I would gladly take my scythe, walk to whatever meadow I hadn't already mowed, and attack the thistles. It was satisfying work. I saw these plants as my imaginary enemy and rejoiced in the swish of the scythe as I mowed them down. On my 21st birthday in July 1940, to the amazement of everyone at Dale Barns, old Mr Whittaker gave me a pound note and told me to take the weekend off. I immediately went to the village on my bicycle, telephoned Mary, and arranged to meet her in Blackpool on that next Saturday. The purchasing power of £1 in those days was equivalent to about £100 now, so the weekend in Blackpool was not stinted. The boys told me that their father had never previously made such a gesture, and I can only assume that my diligence with the thistle mowing had moved him deeply.

Mary Delahunty and I spent my twenty-first birthday in Blackpool. We saw a Spitfire fly by at a hundred feet or so above the beach. The sight of it made us think how beautiful it was, yet we were pacifists, and what we saw was a perfectly constructed killing machine. Like Blake's tiger, it had a perfect symmetry. I remember the spirited but outrageous reply of a Cambridge don in the First World War. A super-patriotic woman gave him a white feather, symbol of cowardice, because he was young, apparently fit, but not fighting at the front. He replied, 'Madam, I represent the culture the other men are fighting to save.' In the civilized atmosphere of the Second World War, white feathers had no place, but in a way, their absence was just as hard to bear. It really was our finest hour, although few then knew the cost. The war brought the nation from the status of a superpower to a state of impoverishment, barely better than that of a developing country now. In a way, it left us worse off than the vanquished, for we still had to keep up the appearances of a superpower, and pay the costs expected of one, from almost no reserves.

August came, and soon we encountered the hardest work of all: harvesting the oats by hand. It had been good summer weather for northern England, but even so, enough wind and rain had beaten down a great deal of the crop. The horse-driven side-cutter could manage only a part of the cutting; we had to do the rest by hand with scythes and sickles. I soon learnt that wonderful swaying motion and movement needed to cut a flowing swathe through the oats. Much harder was the gathering of the sheaves of cut oats, which we tied together by two stems of oats, forming a kind of string. I was hopelessly inefficient at this and they left me to scythe on. The sheaves of oats were stacked in piles of six, with two on top acting as a kind of thatch to stop the rain from rotting the crop beneath. The hardest job of all was the pitchforking of the sheaves onto the cart. Hard, because in the fickle weather of this mountainous oceanic region, we had to do the job immediately the sheaves were dry. We started at first light one day in late August and the job was not finished until midnight. I did not see the end of it: the boys told me I passed out in the field in the evening and they carried me back to the house to bed. I can only remember waking the next morning, stiff and still feeling tired.

September, after the harvest was over, was by comparison a wonderful month. Work eased off and there was time to visit the delightful small towns like Silverdale, and for picnics on the River Lune. One job for me in this month was taking the milk round, or, should I say helping the horse to deliver the milk. The Whittaker boys harnessed this wonderful intelligent animal to the milk-cart and, as soon as I shook the reins, it set off for Bolton le Sands. It knew the way and stopped of its own volition at the first house where milk was due to be delivered. All that I had to do was ask the woman at the door how much milk she needed and then ladle it from the churn into her jug. After collecting the payment I went back to the horse, shook her reins, and off we went again to the next house. This went on until the horse decided, not me, that the round was over and that we should go back to the farm. I have rarely felt so redundant as on this occasion when I served as an assistant to a horse. The Whittakers were farmers who were unusually compassionate and understanding of their animals. They were concerned for their pain and seemed to know them all as individuals. The farm dog was intelligent enough that when called from the bedroom window at 7 am she would go out into the fields and round up the milking cows from the rest of the herd. She would drive them back to the byre unaided so that they were there waiting to be milked by the time we had washed, dressed, and shaved.

When it was time for me to go back south in the middle of September, Peggy arranged a special dinner on the Sunday to send me on my way next morning. I had grown very fond of the family and of Dale Barns and thought of it as a home. The parting was painful. Next day I rode my bicycle into Lancaster to catch the train to Manchester. I badly wanted to see Mary but I knew that I had to move on to my home in Kent. I had promised my mother and father that I would see them for a while before starting the autumn term, and I compromised by spending just a day in Manchester. I then hitched a ride with a friendly lorry driver I knew who regularly travelled between Manchester and the London suburb of Mitcham. I went to a factory in the east of Manchester to pick up the lorry. The business of the firm was packaging. Packaging is usually associated with the wasteful extravagances of marketing—think of the ballpoint pen displayed in what looks like an acre of white card emblazoned with hyperbolic advertising. In spite of wartime austerity, some products still needed packaging, and my friend the driver spent his days and nights moving the material of packaging between Manchester and London.

It was early in the morning of 14 September when I boarded his lorry; a medium-sized panel truck with a diesel engine separating the passenger and driver's seats in the cab. When moving, it was intolerably noisy and smelly and the seats hard and uncomfortable. It was so miserable as to make long-distance charter flights in economy seem like an orgy of hedonism. We slowly trundled south along the narrow roads of England, and I remember passing through the beautiful town of Lichfield but skirting Birmingham. We stopped to eat at my driver's favourite diner called Clifford's Closet on the Cliff. It was at Bromsgrove, and an island of prosperity in a heavily rationed landscape. Almost anything to eat was there and consumer goods were exchanged freely. There were prostitutes also, plying their trade discreetly. Wartime truck driving was a miserably stressful job, but an essential one. I guess the authorities knew what went on at Clifford's Closet but ignored what was a small matter nationally, just as they never attempted to ration the farmers. Rationing worked well in wartime United Kingdom. We never were indignant about these minor cheats by the producers and carriers of food. What brought community disapproval and anger was cheating by wealthier neighbours; happily, this was rare.

After a farm-style lunch, we drove on. By evening, as the sun was setting, we were near Luton and on the Dunstable Downs, looking south towards London. The sky was red in the west but to our surprise, it was red in the south also. At first we thought we were looking at mock sunset, a meteorological phenomenon. Then we realized that it must be a large fire. So free of action had the first year of war been in England that our first thought was not of a fire caused by bombing but one that had happened naturally. Nothing was further from our minds than the fact that London was burning because of a large bomber raid. As we moved south through Watford and darkness fell, the southern sky glowed red. We began to wonder what was in store for us. We crossed London on the western side, as this was our route to Mitcham, and it was then clear that most of the fires were to the east. We encountered only occasional evidence of bombing: crumbled houses, blocked-off roads and the occasional fire. We crossed Hammersmith Bridge and went on to Mitcham, where all was relatively quiet. I had planned to take a train from there to Orpington, where my mother and father lived, but no trains were running. This was the first large air raid and the disorganization was far worse than it was later with even worse raids.

To me the greatest military blunder of the Second World War was the blind belief of all participants in bombing as a means of winning the war. It almost equalled in cruel stupidity the blunders of the First World War, when men died horribly by the millions in the noxious mud of the trenches. All of us, military and civilian, had drawn wrong conclusions about the effects of bombing. What misled us were the events of the Spanish Civil War, where almost unopposed fleets of bombers defeated the defenders of small, tight Mediterranean towns like Teruel and Guernica. The larger European war was not like this, and in addition the emotional impact of the Spanish war was for many of us, especially those of Leftist inclinations, so great that the Second World War seemed quite tame by comparison. The Spanish war was for the Left almost a holy war; the Second World War was merely a job to do. Both sides believed in the myth of the all-powerful bomber and that strategic bombing would certainly lead to capitulation. The evidence of the bombs in the Second World War is quite to the contrary, and it was only when there was a qualitative change in intensity, with the dropping of the first nuclear weapons, that they had the expected result. In London, most of those who were seriously frightened by bombing left for safer places, and the remainder adapted stoically. The only time during that war when I can recall a sense of real unease about military action was towards the end of the war when the V-weapon missiles were used. I think it was the absence of any definite respite, the period of peace between raids, that made the difference. Bombs dropped by aircraft can be withstood because the event is never continuous; with missiles you never know when another one will fall and there is no spell of quiet and safety for recuperation. We have heard far too little about the feelings and plight of average German and Japanese people. They suffered bombing at a higher intensity and for far longer than ever we did. That their spirit was never broken is surely proof of the inefficiency of bombing civilians as a practical way of winning wars.

The visit to my Orpington home of a New Zealand relative made easy my return to Manchester. He was a Major in the army and he came in a Land Rover driven by a Maori driver for a brief visit to my mother and father. He broke the journey between his base in Kent and another in Hertfordshire and was able to take me to Mitcham to keep my appointment with the lorry driver. It meant only the slightest detour and, on the way back through London we saw more damage from the bombing, but remarkably the greater part of the city seemed as usual. A journey through Docklands at that time would probably have revealed a different scene. We encountered a few streets closed by signs saying 'unexploded bomb' and it was a wonderful excitement to have my New Zealand relative, the Major, override the police and just drive past whatever was waiting to explode. The Army delivered me to my friend the lorry driver and we set off on the tedious journey back to Manchester.

The teaching lab for third year students was a long room with teak benches arranged in parallel rows. Each bench was about twenty-five-feet long and split longitudinally by a central wooden wall with shelves for reagent bottles. There were, of course, Bunsen burners, without which no lab seemed complete. But new to me was steam heat with taps to the steam supply at every student's position. Around the walls were fume cupboards—glass chambers in which we did experiments that produced noxious or toxic fumes. At each student's bench, there were small sinks with a swan-necked tap. These taps fed cold water to the condensers—those elegant blown-glass constructions that are so much a part of organic chemistry. Most of the year's work was to analyse the composition of mixtures made up from three different organic compounds, and there were ten or more of these mixtures to analyse. I thought them a fascinating puzzle and soon found that the first step was to separate the mixture into discernible parts. We could distil it and so separate it into portions that distilled at different temperatures and put these aside for identification. We could mix it with water or some other solvents to see if it separated into two layers. We could add acid or alkali to see if something precipitated. When the mixture was finally separated into three single substances these had to be identified by measuring their boiling or melting points and then checked against a table of melting and boiling temperatures. Sometimes it was necessary to go further and characterize the compounds isolated by making special compounds from them. Thus, if we suspected that a ketone or an aldehyde had been isolated, we used the reagent 2,4 dinitrophenylhydrazine to make the hydrazone, which was usually fine red or orange crystals. The melting point of these crystals helped to identify the ketone from which it had originated. There was a list of the melting points of the dinitrophenyl hydrazones and other compounds on the instructor's desk at the end of the lab. It was a delightful and challenging way to stretch the student's mind and analytical skills. Here again my apprenticeship at Humphrey Desmond Murray's laboratory came to my aid. I knew the smells and appearances of an amazing range of organic chemicals. We started the course with easily separated mixtures, such as acetone, butyl acetate and methylene dichloride. We moved on to more difficult mixtures, such as picoline, xylene and acetophenone. Then finally to the stumper: a mixture of cyclohexene, cyclohexane, and benzene, all of which were hydrocarbons and all of which boiled at the same temperature and therefore could not be separated by distillation.

Knowing the strangely evocative smell of picoline and the penetrating odour of cyclohexene, I was usually ahead of my fellow students. Instead of wasting a futile week trying to separate a mixture by distillation, something impossible to do, I was busy removing such compounds as cyclohexene by its reaction with bromine and then identifying the dibromocyclohexane. I was through the entire collection of mixtures intended to keep us occupied until the Spring of 1941 by Christmas 1940.

The months from May 1940 until January 1941 spent in Mary's company taught me more than a lifetime at a university could have done. My dear, myopic, politically conscious mother had looked after me in my adolescence with all the intensity of a Jewish mother. With the very best of intentions, she had provided me with little room to grow. I think I was the last boy of my year in 1936 to stop wearing short-length trousers. I was oblivious that I cut an absurd figure. I just liked the freedom that shorts gave for walking, and my mother never noticed. My love for Mary made me a part of the Delahunty family. The Delahuntys were a wondrously warm and human family and soon, with subtle suggestions, made up for the lost and lonely years of adolescence. Mary's uncle, Ted Doran, was a drama critic for the Manchester *Guardian*, as it then was. He would sometimes have a pair of free tickets for the better seats in the opera house. We lived a life that seemed almost sybaritic in the otherwise utterly grim environment of wartime Manchester. We saved enough for the occasional night out at the Squirrel Restaurant in Manchester, where the standard of food supplied, at a price, was far above that of the rations. Manchester was, until Christmas 1940, spared most of the bombing. London and Liverpool were the prime targets of the German bombers, but a few bombs did fall on Manchester and to these, I am eternally grateful. They gave me the reason and excuse to stay the night at Mary's flat, and soon I gave up my digs in Fallowfield. I had never been at any time in my life the kind of male who wished to play the field. I was in love with Mary Delahunty and I wanted to marry as soon as we could. I knew that I would have to wait until I had my degree and the means to keep her. In those days, students were never married. They rarely ever lived together as lovers, but in 1940 bombs arriving at random from the sky were a fine reminder that life can be short and should be lived now, not postponed and taken later like a pension.

So much was I learning in those days about life, about love, about decent human relationships, that there was no place in my mind for the excellent chemistry that was being taught at the university. The final year at Manchester was mainly about the research program that Professor Todd had made famous. The chemistry was the nucleoside bases. These are the links of the molecular chain that is DNA—that wondrous double helix and the living program of all organisms. Of course, ten more years were to pass before Crick and Watson discovered the nature of DNA itself, but Todd and his colleagues were setting the scene so that when it came the discovery was inevitable. Quite rightly, Todd received the Nobel Prize for this work. Yet, here was I, with this wonderful opportunity to learn from such a master, so bemused with Mary and her family and all they had to teach me that I turned aside from the best organic chemistry in the world.

There was more to it than this. My love for science was all embracing. I had always been repelled by intense specialization, such as was the nature of nucleoside chemistry. I did no more than commit to memory just enough of it to ensure that I got some sort of degree. As a subsidiary subject, I attended bacteriology classes at the Manchester Infirmary. This I found entrancing and I never missed a single lecture or practical session. Perhaps it was the background of fear when handling live tubercle bacilli or typhoid organisms that kept me interested, in addition to the discipline of sterile working that has to be learned until it becomes instinctive. It all seemed so much more real to me than the intricacies of a chemistry that had no 'hands-on' content. I did not know it then, but the bacteriology I learnt was to be an important part of the biology that helped me in the quest for Gaia twenty or more years later.

The idyllic time with Mary ended in early 1941. Mary had gone to stay with a strange couple called the Stormont Murrays, who lived near High Wycombe. The sculptor, Eric Gill, who lived at Piggots, just near there, had entranced her. She had taken to me somewhat less intensely than I to her and on the rebound from a betrayal by a previous lover. He was an architect at the University Department of Architecture, where she had worked as a secretary. I think the last straw that severed our relationship was an encounter with my mother in a tearoom at a London railway station. Mary told me later that on her way to meet her she bought a posy of violets as a gift. My mother's response to this warm gesture was not pleasure but complaint—they were she said, a waste of money. This was followed by a lecture on the evils of Catholicism, and the statement that her boy was not to have his career blasted by an early marriage and a string of children. It must have been an awful tea. Nell Lovelock was a formidable woman and utterly set in what she knew was right, or thought was right. Soon after, I received the letter from Mary that was to close our affair. I was devastated for quite a while in spite of the support I received from the Delahuntys, especially from Mary's mother. By spring 1941 the need to prepare and organize an Easter holiday walk in the Lake District took my mind off my troubles. I had offered to escort a party of students belonging to the Ambrose Barlow Catholic Society . We planned to stay at youth hostels. Among the students was a Delahunty relative, Moya Kearney, who knew of the break between Mary and me and was warm, sympathetic, and kind. The last I saw of Mary, until we met again forty-five years later, was in July 1941, just after I had learned that I had passed my degree examination, but only as a bottom second. On that day, we spent a heavenly time bicycling from her mother's house in Moss Side to the village of Delph, near Oldham, where her Aunt, Ciss Seed, had a cottage. I can still recall that last kiss in the warm sunshine outside the smoke-dark brick of the bank house where the family lived on the corner of the road in Moss Side.

The books read at my family home at Orpington tended to be political: Gollancz's famous Left Book Club made up many of them, with their characteristic yellow jackets and black print which stood out like grounded wasps on our bookshelves. I was well versed in the socialist litany and swallowed without qualm books like Edgar Snow's *Long March* and, of course, anything good about the Soviet Union. Even the novels at home tended to be political, like Cronin's famous book, *The Citadel*. It was only after working for several years for the Medical Research Council, target of much of Cronin's diatribe, that I realized that things were not so simple as portrayed in his book. Shaw was my mother's bible and prayer book combined. My grandmother happily was less intellectual. She would walk at least twice a week the mile or so downhill towards Orpington High Street to visit the Penny Library. She borrowed what she called her 'little bit of love', what she read were the Mills and Boon books of her day. The Delahuntys gave me the other side of literature, not the political other side but the reading for pleasure rather than for instruction. Mary opened my mind with Yeats and such craftsmen of literature as CE Montague, and such light-hearted books as the Penguin *Weekend Book* and *Cold Comfort Farm* by Stella Gibbons. I think that, by taking in this and missing much of Todd's expertise in the specialist branch of chemistry, I lost little. So few scientists are able to express their science in a readable and interesting way, and I owe the Delahuntys a debt for opening my mind to literature. More than this was the way that they gently plucked away the prickles and thorns of a childhood in the wild.

One Sunday morning Mary's mother, Helen, insisted on coming with me to the Friends Meeting House. Instead of walking, as was my usual way, we took the tram to the centre of Manchester. The Meeting House was an imposing building with a large central hall, containing pews arranged in a square several rows deep. The Manchester Friends were good speakers and when moved by their internal voice of conscience would rise and give forth, sometimes for as long as twenty minutes, an amazingly coherent and relevant comment on some contemporary affair. I was envious of their ability to speak so well and was never able to get up and contribute myself. It was not until many years later that I discovered that such extemporary speaking needs a lot of prior preparation. After the meeting Mrs Delahunty was grateful and revealed how she had always wanted to experience a religious service other than in a Catholic church. She expressed the wish that her own priest would talk even half as much on interesting topics as those that she had just heard. It was not fair, though, to compare the capacity to entertain of the elite of the Society of Friends in Manchester with that of a humble parish priest.

In 1941 Mary's mother asked me what might happen now that Germany was at war with the Soviet Union. I replied, 'It is wonderful news for us. There will be a lot less bombing, as they will need their planes for the Russian campaign. War with Russia defeated Napoleon; perhaps it will be Hitler's ending also.'

I have wondered how I passed my degree examination and, still more, why Professor Todd should have recommended me for employment at the National Institute for Medical Research. It was an institute run by his father-in-law, Sir Henry Dale, at that time President of the Royal Society, and one of the most distinguished labs in the country. Did he see in me a good chemist who had done poorly in examinations because of privations or did he see me as a superb technician? Professor Todd was the best of professors—an outstanding, active scientist, yet one who cared for his students. He would appear suddenly in the teaching lab and move around the benches like the hospital consultant visiting the beds of his patients. When he came to me, our conversation was never about chemistry, always about politics or the war. I remember him coming in one morning carrying a frown of considerable disapproval on his face. He towered above me. 'Lovelock,' he said, 'is it true that you're a conscientious objector?' 'Yes,' I said, 'I'm a Quaker.' His prepared lecture, no doubt intended to bring me to my senses, crashed before it had even flown. I think he saw conscientious objectors as the cowardly who used a legal loophole to escape fighting for their country. But in his mind also was a belief that Quakers were brave dissidents who had odd views but which were acceptable and civilized. The conversation began again, Todd now in his lively role trying to flesh out the curiosity, 'What do Quakers really think?' asked he. Students rarely ever realize that such encounters are the real examinations. Todd had little respect for set examinations and said that he would not ask questions at the examination on anything in his class lectures. I think he saw the degree examinations as a mere formality. My rapid passage through the maze of set analyses may not have passed unnoticed.

It is good to have a short spell as a student, but I found my eighteen months at Manchester enough. The thought of the seven-year stints to a medical degree or a PhD, which are now the lot of the average student, appals me. For those aiming towards an expert profession like medicine or law, I suppose it is not so much of a problem, and better than employment in a factory or an office, but for the creative, it is a cruelty. It is, from the nation's point of view, a near criminal loss of their skills. For me the mix of daytime employment as an apprentice and evening class study was ideal. Full-time study at a university certainly supplied my social needs but, apart from the job recommendation, added little to my capacity as a scientist.

Near the end of my time at Manchester University, local firms invited students to apply for jobs. This nearly always meant a free lunch, so of course we went willingly. Professor Todd, as ever solicitous of his students' welfare, insisted that we take no employment offering less than £300 per year. Inflation adjusted, I think this corresponds to something approaching £20,000 to £25,000 a year now. Among the firms offering jobs were ICI, Thomas Hedley—a branch of Proctor & Gamble—and British Celanese. I took the tram to the factory of Thomas Hedley in West Manchester to arrive there at

9.30 am, and along with other students we went to a room full of desks. They gave us the thick books of a psychological profile test with multiple-choice questions. Compared with the university examination in those days it was an easy task with which to earn a lunch. The questions took an hour to complete, and then we toured the plant in groups of one or two and were quizzed about our interests and why we wanted to work for the firm. It was so different from the casual interview that one had with a British firm; at these a small panel, rarely more than three people, judged the applicants by their accent, demeanour, vitality and so on. Two weeks later, they invited me back to the plant and told me that the tests confirmed their personal decision to offer me a job. I was amazed. It was not what I had been expecting. As a young idealist and socialist, I was full of the dogmas that work for an industrial firm was a form of slavery: a bondage where I would be obliged to sell my talents for a pittance while they made profits from them. In truth, they were offering a well-paid industrial job doing a skilled necessary task. My disdain, though, was increased by the thought that it was also unexciting science. As a southern Englishman, I was by culture polite, whatever were my inner thoughts, much as the Japanese are now. Before I could say diplomatically that I had prospects elsewhere to consider, they added that their tests showed that I was an ideal choice for employment in marketing. They also said to me that the same test showed that I was quite unsuited to scientific research. This incredible news gave me an honourable exit, for I truly wished to do nothing but science. I had certainly not come this far to be diverted into a purely capitalist occupation: marketing. Many years later, in 1959, the American Company, Proctor & Gamble, that owned Thomas Hedley, invited me to their headquarters in Cincinnati to give a lecture on lipid biochemistry. It was in their Distinguished Scientists series of lectures. The story of my encounter in Manchester gave me just the opening I needed. It received a good and cheery laugh from the audience, who had their own experiences of psychological profile testing. I still sometimes wonder, though, if Proctor & Gamble were right. Maybe I have wasted my life in the wrong job. Perhaps if I had become a marketeer, Proctor & Gamble might now rule over more than the world of soaps and detergents.

3

Twenty Years of Medical Research

The second stage of my apprenticeship began one morning in June 1941, when they called me to the student office and asked if I would be interested in a job working for the Medical Research Council in London. This seemed much more to my liking. It was research and it was medicine, something needed but posed no conflict for me as a conscientious objector. In a few days, I received a letter from Robert Bourdillon of the National Institute for Medical Research at Hampstead (NIMR) in North London, an Institute established by the Medical Research Council (MRC) in the 1920s. The MRC was an unusual governmental body in that it was responsible directly to the Crown through the Privy Council. This gave it an independence from political meddling and, more importantly, from the Treasury.

I travelled down to London for the strangest interview yet. The National Institute was at that time housed in a disused hospital on the top of Holly Hill in Hampstead. It was a pleasant, warm, red-brick edifice with the Victorian embellishments of towers and turrets and sited in its own spacious, shrubby grounds. It even had a croquet lawn where we played in the summer after lunch, and tennis courts. I went in at the sandbagged front entrance and announced myself. Helen Hyslop, who was then receptionist, telephoned Dr Bourdillon and asked me to wait. While I waited the few minutes before entering the Institute, I had no thoughts for the girl there, yet in less than two years we were to be married. Robert Bourdillon appeared: a tall lean man in his late forties, with an angular face and a warm smile. 'Come

69

along with me,' he said, and we went to his office in one of the Gothic turrets at the south end of the building. He started by saying that Professor Todd, the Institute director's son-in-law, had recommended me for the job. He then told me about the work that he was doing to prevent the spread of infectious diseases. He and the authorities were much concerned that under wartime conditions, an influenza epidemic like the one in 1918 could occur again. It could be devastating if it happened in the packed conditions of the air-raid shelters. He and his colleague, Owen Lidwell, were trying to combat this threat by devising barriers to the spread of airborne infections. Did I think I could contribute to this work? I replied, 'I'd love to try.' Then he started to ask questions about me. He was obviously worried about my conscientious objection. He had himself fought in the First World War as a pilot and was decorated for his bravery. He tried the usual impossible-to-answer questions such as 'What would you do if a German soldier entered your house and tried to rape your mother?' The standard pacifist reply to this one was 'anything I could do to stop it happening'. As always this line of questioning reveals little and he went on to ask me what were my hobbies. When I said mountaineering, his face, which was marvellously expressive, lost its look of concerned irritation and expanded into reminiscent delight. 'Where do you climb?' he asked. 'Wales and the Lake District, and sometimes Derbyshire.' 'Have you climbed the Idwal Slabs?' 'Yes,' I replied, 'but I never got far up the Holly Tree Wall.' He knew that those are moderate and difficult climbs respectively. He quizzed me about the details of them and when I had satisfied him, it was clear that the test was over. He had, I think, been worried that conscientious objectors were cowardly people, rather than those with awkward principles. You could not be a coward and a rock climber, not for long that is.

We then went to the lab where I met Owen Lidwell, and found him to be an Oxford physical chemist with a DPhil. He looked like a young farmer, but I came to know him as a talented scientist and mathematician. He showed me the equipment they were using, nearly all of it made in their workshop on the same floor. There was an ingenious device for collecting and counting the number of bacteria in the air. They called it a slit sampler because it drew air rapidly through a slit, which impinged the bacteria onto an agar culture plate that rotated slowly under the slit. It recorded the bacterial abundance of the air as it varied with time just as does a CD writer, or a tape recorder, record sounds. In another part of the room there was a giant photographic flash tube several feet long, which when discharged could illuminate the droplets of a sneeze. Owen Lidwell told me that he was having problems with the accurate measurement of air pressures. The rate of flow of air in their slit sampler depended on the pressure difference across the slit. He used a water manometer to indicate the air pressure, and the column of water was in a narrow glass tube, about twelve inches long. The water tended to stick to the walls of the glass tube making accurate measurements difficult. I remember suggesting to him that he try adding a little of the surfactant, Aerosol OT, to the water, something I had learnt in my apprenticeship but which is almost never taught at a university. It worked, of course, and made my welcome that much warmer.

Robert Bourdillon then took me to see Christopher Andrewes, head of the Virus Division, for whom I should have to work as well, and we then went to the Director of the Institute, Sir Henry Dale. Dale was a Churchillian character, bluff and direct. He challenged me straight away about my conscientious objection saying, 'This is a government institute and you may be directed to do work that conflicts with your conscientious objection. What would you do about that?' I remember replying that I recognized that life in wartime involved everyone and that I had to make fine distinctions about behaviour at the time and on its merits. I saw no reason, I said, from talking with Dr Bourdillon to expect any conflict over what he expected of me. Having, like Bourdillon, applied what he considered a test of integrity, he then moved on to tell me about the Institute and its structure. It was, for its time, a wonderfully democratic place, in the Greek sense, that is. If you were a member of the scientific staff, which is what I would shortly be, there was a great deal of freedom to do whatever seemed right scientifically. Technicians and office staff, on the other hand, were treated like other ranks and were there to do what they were told. We were the officer class and expected to show initiative. I realized that the job was mine when Sir Henry Dale asked abruptly, 'Can you start on Monday?' And so began the final twenty years of my apprenticeship as a scientist.

'Coughs and sneezes spread diseases, trap the germs in your handkerchiefs.' These words were on posters everywhere in the UK and their message showed the flash photograph of a cloud of fine particles coming from a sneeze. The photographs were taken in the Hampstead lab, and they illustrated the nature of our work. We wanted to know what organisms were floating in the air that Londoners breathed.

Using Bourdillon and Lidwell's slit sampler, I was soon collecting airborne micro-organisms in the London air. I remember using the sampler in a hospital ward and recording the effects of bedmaking and the shaking of blankets. It was scary sometimes to find that the blanket shaking had released billions of such pathogenic organisms as haemolytic streptococci into the air, the air that I, as an experimenter, had been breathing. One of the many places I took the slit sampler to do measurements was a deep underground shelter. It was an old disused tube tunnel near London Bridge and on the south side of the River Thames. It was about half a mile long and had been fitted with lights and two-tier bunks, and housed tens of thousands during the bombing. The air in the shelter was foul to breathe but, as with all bad smells, after a few minutes' exposure, the nose adjusted and it became at least bearable. They told me that during the height of the Blitz in 1941, the air in this tunnel was so bad that a cigarette would not burn. A match would strike but the wooden shank of the match went out. I now know that this meant that the oxygen in the air was lower than thirteen to fifteen per cent, although more than ten per cent, otherwise some of the inhabitants would have died. It is odd that combustion is more sensitive to oxygen deprivation than we are. The shelter seemed to be just the place where epidemics could start and spread.

There was reason behind the fear among my medical colleagues of an influenza epidemic. The one in 1918 killed over seven million people, more than the number of casualties of the First World War. I would spend nights in this mephitic place sampling the air. The inhabitants, working-class Londoners, tolerated me and even drew me into their strange lives. Here was my first experience of birth. A young pregnant woman went into labour one night and the well-qualified nurse from the first-aid rooms built into the tunnel came to her assistance. When someone asked, 'Where's the father?', the young woman replied, 'I don't know anything about a father; it was just a come and go in the shelter.' I cannot remember whether this event was the stimulant but soon I found myself coming and going, in between sampling, with a warm and passionate nurse from Guy's Hospital. We made love behind the locked doors of the first-aid room. It was an exciting but exhausting life. I rarely ever seemed to find time to sleep. I counted and recorded the samples from the night's work after twenty-four hours' incubation in the Institute's hot rooms. These were large rooms kept at 37° C, with shelves on which were spread the culture plates. There always seemed to be plates that needed counting immediately. Fortunately, it soon became apparent that, bad though the air in the shelter was, the inhabitants were incredibly healthy.

My bleary-eyed appearance at the Institute was noticed by my friend David Evans. He was a dark Welshman and a distinguished bacteriologist who later became famous through the development of a vaccine for whooping cough. He was one of a family of scientist brothers that included the able physical chemist AG Evans. David, along with the physiologist Hank McIntosh, decided that I needed taking in hand. Unwisely, although with good intentions, they arranged a match between the Institute's receptionist, Helen Hyslop, and me. As they put it to me, 'If you want to become a scientist you will have to stop behaving like a tom cat and then sleeping all day. You will have to settle down with a nice girl.' At the time, it seemed to me that they were right and Helen and I began a low-key courtship that ended in our marriage on 23 December 1942. Looking back it seems that our marriage was in some sense arranged. We were both so encouraged by the Institute staff that it just happened. We were not really in love, we were just fond of each other, and we both believed that love would come in its time. We spent our honeymoon at a small hotel in Keswick in the Lake District. It was a wartime marriage solemnized at a Registry Office in London's Euston Road. David Evans was the best man and the Institute's chef, Madeline Scott, the maid of honour. The wedding reception was stark and held in the buffet at Euston Station.

Travel by train in wartime was unrestricted but made so uncomfortable that only those who needed to travel did. The train to Keswick took nearly twelve hours to reach its destination. It was packed with troops as far as Crewe, midway through the journey, but from then on almost empty of other passengers. When at last we arrived at our hotel in Keswick, we found it far better than we had expected. We were welcomed warmly and, although by now it was past midnight, the hotel provided hot cocoa and a fine choice of food. We retired to a warm and comfortable bed at about 1.30 am. In spite of Helen's virginity we started our marriage well and spent a pleasant and fulfilling honeymoon walking the Lakeland mountains.

On returning to London in January 1943, Basil and Mary Large, friends of David Evans, invited us to stay with them while we hunted for a flat. Basil was then editor of the communist paper the *Daily Worker* and Mary his wife was a trade union organizer. They were both wonderfully kind and unstinting with their help and advice in finding a home. We soon settled in a flat in Willow Road, on the edge of Hampstead Heath and only a short walk from the Institute.

As the German bombing of London lessened during 1942, the population of the shelters also diminished. I spent my time testing aerial bactericidal substances designed to destroy the bacteria in the air without harming or irritating people. This was my first encounter with dogma in science. The conventional wisdom among my colleagues was that aerial collisions with the fine particles of disinfectant floating in the air killed the bacteria. My upbringing led me always to question certainties. Partly, I doubted my father's dead cert of a horse bound to win the race. He was a hopeless gambler, even though his bets were always modest and did not adversely affect the family income. Partly, it was the endless political arguments and the religious dogma of those times that inoculated me against belief in the certainty of anything. My scepticism led me to calculate the probability of a collision between an airborne bacterium and a droplet of the disinfectant we sprayed in the air to kill it. The calculation suggested that even with the densest disinfectant aerosol we could sustain, collisions would be so infrequent that the bacteria would survive for as long as a day. We knew that the sprays did work and killed bacteria in seconds, not days. The agent most used in the experiments was a solution of hypochlorite. I began to wonder if the bactericide worked, not by collisions between bacteria and bactericide, but by the condensation of gas or vapour in the air on the airborne particles. To test this idea I sprayed some strong disinfectant, a cationic detergent that was not volatile, into the air. At the same time, I sprayed a suspension of mouth bacteria, *Streptococcus viridans*. The spray of non-volatile disinfectant had no effect whatever on the organisms. Next, I tried volatilizing some lactic acid, a harmless acid that is part of our normal metabolism but which, when it condenses on a bacterium, will make it so acid as to kill it. This did kill the bacteria, and far more effectively than anything else we had tried. This and some other experiments confirmed that it was the vapour, not the aerosol that acted as a disinfectant. Lidwell was a much more accomplished mathematician than I was at that time and he analysed the conditions under which the bactericide condensed on the particles. With this model, we established the vapour condensation theory of aerial disinfection.

The English by that time of the war had entered a state of grace that had not existed earlier and certainly has not existed since. Bourdillon

74

was an old Tory, yet he told me that I must publish my lactic acid experiments as a Letter to the famous science journal, *Nature*. The reason for publication was not to help our reputations but to block the possibility that someone might patent the discovery and make money from it. So, my first paper to *Nature* was 'Lactic acid as an aerial disinfectant', and published in 1944. Later I synthesized a series of acids similar to lactic acid to see if one of them was a better aerial disinfectant. I published this also as a patent-blocking *Nature* Letter. The English distrust of entrepreneurs and of successful businessmen is much older than socialism. In the complex hierarchy of England the middle classes, professionals, and office workers looked comfortably down on the working classes but angrily disliked those in business—trade as they called it—who bypassed the normal routes to preferment. They saw it as queue-jumping and therefore wholly amoral. Continentals and Americans find this trait difficult to understand, but then their societies have not enjoyed the long period of internal peace that England had, during which there was time for social structures to evolve. Looking back, I find this refusal to market our inventiveness and so help establish advanced industries post-war in Britain, both perverse and unrealistic.

The Londoners were surprisingly non-tribal. Whatever Churchill, the old war horse, might say otherwise, many of us viewed German aircrews, especially when caught by the searchlights, with more compassion than anger. They were clearly targets, but few of us regarded the bombs they dropped as personally intended. The war was against the Nazis, we said, not against the German people. Lunchtime talk at the National Institute in Hampstead often involved the war, but usually in a strategic sense, such as the victories and reverses in North Africa, for example, and it was rarely about air-raids—they were too close at hand. M Van den Ende, a virologist, was the exception. He was an Afrikaner and a committed nationalist. He would often tease the more stolid Englishmen by taking a pro-German stance. I well remember two bruising rows over lunchtime. Van den Ende and his English opponent, a physical chemist named Elford, almost came to blows. We had few doubts about Van den Ende's commitment to the war against the Nazis, but equally we knew he disliked the English as a tribe.

Perhaps because I was twenty-two, young compared with the other staff members, or perhaps because he knew I was a Quaker, Van den Ende became for me a confidant and a friend. I grew to respect him and soon discovered that he had the cool bravery of a professional warrior. At this time, the Institute became involved in an extraordinary and dangerous project. The war had progressed to a point where the allies contemplated the invasion of Southeast Asia and there was not just the enemy to consider; some parts of that vast region carried a high risk of infection with scrub typhus, an often-fatal disease. The government ordered the virology department of the Institute to develop a vaccine against the scrub typhus organism. In the 1940s, there was no Health and Safety Executive to oversee dangerous experiments and, in any event, the daily risk to life of the war itself made us all less finicky about risk-taking. In fact, the scrub typhus project started with a rehearsal using murine typhus, a comparatively mild disease in humans.

Because of the deadly nature of the organisms, the virologists took unusual precautions. All work was in sealed chambers through which air was drawn and vented through disinfectant-laden filters. Here they inoculated experimental animals, rats, with the virus by pipetting a small quantity of a virus suspension into their nostrils. In spite of the precautions, several members of the virology department caught the mild infection of murine typhus. There was a post mortem on the experimental procedures and they made all apparent steps at which infection could have occurred virus-proof. The team now decided to do a second rehearsal, this time with human typhus, a serious but rarely fatal disease, before going on to scrub typhus. Again, several virologists, including Van den Ende and the departmental head, Christopher Andrewes, were infected and were seriously ill, and the prospect of moving on to work with scrub typhus was daunting. An unknown leak of virus existed somewhere and it placed the whole team in hazard. At this stage, they began to wonder about the risk to all of us in the Institute, and to those living nearby, because the Institute was an old hospital building with no ventilation, other than by air movements from open doors and windows, and there was no way to isolate the virology department. In peacetime they would have moved the experiments to an isolated safe unit in the countryside, but the pressures of war gave no chance to do this. Instead, our group—Bourdillon, Lidwell, and I, now joined by Frank Raymond—were given the task of finding the source of the infection. We suggested that they try inoculating their animals with a suspension of the organism *Serratia marcescens*, a more or less harmless bacterium, but one that we could grow on agar culture plates. Its bright red colonies distinguish it from other naturally occurring bacteria and a single bacterium collected from the air will grow on the culture plate into billions of organisms and become a colony—bright red—visible to the eye. By this means, we could detect the escape of even a small number of potentially infective organisms. The virologists ran through their rehearsal again using our scarlet bacteria. We soon found that these organisms were in the air of the lab and the corridor outside that led to the rest of the Institute and to the animal house. We found that the recently inoculated rats sneezed as they sat in their open cages awaiting transfer to the animal isolation unit. Their sneezes spread the organisms through the air. The virologists then constructed sealed cages and repeated their rehearsal. This time they found no organisms in the lab or Institute air.

Van den Ende and his team immediately went on to work with scrub typhus and soon had developed a vaccine, but there were casualties. An Australian scientist, Dora Lush, died after accidentally injecting herself with the virus, and a technician named Joyner also died from the disease. We all felt that this brave man and woman who had given their lives in this cause, who had spent their days in the company of so deadly an agent, should have received more acknowledgement. The authorities rewarded Van den Ende by making him responsible for the safe manufacture of scrub typhus vaccine on a scale sufficient to inoculate the troops who would invade South-East Asia. He had the awesome task of setting up a plant in the village of Frant near Tunbridge Wells to grow this deadly organism in cotton rats on a near industrial scale. They called us in again to help design a safe procedure and building. Bourdillon and Lidwell did some pioneering research on the air temperature needed to destroy all organisms, including this virus. They discovered that heating the air to a temperature above 120° C was effective, and from this information, they designed a ventilation unit for the Frant operation. It drew air from the building through a furnace that heated the air to over 120° C and then passed it through a heat exchanger so that the heat was not wasted. The air, now free of infectious organisms, escaped to the countryside. Women soldiers who had no previous virology training were taught to handle the virus and the rats by Van den Ende and his team and they made the vaccine without a single casualty. They never used the vaccine in military operations: the atom bomb ended the war and there was no invasion of South-East Asia. With today's morbid fears of pollution, we would never have attempted this dangerous project, but then we obeyed orders and faced the risks of war, whatever form they took.

There was a series of dining rooms on the top floor of the Institute. One for members of the scientific staff, which included all qualified staff from the Director, Sir Henry Dale, down to the youngest and newest, a bottom-second graduate from Manchester. We were the officers and our dining room was the best. There was a dining room for the administrative staff, which included the librarian, the office staff, and the Director's secretary; and there were dining rooms for the technicians and maintenance workers. The social apartheid of those days was as intense and unbreakable as was the racial segregation of South Africa. Few among the socialist majority of the scientific staff, even Marxists, complained about or suggested changing the dining arrangements. My seniors and I gathered in the coffee room after lunch and were unrestrained in our conversations. Socially and politically incorrect it may have been to have no women or other ranks present, but for me it was fulfilling. We freely discussed good things and terrible things without thought of the needs for security. I first heard of the Manhattan Project, the source of the first atom bombs, in 1944 from a biologist who had just returned from an operational research posting. Soon it was all round the Institute. The idea fascinated Robbie Bourdillon, who had the idea that atom bombs were small things about the size of a pea but with the explosive power of a blockbuster. We did not have detailed information about design or critical masses but we did know that neutrons and uranium-235 were involved. One of the more awful things discussed was a suggestion from an Anglo-American source to use Arabs in the North African desert as experimental animals in the testing of the scrub typhus vaccine. Fortunately, it was never more than a suggestion. There were strange things also. The after-lunch coffee was diluted with bull's milk. Yes, under wartime conditions of scarcity we feminized experimental bulls and turned them into milk producers. Then there was the suggestion that we should use stilbestrol, the synthetic female hormone, as a chemical warfare agent. The proposer of this idea wanted stilbestrol powder dropped from the air over German troop concentrations. The conversion of tough soldiers into quasi women, he said, would sap their morale. Moreover, its effects were reversible and it would therefore be a most humane weapon. This idea also never flew. I do not know why, but guess that the idea was discarded because it could have been seen as chemical warfare.

My senior colleagues were wonderfully kind to me. I think now they saw me as their personal graduate student, for as an apprentice I was always eager to learn and would listen and sometimes help them by inventing something for their own problems. I spent a lot of time with M Van Den Ende and he unstintedly completed my bacteriological education. Whenever there was spare time, I would go to his lab for a tutorial on topics such as Koch's Postulates, the scientific criteria used by bacteriologists to confirm that an organism and a disease are causally connected. The physiologists, led by GL Brown, soon took me to their bosom also, as a fixer of electronic apparatus and an inventor. One day Hank McIntosh of that department, a Canadian physiologist over in Britain during the war, came to me and asked, 'Can you make something to measure mercury vapour in the air by this evening?' It was quite a challenge. It meant parts-per-billion analyses and I could think of no chemical way to do it in this short time. Then suddenly I remembered that we had made and used an ultraviolet absorption instrument for measuring ventilation rates. It used ultraviolet-absorbing tracer substances. I knew that mercury vapour is the strongest absorber of ultraviolet coming from a mercury vapour discharge lamp. So I asked my colleague, Lidwell—who had actually constructed the apparatus, although the suggestion to make it was mine—if it was still working. It was and Hank McIntosh took it into their diving chamber to see if it was safe to spend hours there in a simulated deep-dive experiment. Our equipment found the chamber air saturated with mercury vapour. It came from a broken manometer, which had spilled liquid mercury on the floor. To breathe this air for several hours could have led to irreversible brain damage, if not death. It was a joy when in Canada, forty years later, Hank McIntosh, by now Professor of Physiology at McGill University, greeted me with the words, 'Here is the man who saved my life.' During the war, Hank and I spent time making a thumb sphygmomanometer to measure continuously the blood pressure of divers. I discovered using it that my own blood pressure at age twenty-three was high, 150/70, something that seemed to worry McIntosh, who was medically qualified. He said I ought to do something about it. It increased over the years until the onset of angina nearly thirty years later convinced my reluctant GP that something indeed should be done about it. He then prescribed anti-hypertensive medicine, which I have taken ever since.

Towards the end of the war, there was an open day at the Institute where we showed off our inventions. My bacteriologist friends were always complaining of the difficulty of writing with coloured wax pencils on cold damp glassware. They often needed to write on the glass of culture plates and tubes, which came straight from the refrigerator. In the damp air of England, a film of water immediately condensed on the cold surface. It was almost as difficult to write on these cold wet plates as it would be to strike a match on a piece of soap. I made a batch of special wax pencils which would write on cold wet glassware. They were a roaring success, and I could have spent the rest of my time at the Institute making these pencils for the staff and their friends in hospitals around London. The new Director, Sir Charles Harington, suggested that I publish the formula in a Letter to *Nature*. This I did and within a month received a letter from a pencil firm in the United States asking if I would sell the patent to them. Of course, I had to reply that there was no patent.

Hampstead is hilly and anyone living as far down the hill as we did in Gayton Crescent enjoyed aerobic exercise walking up the narrow steep streets to the Institute. One of the joys of wartime was the absence of cars. All streets were pedestrian precincts and life conformed to this pattern. It was not so easy, though, on dark moonless nights as I stumbled my way upward to my weekly firewatch duty at the Institute, where all staff were required to spend one night a week. Our main task was to be ready to extinguish the small but numerous incendiary devices dropped by German aircraft. When off watch, we slept in a room on the ground floor, which had about eight bunks in it. On watch, we either patrolled the building or spent time on an upper balcony looking south towards central London. There was a button on this balcony connected to the fire alarms of the building. It was on firewatch duty here that I enjoyed some of the most valuable teaching of my apprenticeship. Old and senior scientists did their firewatch duty, and when bombs or missiles came close by, they would in their relief afterwards turn to me and do what I can only call a brain dump. Taciturn, uncommunicative scientists in their post-fear relief would start talking to me as if I were a combination of an old friend and a father confessor. They seemed to feel a need to pass on the secrets of their scientific craft to the nearest young scientist. Once a V1 flying bomb passed by so close that I could see the rivets that held it together. It passed on and I was vastly relieved. Just being there on the balcony was enough; in the aftermath my distinguished companion told me those essential parts of his scientific life, and it was those revelations that prepared me for a life as a cross-disciplinary scientist.

One of these famous older scientists was the eminent bacteriologist, Bruce White. He was a rotund and cheerful man who, when elected a Fellow of the Royal Society, said his ambition was to retire and open a pub called The Jolly FRS. He had a room in the basement where he would often sleep and eat. He invited me to dinner one night and said to me as I sat down, 'Do not cross the white line on the floor—on the other side of the line anything you touch may carry typhoid organisms.' He added as an afterthought, 'Of course, the flies won't obey the rule.' I never knew to what extent he was joking, but my skin itched as we ate. He was a model for me of the lone scientist, one who, like the artist or the novelist, does his creative work best alone. Because of his unusual skills, they gave him the puzzling problems of wartime that others had failed to solve. Thus, when the police found some white tablets strewn across a field in Somerset, first they tried to get them analysed by their forensic chemists and, when they failed to identify them, the problem came to Bruce White. What were they? Were they some subtle poison put there by the enemy or saboteurs? The chemists could only say that they were tablets of some unknown alkaloid. Bruce White reasoned, 'They are probably a medicine, and one tablet will not be a harmful dose. I'll try by taking half a one and see what happens.' He tried this experiment after supper one night and told me he spent the night pacing the corridors of the Institute with an irrepressible erection, almost a priapism. The tablets were the drug yohimbine, accidentally dropped in the field by a vet who had been using it to enliven a reluctant stallion.

I worked for a while during the war at an American Air Force base in East Anglia. It was not far from the market town of Kettering and close to the small village of Grafton Underwood. Here in 1943 was a new airfield from which flew B17s or as we in England called them, Flying Fortresses, on their daylight raids on German-occupied Europe. RB Bourdillon's small group was asked to investigate and try to prevent the spread of common colds amongst the American aircrew. For reasons I do not know, this work fell mainly on me. My colleagues, Owen Lidwell and Frank Raymond, were engaged on other jobs. You may wonder why anything so trivial in wartime as a cold was worth wasting time on. Surely, we could do things that were more important at this time in the war when our very survival was threatened? No, it was not the consequences of a bureaucratic blunder; the common cold can be a miserable, agonizing handicap to a crew member of an unpressurized aeroplane at 20,000 feet or more. Remember also that all the crew of a B17 wore oxygen masks—can you imagine sneezing while wearing an oxygen mask? Worse were the agonizing pains of eardrums distended because the Eustachian tubes blocked by the cold prevented the normal release of excess pressure in the middle ear as the plane ascended. Most of us have felt this when travelling on ordinary aircraft with a cold, but for us, except in emergencies, the internal pressure of the aeroplane never falls below that equivalent to a height of 5000 feet. A small change compared with that experienced by the bomber crew. After a recent radio programme in which I described my working on the common cold at an airbase in wartime, a commentator asked if there was not something better that I could have been doing, for this was such a trivial illness. Among the listeners was the navigator of a Halifax bomber, which flew over Germany in those days. He sent a warm letter telling me how utterly miserable it was to fly with a cold, and how glad he was to know that someone at least had tried to do something about it.

Robert Bourdillon was allowed to use his car during the war for our journeys to military establishments. I met him at his home in Frognal in Hampstead early one frosty morning in 1943. Cars were unheated in those days and driven with the side windows open to stop the windscreen from misting. An army-issue balaclava helmet framed Robbie Bourdillon's gaunt face and we were both wrapped in cast-off army clothing so that we must have looked like a pair of caddis fly larvae as we travelled north. Our journey took us along near empty roads through Hitchin and Bedford until we came to Kettering and then turned off down country lanes to the flat fields of Grafton Underwood. We checked in at the gate to the airfield and were met and taken to the station hospital by the medical officer, Captain Mitchell Spyker. Mitch, who was soon to become a close friend and regular visitor to our home in Hampstead, was a rotund little man who survived the war and became a coroner in Columbus, Ohio.

In the Second World War there was a fair amount of envy from the native population of the pay and conditions enjoyed by our American guests. Over-sexed, overpaid, and over here was a common complaint, which of course was quickly met with the pointed response: maybe, but you are under-sexed, underpaid, and under Eisenhower. Yet, in my days at Grafton Underwood I felt nothing but a deep sympathy and compassion for the appalling lot of those brave young men who flew their B17s, and I found them surprisingly good humoured considering their conditions. At one time, their life expectancy was no more than five missions, so dangerous was it to fly in daylight over Germany. They lived in long cold Quonset huts—tubes of corrugated iron lit by no more than two 60-watt bulbs and heated by a single coke-burning stove. The huts existed in a sea of mud extending in all directions. What an appalling place it was in which to wait for death.

The moral problem of my conscientious objection haunted me in the first years at the NIMR. In 1944 I decided to give up my exemption from service. I had not the heart to stand by nursing my convictions while the rest of the community, not least the brave merchant sailors, brought in the food that fed me. Not logical, and perhaps no more than a response to tribal pressure, but the urge to resign my objection was so strong that I applied for my exemption from military service to be cancelled. Quite soon, they called me to an induction centre where an army officer quizzed me. After some quiet questioning, he told me that I would soon receive orders directing me for training as a medical orderly. This was somewhat of a shock, but logical from the viewpoint of the army. I had expected at the least to join my friends of student days, Teddy Hesketh and Geoffrey Elias, who were in the Royal Air Force as radar specialists. I doubted if I would make a good orderly. When the orders eventually came, I asked to resign my post at the Institute. Within minutes, the new director, Sir Charles Harington, a famous biochemist and the discoverer of the thyroid hormone, called me to his office. He looked at the orders and said 'What's this nonsense? You, a medical orderly, ridiculous.' 'But I am due to report to the barracks in two days' time,' I replied. 'No, you will not. The work you are doing here is much more important and I will see that they exempt you on that account.' Sure enough, they did exempt me and, somewhat bemused by it all, I continued working at the National Institute for the rest of the war.

Robbie Bourdillon's small back room of science worked on other wartime problems as well as cross infection. We became experts on the effects of heat radiation and devised ways to lessen the painful burns of servicemen exposed to flash or flame. We travelled to army sites where flame-throwers were tested. I shall not forget the fierce radiant heat from the wall of flame projected by one of these weapons. At twenty yards from the flame, the radiation was enough to burn exposed skin. Lidwell and I were ordered to measure the radiant heat flux that would cause burns by using the shaved skin of live rabbits. Neither of us was anti-vivisectionist but the thought of burning even anaes-thetized rabbits was more than we could stomach. We came almost instantly to the same conclusion. We would have to burn ourselves. At first, it was exquisitely painful. Then, quite remarkably, after about a week of burns the pain lessened and became a sense of pressure, not pain. Perhaps we were so interested in the science that excitement caused our endorphins to flow and act as natural analgesics. There was some fieldwork as well as these ordeals in the laboratory. We measured the radiant heat and the protective effects of woollen blankets. These, to our surprise, were as or more effective than asbestos. Animal hair seems to have evolved to protect its wearers against heat radiation in forest fires. Hair or wool does not easily burn and when it does the superficial fire leaves a protective coat of carbon bubbles. Strangest among our workplaces was a bombed-out set of streets in Canning Town, East London. Here the army was trying out street fighting techniques.

Our first daughter Christine was born on 16 September 1944. The twin boom of the first V2 weapon to hit London marked her a child of the coming Space Age. The V2 was the forerunner of all the large launch rockets that have carried instruments and men into space. Londoners recognized it by the two consecutive bangs, the first of its sonic boom as it re-entered the atmosphere, and second the explosion of its warhead. We had all that summer endured the deadly but less frightening V1 flying bombs. These were an early and in-accurate version of the cruise missile. The V1s were bearable because they flew in a straight path, never deviating—so long as the path did not cross your position the bomb was obviously going elsewhere and you could relax.

When peace came in 1945 we returned to full-time work on air hygiene. As a junior, I knew nothing of the Institute politics, but it soon became apparent that there was competition for space in the small Hampstead laboratory. Scientists returning from the war needed room, and air hygiene was low on the list of priority topics. Bourdillon moved to Stoke Mandeville Hospital to work on neuro-logical problems, and Lidwell and I were moved to work in a depart-ment of the London School of Hygiene and Tropical Medicine run by Ronald Bedford, an air pollution scientist. Air hygiene now had an MRC committee to oversee our work and Lidwell and I were both members. The main concern of the committee was an attempt to control the spread of childhood infections in primary schools of the borough of Southall. The idea was to irradiate the top part of each classroom with UV. The committee hoped that passage through the irradiated region would destroy the virus- and bacteria-carrying particles from the children's coughs and sneezes. Measles, mumps, chickenpox and streptococcal infections were among the target organisms. It was a set of experiments well suited to Lidwell's talents and inclinations. The problem was that he wanted to use me, the junior colleague, to do the legwork while he did the statistics. I made it clear that if he expected me to spend most of my time taking air samples in the Southall schools I would find a job elsewhere. Fortunately for me, the MRC agreed that it would be wasteful to use me that way and they gave me the chance to complete and submit my experiments on the killing of airborne bacteria by chemicals as a PhD thesis. In this way the London School of Hygiene and Tropical Medicine served as a second university for me. The fact that I was a fully paid MRC staff scientist made the studentship unusually easy, especially since by now our second daughter Jane had been born.

At the end of a year at London University the MRC offered me a stark choice. I could return to Hampstead as a junior member of the biochemistry department on a three-year contract at my present salary of £400 per year. Alternatively, I could transfer to Harvard Hospital at Salisbury as a member of the virus division led by CH Andrewes at a salary of £600 and with tenure. Without hesitation, I chose the move to Salisbury and it was not the higher salary and tenure that made me do it. Had the untenured poorly paid job been in Salisbury I would still have chosen it. The attraction was the chance to live and work in the country. Post-war London was a dreary place and neither Helen nor I wanted to bring up our two daughters there.

One day in September 1946 a large Ford station wagon drew up outside our twenty-room barn of a house in Gayton Crescent, Hampstead. Keith Thompson, the genial driver from the Common Cold Research Unit (CCRU), had come to collect my family and our luggage for the journey to Salisbury. It was all a dream come true. We would have a warm, centrally heated flat at a site on the edge of the then heavenly Wiltshire countryside. I would have a seven room well-equipped laboratory all to myself and medically trained colleagues in the lab next door.

The CCRU was just outside Salisbury on the road that runs to Blandford and Dorchester. During the Second World War, it had been an infectious disease hospital of the United States Army. In the early stages of the war, Harvard University approached the UK Government with the generous offer of a civilian research hospital intended to cope with the epidemic infectious diseases that war might cause. Their offer was welcomed and the prefabricated units were built on the outskirts of Salisbury. However, by this time the United States had entered the war and it was used as a military hospital. At the end of the European war, Harvard University donated the hospital to the UK with the single condition that it remain a research hospital for infectious diseases. Their generosity was gratefully accepted and it fell to the MRC to find a use for it. Christopher Andrewes proposed that it serve as a human volunteer hospital for experiments with the common cold. To some this use of the Harvard University gift seemed frivolous, since the common cold was so trivial an infection. In fact, the common cold is a serious source of lost working time, and knowledge leading to its cure is a prize well worth the effort. The hospital itself was well-constructed from prefabricated wooden units. They were wonderfully equipped by the standards of the time and supplied with efficient heating. There was ample accommodation for the staff, good laboratories and numerous isolation wards for housing the volunteers.

The next five years were idyllic and shared with my medical colleagues Edward Lowbury and Keith Dumbell. We worked on topics such as the spread of infection from pocket-handkerchiefs. It is hard now to recall that once almost everyone with a cold used a cotton handkerchief to mop up his or her running nose. This rag soon became sodden with nasal secretion and was a potent aid for organisms wishing to find a new host. I like to think our paper in the *British Medical Journal* helped to replace the cotton handkerchief with the disposable paper tissue. This was something better destroyed than recycled.

Living at Harvard Hospital gave me a chance to return to Bowerchalke, the village that had so entranced me as a schoolboy. I went there again on a bicycle, this time with Helen, and in the spring of 1947. The hospital was on Coombe Road, which ran southwest from Salisbury and in the direction of Bowerchalke, some ten miles away. In 1947, the United Kingdom was as poor as an underdeveloped country is now. Food and fuel were rationed and there were few cars on the roads. It was a cyclist's delight. The journeys up the Chalke Valley to Broadchalke and Bowerchalke were wholly unimpeded by traffic and the air was fresh and free of exhaust fumes. More than this, in spite of an easterly air stream from Europe, the sky was a clear and sharp blue, free of the obstructing haze that spoils fine weather in Europe now—a haze that represents the exhaust fumes of the tens of millions of vehicles in that densely populated continent. Bowerchalke was just as it had been, except that no teas were on offer anywhere. We went through the village and up the hill to Wood Yates on the main road, and turned left back on the main road to Harvard Hospital and Salisbury. I took comfort in the thought that Bowerchalke was now only twelve miles away. Maybe one day we could move there.

There was a prevalent notion among common cold virologists that immunity to the disease was short-lived and this was why we catch colds so often. One evening in a discussion on this topic, Christopher Andrewes suggested that we do an experiment with volunteers on a desert island. We could isolate them for three months and then test their immunity. It so happened that there was a small deserted island off the north coast of Scotland near the small town of Tongue. In the summer of 1949 we rented the island and refurbished the cottages still standing to make them suitable temporary homes for the student volunteers and MRC staff. It was hard work and involved frequent trips by boat carrying the three months' supplies of food and equipment.

We had just moored the village boat at the decrepit stone quay of Eilean Nan Ron when Mr Anderson, the boatman, took me by the arm and asked quietly, 'Tell me, Doctor, what is it that you are all doing here on this island?' He spoke that clear precise English that is a joy to listen to, the tongue common on the northern and western fringes of these islands. Mr Anderson was no Celt; his tall lean figure, blue eyes, and light complexion spoke of Scandinavia. We often forget that Scotland was once a Norwegian colony. He was also the headman of the village of Skerray and looked the part. His question, what were we doing, had been simmering a long time. Here we were spending what was, to the villagers in the austerities of 1949, a fortune refurbishing the houses on the island that had been deserted for decades, and just for a few months' use. We were there to do an experiment on the common cold and we needed temporary accommodation for the student volunteers who would spend their summer in total isolation on the island. When we told Mr Anderson our true intentions, he did not believe us. The idea that we civil servants were spending taxpayers' money investigating the common cold was too absurd, an insult to his intelligence. 'So come clean, Doctor, what are you doing here?' There was no use in my saying, 'But we really are studying the common cold here on this remote place. We expect to find a decline of the immunity to common colds of our volunteers as time goes by and we will test it at the end of the season by exposing them to a cold virus.' Nothing I said like this, however true it was, would be believed; truth is so much less credible than fiction. Without conscious intention, I turned to Mr Anderson, after I'd stepped onto the quay, and said, 'We are searching for uranium in the rocks here.' His eyes lit up and a smile came across his face. 'Of course, Doctor, I understand your reluctance to speak of it, but do not be concerned, I will tell no one what you've told me.' As I looked down at the clear sea sparkling in the sunlight with the rich growth of *Fucus* and *Laminaria*, an anemone opened its swaying fronds and seemed to wink at me. I wondered how long it would be before my fable reached Inverness.

I would like to think that my small fiction so impregnated the culture of northern Scotland that before long it gave birth to the fast-breeder reactor at Dounreay. One could have said that my words were a self-fulfilling prophecy. I do not mean by this that there was any link connecting my careless remark and the decision of government ministries in London, nearly a thousand miles away to the south, to build a fast-breeder reactor at Dounreay. No link was needed; in the minds of the locals the connection was readily made. There is no better fertilizer for a newly planted myth than secrecy, real or imagined. In those days, anything atomic was secret.

In a like manner, the 20th century legend of flying saucers received sustenance from inappropriately applied secrecy. The more the truth is guarded, the more the fiction grows and, as we say in England, 'Never believe anything until it is officially denied.' Some American government agency or one of its contractors decided to do experiments using mannequins as surrogate victims of parachute accidents, much in the way that car manufacturers test their new models by deliberately crashing them at speed into brick walls with dummies in the driver and passenger seats. From the damage sustained by these dummies, safety features and preventative designs can evolve. A wholly reasonable and scientific operation and one whose intentions are, of course, benign. Car manufacturers publicize their experiments as part of their advertising campaign, but bureaucrats hate publicity and given half a chance will make any information secret. In July 1947 in the USA they were in the mood to classify even the directions to, and the gender of, their lavatories.

The locals of Roswell, New Mexico noticed the sudden appearance of broken mannequins on the scrubby desert landscape near their town. They were puzzled, and when they saw soldiers gathering them up and placing them in body bags, their imaginations inflamed and the great myth of a failed alien invasion was born. The unwillingness of the authorities to explain the truth sustained and fed the myth until its growth became unstoppable. A recent Gallup poll showed that forty-two per cent of American college graduates in 1997 still believe that flying saucers have visited the Earth. Seventy per cent of Americans believe that the US government knows more about UFOs than it lets on and, of course, they are right. Bureaucrats, once they have a secret, gnaw and growl over it like a dog with a bone, and their one wish is to bury it and keep it from everyone. Like the dog they unearth it again after burial and guard it with a solemn seriousness, even when all shape and substance of the bone has gone.

Once science fiction or highly improbable events are sanctified by official or expert denial, they become a public myth. Even trained scientists and engineers become as gullible as do the lay public. One such myth, or remote improbability, is ball lightning, described as a glowing ball the size of a football that floats in the air or darts about like an insect and is usually associated with a thunderstorm. Sometimes it fades quietly; other times it vanishes with a loud bang. In the spring of 1979 I was returning to London from the United States by Northwest Airlines. I was sitting in my seat in the upper cabin of a Boeing 747. My seat companion had recently left his seat to go to the loo just above the helical stairway leading to the main deck. As he returned from the loo, making his way back to the seat, there was the most vivid flash and a deafening detonation. Lightning had struck the plane, not uncommon and usually harmless to large, modern aircraft. My friend of the journey regained his seat, turned to me and said, 'Well, at least we're still flying straight and level.' He was an off-duty captain of the Northwest fleet and travelling to pick up an aircraft for a return to the USA. He was a cool, competent man, as one would expect of an experienced pilot. He turned to me again and said, 'Did you see it?' 'See what?' I replied. 'The ball lightning,' said he. He went on, 'I saw it coming up the stairwell and it exploded with a loud bang near the top.' 'No, I didn't see it,' I told him. 'I thought it was just a lightning strike on the plane.' But my pilot friend was quite sure that he had seen ball lightning and he was believable. Maybe he had seen it.In a court of law, he would have been a convincing witness. I wondered then, and still wonder, whether he was mistaken. My memory was of a vivid flash brighter than a photographer's flashgun straight into my eyes, followed by a lingering afterglow like a ball of light superimposed on the view of the cabin. Could my companion have mistaken this afterglow for ball lightning and confused unconsciously the history of the event? In his memory, the bang came after and not simultaneously with the flash. Despite anecdotal evidence from distinguished physicists, I put tales of ball lightning in the same category as those of the spontaneous development of crop circles, or the spontaneous combustion of humans. I regard them all as almost certainly untrue.

What bothers me is not that the public believes these myths as much or more than they do the facts of science, but that so many scientists believe them also. Far too many British and American scientists seem either to believe or to want to believe in life on Mars. Few are objective on this topic. At a Royal Society discussion meeting on Life on Mars in 1997, I was surprised to discover how many of the scientists gathered there were ready to accept that pieces of rock gathered from Antarctica bore evidences of life on Mars. Any sensibly objective scientist would have regarded the tenuous chain linking those pieces of rock with the possibility of ancient life on Mars as so stretched as to be worthless. But faith overcame scepticism and all too many of the participants used the fiction of *Star Trek* as their source of metaphor. There was even a government minister, Ian Lang, attending the meeting, as if it were an important event in science. Norman Horowitz of Cal Tech said, 'The discovery of life outside the Earth would be a momentous event and change our view of the universe and ourselves.' No one doubts the importance of such a discovery, but let us face it: founding a science programme as large as a space mission on the chance of Martian life is about as foolish as playing the National Lottery to fund a business.

As well as experiments on remote Scottish islands I found time at Harvard Hospital to improve my skills at instrument building. Among the instruments I made were two anemometers. One was an ionization device, the other an ultrasonic anemometer. I made these instruments in response to the experimental need of my medical colleagues to measure very low air movements, or draughts as the English call them. The public firmly believed that colds were caught by getting cold, hence the name. They needed objective, experimentally repeatable criteria for defining the coldness of an environment and this meant measuring the temperature and the humidity of the air, which is easy, but also measuring the speed of air movement, which was difficult. At the time, there were no instruments in existence capable of measuring air velocities as low as five millimetres per second. The ionization anemometer met the need. More important for me it was the inspiration behind several important ionization devices I invented ten years later.

The Voyage on *HMS Vengeance* in 1949

The invention of the ion anemometer also led to an exciting voyage. I have always loved travel by ship and in 1949 my smouldering itch to go to sea ignited. I was at a committee meeting at the MRC headquarters in London. In those days, the council occupied an elegant old house in Old Queen Street, Westminster. We met in a gracious room with a large window looking out on to St James's Park. It was a pleasant enough place to be in but we were discussing what, to me, was a dull and pointless experiment in air hygiene in some schools in Southwark, a London suburb. One of the committee members was also a member of the Royal Naval Personnel Research Committee. During 'any other business' he asked if any of us would be interested in making air hygiene measurements aboard the *HMS Vengeance* on its cold weather winter cruise into the Arctic. I was suddenly awake. Here was my chance to satisfy my longing for a ship voyage. After the meeting I buttonholed the naval colleague and said, 'Look, I would be glad to go. Please include me on the ship.' Fortunately for me, ship journeys are not popular with scientists and there was no competition. I rediscovered this reluctance to leave dry land years later when I was a member of the Marine Biological Association's Council, and later its President. Few marine scientists seem to want to go to sea. To me, this is extraordinary. My employers, the MRC, were reluctant at first but the Navy, having a willing volunteer, would not let go. Soon my naval friends and I were planning the experiments we would make on the voyage.

Preparing for a scientific expedition is not usually part of a scientist's training but it is something that must be done right. Nothing, not even the small things usually taken for granted, can be forgotten if you are off on a trip to distant places. More than this, one must duplicate all essentials whenever possible. Murphy's Law rules supreme: if anything can fail, it will. The scientist and well-known science writer Robert Matthews recently demonstrated by good experiments that toast does indeed nearly always fall on the buttered side, and that the supermarket queue we choose is more often than not the slowest one.

For the six-week Arctic cruise of *HMS Vengeance*, they were letting me off lightly. This was to be my expeditionary apprenticeship. Here I had the thorough and painstaking support of Frank Smith, a member of the Royal Naval Personnel Research Committee, who had served in the Navy as an engineering officer. Fortunately, the *Vengeance* carried ample stocks of most of the things that we might need and, in addition, had an engineering workshop able to make and repair anything we broke. We were taking to the ship our slit samplers to collect the bacteria-laden particles from the air. We intended to sample the sailors' quarters and mess decks; we were also taking some medium-sized forty-cubic-foot cylinders of helium to use as a tracer gas to measure the ventilation rate of the ship's compartments. There was as well my ionization anemometer to measure air movement and so decide whether the spaces the sailors lived in were or were not comfortable. There were also all the small things of a laboratory: Pasteur pipettes, glass-marking pencils, stopwatches, chemicals, batteries, electronic spare parts, and so on, to say nothing of notebooks and pens. Because of these preparations, the voyage filled my mind for weeks before the ship set sail. I was still young enough then, twenty-seven years old, to lose sleep with the excitement of the prospect.

At last February came round, and after breakfast, I said my goodbyes to Helen, Christine, and Jane and set off with Tom Thompson and Frank Smith in the Harvard Hospital station wagon. Frank Smith, the retired naval officer, was to be my colleague and guide aboard the ship. Our equipment and luggage completely filled the back of the car. It is only fifty or so miles from Salisbury to Weymouth, which in those days was still a place of naval significance. From the dockside, we could see the huge bulk of the *Vengeance* lying in the middle of the calm water within the breakwaters. We loaded our gear onto a cutter, helped by sailors, one of whom made me immediately feel at ease when he called our helium cylinders boffin bombs. Soon we were at a sea-level platform lowered from the ship's quarterdeck and they started the boarding ceremonies. The ship's company piped the naval personnel on board and they saluted the quarterdeck. This caused me concern because my dyslectic tendencies would cause me both to face in the wrong direction and do the salute incorrectly. But

Frank Smith calmed me and said, 'No need to salute, you're a civilian and as far as the ship's concerned, you're invisible.' He was a wonderful companion, just the guide I needed for such a voyage. It is agonizing to be a virgin in a new ceremonial environment and he saved me an immense amount of embarrassment.

Our cabins for the next six weeks were in the officers' quarters towards the stern of the ship. They were cramped quarters and in our six-bunk cabin there were only two wash-hand basins. There were more than enough cupboards and drawers to stow our clothing, which included Arctic gear. It was lunchtime before we had settled ourselves and arranged the equipment in our lab—a spacious suite of rooms in the ship's sickbay. We expected no enemy action on this voyage so these quarters seemed a natural place for us. The officers' wardroom of the *Vengeance* was forward and was a room of luxurious spaciousness. Tables with white linen and good cutlery were there to welcome us. The food, after the privations of post-war rationed England, seemed almost like a daily banquet.

After lunch, we went on deck to see the ship leave port and go into the Channel to commence sea trials along the Dorset coast before setting sail for the Arctic. It was strange to watch the so familiar Dorset coastline from Lulworth via Brandy Bay to Kimmeridge and on to St Alban's Head as we travelled past about three miles away. Those high cliffs I had climbed so often seemed no more than the saucer rim of a quiet sea. It was a mild and weakly sunlit February afternoon. Later that same day we began our journey down the Channel towards Land's End, and then turned north past Wales. It was calm and easy progress at a speed of not more than about 14 knots (16 mph). The weather was unusually quiet as we sailed past the west of Britain and we were able to go on deck to see the snow-covered mountains and islands of Scotland. We sailed on north through the Minches and up past Cape Wrath. The next day the Faroes came in sight as more snow-covered mountains.

We were now well into the routine of our work. We went onto the seamen's mess decks and negotiated with them for a table on which to set up our gear and start taking measurements. I must admit that this kind of science is not my favourite occupation. Had I not had the joy of being on a ship I would not have been doing it. I always have found tedious the endless repetition of comparatively easy measurements. Nevertheless, I knew that we must do them if our observations were to have significance. It was easy to be distracted by conversation with the sailors and by watching the hobbies they enjoyed in their off-duty periods. Who would have thought that knitting and embroidery were amongst the pastimes of a warship crew. To me and to Frank Smith, who knew much more about ships than I could ever know, the *Vengeance* was a contented ship. The crew could have seen us as uninvited intruders, like social workers; instead they accepted us kindly and courteously.

Walking through the ship carrying our equipment was our greatest difficulty. The curse of a naval ship is its need for watertight compartments to keep it afloat after the enemy has shot it full of holes. The oval doorways with heavy clip fasteners every few yards and the vertical steel ladders between the decks made travel across the territory of the *Vengeance* hard and painful. Novices like me always barked shins. However, compared with the naval ships to come, like the aircraft carrier *Victorious* that I went on ten or so years later, the *Vengeance* was spacious and enjoyable. A journey on a present-day large aircraft carrier is like living in a nightmare version of a London Tube station in a permanent state of rush hour.

We spent our evenings in the wardroom playing cards, drinking modestly and telling stories. On British ships liquor is freely available, but something about shipboard life seems to hasten the metabolism of alcohol and lessen its capacity to stupefy. As one sailor said to me, 'You never need exercise on this ship; even in bed you have to work to stay put.' Sailors had it easier than the officers did; they slept in hammocks, which insulated them from the ship's considerable motion. It was winter when we left England and our course was into the Arctic almost directly toward Spitzbergen, which is a mere 800 miles from the Pole. We expected cold but for the first part of the journey, we did not get it. Even at latitude 70° N, close to Bear Island, it was merely damp, wet, and about 40° F, typical of English December weather but not what I expected well within the Arctic Circle in February. Not until the eleventh day of our voyage close to latitude 75° N, did we see ice in the sea; even then the wind was still from the south and west and unusually warm for the Arctic. All the time, though, imperceptibly but on a daily basis, the weather had grown stormier.

The *Vengeance* was nearly as long as the *Queen Mary*, with only about a sixth of the mass of that great liner. It was also a welded ship. This gave her a vicious motion in a rough sea, especially if it was a following sea, with the waves racing to catch up the ship from behind.

As one seaman put it, 'It was like being dragged down a flight of stairs in a tin bath.' In the wardroom, the curbs were now around the edges of the dining tables almost all of the time. One of the naval constructors travelling with our party was so seasick that the ship's physician had to ask the engineers to rig a bed for him suspended in gimbals, a clever mechanical contraption that ensures that whatever the ship's motion the suspended bed remained level. It was a large version of the gimbals used to hold a ship's compass level. The bed was in the sickbay, which was near the metacentre of the ship, the place where the movement is least. He spent most of the voyage in this bed.

As our course moved west and south towards Jan Mayen Island and Greenland, the wind grew stronger and was often storm force or higher. The naval purpose of the cruise was to see if an aircraft carrier like *Vengeance* could operate and fly its aircraft under winter conditions in the Arctic. Flying was, in fact, limited to the few quiet spells, and even then expensive in both lives and aircraft.

In London, before the voyage, I had foolishly volunteered for a dangerous experiment on the ship. I was so keen to go and to make myself acceptable to the Navy that I ignored common sense and my survival instinct. The Navy wanted to know if it would be possible to warm up the piston engine aircraft in the hangars inside the ship. Warming the engines by running them on the icy open decks would waste time and fuel and under battle conditions such a time waste could be fatal, but the hangars were large and full of planes, and to let them start and warm up their engines inside the ship raised the worrying possibility of fire and pollution of the ship with dangerous amounts of exhaust fumes. There was particular concern that carbon monoxide would build up to a toxic level inside the hangar—even to a level where lives were in danger. The Navy needed a volunteer to measure the carbon monoxide in the hangar as the planes warmed up and this is what I volunteered to do.

On a relatively quiet day as we sailed between Spitzbergen and Jan Mayen Island the Captain decided to do the warm-up experiment. It was scheduled for 10.00 am and at 9.45 I went to the stern end of the hangar, just below the great open doors of the ship's lift that carries planes up to the flight deck. The only protection I had, apart from my Arctic gear, was earmuffs, for the sound level with all of the engines running would be deafening. By 10.00 I had my meter running and checked. I raised my flag as a sign and the first of the engines started up. There were clouds of smoke and a fair amount of fuel from the priming splashed on to the floor of the hangar. As they started more and more engines, the smoke grew thicker and so did the wind. With all the engines running, I had to kneel down and hold a ringbolt on the deck to keep position. To my relief, the carbon monoxide level barely rose above zero on the meter. There was so much fresh air drawn in by the planes' propellers, acting like giant fans, that the fumes were swept away almost as fast as they were produced. Pollution was no hazard at all. Fire was another thing, and several of the flying crew came to me afterwards and said that the venting of fuel during the start-up made the experiment foolhardy and hazardous. This, coming from men who served in perhaps the most dangerous of peacetime naval tasks, made me feel glad that they spoke after the experiment and not before. As an experiment, it worked well. I did not have to lift my flag the second time to warn that the carbon monoxide had reached danger level. They stopped their engines when they were warm. We had gained some useful information and it helped me personally. Courage is the quality most valued instinctively in groups of men and, although to me it had seemed no more than a very uncomfortable and slightly risky experience, to the ship's crew I had passed some kind of test. From then on, I no longer felt myself an invisible civilian boffin who intruded on their lives at sea.

The most frightening period of the voyage began mildly with some conversation in the wardroom after dinner and while we were playing poker with dice instead of cards. The winner of each game bought the other players a round of drinks, an interesting negative feedback on the rate of play and the amount of drink consumed. Among the players were two naval architects from Bath, who proceeded to tell us about the inevitable fate of welded ships: how once a crack occurs in a welded plate it spreads across the plate and through the weld to the next plate. In this way a crack propagates right around the ship and severs it into two pieces as if sliced by a giant knife. They told us how the welded Liberty ships built in the Second World War often sank suddenly and without warning and the *Vengeance*, they said, was a welded ship built during the war. This good bedtime story stirred us but did not cause any loss of sleep.

A few days later, we at last encountered cold weather and the ice pack. It was also calm, and the low Arctic sun shone brightly. I had expected, wrongly, when we set sail, that at 70 – 80° N there would be no daylight in February. In fact, there was no day even at 75° N without light between 10 and 2 during the day. In the farthest north, the sun rested level with the sea rim all of the day, a kind of frozen dawn merging into sunset without full daylight in between. Never was it wholly dark.

After the week of storms, the bright sun drew us on to the deck to bask in its apparent warmth, and to enjoy the Arctic scene. Peculiarly, in the wet and mild weather of the previous days we had felt cold enough to need our anoraks and Arctic gear. Today, with the sun shining, many went out with just the clothes they wore in the warmth of the ship. The air temperature was now near 15° F, some 25° F colder than on the previous day, but perversely it felt warmer. The ship then began to move into the pack ice. All went well until there was a sudden noise and a jerk in the ship's motion. We had hit a larger floe and the bows of the ship were damaged enough to let some sea in. It was nothing serious—not a re-run of the *Titanic* disaster—just a minor mishap like a shunt collision in a car park. It was a result of a scheduled test of the ship's abilities, not an accident. The ship moved back into open sea and hove to and the engineers repaired the damage by filling the small leaking compartment with concrete. It seemed to us that it was not serious for the ship but we had forgotten our friends, the naval constructors. In the wardroom that evening, the Jeremiah of them told us that the collision with the large ice floe had cracked one side of the flight deck just ahead of the bridge. He seemed to relish telling us that this was the strength deck that held the ship together and that in the cold the steel was much more brittle and liable to further cracking. We went to bed that night less easy in our minds.

A few days later, the storms were back fiercer than ever. We had travelled up and down in a short circular path on the northern and leeward side of the volcano, Jan Mayen Island. This small island, a Norwegian possession, formed a large natural breakwater in the stormy northern seas. We were not alone. Two frigates accompanied the *Vengeance*, the *Loch Archaig* and the *St Kitts*. We could see that they were having a much harder time in the rough seas than we were and on the evening of 25 February the Captain announced that we would leave the lee of the island and sail south to give the men on the frigates, as he put it, a good night's rest. As we left the island shelter and turned into the wind, the ship's motion became wild enough to be disturbing. The wind must by then have been blowing with hurricane force from the south. We stayed much of the day in our sickbay laboratory near the ship's metacentre where the movement was mostly a rotation, not up and down. In the wardroom near the stern, the pitching was so great that it was like being in an express lift forever going up and down at the whim of a hyperactive child in charge of the buttons. A few of us were seasick but eating was in any case an ordeal and our chairs would topple over mid-meal.

The *Vengeance*'s own peculiarity was the longitudinal flutter of the whole ship as if it were a long and thin metal bar. This flutter was rapid and gave the feel, as the seaman said, of sliding down a flight of stairs. This uneasy motion superimposed upon the pitching and tossing made useful work all but impossible. The crack on the deck became more than just a doom story in the naval constructor's mind. It started spreading across the deck and soon we heard that seamen were drilling holes ahead of the crack. This is sound engineering practice: a hole imposes less stress on the metal than the sharp growing point of the crack itself. Other seamen, we heard, were welding strips of metal behind the crack to hold it together. Everyone on deck was roped as climbers are, so great was the wind and the danger of slipping off into the icy sea.

The ship continued on its southerly course into the storm for two days. Then the north coast of Iceland came into sight and there was no choice other than to turn back north again. This meant the ship would have to turn across the wind and the bridge warned us of the dangers of the manœuvre in such seas, with the ship in the state it was. The turn was an awful minute during which our cabin cupboards crashed over, ripped from their mountings by the motion of the ship. We sailed north and the storm continued; the motion more uncomfortable still by the following sea. That evening in the wardroom I overheard the Captain say to the Chief Engineer, 'Well, Chief, which end drops off first?' It was not good bedtime news. Frank Smith was, as usual, his calm and wonderful self. When I said, 'Shouldn't we stay in the wardroom for the night?', thinking that our cabins in the stern were a trap should the ship, in fact, break in half, he said, 'Nonsense, we'll sleep there as usual,' and we did. Next day the storm had lessened and we were able to resume our researches.

One evening, back behind the shelter of Jan Mayen Island, the Captain invited Frank Smith and me to dinner in his spacious cabin. He made us welcome and at home so that we felt that what we were doing was important for the ship. He was keen to know what we had found out so far in our tests. Because of the ship's size and spaciousness, our news was good: our measurements showed a low level of airborne bacteria, and confirmed the sailors' opinion that their quarters were comfortable. The *Vengeance* seemed to be a healthy ship to be on, except of course for the crack. Here Captain Terry was reassuring and we left for our quarters with a sense of warmth and security. Perhaps the knowledge that they may someday be responsible for starting a major war is what gives senior diplomats and service officers that quality of calm authority.

Five weeks had passed and the weather was warmer and calmer, and the trials were completed. We set sail south for Scotland, this time heading for Rossyth, the main naval port and dockyard. As we approached the north of Scotland, most of the planes took off for airfields there. The wardroom then was half empty, with the flying crew gone, but it reminded us of the dual nature of the ship that we were sailing on. Frank Smith and I spent the last day of our sailing, as we travelled down the east coast of Scotland, preparing the draft of our report on the voyage. It was later polished on shore but it was good to have what was then for me the hardest part of the whole voyage, writing the report, done before we reached port. We arrived early next morning at the dock in Rossyth and disembarked. We carried with us a generous allowance of dutiable items like liquor and cigarettes. News of our ordeal must have gone ahead for when the customs officer asked which ship we came from, and we replied the *Vengeance*, he just smiled and waved us on our way.

Back at Harvard Hospital my own particular task in the common cold project was to try to find the paths along which colds spread between people. Together with Edward Lowbury and Keith Dumbell, we had made experiments to show that colds spread mainly by direct contact. Contact such as shaking hands could cause the transfer of substantial quantities—milligrams—of nasal secretion from person to person. We doubted that colds were spread, as previously thought, by the fine airborne droplets of a sneeze, and our main effort was to try to quantify the transfer of infectious secretion from one person to another. I used fluorescent substances to label the nasal secretion of volunteers with colds and followed the spread of the secretion by illuminating their surroundings with long wavelength UV. In this way we showed that airborne fine particles conveyed, to those that breathed them in, only fractions of a microgram of secretion. Direct contact from shaking hands or large droplets from a cough in the face conveyed over a thousand times as much. We also made field observations on the London Underground, watching how often travellers touched their mouths and noses. We concluded that most respiratory infections occurred either by imbibing the large droplets of a close encounter with a sneeze or by touching some previously infected surface and then transferring the infection to the mouth. Infection by breathing fine airborne droplets could occur but would require a highly infectious organism. Measles or tuberculosis could spread this way, especially in the confines of a passenger aircraft, but even here, the opportunities for contact transfer are much greater.

A direct experiment supported these views. We took a small room and divided it in the middle by means of a large blanket suspended between the walls of the room. On one side of the blanket was a group of five children who had streaming colds, and on the other side of the room were ten volunteers who came to the hospital and offered their services as human guinea pigs. A large fan stirred the air of the room so that fine airborne particles sneezed, coughed, or talked out by the children would be transferred rapidly round to the side of the room where the volunteers were. We also had sampling apparatus to sample the bacteria and virus particles in the air. In this experiment, colds were not transferred from the children to the volunteers. In another experiment, we took the blanket down and let the children play card games with the volunteers. The contact of the volunteers' hands with the nasal secretion deposited on the cards by the children effectively transferred the infection. We concluded that we catch colds from others by direct contact. Something useful, I suppose, but I do not think that in practice our discovery has helped to stop the spread of the disease to any extent.

In the last years of my time at Harvard Hospital I grew curious about the role of calcium in blood clotting. I had the idea that calcium was not so much an active essential part of clotting but acted to bring in contact negatively charged blood components that would otherwise be repelled by their negative polarity. I started collaboration with Betty Burch and with James Porterfield. It turned out that the idea was sound and we published our research in the *Biochemical Journal*. James Porterfield and I went on to pioneer the production of plastic surfaces that would keep blood from coagulating almost indefinitely. This work we published in *Nature* but we were about ten years premature; the need for such an invention did not come until DeBakey and others first made artery replacements in the 1960s. A happy consequence of the collaboration was the romance that developed between James Porterfield and Betty Burch that led to Harvard Hospital's first marriage.

Frank Raymond, a wartime colleague in Robert Bourdillon's department, now worked for the Agricultural Research Council but we kept in touch. He asked me if I could help by designing an instrument that would monitor the movements of cattle as they grazed. I was ready for a break from biochemistry and willingly agreed, but it led me to participate in the removal of hedgerows— one of the most destructive changes that happened to the English countryside after the Second World War. Hedgerows are linear forests that act as fences between farmers' fields and serve to provide a habitat for birds and for numerous species of plants and insects. They are the refuge and reservoir of bygone ecosystems, but since 1946 we have lost 150,000 miles of hedgerow, and I regret to say I played a small part in this act of national ecocide.

We had nearly starved in the Second World War and we knew that our farmland could not produce enough to feed us, so it was inevitable that the improvement of farming efficiency should be high on our list of national priorities. What we would lose in the way of scenic beauty and a country way of life never occurred to us. As a nation, we behaved just like those in charge of a famous national museum during a time of recession when the only way to survive is by selling its treasures. I loved the English country scene passionately, yet I was as thoughtlessly responsible for its destruction as was a greedy shareholder of an agribusiness firm, or a landowner out to maximize the return from his broad hectares. This is how it happened with me.

The Grassland Research Institute was at Stratford-upon-Avon, about 120 miles from Salisbury. In 1947 the Medical Research Council had provided Owen Lidwell and me with a car, a Morris ten, registration JMM 540, and it was for our travels to sites where we did air hygiene experiments. Owen, as the senior partner of the pair of us, had charge of it. He also needed it for travelling from Salisbury to London, where his home still was. Generously, he allowed me to use it for journeys such as this one to the Grassland Institute. The problem was that there were coupons only for two gallons of fuel and only about one gallon in the tank. At thirty miles per gallon, I was short by thirty miles of my destination, Stratford-upon-Avon. However, at twenty-seven I was still under the influence of abundant testosterone and a risk-taker and was sure that I could drive to Stratford-upon-Avon and back with the limited fuel available. There were competitions where the winner was the one who travelled furthest on a fixed quantity of fuel and they left in my mind the possibility that I could also drive as efficiently. The journey had been planned with my friend, Tom Thompson, Harvard Hospital's capable manager and he thought that I could do it. We agreed that the best plan would be to keep an average speed of forty miles an hour, and to do so by accelerating to fifty and then coasting back to thirty, then repeating this saw-tooth pattern of driving throughout the journey. Nowadays such a plan would be impossible to put into practice; then, even the main roads were all but empty of traffic.

I set out from Harvard Hospital on a clear, bright sunlit May morning. The blackbirds advertised the excellence of their genes to potential mates and the scent of hawthorn blossoms filled the air. I should have spent the day walking in the countryside to enjoy it while it was still there but I was in the honeymoon stages of driving. The meadows were full of wild flowers, there was even pheasant's eye, the scarlet buttercup, in the field below the hospital and the hedgerows were full of birds' nests. Ten years later, it would be well on its way to a desert full of weed-free grain, bounded by barbed-wire fences.

The journey took me up the Avon valley through Amesbury, just missing Stonehenge and on through the Savernake Forest, with its fresh new leaves, to Marlborough. I then drove on over the downs to Swindon and to Burford in the Cotswolds, and from there I was soon at the Grassland Research Institute at Stratford-upon-Avon. The fuel gauge registered that I had used less than half the fuel allocation, so the return journey would be less exacting. My friend, Frank Raymond, was then a young scientist working diligently to improve the 'backward' farming practices of Old England. Even bread was rationed. In theory we could grow all of the food we needed; in practice, English farming seemed to use the land inefficiently and we were able during the war and immediately afterwards, to grow no more than sixty per cent of our needs.

At the Grassland Research Institute, they pioneered the practices that now allow even a small part of England to grow all of the food needed to feed the whole country. They specialized in grass farming and were telling young farmers how much more efficient their farms would be if they took out most of their hedgerows. Hedgerows are made of woody plants entwined with brambles; they are natural fences festooned with natural barbed wire. They included all of the woodland trees: oaks, ash, beech as well as holly, blackthorn and hawthorn. It is said that in some places the age of a hedgerow can be guessed by counting the number of woody plants per thirty-yard run. Ten different species implied an age between one and two thousand years old. Hedgerows represent the most amazing symbiosis of human and woodland ecosystems, and they are places where birds can nest. They are the habitats of predatory insects—ichneumon flies, small wasps, and ladybirds—that are the natural means of keeping pests in check. Hedgerows evolved in the days when mass-produced farm machinery was non-existent. Horses were the power sources and small fields enclosed by hedgerows were the norm.

What we were doing at the Grassland Research Institute was providing essential information to the civil servants of the Ministry of Agriculture and Fisheries and the farmers. They then used it to plan their campaign to replace the old English countryside with an efficient agribusiness operation. We took the breath-taking beauty of our land as much for granted as would a peasant farmer that of his young wife, and we expected it to work for us, not realizing that a life of drudgery is incompatible with beauty. In the pursuit of agricultural efficiency we were concerned with choosing the breeds of sheep and cattle that most efficiently converted grass to meat, and Frank Raymond had the notion that the more placid an animal was the more weight it would gain during grazing and that unnecessary movement wasted energy. He had asked me—in my role as an inventor—if I would design and make a device that cattle could wear that would continuously monitor their movements. It would have to record how much time an animal spent walking, running, sitting down, chewing the cud, and so on. To meet this need I designed a small battery-operated radio transmitter that broadcast information on the animal's movements as notes at different audio frequencies. The senior technician at Harvard Hospital, Ron Canaway, converted my rough breadboard design into a neat package that fitted on the back of a young bullock. I had brought the first model of this device with me for trials at Stratford-upon-Avon.

In the 1940s, unlicensed emissions of radio frequencies were forbidden and we needed a licence to operate our transmitter. Here we encountered an odd problem. The law required all transmitters to start and finish operation by sending their call sign in Morse code. How were we to train our bullocks to use a Morse key? When I explained our problem to the officials of the licensing authority, which was then the General Post Office, they laughed, relented and gave us a licence. I then went on to request a frequency of 175 megahertz for the transmitter. Higher frequencies would have been beyond the capacity of the simple devices then available and lower frequencies would have required an aerial (antenna) so long that the animals would have broken it off when they walked under trees. The civil servants at the General Post Office wisely saw that this was a genuine need, even though a peculiar one. They granted us a licence to transmit and waived the need to use our call sign, G9OO, which nevertheless they assigned. By present-day standards, the transmitter was heavy, bulky, and inefficient; the transistor had not yet been invented. For the technically minded, I used a DCC91 double triode as the output stage of the device. It was power hungry and batteries were much less long-lived than they are now, but it worked, and I played my small part in the destruction of the English countryside. The scientists, the farmers, the agribusiness men, and, most important, the civil servants who drafted the legislation that gave grants to farmers to take out their hedges, all of us were ignorant of the consequences. I am ashamed and now regard myself as part of the unconscious vandalism that has all but destroyed the beauty of my country.

4

The Mill Hill Institute

My boss at Harvard Hospital was a gentleman as well as a distinguished virologist; later he was knighted, but in the 1940s was just Christopher Andrewes. He was the co-discoverer of the influenza virus and a talented amateur entomologist. Often when he visited Harvard Hospital he would take me with him on expeditions to the New Forest where he collected specimens of his favourite insect, the sawfly. How different science was in those days. The two of us walked as companions enjoying the quiet delightful countryside and discussing our researches. Sometimes he would ask me to walk a few yards ahead on the path. It took me some time to discover that he was using me as bait for his beloved flies.

One day in September 1951, on the way back from one of these expeditions to the New Forest, I voiced my doubts about continuing to work at the Common Cold Research Unit. Perhaps it was the slight pique of having been used as mere bait or, more likely, because I sensed that for me the virology chapter was due to come to a close. Andrewes was shocked to hear that I was thinking of resigning from his division but he was a good man and he promised to discuss my wish with the director of our parent Institute in London, Sir Charles Harington. He was true to his word, for within a day Sir Charles summoned me to London. He was a man who resembled the Prime Minister of that time, the Labour leader Clement Atlee, or, indeed, the US President, Truman. He was a small, perhaps shy man, with a limp caused by a tubercular infection of his hip as a child. His slight

105

stature belied the strength of his character: they said he was descended from a line of judges. Whether or not this was true, he was one of those few people I have encountered in life whose presence was immediately and tangibly felt, who could exert authority even without speaking. Without preamble he said, 'I am so glad you are coming back to the Institute. You have been much too long in the wilderness of Harvard Hospital. I have a problem for you and it is urgent. Can you start next week?' He didn't expect me to disagree. He was a man with an attention to detail that now you would think of as Japanese, and had already arranged that Helen and my family could stay at Harvard Hospital for as long as it took me to find somewhere for us all to live in London. He made a lab available for me on the first floor of the institute. It was like falling over a small waterfall, exhilarating but with the knowledge that there could be no going back, no indecision. The National Institute for Medical Research (NIMR) at Mill Hill in North London was an odd building. Its design reflected the chemical structure of a benzene ring. In the 1930s, so many drugs and important natural compounds had the hexagonal shaped benzene molecule as an important part of their structure that chemists and biochemists felt the need to recognize this fertile shape in the lab they hoped soon to occupy. In fact, it was not opened until 1950 and this was because during the war years, it was a barracks for women enrolled in the Navy and it took five post-war years to equip it as a medical research institute. By 1951 the hexagonal main building had four wings which made it more like the structure of the hydrocarbon durene (tetra methyl benzene). It was a wonderfully well-equipped institute with a first class library and a spacious lecture hall as well as having mechanical and electronic workshops and a vast animal house. In the spacious grounds was a small farm; the fields and woods of London's Green Belt surrounded it. The whole of the administration occupied a few rooms on the first floor of the main building and only a few per cent of the annual budget of the Institute went for administration. This meant that often we had to type our own letters and papers but there was a great freedom from bureaucratic interference.

Soon I was living during the week with my beloved mother-in-law, Queeny Hyslop, in her flat at the foot of Highgate Hill near Parliament Hill Fields, in North London. I walked each day through the back streets to Archway Tube Station and took the tube from there to Mill Hill East and then a bus to the Institute, which was at the top of Mill Hill. I travelled by train to Harvard Hospital on Fridays and returned on Monday mornings.

On my first day back, they gave me a roomy personal lab looking out over the front lawn of the Institute. It was in the experimental biology division, sited on the first floor. Here I met my colleagues, Alan Parkes, the divisional head; Audrey Smith, the Cambridge biologist; Chris Polge, a veterinarian; a visiting scientist from America, a haematologist, Henry Sloviter; and the senior technician of the department, Fred Crisp. Before long, the director summoned me and gave me my brief. 'Lovelock,' said Sir Charles, 'Parkes and his colleagues are doing important work. Their successful freezing of a variety of cells and tissues will affect medical research and benefit it everywhere, but I'm concerned that these competent biologists are almost wholly ignorant of chemistry and physics. I doubt if they know one end of a thermometer from the other. Your job is to see that they do not make mistakes and bring discredit upon the Institute. Of course, you will want to do your own research so what are your plans?' Fortunately for me, I had a clear idea of what I wanted to do because in the days before returning to London, I had thought of nothing except what could happen to cells during the process of freezing. I used my usual technique of empathy; that is, imagining myself to be a cell and wondering what would happen as I froze, and I had concluded that the worst thing that could happen would be an ever-increasing salinity as water was taken from the cell itself and from its medium to make ice. Ice always separates as a pure substance, and the dissolved solids are left behind concentrated in the remaining water. Interestingly, this meant, in effect, that freezing was the same as drying.

Everyone knows how easily lack of water kills plants and animals, but I knew that it was too soon to venture so odd an idea. The conventional wisdom was that freezing kills cells by literally spearing them with sharp ice crystals, and Audrey Smith herself had made a remarkable film of cells freezing on a microscope slide. She had travelled the world with this film and shown the growing ice crystals apparently penetrating the cells. I didn't think it was appropriate for me to come out with a rival theory just at that moment so all I said was, 'I have thought about it quite a bit and I have some ideas on what the mechanism of damage might be and how glycerol protects the cells against this damage. I'd like to try a few experiments before confirming these views and producing a research plan.' He said,

'Good, that's fine by me.' He was a good scientist and knew that I would have to do it that way. He then went on to the important things, to me, namely salary and finding a house for my family. In spite of his formidable air, he was a humane and kind man. He dismissed me, saying, 'Well, if there's anything you need or any support, just let me know.'

Unfortunately for me, some of his thoughts on the capacity of my biologist colleagues to handle the physical chemistry of freezing must have got back to them, and the first few months I spent at Mill Hill were rather strained; on bad days they saw me as a spy for the director. I worked mostly with Christopher Polge and Audrey Smith; Audrey resembled the actress Margaret Rutherford. She dressed in tweeds and sensible shoes and had a loud voice and bossy air. In other ways, Audrey was like my mother and, having grown up with one formidable lady I had no great difficulty discounting the externals and enjoyed working with the real and very able person that was underneath. I did not like the way my biological colleagues treated me as a useful technician and no more—one who could do wonders with thermocouples, diathermy and other physical devices but was, in their eyes, not a proper scientist. Like all specialists, they had disdain for the other disciplines of science. For them real science was biology. Chris Polge, although just as good a scientist, was easier company. He looked like a young farmer and, since he was in charge of the department's livestock, which included twin bulls called Castor and Pollux, it seemed right that he should. The work he did was probably the most important. His pioneering success with a technique for preserving animal spermatozoa in the frozen state affected the conduct of farming worldwide. Rightly, the Royal Society elected him a Fellow in 1983 and he was awarded the Japan Prize in the 1990s.

When I was not helping them, I was able to pursue my own researches into the damage done to human red blood cells by freezing and how glycerol protected them, and it turned out to be exactly as I had imagined. My colleagues had developed a technique for freezing living cells that was quite slow and it took several minutes before the cells were frozen. At this slow rate of freezing, the water around the cells froze, but the cells themselves merely dried—and drying was the cause of their damage and death. I was able to show that glycerol and similar substances exerted their protective action by preventing this drying process from taking place. These solutes stopped it proceeding beyond what was a sharp critical point. This finding was published in two papers in the journal, *Biochimica et Biophysica Acta*, and has now become part of the conventional wisdom of cryobiology. Indeed, one of these papers 'The mechanism of the protective action of glycerol against damage by freezing and thawing' was the most cited paper in biological science for the year following its publication.

To confirm my ideas about the effects of freezing on cells I had to separate the mechanical effects of the ice crystals from the toxic effects of the concentrated salt solutions. The way I did it was to suspend cells in salt solutions of various strengths. I soon found that salinity greater than five per cent damaged almost all cells, whether from animals or plants. The strong salt caused lipid components like lecithin to leach from cell membranes. When this happened the membrane became fragile and it easily split when stressed. Freezing exposes cells to concentrated salt solution and thawing from the frozen state subjects them to stresses great enough to break open the salt-damaged cells. This knowledge stayed with me and when later the idea of Gaia, a self-regulating Earth, first came into my mind, I began to wonder how the salinity of the sea had always kept below five per cent. It has done so for over 3 billion years, otherwise marine life would not have survived. We still do not know what regulates salinity. Maybe the burial of salt goes on at just the right rate by chance. Much goes to form the lagoons of salt that exist on the shorelines of continents. These are the evaporite deposits and, when they are buried under sediments, become the ubiquitous salt beds of the Earth. I still do not know how ocean salinity stays below five per cent; it is one of the puzzles posed by the notion of Gaia.

In the first months back at Mill Hill I had to buy a house for the family to live in. Helen, who otherwise would have helped me, was in the last months of pregnancy and Andrew our third child was born in early November 1951 at Salisbury Infirmary. Alick Isaacs, a young virologist in Andrewes's department gave me generous help in finding a house. He was a small, dark, mercurial man of about my own age and with a Scots accent. He knew Finchley well and he introduced me to estate agents and a solicitor and gave me wise advice about mortgages. I knew him a little from his visits to Harvard Hospital but soon we became close friends and I joined him on weekends in his search for flint implements and arrowheads in the quarries of Kent. Alick was the discoverer of Interferon; indeed, he named it and the name has lasted in spite of objections by purists who seem shocked by any new name. Sadly, he died before they successfully applied his discovery in medicine.

The road from Edgware to Mill Hill through north London was typical of suburban development. Graceless uniform shopping centres separated the ranks of semi-detached villas with tiny gardens; the shops and dwellings looked as if they had been factory-built to the plans of a council committee. They lacked the rich diversity of shops and houses of our older market towns. So dull was the journey that morning as I drove my old Rover car that I failed to notice I was speeding. The limit was 30 mph and I was travelling at over 40. Suddenly a police siren and flashing lights just behind me startled me. It shattered my deep thoughts of the experiments waiting to be done with the blood I had just collected from the Edgware blood bank. I pulled over, feeling that wretched guilt that comes with law breaking no matter how trivial. A young PC came to my open car window and said, 'Can I see your licence sir?' I handed him the small red book and awaited his admonition, but instead he looked at me, then back to my licence and gazed at the litre bottle of blood sitting on the passenger seat. His manner changed from prefectorial to professional. 'Sorry sir,' he said, 'I did not realize that you were on your way to an urgent case. Would you like us to escort you?' I declined his offer as convincingly as I could. I feared the consequences of a high-speed drive back to the Mill Hill Institute with the sirens sounding. I took off decorously at just above the speed limit and was relieved to see the police car turn round and retreat down the road to Edgware. I had never thought that a PhD in medicine was such a powerful token. In fact, I was returning from my weekly visit to the blood bank not, as most do, to donate my blood, but to collect some for my experiments in the frozen state.

We donate our blood without charge in the UK. This generosity pre-dates the Health Service but is now an essential part of it. We need a constant supply of fresh blood to replace the losses that happen in accidents and in surgery and to maintain the stocks. The red cells that give blood its colour and capacity to carry oxygen to the tissues do not survive long in or out of the body. Even in their normal habitat, the life span of a red blood cell is only 100 days. After three weeks' storage at refrigerator temperature they reach their use-by date. After this, only the plasma is used, and the red cells are discarded because blood cannot be stored in a deep freeze. The acts of freezing and thawing both cause the red cells to burst open. My colleague, Audrey Smith, had found empirically that after the addition of fifteen per cent glycerol, blood would keep for a year or more at −80° C. Unfortunately, blood containing fifteen per cent glycerol cannot be transfused. My job at the time was to try to find a way of removing the glycerol without harming the red cells.

I could have used a dialysis machine of the kind that extends the life of those whose kidneys have failed. This machine would have removed the glycerol without otherwise affecting the blood, but it was too slow, too cumbersome, and expensive. I was trying a crude and simple quick fix. Add some strong sugar solution to the blood and it squeezes the red cells free of most of their fluids, including the glycerol, and they can then be resuspended in saline or plasma and used for transfusion. It worked, and I was able to publish a short paper on it in the *Lancet*. I do not think it was ever used in practice. There is still no satisfactory and practical way for the long-term storage of blood cells for transfusion.

To the annoyance of my biologist colleagues, I chose to use red blood cells for all my experiments to discover the harm done by freezing. They chided me, saying that I was wasting my time and theirs. Red cells, they said, are not alive and therefore any conclusions drawn using them are not valid for living cells generally. This was my first quarrel with biologists over the meaning of life. They asserted that reproduction was the essential criterion of life. Red cells, they said, have no nucleus or DNA and certainly do not reproduce; therefore they are dead, no more than floating tiny bags filled with haemoglobin. I agreed with them that reproduction is an essential property for the evolution of life, but I thought that such other properties as metabolism and the active maintenance of homeostasis were also things that distinguished living things from dead matter. Red cells certainly metabolized and they kept their internal composition in homeostasis.

My preference for the red cell as a model cell for freezing experiments did not come from mere perversity—a wish to be different for its own sake. I saw red cells as a simple and elegant model of living cells generally. Freezing is specifically damaging to cell membranes, and red-cell membranes are just like those of other living cells. The balance tipped in their favour for me because damage to red cells could be measured quantitatively by observing with a spectrophotometer the amount of red pigment that leaked out. I could do hundreds of experiments with red cells in the time it would take to do one where the ability to reproduce was the measure.

The absurdity of the objection to my use of red cells as a model revealed itself when I moved on to work with Chris Polge on spermatozoa. These, the biologists said, were alive. 'You can watch them swim,' they added. To me this was nonsense. Spermatozoa may be a key part of reproduction but as cells, they never reproduce. What if red cells had possessed cilia that allowed them to move? Would that make them more alive?

Of course, reproduction followed by the natural selection of the progeny is an essential part of the evolution of living organisms but the insistence by biologists that reproduction is the only criterion for life has plagued me throughout the years. It was the argument they used to reject all of Gaia theory. The Earth cannot reproduce, therefore it is in no way like a living organism; moreover, because it cannot reproduce it can never evolve by natural selection. Their argument is as flawed as it would be for me to argue that grandmothers, Lombardy poplar trees, and anyone, like me, who has had his prostate gland removed are not alive. More seriously, is it sensible for biologists to exclude metabolism and homeostasis as attributes of life?

Perhaps I am too hard on biologists. In the six years I spent—from 1951 to 1956—doing cryobiology, I learned to understand and respect my biologist friends. Their approach to their science was not so different from mine. We both did science by intuition and then spent ages testing and rationalizing what we had done. A widespread foolishness among scientists and their administrators pretends we know what we are going to do before we start, that we can plan the details of our research. It may be commonplace with the i-dotting and t-crossing research, which is the great bulk of science done these days, but it rarely ever happens in pioneering research. Perhaps the wish of fund-holders to know exactly what the recipients intended to do with their money has played a part in bringing science down to today's pedestrian levels.

The experimental biology division at Mill Hill was, even in the 1950s, media conscious. Parkes was always good for a quote on some aspect of reproductive physiology or, as the media had it, sex. It could be on the possibilities of a contraceptive pill, or if the sex-ratio at birth could be changed, and the ethics of it all. With his striking features and wonderful silver hair, Parkes was a well-known television personality. In spite of it all he had a prudish side to his character.

Once he asked for my support when two senior managers of the London Rubber Company—makers of condoms—came to visit. They were concerned that the Pill would severely affect their business unless they could have control of its marketing. Parkes bothered about the thought that these private talks with the condom makers might become public and he would be the subject of sniggering comment. 'Have you heard Parkes is the adviser to a firm that makes "French letters"?' It is difficult now to imagine how repressed the older generation was in those days about anything to do with sex. On another occasion, I was working on the freeze preservation of human spermatozoa. I complained that it was a waste of time for me to travel daily across London to the fertility clinic to work with aged sperm from used condoms. Would it not be better, I suggested, to use my own—at least they would be fresh. I had never seen him so shocked. 'I'll not have a wanker in my division,' he shouted. 'Don't even think of it, Lovelock.' I was surprised that Parkes, the sex guru, should be so touchy over the manual acquisition of a sample of semen for research.

Media interest intensified when we moved on from freezing blood and spermatozoa to freezing whole animals. Audrey Smith reduced to practice a technique pioneered by the Yugoslav biologist, Andjus. She cooled and froze hamsters and then reanimated them from the frozen state. The animals were truly frozen and all their organs transfixed with ice crystals, yet once we had perfected the re-warming technique, they returned to normal unharmed.

The method Andjus first used to reanimate small animals from just above the freezing point was to apply a piece of hot metal to the animal's chest above its heart. This procedure warmed the heart and started it beating while the rest of the animal was still cold. If cold or frozen animals are warmed from the outside by placing them in a warm bath they never recover. Andjus and Audrey Smith both thought that this was because the skin, when warmed, consumed the oxygen remaining in the blood, and when later the heart started it drew in anoxic blood and so failed. Audrey drew on Andjus's experience and warmed her frozen hamsters by applying a teaspoon heated in the flame of a Bunsen burner to their chests. This technique worked with some of the frozen animals, but at the cost of badly burned chests. The experimental biologists at Mill Hill were tough and unsentimental about animal suffering. They were not consciously cruel and did try to avoid suffering so long as it did not interfere with the scientific objective of their experiments. This was, I think, the usual attitude of almost all scientists who used animals in the 1950s. I had to be there to monitor the physics and chemistry of the animal as it went through the freezing and re-warming. I soon found that I was made of softer stuff and was repelled by what I thought were cruel experiments.

It was not long before I decided to make a radio frequency diathermy apparatus with which to warm the animals' hearts from the inside without burning the skin of their chests. I took an afternoon off and went by tube train from Mill Hill to Leicester Square in the centre of London. Just outside the Tube station at Leicester Square is Lisle Street. In those days, it was the market place of two ancient industries, prostitution and the sale of used military hardware. The girls who paraded the street in search of customers had an uncanny ability to distinguish those consumed by lust from those, like me, who were seeking surplus radar equipment. They never accosted me on these expeditions. Lisle Street was a cornucopia of equipment. I was soon able to find an aircraft radio transmitter complete with its 807 vacuum tubes. It cost about ten shillings. I took it home, dismantled it, and from the parts made a simple fifty-watt diathermy apparatus on my kitchen table. It was no more than an evening's work, but with it, Audrey could reanimate her hamsters decently. When I gave it to her the next day she accepted it with enthusiasm and used it from then on in her experiments. It made life difficult for me because the measurement of temperature using thermocouples was near impossible when the diathermy was on and radio frequency currents were flowing in all the nearby wires. We compromised by turning off the diathermy briefly for temperature measurements.

The main proponent of the ice-crystal damage theory—the rival theory to my own view that it was salt damage that harmed the cells— was an American scientist who was also a Jesuit priest, Father Luyet. He came to visit the Mill Hill labs in 1954. I found him a courteous and engaging fellow and we differed without rancour. A much deeper exchange occurred when we showed him two frozen hamsters. One was intact and was shortly to be reanimated by diathermy; the other was sliced with a sharp knife through the heart and through the head. In theory, a skilled surgeon could have repaired the sliced animal. The slicing was to demonstrate that the animal had ice crystals transfixing all organs including the brain. We asked Father Luyet his opinion on the state of these two frozen hamsters. Were they both dead? If the sliced animal was not yet dead, how much more slicing would be needed to kill it? He thought for a while and then replied: 'The questions are meaningless because animals do not have immortal souls and therefore cannot experience death as we do.' Death, like life it seems, describes several different states. This brief encounter with a man of faith stayed with me. I was sharply reminded of it in the 1980s when the neo-Darwinist biologists were so insistent that the Earth could not be compared to a living organism. Both the priest and the biologists seemed to argue from the certainty of faith.

At the beginning of 1954 the United States National Academy of Sciences invited me to a meeting in Washington on freeze preservation. This was my first invitation to another country and my first trip abroad. I flew to Washington by US military air transport, travelling with Pat Mollison, a distinguished haematologist then working at the Hammersmith Hospital. We stayed at the home of the haematologist Hugh Chaplin, who had worked with Pat Mollison. It was a delightful suburban house in Chevy Chase. Coming from London, still then unkempt and with rationing still in place, America was a fairyland of plenty. I marvelled at the supermarkets, to which Mrs Chaplin took me, and at the beauty of Washington as a city. Pat and I were the stars of the meeting and afterwards they deluged me with job offers. I was attracted by two offers of a year's visit—something I knew would be possible as part of my Mill Hill job. One was to Duke University at Durham in North Carolina and the other to Harvard Medical School in Boston. Pat advised me to have a look at both places. I had hopes of receiving the award of a Rockefeller Travelling Fellowship in Medicine and later that year I did receive it.

The airport at Durham was a wooden hut set literally in a field of grass. Dr Ivan Brown met me and took me to the hospital guest quarters. I soon found him to be an unusual medical scientist. He had pioneered a method of freezing blood products for haemophiliacs. The medical bills of their unavoidable accidents could quickly ruin families who had the misfortune of a haemophiliac child. Brown arranged for them to keep a store of Factor VIII in their deep freezes and then instructed them how to prepare and inject it when an emergency happened. It was good to see a decent kindly physician at work in this way. I was sure in my mind that Durham was where I would like to spend the year with my family but it was not to be because my employers, the MRC, insisted that Harvard was the right place for me to spend my Rockefeller Fellowship.

When one first visits a new country, everything is magical. Euphoria brings a sensory enhancement almost like falling in love. I marvelled over the small differences. The green mail boxes that opened to receive a letter—how different from the red pillar-boxes of home; the layout of the railway stations—cathedral-like buildings of elegance but no platforms. I returned to Washington by air and then took the train to New York. I took a day off as a tourist to see the sights. It was a good time to do it, for New York was relaxed and easy then to enjoy. I even saw horse-drawn wagons taking beer kegs to the bars. I took the Staten Island Ferry and called on some of Helen's Scots relatives. Next morning I made my way to Penn Station and the train for Boston. What a slow and bumpy ride it was, and looking out at the New England scene I was surprised to see how brown and grey it was. There were no green trees or grass anywhere. I stayed in Boston at the home of Dr Alan Richardson Jones and his wife. The department at Harvard Medical School, where I was to spend my Rockefeller Fellowship, were affable and offered a $2,000 supplement to the Rockefeller stipend. Bill Jones asked me if they had put it in writing and when I said no, warned that I should not expect them to honour their verbal offer. But I could not believe that a reputable university like Harvard would renege. I returned overnight to Washington on a sleeper and took the Military Air Transportation Service (MATS) flight back to London. There was plenty to do on my return, completing the experiments on the freezing and thawing of live hamsters. We had a film taken of the procedure and, when in America again for my year at Harvard, this film was a passport for travel around the USA.

The Year in Boston

The cost of travel by ship across the Atlantic for the whole family was about £300 one way. The only way we could raise the fare was by selling our house. All through the summer of 1954, a succession of would-be buyers came, attracted by the £3,000 we were asking for our house in Finchley. But one after another their surveyors gave them damning reports on its condition. The would-be purchasers turned it down, often reluctantly, saying it was just the house they wanted. The surveyors all found subsidence and warned that it might not be cured and could lead to expensive structural repairs. I was just about to cancel our American trip when a young couple made an offer: 'We'll take it on, warts and all, but for £200 less than you're asking.' With the return of our deposit to the building society this left us with just enough money for the fares to New York but not to return, and we arranged then to travel on the *Queen Mary*.

Our first glimpse of the formidable bureaucracy of the United States was at their embassy in Grosvenor Square, London. To get an exchange visitor's visa for a year's stay at Harvard involved many visits. To make matters worse, in 1954 that grim and unusual man, Senator McCarthy, had undue influence over the politics of the United States. There was more stringent and difficult questioning than was usual at that embassy: questions like, did we intend to overthrow the government of the United States of America by force? It was difficult not to laugh at such absurdities, but we had been warned beforehand that laughing at them was the last thing we should do if we wanted to get a visa. Even odder and more insulting was the question, 'Is the purpose of your journey solely to set up a house of ill repute and exploit women in prostitution?' We even had blood taken for the Wassermann test so that they could know whether we were syphilitic. In dear old failing England with its socialist tendencies, we had never encountered anything so demeaning, so crass, as this inquisition from an erstwhile ally. Eventually it was done and we had our visas and tickets. Our home was gone and we were staying in Salisbury for the night before we travelled with Tom Thompson in the Harvard Hospital station wagon with our luggage to Southampton and the *Queen Mary*.

On the morning that we left it was all excitement and we were full of wonder at the thought of our coming journey. Compared with an airport today, the ocean terminal at Southampton was not impressive. It had the appearance of a railway station trying to put on airs. The ship's crew took our luggage and we were on the gangway to the ship within minutes of arriving. The only time spent on land was in saying goodbyes. On the ship they took us to our cabin, large enough and with bunks for all five of us. Our youngest, Andrew, was now almost four years old, Christine ten, and Jane eight. We then walked to the tourist-class dining room for lunch. It seemed to take us an age to reach it, passing along the vast old passageways of the ship. We were soon well aware that she was the largest vessel afloat, so great was the distance to walk around her. In 1954 the UK was still rationed and we were used to short supplies of food, for there had been fourteen years of privation during and after the war. Our stomachs and our tastes were unprepared for that first meal on the *Queen Mary*. It was truly gorgeous, and we gorged. Even in tourist class, the cheapest way to travel at £60 a head to New York, the food was plentiful and of good quality, and delivered by waiters who provided an excellent service with several courses to the meal.

Walking around that floating ants' nest of a ship we encountered frequent barriers saying, 'Cabin class only' and, more rarely, 'First class only'. But the space available in tourist class was sufficient and included an area on most of the ship's decks, even at the top. The top deck was near the ship's funnels and when the ship sailed from Southampton to Cherbourg, her first port of call, we were up there to watch. We forgot that ships always announce their departure by a blast from their hooters, and those of the *Queen Mary* were claimed to be so loud as to be audible ten miles away. To Helen, Andrew, and me it was the most terrifying sound. A low deep throbbing that seemed to be measured in bels not mere decibels, it shook our bodies as well as our ears. Andrew screamed in terror and we staggered to the shelter of the stairway. We did not return to that deck again for the whole of the trip, but it was a pleasant journey. The five days to New York, even in tourist class, were more comfortable and relaxed than anything the airlines can offer. The shift in time of one hour daily is much easier to cope with than the sudden jerk of five hours. Eating in comfort at dining tables was a joy after so much privation. The ship's library and cinema had much to offer and there was no difficulty finding space in the ample recreation areas.

Typically, as young socialists, we resented our exclusion from the first-class territory. What justification was there for these bloated plutocrats and faded gentry to travel so extravagantly? Typically also, we were determined that as soon as we could afford it we would not travel classified amongst the poor but would be amongst first-class also. Such is the contradiction of socialism. To citizens of sensible nations, I must explain that in those days the English were so class-oriented that questions of status were ubiquitous, but it was not all bad. We knew instantly from the class system, from dress, voice, and deportment, just where anybody belonged on the pyramid of our nation. Many, if not most, were contented to know this place and lead their lives at its level. This was true to some extent of us also, but the segregation of classes on a ship somehow seemed to ignite the politics of envy. All this must seem odd, if not mad, to wealthy Americans who choose to travel economy on the flight from America to Europe or even farther. They do so as part of their puritan ethic. I knew American millionaires, at a time when a millionaire was seriously rich, who would never waste money on the greater comfort of business or first-class travel.

The journey to the United States in early October was pleasantly enhanced for us by rough weather. This kept many in their cabins sea sick and there were few in the dining rooms and recreation areas. There were gales blowing most of the journey, and the Atlantic swell made the bows of the ship rise and fall through sixty feet or more. The tourist class lounges and bars were in this part of the ship. This we didn't mind in the least; indeed, we enjoyed it.

Looking out from a ship on a transatlantic voyage there are three great sights: the green countryside of England as the ship passes down Southampton water into the Solent; the sea in all its moods; and the splendid arrival at New York past the Statue of Liberty and to the white cliffs of the skyscrapers. The airlines can never offer so magnificent a prospect. As the ship berths on the East Side, its large, functional, but seemly bulk is a true match for the architecture of New York. The stopping of the ship's engines punctuates the journey's end. Then comes the anticlimax. On the *Queen Mary* this involved for us a long and wearying wait in queues in the ship's lounges for the attentions of the immigration officers.

My experiences of public servants like police officers and tax inspectors came from my growing up in London. This was a time when policemen, even in the rough area of Brixton, were friendly men who walked the streets and who seemed to spend as much time holding up traffic to let children like me, or the elderly, cross the road, as in deterring crime. I never saw in all my childhood, especially with the poorer children of Brixton, anything that would fit the academic Marxist image of an oppressive force that kept the poor in their place. Indeed the police were mostly working-class themselves. If the Marxists were right and the function of the police was oppression, then they did their job with such tact and sensitivity that no one on the ground, except criminals, was aware of it. But London in those times, in spite of profound racial differences, was only stratified by class, and it was otherwise a homogeneous society. It was so different from the mix of cultures that London is now and New York was then. An Austrian living in Boston in those days said to me, 'I would never live in America if the police were unarmed or in Britain if they were armed.' Waiting in the vast dockside customs sheds for our luggage to be checked, we saw the armed police around and immediately were made aware how different from our own was the society in which we would spend the next year. Two officials from the Rockefeller Foundation met us in the customs shed and eased our way through customs and into a taxi. They took us to the Abbey Hotel in Manhattan. It was not far from the Penn Station from where we would be travelling to Boston the next day. Travelling with my family gave a wholly different perspective from my solo journey earlier that year. Everything we saw in New York during our brief stay was strange, fascinating, yet slightly threatening. How odd that the hotel had no public rooms at all, just a small entrance hall with a reception desk and a row of lifts. Meals were in restaurants somewhere in the streets around. In the evening we chose an automat to eat in; we were too insecure to want to interact with these strange and inscrutable New Yorkers. They were so unlike the men we had known in the American Forces during the war. To add to our feeling that we were indeed alien, Andrew had a nosebleed during the night and bloodstained his bed. We left in the morning in a hurry and embarrassed, imagining that shortly afterwards there would be an encounter with the police and the problem of convincing them that the blood had come from nothing more serious than a nosebleed.

Soon we were in the magnificent Penn Station and ready for our journey. We had our tickets and we boarded the Boston train for the 250-mile journey from New York to Boston, about the same distance as from London to Newcastle. In England, a fast steam train in those days did the journey in about three hours. We were surprised to find that our 9 am train did not arrive in Boston until 3.30 that afternoon. It was a dismal journey, creeping past dry, barren-looking countryside and numerous small industrial towns. If this was New England, presumably therefore most like old England, whatever must the rest of the United States be like? Later we found that in many ways New England—in landscape, culture, and peoples—is the least English of all the regions. It was different from the countryside and small towns of Texas, which later we found was much more familiar and pleasant to live in.

We eventually arrived in Boston hungry and thirsty, for there was no restaurant car on the train, just a vendor selling peanuts and Hershey bars. We took a taxi to Harvard Medical School and went with our entire luggage to the Department of Biophysical Chemistry, in which I was due to work for the next year. They seemed quite unprepared for our arrival, although I had written on several occasions telling them exactly when and on what date we would arrive. After a while someone managed to find another Englishman, Kenneth Walton, who was also spending a year in the department but had arrived earlier, and he took us to the Peter Bent Brigham Hotel just nearby. It was an ancient faded wooden structure with miserable rooms, more like a doss house than a hotel but, as he said, it was cheap. We were rapidly discovering that the $3,000 a year fellowship that Rockefeller Foundation was providing was wholly inadequate to support Helen, the three children, and me.

We had to find somewhere to live quite soon, and the next day we spent visiting a round of realtors. All were unable to offer anything that we could afford until the last one—a Jewish realtor—mistook me for a Jew, not just a quarter of one. He offered us a flat in Brookline, conveniently near the university and in the Jewish quarter of Boston. The rent was $140 a month, which was more than half our stipend. But since the department at Harvard University had promised to add $2,000 a year, our difficulties would merely be temporary. We discovered later that the size of our family had prevented easy access to rented accommodation. Our three children were seen as a threat and no one wanted to rent their property to us. The Jewish realtor who finally did said afterwards that it was because we were English that we got the flat. I think that this was because at that time English children were seen as well behaved. After visiting the nearby supermarket and settling in, life seemed less stark.

The next morning I went to the lab to start my year's work. I found it was oddly disorganized. The labs were poorly equipped compared with those at Mill Hill and money seemed to be in short supply. I went to see the staff member who had invited me to Harvard. High on my agenda was the $2,000 a year that Harvard, through him, had offered to supplement my Rockefeller stipend. To my dismay, he said that Senator McCarthy had introduced new regulations concerning the employment of aliens, which made it impossible for the university to help me. I had no way to check his statement and the first few days in the United States, with hotel bills and purchases to equip our flat, had reduced the tiny sum of two weeks' salary, $114, to almost nothing and there were two weeks remaining. We found near complete inflexibility. When I asked how we were to live, the reply was 'Well, give up smoking, you'll survive.' The Rockefeller Foundation was equally unhelpful. When I pointed out that the two weeks' stipend given me in New York was not enough to live on, their response was to say, 'You should not have come with three children and a wife. Why have you not left them in England?' They refused to give an advance to tide us over. We began to realize how cosseted a society socialist Britain was and that America was a world of harsh reality for which we were wholly unprepared. I mentioned my plight to an English colleague, Bill Jones, who I had met in Washington in January and who worked in the blood-grouping laboratory just down Longwood Avenue from Harvard Medical School. He snorted and said, 'I warned you about that bunch.' He suggested that I sell a pint of my blood. The rate then paid was $10 a pint. I had given many pints in England for experimental purposes so I thought why not sell my blood to feed the family until our next pay cheque comes in two weeks. Bill had the technicians check my blood group while I chatted with him about his invention, a blood-cell counter, which he called an 'arith-mometer'. When he saw their report he said, 'You are in luck. Your group is so rare that we will pay $50 a pint.' I was delighted to give my pint of blood, for they were paying me almost a week's stipend and in cash. Bill explained that my blood group was common among Baffin Land Inuits but extremely rare elsewhere. It was no use for transfusion but valuable for typing other bloods. We celebrated that night in our Brookline flat on Beacon Street with a good meal, our first since we had arrived.

At Harvard Medical School, I learnt how to separate the lipoproteins of the blood and then I examined their response to freezing and thawing. The Department of Biophysical Chemistry, where I was to spend my year's fellowship, had recently lost the man who founded it, Professor EJ Cohn. He pioneered the separation of the proteins of the blood by a technique he called cold ethanol fractionation. He was a good scientist but with a difficult personality, caused perhaps by the disease that caused his death, a pheochromocytoma. This is a tumour of the adrenal gland and it causes an excessive secretion of adrenal hormones, which kept him permanently switched on. To perform the separations of the proteins he had built a large cold room kept at $-20°$ C. His graduate students were obliged to spend their time in this arctic environment. Because of his disease, he slept little and would telephone the cold room at any hour during the night seeking news of the progress of the latest separation technique. Surviving students told me that their progress towards a doctorate depended on their prompt answering of the cold-room telephone whenever it rang. They seemed to live in terror of their professor and I was concerned at how little had been done since his death to improve working conditions.

I was not keen to work in the cold room and managed to persuade the department to buy two top-opening deep freezers from Sears Roebuck. We could then keep our solutions in the cold while we were in the warmth of the lab. I began to realize as the fall of 1954 moved towards winter that it would take time for the department to recover its poise. The new professor, Dr Oncley was personally kind but offered no practical help with funding. An odd episode took place at Christmas. A letter came in the post to the department from a distinguished physician, Dr Henry Forbes, known for his strong stand in favour of birth control. It was a personal letter to me and it enclosed a cheque for $50. He had heard from his friends in England that we were having a hard time and had enclosed something so that we could at least enjoy a good Christmas. There was also an invitation to bring the family to his home in the Blue Hills near Boston. The effects of this gift and letter astonished me. Suddenly we became persons of consequence. The Forbeses were one of the old Harvard families and such condescension (in Jane Austen's parlance) greatly elevated our social standing. I had always thought of the United States as a place free of snobbery. Yet, here was a piece of almost 19th-century class distinction. Michael Crichton's semi-autobiographical book of his days at Harvard Medical School, *A Case of Need,* confirms our experience as far from singular.

By Christmas 1954, things were looking up for us in Boston. We had found it impossible to survive in Brookline with so much of our income going on rent and we moved to a twenty-roomed Charles Addams style house for rent at $90 a month in the suburb of Auburndale. The owner, a true Old New England lady named Pockwince, let it to us on the basis that we would allow prospective buyers to see round. The capacious basement was full of old furniture. She said, 'Go to the hardware store, buy yourself a cross-cut saw and you will have all the fuel you need for the winter by burning these old pieces here.' This I did, which was as well, for it was a truly cold winter with temperatures down to −20° C.

Through Bill Jones, the Jarrell family befriended us. Dick Jarrell, still a friend who writes yearly, was President of an instrument company, Jarrell Ash, that made spectrometers and other scientific instruments. He and Kiffy, his wife, were unstintedly generous and invited all the Lovelocks to spend Christmas with them at their home in Waban, a Boston suburb. They also had four children, so it was a noisy but delightful Christmas. As our year in Boston passed the Jarrells became close friends, and we spent a two-week holiday with them at their beach house at Surfside in Nantucket. I think that I was able to repay Dick in part by the advice I gave him on instrument science.

The research I did at the Department of Biophysical Chemistry was mostly on the effects of freezing and thawing on lipoproteins. My earlier work had led me to believe that the damage suffered by living cells when they froze was mostly to the structures of their membranes and these were made of lipoprotein—a combination of fatty substances like lecithin with protein. Using a technique developed by another Rockefeller Fellow, Dr Kenneth Walton, I was able to harvest beta-lipoprotein from blood. I did this work in collaboration with an American postdoctoral student, Dr Al Keltz. We found that beta-lipoprotein was only slightly damaged by freezing and were able to devise practical methods for its preservation in the frozen state. We tried without success to publish the work and eventually a summary of it appeared in a paper I gave before a Royal Society discussion meeting in 1956.

As we moved into 1955 I began to fret about how we would be able to pay the fare back home. The least expensive way was on the *New-foundland*, a 5,000-ton cargo liner that sailed from Boston via Halifax, Nova Scotia and St Johns, Newfoundland to Liverpool. It would cost £250. There seemed no chance of saving this much from our meagre stipend. Then I saw in a copy of *Nature* an advertisement from the CIBA foundation about a prize for an essay on Research in Ageing. The prize was £250, just what we needed, and I bought with the cash for my next bleed a second-hand typewriter and wrote the essay sitting in bed at our Auburndale home. Helen transcribed it on the typewriter and we sent it off to CIBA in February. In July we heard that I had won: soon the cheque came and we were able to confirm our bookings on the ship. It was a joyful return in September 1955 on a delightful small ship and the journey gave us the opportunity to see those rarely visited places, Nova Scotia and Newfoundland.

I have mixed memories of Boston. On the bad side are my experiences at Harvard Medical School. For the first three months I was there in 1954, they treated us as American universities in those days treated their graduate students. They expected us to survive on $3,000 a year, not easy for foreigners with three children to support. The department needed me badly to bring to them the know-how of blood freezing. I did this so well that the department, or one member of it, won the Glycerol Prize for their work. What I did not know, and no one had explained to me, was that at an American university you often have to bargain for your salary. When it came to the end of our year in Boston, and we were longing to return home, the Harvard department suddenly realized that they still needed me and offered $6,000 a year if I would stay on. I was incensed. We had suffered privation but had survived, in part, by selling my blood, and through the kindness of our friends and I now realized that the story about Senator McCarthy preventing the department from keeping their promise of extra salary was fiction. After that, I had no confidence in them and no intention of staying on. Not understanding, they raised the offer to $10,000. Uplifted by our righteous indignation, perversely, we returned to the poorer but gentler welfare-oriented socialism of the United Kingdom, where salaries could not be negotiated, at least not at the MRC.

The other side of Boston was the personal kindness of our neighbours, who sensed our difficulties and remembered their own hard times in the Great Depression. Because we were poor, we met many ordinary Americans who had the same problems as we did. Class divisions there are as large as they are in the UK, but the segregation is by income, not status, and the separation of the classes is geographic. Where you live depends on what you earn and to some extent on your race.

My Last Years at the Mill Hill Institute

When I returned to Mill Hill from America in 1955 I found that Parkes's department was still deeply involved with whole-animal freezing and reanimation. Audrey Smith had carried the technique, still using my homemade diathermy, to the point where it was almost routine to freeze and reanimate hamsters. She presented her work in three papers in the *Proceedings of the Royal Society*, and I think that Parkes submitted them for her because, generously, he wanted to reward Audrey for her success and the status that it gave to his department by promoting her election as a Fellow of the Royal Society. My own contributions to this success, through the diathermy equipment and the physical measurements during freezing were recognized by my appearance as a second author on the third paper. To be fair on Parkes and Audrey, they did not understand the amount of hard science involved in the physical-chemistry of cryobiology. Also, I think that they both felt about me in the same way that a car driver regards a police car that keeps station behind him. I was a representative of the law sent by the stern figure of the Institute's director. My presence was a constraint on their freedom to act like happy biologists and ignore physics and chemistry, or so they seemed to think. In practice, Sir Charles Harington only asked me if I was happy working for them, never about what they did. I was content, for they were kind enough personally and the work that I did was fulfilling.

In February 1956 our fourth child, John, was born. Sadly, he suffered a birth defect, an oesophageal atresia, that caused anoxia soon after he was born. The defect was corrected by surgery within hours but too late to save him from brain damage. John was delightful as a baby, but after one year, he became a hyperactive and an unusually difficult child to rear. His first ten years were hard for all of us, but we coped. After this, a Rudolph Steiner school in Sussex in southern England did wonders to bring out his potential and now he manages his life at least as well as many of his contemporaries with normal brains.

Early in 1956 Parkes had arranged a discussion meeting on freezing and reanimation at the Royal Society. He asked me to present my own work as a paper. This was my chance to close my freezing research at what seemed to me to be a definitive stage and I took it willingly. I knew that there was much still to be done to unravel the physical chemistry of freezing and thawing, and soon afterwards the American scientists Peter Mazur and Henry Merryman took it on. For me the science of cryobiology had ended. I had no wish to continue filling in the details. My last paper in Parkes's department was with Marcus Bishop, a biologist. It was on the use of dimethyl sulphoxide (DMSO) as a freeze-protecting chemical. Bishop and I had tried it as a protective agent against freezing damage for the red cells of cattle, which were impossible to freeze using glycerol. It worked perfectly and we published our work as a *Nature* Letter. I was proud of this discovery. Dimethyl sulphoxide was chosen from a number of candidate substances by prediction. It had all the properties needed according to my theory of freeze damage by electrolyte concentration to provide near perfect protection.

My last act in Parkes's department was to serve as science adviser to a BBC producer, George Foa. This happened because Sir Charles Harington's personal secretary, Lorna Frazer, had written a play that the BBC was about to produce. Lorna, feeling an urge to write, had attended a BBC course on playwriting and soon after resigned her job and wrote her play, *The Critical Point*, based on the work of Parkes's department. The Institute gave me six weeks' leave to work with George Foa and Lorna during the rehearsals. It was an exciting experience to be part of a team that included, in the two separate runs of the play such actors and actresses as Leo McKern, Lana Morris, Joan Greenwood, and Mervyn Johns. To watch the development of the play through its rehearsals is something I still remember with pleasure. My job was to see that the scenes presented were a faithful representation of the Mill Hill laboratory, and in this I succeeded far too well. The lab was indeed like that of Mill Hill but the public and the critics knew better. They had expected something like the interior of a nuclear power station or else a rerun of 'Frankenstein'. A real laboratory was to the public and critics unbelievable; truth is indeed so strange as to be incredible. On the second production, we let the public have their way and all was well. The play was about the freezing of the actor, Eric Lander, and the consequences of failed reanimation: was it an accident or murder? I made a tape using a homemade electronic sound generator that simulated the dying breath, the death rattle, and the failing heartbeats. The BBC told me later that it inspired them to form their radiophonic workshop for artificial sound production. Proof of their approval was a cheque for £50 for the tape, something that I had neither asked for nor expected. After the play was over, Lorna, Helen, and I celebrated at an Indonesian restaurant near Leicester Square.

This exposure to the outside world started my slow move over the next few years to independence. In 1956 I told Parkes that I wanted to move to the biochemistry department to work on detectors. I felt also that I had reached the end of my usefulness in the freezing work. He was not pleased and he said, 'Maybe it means little to you but if you go on like this, moving from one department to another, you will never be elected a Fellow of the Royal Society.' It was difficult for me not to laugh. I did science for its own sake; the rewards at that stage seemed so distant that they were no spur for me. And, in any case, my low self-esteem had convinced me that there was no chance of my ever being elected to so distinguished a society. Sir Charles Harington, as

I expected, welcomed my wish for a change, and took me into what had been his own department, biochemistry, now run by Tommy Work. He was an entirely different man to Parkes and was an Orkadian, that is, someone from those northern isles, the Orkneys. I found him to be thoughtful, considerate and a thoroughly decent man.

During the early 1950s Archer Martin and his colleague of those days, Tony James were busy establishing the science of chromatography. Their work was truly important and made possible so many of the great advances in reductionist science that took place in the 1950s. The MRC's greatest triumph was the worldwide expansion of biotechnology which grew from the support it gave to pioneers of molecular biology and to these instrument scientists. I first heard news of the new and exciting method of chemical analysis called gas chromatography from Keith Dumbell early in 1951, when he returned to Salisbury after a visit to the Mill Hill Institute. I knew all about chromatography. It was a method of separating substances by passing a solution through a tube filled with some inert absorbent powder like starch or silica. A distinguished Russian botanist, Mikhail S Tswett, had invented chromatography in 1906 and he used it to separate and identify the pigments of flowers. He dissolved the pigments that colour flowers in alcohol and then placed a few drops of the alcohol solution on the top of a tube filled with powdered chalk. When he washed the chalk column with a hydrocarbon solvent, the pigments moved down the chalk and separated as coloured bands; each one a different substance. It was the separation and recognition of the pigments by their colours that gave the technique the name chromatography. In fact, it was merely the separation of different substances, and since most substances are not coloured, the word chromatography is a little odd. All chemists knew about chromatography and I had often used it to separate otherwise inseparable substances. But what was gas chromatography? In my mind, I pictured a tube full of tiny bubbles, a froth of gas. Somehow, liquid solutions percolated through these bubbles and in the process components of the solution separated. This image was quite wrong but typical of me at that age. In fact, the gas chromatograph column is filled with fine powder, usually coated with an involatile liquid. An inert gas like nitrogen passes through the column just as liquid passed through Tswett's original column. Vapours carried by the moving gas separate by absorbing differently on the material of the column. Scientists worldwide were soon using this powerful technique to separate and identify the numerous substances that go to make up a flavour or a perfume, the fatty acids of the blood, or the hydrocarbons of petroleum. The name chromatography stuck, even though the separation of coloured vapours was a rare event indeed.

His friends knew Dr AJP Martin as Archer, the inventor of many important developments of Tswett's original method. Most deservedly, he was awarded a Nobel Prize for this work, along with his collaborator Dick Synge. Archer was the kind of scientist with whom I could empathize. He was oblivious of dress and would come to the lab on hot summer days dressed in shorts, an open-necked shirt, and wearing sandals. The National Institute of Medical Research was a government laboratory and in the early 1950s it was bad form to appear so dressed. We were free to dress casually and were not, like most civil servants, required to wear suits, but it would have been out of place for one of us to dress as Archer did—almost as inappropriate as a hospital nurse wearing heavy makeup and a mini-skirt at her duty on the wards. It says something about the management of the Mill Hill laboratory that they tolerated such behaviour from distinguished eccentrics like Archer. We are freer now to dress as we like but somehow in discarding the constraints we have lost a sense of anticipation—the joy that comes from earning the rewards of seniority. As a young scientist I knew that I could not dress like Archer but I knew that fame, if it came, would let me throw away my stifling shirt and tie. That feeling of anticipation and the security of a place in society are missing from the untidy egalitarianism of today. Archer Martin was no father figure for me but in the many encounters we had in the next few years he gave me confidence in my own odd way of doing science, which was not so different from his. I was especially grateful for his insistence that the first experiment in a new subject should be a rough one and intended only to get the feel of it. Exact science should come second, not first.

I started collaborating with Martin and James to make new detectors for their gas chromatograph even before leaving Parkes's department; this work was successful beyond all my expectations, and soon we had a range of new detectors that enhanced the power of the gas chromatograph. Among these was the argon detector that made gas chromatography accessible to scientists in many different fields, and the electron capture detector, ECD, which was to prove so important in the environmental revolution soon to come. Chapter 7, later in this book, is entirely about the ECD. I continued working with red cells and, with Tony James, fed them ^{14}C-labelled acetate to see if the blood cells synthesized fatty acids. They did, although by the time I left Mill Hill it was not clear whether the red cells were active in this way or whether it was only the white cells that synthesized fatty acids. We were surprised to find that the cells of human blood synthesized the so-called essential fatty acids, linoleic and arachidonic acids. Detector development took up so much of my time that the red cell experiments took second place and the pressure of work made me feel the need for somewhere to escape to for weekends in the quiet of the countryside.

I was now receiving a good salary as a tenured member of the scientific staff, enough indeed to contemplate a mortgage on a small cottage in the village. We did not have enough spare cash for the required deposit but could afford the monthly payments and with the help of a colleague, Thomas Nash, a bachelor, who put up half the price of the cottage, we bought it. Pixie's Cottage was on the Wood Yates Road at the top of Bowerchalke village. It was a tiny thatched cottage with a small well-tended front garden. Strangely, thatched cob walls surrounded the house and garden and enhanced its privacy. On the ground floor were a living room with oak beams and a tiny kitchen. Upstairs were two small bedrooms and an even smaller bathroom. Neither Helen nor I cared for London, still less for the suburban living in Finchley. Our cottage at Bowerchalke was a refuge and we went there whenever possible.

We grew to know and love the village, the villagers, and the glorious, still unspoiled countryside around. We were not churchgoers and so we met villagers in the shop or the post office or in the pub, The Bell. Chris and Arthur Gulliver ran the village pub and their families had been in the village since time beyond imagining. The pub was a place for social encounters rather than for heavy drinking. Indeed, the landlady made it clear she disapproved strongly of drunkenness and would not hesitate to turn drunkards away. We found little difficulty in getting to know most of the villagers, and the notion that country folk are hard to make friends with, or that it is necessary to live for generations in a village before one is accepted, is rarely true. More often, those who complain are expressing their own inability to change and become amenable.

The Bowerchalke community was alive and had been so for hundreds of years. It was complete with a fine village school which Mrs Adams, its capable Welsh schoolteacher, ran with an assistant. There was a village cricket team good enough to win against the county team of Somerset. There was a bus service into Salisbury several times a day. The bus was another meeting place where villagers gossiped and shared the news. One of the bus drivers was rumoured to have a lover in a village, Bishopstone, half way to Salisbury. Here the bus would stop for brief encounters while the driver slaked his passion, and then resumed, as before, the journey to Salisbury. This idyllic existence in Bowerchalke, as in other villages across the south of England, was doomed, but we did not know it then in the 1950s. Agribusiness and the car culture were preparing their deadly assault that was to overwhelm and destroy the villages and the countryside of southern England. Like many a successful campaign of conquest, it did not begin with outright war. The long years of privation softened our resolve.

Back at Mill Hill, in order to concentrate on detector development, I took on a post-doctoral scientist, Charles Rowe from Birmingham, who then took over my blood experiments. They gave me a spacious lab on the third floor at the north end of the Institute with an office in a separate room from the lab. To work on this floor was quite an honour; a sizeable proportion of the labs were the workplaces of Nobel Laureates or those who would later receive the prize. Archer Martin, who had now moved to the other end of the floor, had previously occupied my lab. These were near ideal working conditions and I was lucky to have the infant technique of gas chromatography to exercise my inventive talents. I made too many inventions, for I had during that period no chance to fully develop or understand any single one of them. I was like a keen gardener presented with all the plants at the Chelsea Flower Show—delighted and at the same time frustrated by the lack of ground in which to plant them. One invention I made but never reduced to practice was super-critical fluid chromatography. This analytical method makes use of that strange state of matter that exists between gas and liquid. If water is heated to above $374°\,C$ or carbon dioxide to above $31°\,C$, no amount of pressure will keep them in the liquid state. What is interesting for chromatography is that these dense gases will dissolve solids as well or better than the liquids from which they came. Super critical steam will even dissolve rocks. I went as far as notarizing an invention record when I visited Yale in 1958, but there was no time when I was back at Mill Hill to develop the invention. It has subsequently become one of the main branches of chromatographic science.

I spent most of my time developing the argon detector, which was the first practical device that could analyse sensitively and quantitatively the compounds emerging from a gas chromatograph column. It took advantage of the property of rare gas atoms, such as those of argon, to form short-lived highly energetic metastable states. When a vapour molecule collided with a metastable argon atom it was ionized. In my argon detector the ions were collected and measured. It was exceedingly sensitive and much needed because the application of the Martin and James gas chromatograph in biochemistry was hindered by the lack of a general-purpose sensitive detector. I discovered the argon detector by one of those happy accidents that are part of a scientist's life. I had been trying unsuccessfully to apply a device called an ionization cross-section detector to the gas chromatograph, and although it worked it was miserably insensitive. The American scientists, JW Otvos and DP Stevenson had invented it at the Shell labs in California several years before and they recommended that hydrogen or helium be used for the carrier gases. Now, Institute rules required me to use nitrogen because hydrogen was too much a fire and explosion risk for apparatus left on overnight and unattended. Helium was in those days too expensive for use in Britain. Nitrogen worked well with Martin's gas density balance but was hopeless with the device I was trying.

In late 1956 I had one last set of experiments planned before I gave up trying to make an ionization detector work for gas chromatography. At that moment, my nitrogen supply ran out. My technician went to the stores to pick up another cylinder and returned saying that they were out of nitrogen and would argon do instead? She had sensibly brought up a small argon cylinder for me to try and I thought, well, why not? Theory suggested that the detector would be slightly less sensitive with argon than with nitrogen but this should not affect the experiments I intended to do, so I joined up the argon supply and started my last set of experiments. These were running the detector at a potential of between 500 and 2,000 volts. I added a three-microlitre sample of fatty-acid methyl esters to the top of the gas chromatograph column, reconnected the argon supply, and waited. Old-style gas chromatography with packed columns was a slow business requiring much patience, for substances could sometimes take hours to pass through the column. On this occasion, the air peak, representing the air that had leaked in with the sample appeared first. Then, to my amazement, the recorder pen went off scale. At first,

I thought there must be a short circuit, but on turning down the gain, I saw a series of large peaks emerging. Here was a detector incomparably more sensitive than anything I had expected, and I repeated the experiment several times and at different voltages until I was sure that argon gas had somehow amplified the signal hundreds if not thousands of times. Better still, the analysis of the fatty-acid esters was in more or less true proportion to the quantities expected.

We now had the detector Archer Martin and Tony James had sought, one that would allow them to exploit in full the potential of their wonderful invention. For the next two years, I was overwhelmed by the interest stirred by this discovery. I found myself describing it at laboratories in almost every state of the union and it took me to places like Peoria, Illinois and Bismarck, North Dakota. It was hardly an invention, for I had not planned to use argon; I did not want it named the Lovelock detector, so we called it the argon detector. Naming things is often difficult and to call it an argon detector was not a good idea, because argon was the only thing it did not detect. It is good to have recognition for a job well done, or a creative achievement, but in science I dislike the thought of rewards as the prime motivation for work. The joy of science lies, for me, in the sense of adventure and the retention of a child's sense of wonder, even to my dotage.

About two years later an even better invention—the flame ionization detector, FID—superseded the argon detector. It was more accurate and did not require a radioactive source of ions. This invention by IG McWilliam and RA Dewar was so successful that it is now the principal detector for analytical gas chromatographs. But the argon detector gave me two years of excitement and established gas chromatography as a key analytical method in biochemistry. On one occasion during my work on detectors, and when the ECD was proving to be a fascinating distraction with no apparent use, I asked the Institute Director if he disapproved of my working on ionization physics, for it then seemed most remote from medical research. Sir Charles replied, 'All I care about is that you continue to do good science; I am not concerned that your work is in physics instead of medical research.' Looking back I see how right he was, for nothing I did at Mill Hill had as great an impact on medicine as did the ECD, but that is the story of Chapter 7.

Another detector I invented was the photoionization detector. In this device, a low-pressure electrical discharge in argon, helium or hydrogen generated hard ultra-violet radiation that ionized vapours coming from a chromatograph column, and it was described in a Letter to *Nature* in 1960. The great practical utility of the flame ionization detector satisfied most analysts' needs and the photoionization detector was only occasionally used.

It was a glorious May morning in 1960, and as I walked across the fields to work at the Mill Hill Institute, birds were in full chorus and the wildflowers bloomed. The scent of May from the hawthorn hedges filled the air. This island of countryside in suburbia was part of London's Green Belt and off limits, then and perhaps even now, to conniving developers. I should have been counting my blessings, fortunate to be securely placed in a well-paid tenured post at one of the world's most distinguished scientific institutes. I could do whatever science I felt inclined to follow within the wide field of medical research. I was accountable only to that benign authoritarian figure, Sir Charles Harington, the Institute's director. My post was equivalent to that of a research professor at a famous university. I had a large, well-equipped laboratory, two technicians and a postdoctoral scientist, Dr Rowe, working for me. In many ways, it was a scientist's dream employment. My salary was then edging towards £3,000 per annum. Our five-bedroom house in Westbury Road, Finchley, was in good condition and spacious, and with an outlook over the Dollis Brook and the small park that lined its banks. The house cost us £3,500 when we bought it in 1959 and with house prices rising yearly, our equity was sound. The same house would now cost fifty times as much. It would require a salary of over £50,000 a year to sustain the mortgage payments. In addition to all this, we had a new car, a Riley, costing between £800 and £900, and paid for from the fees of American lecture tours. Best of all was our cottage in Wiltshire where we could escape for weekends and holidays. The Medical Research Council allowed six weeks' paid holiday a year and one week of so-called uncertificated sick leave. In spite of all this, I was uneasy, and as I walked along the footpath to work, I wondered how I could honourably resign and start an independent practice of science.

There were many unsettling things. My mother's presence in a nearby flat, to which she had moved after my father died, led to endless quarrels involving Helen and the family. They were both good women, but obstinate and as bitterly opposed as members of warring tribes. We would spend weekends and holidays at our cottage in Bowerchalke, but this was no substitute for a full life in Wiltshire. We placed the cultural benefits of working in London below that of country living. To cap it all, I had a vague and ill-defined ambition to widen my scientific horizons beyond that of medical research. I could not have known it then but somehow Gaia was beckoning me away from the security of the civil service. The peculiar physiological changes that seem to affect men approaching forty years old amplified this urge to escape the nest and the phrase, 'life begins at forty' sums it up. Some men change their wives, some their jobs; I felt the urge to make a complete change in my way of life. There were formidable obstacles. First, where would the money come from? Perhaps I could write science fiction; perhaps I could start as a consultant to one of the firms who forever sought my advice on gas chromatography detectors and other inventions. And then, as a deterrent, there was the scorn and powerful persuasion against taking so foolish and insecure a path. This would come from Sir Charles and from my colleagues at the Institute. My mother would be even more difficult to persuade. To her nothing was better for her son than a secure and safe government job and the idea of an uncharted future working privately was anathema to her. As I walked, these thoughts jostled for attention in my mind and I could find no easy answer. Although we were comfortably well off, there was no reserve; far from having a private income or a rich family to fund the new life, I had Helen and four children to support and, in addition, my mother needed five per cent of my net income to supplement her pension. I shrugged as I climbed the hill to the Institute and tried to turn my thoughts to the work of the day. It was no good—the need to make a decision about my future nagged in my mind like the unforgettable itch of the malignant pustule of anthrax.

Three weeks later my mother came to spend an afternoon and evening with us. Over the teatime meal, a fierce row developed over the trivial topic of Christine's homework. Christine, my elder daughter, was as much at odds at her grammar school, the prestigious Henrietta Barnett School in Hampstead Garden Suburb, as I had been twenty-five years earlier with the Strand School. She could see no point in homework that they insisted she do; she remembered all she had been taught that day and saw no need to recapitulate it. I supported her. My mother invested education with near magical properties and saw Christine's rebellion as a wicked rejection of a wonderful opportunity for betterment. My mother was living out her own lost opportunity when, as a young girl, family poverty had denied her the chance of a good grammar school education. A wiser woman would have kept quiet, but not Nell Lovelock, and with blazing eyes and waving arms she shouted her disapproval. Helen, who feared above all any overt show of emotion, was distraught, and pleaded for calm. It went on for at least an hour and left us all cross, unrepentant, and exhausted.

Next morning in bed, Helen and I decided to move at once to Bowerchalke and to sell our house in London. I would stay during the week with my mother at her tiny flat in Finchley. Helen and the children would live in the Bowerchalke cottage until we could find a house in the village. At the back of my mind was the thought that I would never be able to endure the ninety-mile journey each weekend, nor the company of my mother every evening of the working week. The discomfort of such a life would force my hand and make me resign from the Institute. At first, it was bearable; my mother was pleased to have my company, and there was the break from Thursday night until Monday morning in Bowerchalke as something to look forward to. It was usual for senior scientists to do the writing work they had at home, the constant interruptions during the working day at an Institute or university lab make serious thought difficult and, for me, impossible. Many tried an early start before the chatterers had picked up their telephone handsets, but it did not often help. There would be a knock on the lab door at 8.30 am. The caller would enter saying, 'I know you're not busy just now so I thought I would call in to ask if you would mind giving something for our cricket fund. We need two new bats for this year's match against Middlesex Hospital.' Of course, he received the token gift, but his thoughtless interruption had broken thirty minutes of deep thought. To catch the fleeting fragments took another thirty minutes, and by that time, the chatterers were at work. It often seemed to me that there was a conspiracy among the staff of the Institute to stop me working, but I was wrong. Conspiracies are rare events; they take too much effort and organization. It was just that I am odd and do not enjoy the ceaseless verbal grooming of human existence. Perhaps if we had been content to pick nits from each other's fur, and not learnt to groom by chattering, deeper thought would be more normal. Those of us at Mill Hill who preferred thinking to chattering often worked at home. Our wise director knew it happened and turned a blind eye.

One Thursday, at lunch in the cafeteria, I was at a table with Sir Charles and several other scientists. One of them turned to me and said in a loud voice, 'I suppose you'll be off to the country this afternoon as usual, Jim.' Sir Charles gave him a baleful look but said nothing. Indeed, he made no further comment about my four-day working week until I left the Institute in 1961, when he explained that he valued the Institute staff for what they produced, not how they worked to do it.

As the summer of 1960 lengthened, so the battle against traffic along the old and twisty English roads made Monday mornings and Thursday evenings a nightmare. The journey from Bowerchalke was not bad for the first thirty miles, but the remaining sixty involved travel through commuter land and across the whole width of London. I was lucky to survive those journeys without an accident. There was no speed limit then, except the 30 mph in built up areas, but driving at 90 mph or more along the few open stretches of country road was unwise. The stress of this broken existence did not seem to force my hand at resignation; instead, I began to smoke and drink far more than before, until one morning at the Institute an encounter with my technician, Peter Simmonds, brought me to my senses. I had run out of cigarettes and he kindly went to the cafeteria to purchase a replacement package for me. When I thanked and paid him, he replied, 'Think nothing of it: if you go on smoking as you do you will soon drop dead and then I can market your inventions and make myself a fortune.' It was a fair comment about my new way of life.

The biochemist and Nobel Laureate, Rodney Porter, occupied the lab next to mine and further down worked Archer Martin and Tony James. Opposite, across the corridor, was Philip D'Arcy Hart and RJW Rees, who worked on tuberculosis and leprosy. The best and worst of my researches at Mill Hill were done in collaboration with D'Arcy Hart and Rees. Sir John Cornforth, Kappa to his friends, whose laboratory was elsewhere in the building, had produced an intriguing family of compounds. They were polyoxyethylene ethers of alkyl phenols linked together by methylene bridges. It is not what they were that is interesting but what they did. Rees and Hart had found that they ameliorated infections of animals with tuberculosis organisms. I had found that they did strange things to red blood cells. In particular, they selectively removed cholesterol or phosphatides from their membranes according to how many oxyethylene groups were present. I noticed by accident one day that these substances also appeared to protect red blood cells against the harmful effects of acidity. If suspended in a medium that is too acid, red blood cells haemolyse, that is to say, split apart and release their red oxygen-carrying pigment, haemoglobin, to the solution. A small amount of Cornforth's agent seemed to stop this happening. Rees and Hart were interested and tried the same experiment with their organisms and with the same results. We were excited and published our findings as a *Nature* Letter in 1958.

Later, D'Arcy Hart and Nash showed that our remarkable experiments were not due to a specific protective action by these compounds against acidity but to an experimental error. The glass test tubes used in these experiments were contaminated by a film of fatty acids and these came either from soap that was used for washing, from the cotton-wool plugs that we used to stopper the tubes, or from our fingers. Fatty acids are more destructive toward cell membranes when the solution they are in is itself acid. What we had observed was not damage by acidity but by fatty acids. Cornforth's polycyclic compounds inactivated these fatty substances and stopped them from damaging the cells. It was a serious oversight on my part not to have checked that this effect was occurring and it was fortunate that D'Arcy Hart's integrity and persistence led him to make the checks and not someone outside our lab. At his insistence, I joined with him and Thomas Nash in a paper in the *Journal of Hygiene*, retracting our observations. Mistakes like this, a near miss to disaster, are no bad thing. Their heuristic value overcomes the pain of hurt pride and the small harm to one's reputation.

The work I did with Dr Rees on the way Cornforth's compounds protected animals against experimental tuberculosis, for me, made up for this blunder. In a short paper in *Nature* in 1955, we reported our finding that these compounds accumulated in the white cells, the macrophages, of an animal's blood. There they had the potential to act like detergents and strip away the fatty coat that protects tubercle bacteria. Macrophages exist to remove and destroy foreign bodies in the blood and if the tubercle organisms were made bare by the detergents, they would be easier to digest. To confirm this idea we added a small quantity of powdered blue dye to the blood. The dye chosen was insoluble in blood but soluble in the presence of a high concentration of Cornforth's compounds. Macrophages taken from untreated animals rapidly ingested the particles of dye. They could be seen as dark granules inside their cells. When the detergent compounds were present in the blood also, the macrophages showed up as bright blue cells, showing that they had concentrated Cornforth's compounds to a level much higher than in the blood, and sufficient to dissolve the dyestuff. I wonder, now that the tubercle organism has grown resistant to antibiotics, if these odd substances should not be re-examined for therapy, either alone or as an adjuvant for use with regular antibiotics.

I spent much of my last year at Mill Hill fending off instrument companies who wanted my expertise about gas chromatography. By the late 1950s, the Government had allowed us to patent inventions for the benefit of the nation and it was our duty as quasi civil servants to give free advice to firms who wanted to market our inventions, especially where they were using our patents under licence. After a while I found it best to advise one company only and I chose WG Pye of Cambridge, partly because they had taken out a licence on my argon detector patent, and partly because they seemed to be the firm most likely to build a successful gas chromatograph using my detectors. Tony James, who also spent much of his time giving free advice, supported me in this decision. The two representatives of Pye, Ron Evans and a talented engineer, were both honest and considerate men. They were practical but not pushy and never tried, as did the staff of some companies, to bribe. On one occasion, a firm offered me a substantial sum for some simple advice; when I refused to talk further, their response was to increase the offer and say that they would pay in cash. Many of us at Mill Hill were originators of unusually valuable intellectual property. It was hardly surprising that those outside sought to get it by fair means or foul, but we were not tempted because we had a strong sense of loyalty to the Institute and we were in those days well paid and well treated. Now that the profession of science has declined and is poorly rewarded, the temptations must be much harder to resist. One thing that I did get from Ron Evans of Pye was an estimate of how much the firm would pay me as their consultant if I did leave Mill Hill and go to work independently. It was £2,000 a year; more than enough on which to survive.

In 1959, my fortieth birthday loomed and I wondered if it was already too late for me to achieve my ambitions. As I write, forty years older, I cannot help laughing at the foolishness of such a fear, but at 39 my response was to grow ever more unhappy about tenure. Tenure meant that my life ran on predestined tracks; it wouldn't matter what I did, I was sure of a salary and employment and a place there all the way down to the day of my retirement. Even then, my tracks to the grave would be supported by an adequate pension. Every day

I would go to the Institute, do my research, and come home again. I felt like the man in the limerick:

> There was a young man who said, 'Damn',
> It appears to me that I am,
> A being who moves
> In predestinate grooves;
> Not a bus, not a bus, but a tram.

Great as was my wish to break away from Mill Hill's cosy nest, I could not give up a vocation for science just to become a consultant. Instead of expanding my horizons, this would be restricting me to working on a single technique. I may have grown richer but this was not my ambition. I enjoyed working with Pye and seeing their ideas for commercial gas chromatographs evolve into a practical, saleable instrument. It provided a welcome change from academic research. My invention, the argon detector, reduced Archer Martin and Tony James's invention of gas chromatography to practice. It was a simple, easy-to-make, and adequately sensitive device. Biochemists worldwide used it for the analysis of lipids, something that previously had been impossible. In its heyday I was sought after like a bride and could have moved to work for any of several American companies at double or more my salary. I could have taken good posts at American universities and been sure of a rich source of grant funds. Perhaps the one mistake I did make was to decline the offer from Dr Keene Dimmick, the owner of a firm called Wilkins Aerograph. He invited me to become a partner in his enterprise. I went to visit him at his home in Walnut Creek in the early days of their business. It had much to recommend it. Keene and his wife, Adele, built chromatographs in their garage, assisted by their children. They took me into the hill country nearby and we walked and enjoyed talking science in a country environment, much in the way that I did at home. Had I accepted, we would probably have shared some of the many millions that Keene received when he sold his company to Varian Instruments. As it was, I made real friends among the instrument fraternity of the United States of America.

The abrading and tantalizing year of 1960 rolled on into 1961, and in January I found myself worn out and unable to think or to work. The spell lasted about five weeks, but by resting and walking at Bowerchalke, I recovered and resumed my commuting to Mill Hill.

I knew it could not last but could discern no break in the clouds of uncertainty. Around about this time the United States National Institute for Health offered me a grant of $50,000 a year for three years to continue my work on lipid biochemistry and detectors for lipid analysis at Mill Hill. This generous offer did not fit in with my plan to resign, but I had no option but to tell Sir Charles about it. He was enthusiastic. It seemed to him a wonderful way to lessen the damage of the brain drain, the flow of talent from the United Kingdom to America. He promised to discuss it at a council meeting of the Medical Research Council the next week.

I went to his office a week later and, for the first time, found him confused and uncertain. 'I have bad news for you,' he said. 'The council turned down that idea of yours to work here supported by a grant from the NIH. I think they were wrong but there was nothing I could say that would change their minds.' This rejection was a relief to me, for I saw its acceptance as yet another silken rope tying me into the cosy environment of Mill Hill. Instead of showing chagrin or even anger at this reactionary decision by the Medical Research Council, I said, 'Oh, never mind, I'll continue as before.' Sir Charles was amazed; he had expected a difficult interview. He saw me storming out, threatening to take up the offer in Washington instead of Mill Hill. He said, 'You have the most peculiar way of taking setbacks but I am indeed grateful.' He was so surprised that he revealed what ordinarily he would not have done—that it was the Secretary, the Chief Executive Officer of the Medical Research Council, Sir Harold Himsworth, who was most opposed to the idea of external funds coming to Mill Hill. I saw it then as part of the battle between the older science-based Medical Research Council with Mill Hill as its flagship, a world-leading scientific institute, and the new guard led by the clinicians and consultants of medicine. The new men thought that practical medicine, not science, was what the MRC should be doing. They would have preferred to fund an institute dealing with such problems as varicose veins and hernias. The many Nobel Prizes that came the way of the old science-based Medical Research Council were to them just an irritant sustaining what they saw as the wrong way to spend money set aside for medical research. I am sure that had the grant been offered for clinical research, it would have been welcomed. Himsworth and his colleagues won the battle for the redirection of United Kingdom medical research into a clinical not a scientific course and the Clinical Research Centre at Harrow was built at considerable cost. After Sir Charles retired in 1962, Mill Hill sustained its excellence under the directorship of Sir Peter Medawar. Sadly, and like Alick Isaacs, the discoverer of Interferon, he suffered a brain haemorrhage and was unable to continue as its director. In spite of these discouragements, Mill Hill has remained a significant centre for medical research.

The practice of science in the 1950s was much different from the way it is done now. As I have often mentioned, most noticeable was the absence of what I see as an excessive public concern over health and safety. We were qualified scientists and expected to plan our research to be no danger to anyone, including us, and during the time I worked for the MRC there were a few accidents but nothing that made a public scandal. We used radioactive isotopes in profusion, but I would be surprised to learn if anyone working at Mill Hill suffered adverse consequences. During 1956–7, I was using radioactive iodine-131 and chromium-55 to label red blood cells. These isotopes would arrive at the Institute usually as solutions in small glass bottles with rubber seals of the kind used for injectable medicines. The bottles were enclosed in small lead pots to be safe to handle. I would calculate the thickness of glass needed to shield me from the radiation and the time that I could allow my hands to be safely exposed as I drew up the solution into a syringe. I much preferred to do this myself than rely on some appointed health physics officer to take charge. On one occasion, when making the preliminary measurements with a counter, I was surprised to find that the laboratory background was high. My first thought was that I had spilt some of the iodine-131 onto the laboratory bench. I checked with a portable monitor borrowed from biophysics and found that the isotope was not just on the bench but also everywhere in my lab. The levels were not an immediate health hazard, just worrying. Had I somehow been careless?

Next day the counts were somewhat less but I decided to report the event anyway. However, before I could do so, I was called to the director's office. Two other scientists, one from the biochemistry division and the other from chemistry, were also there and apparently, they had had the same experience. Their laboratory backgrounds had risen mysteriously the previous day. Further checks showed that iodine-131 contaminated the whole Institute. Sir Charles was naturally perturbed. He wanted to know if any of us had done anything that could have resulted in such a contamination. A few simple calculations suggested that the quantity of isotope we possessed was much too small to label the whole of the lab uniformly. The fact that iodine-131 has a half-life of seven days meant that our concern rapidly went away by itself. I heard nothing more of this event until about fourteen years later when, in 1971, I was visiting Harwell, the United Kingdom Atomic Energy Research Laboratory. Alan Eggleton, a senior staff member, told me how he had followed the spread of iodine-131 from the reactor fire at Windscale in Cumbria. A graphite-moderated reactor caught fire and spread some of its accumulated radioactivity over the countryside. It was the world's first serious reactor accident, and in a way, a warning of the Chernobyl incident yet to happen. I wonder if the mysterious background increase of radioactive iodine at Mill Hill came from the drifting radioactive cloud from Windscale, 250 miles away. This incident exposed the people of England to what some would now consider a dangerous level of radioactive contamination. I wonder why we have heard nothing of an epidemic of thyroid and other cancers in the years that followed?

The only deaths or serious laboratory accidents at Mill Hill were among the virologists. As I described earlier, several of them were seriously ill with typhus caught in the laboratory during the Second World War, and two died of it. Chemists like me led a charmed life. On our shelves were chemicals that would terrify present-day health and safety officials. Exotic materials such as *Clostridium perfringens* toxin, perfluoroisobutene, nitrogen mustard, beryllium sulphate, and uranium nitrate, all sat in their bottles, or small cylinders, sedately around the walls of my lab. Common poisons like cyanide were everywhere. I would find it impossible to do science under the nanny-like restrictions today. Science, even as we practised it in the old days, is nowhere near so dangerous an occupation as riding a motorcycle or climbing mountains. Those of us who choose science as our life's vocation should plan our own protection and be personally responsible for our environment and that of our colleagues. Recently, I purchased a minute quantity of thorium-232 for some experiments. The amount of the isotope I purchased was less than that of the same isotope on a luminous wristwatch I wore for ten years day and night from 1958 to 1968. In spite of this, the expense and the paperwork now mandatory were so great that it nearly deterred me from starting the work at all. Had the same restrictions operated in the 1950s, I would never have invented the electron capture detector or other ionization detectors. Then Rachel Carson might never have written her seminal book, *Silent Spring*, and it might have taken ten years longer before we became aware of the environment and its problems. I wish that Green politicians who introduce legislation to protect the public from toxic or radiation hazards would exempt qualified scientists working in their laboratories from the restrictions of their laws.

Notice that my time as a journeyman was ending came in March 1961, in the form of an ordinary airmail envelope, which lay on my desk at Mill Hill when I arrived one morning for work. It was from what seemed to be a senior officer of the US Government, the director of Space Flight Operations for the National Aeronautical and Space Administration, NASA. The acronym NASA is now a commonplace and everyone knows what it is. In those days, a mere three years after the first Russian satellite had bleeped its simple manic message, beep-beep-beep, around the world, not many of us were aware of the name NASA. The letter itself was even more intriguing. It was an invitation to join a party of scientists who were about to explore the Moon. I was enthralled. Here was a serious person asking me to join with others in what a few years back would have been science fiction. It was for me like a letter from a beloved. I was as excited and euphoric as if, at the peak of passion, I had received a yes from my loved one. To be asked, a mere three years after Sputnik, to join in a lunar exploration was such a thrill. More than this, I began to realize that this letter was deliverance. The past year I had spent somewhat miserably trying to screw up the courage to tell my director and the kindly people who ran Mill Hill that I wanted to leave. How could I tell them I wanted to work alone as an independent scientist? How could I say that their comfortable, tenured, secure existence, where I was free to do almost anything I wished, was not enough? But they knew my love for the physical sciences and astronomy and this letter gave me the way in which to formulate an honourable explanation for my departure.

At that time, to make matters more difficult, the United Kingdom was suffering from a brain drain, the haemorrhage of talented people from western European countries to America. Large incomes, generous conditions of work and the ability to spend freely on equipment attracted them. It seemed so much more than was available in our comparatively poor and declining state. Talent will always go where the working conditions are best and this is the way of the free world. Our government knew this and was wise enough not to put up any kind of

Berlin Wall, even of the mind, or in any way to discourage the free movement of its subjects. But most of us felt outrage when a colleague, newly elected to the Royal Society, or otherwise honoured, would immediately use the prestige of his newly acquired honour to bargain for the maximum income in the USA. They were, I suppose, the early yuppies, and just as annoying. It was not easy for me to say that I wanted to leave for America, but Sir Charles Harington accepted my desire to join the moon expedition as reasonable. He well understood my thinking, and knew that I was not merely seeking greener pastures. He saw it as an unparalleled opportunity for one of his scientists.

The letter from NASA set me free to become an independent scientist, but there were to be two years and four months of transition. I moved from work as a tenured civil servant to a limbo-like state. When the US Jet Propulsion Laboratory (JPL), which was a NASA laboratory, invited me to join with them as an experimenter on the first lunar mission, Surveyor, I could have gone to work there full time, but that would have merely changed work at one good institute for less secure employment at another. My first step was to seek a temporary post as a visiting professor at the University of Houston, where a colleague, Albert Zlatkis, was Professor in the Department of Chemistry. Here I would fund myself by applying for a NASA grant to do detector development, the kind of work that JPL required of me. This was my plan of action. Then, wholly unexpectedly, I had a visit from Marjorie and Evan Horning, two American lipid biochemists I had met at the National Institutes for Health in Bethesda, near Washington, in the previous year. They told me they were setting up a lipid research centre in Baylor University College of Medicine, also in Houston. Would I join them as a research professor? It was a most generous offer, with a dream salary of $20,000 per annum. Since the detector development I would be doing for NASA was also what the lipid researchers wanted, I thought, why not?

During the summer of 1961 I prepared for our move as a family from Bowerchalke to Houston. The job offered was also tenured, but my long-term plan was to save enough spare cash from my generous American salary to set up an independent laboratory in Bowerchalke. There was sadness about my last month at Mill Hill; now that the stress of commuting would soon be over, I began to see how fine an institute it was. What a wonderful community of scientists they were, but I had no serious doubts about my decision and somehow sensed that before many years passed Mill Hill would cease to be the whirlpool of excellence that I had swum in. We sold our house in Bower-chalke to a retired Canon of the church. He told me later that its efficient central heating gave warmth, which was a joy to him and his wife after the long years spent in cold and draughty rectories.

5

The First Steps to Independence at Houston, Texas

We travelled to New York on the old *Mauritania*. It was almost her last voyage and we were able to savour the grandeur of this impermanent monument of a once great and powerful nation. We stayed one night in New York and then took an early version of a passenger jet, a Boeing 707, to Houston. Ab Zlatkis met us and took us to a motel near the university in downtown Houston. Ab was a lean dark tallish man who looked and moved like Groucho Marx. The Zlatkis family was kind and hospitable to us during our stay in Houston and we were especially fond of Esther, Ab's wife, who freely gave her friendship and practical help. I soon found that the lipid research centre at Baylor was not yet built, so there was plenty of time for house hunting, and it did not take long to find a delightful five-bedroom house being built by a craftsman builder on Stony Creek Drive. This was a quiet road in the wooded Memorial district of west Houston and by far its most pleasing suburb. It would be completed in November, two months ahead; meanwhile, we rented an apartment close to the University of Houston. It was a tough two months for Helen and the family, living in an apartment whose air-conditioning system consisted of buzzing boxes built into a wall below the windows, and with Houston in October and November tropical in its heat. The knowledge that soon we would live in a fully air-conditioned house with a pleasant garden made our stay in the apartment tolerable, and there was much to keep us busy. We had arrived in the United States illegally on a visitor's visa. A helpful United States Consul who operated from Southampton in southern England advised us to do this. He told us that the United States Embassy in London was full of career civil servants forever dreaming up new jobs for themselves, and that the long and tedious process of visa application was partly to justify their existence. 'Have nothing to do with them,' he said. 'I will give you visitors' visas, then when in Houston go to the Immigration and Naturalization Service there and ask to be admitted as resident aliens. There's no hurry to do it; get yourselves settled in and then go.' This we did, and to our joy, instead of having long waits and endless crazy questions at the London Embassy, a kindly official welcomed us and said how glad he was 'that you nice folk want to live in Houston'. The paperwork was over in an hour and we received our green cards shortly afterwards. This, if it still works, is by far the best way for prospective immigrants to enter the United States.

We had furniture to buy for our new house. At first we were surprised to find that the local stores would not take payment by cheque, 'where are your credit cards?' was their cry. In England in the early 1960s credit cards barely existed, and even if they had, the Houston shops would not have accepted them. Zlatkis came to our rescue. He had a relative who was part of the Nieman Marcus organization. Nieman Marcus is a department store with branches in the large cities of Texas, very upmarket and somewhat like Harrods once was. Soon we had a Nieman Marcus credit card and suddenly financial doors were open to us.

Before Christmas 1961 we settled in at Stony Creek Drive. Our plot of land had recently been wild wood and our garden terminated at a creek leading to Buffalo Bayou. It was rather like living in a tropical forest without the inconveniences. Armadillos would wander up to the door at night and the most amazing varieties of insect life buzzed and flitted before our eyes. There were over twenty species of snake in our garden, including coral snakes, water moccasins, copperheads, and several kinds of rattlesnake. None of these seemed to mind our presence and they were a source of endless fascination. On Christmas Day we sat in the newly planted garden, enjoying warm sunshine and a temperature of 84° F. I had invited my Mill Hill technician, Peter Simmonds, who had just graduated, to join me at Baylor and use the time there to take a PhD degree. He and his wife

Tina stayed with us for the Christmas period whilst they house hunted. The Lipid Research Laboratory at Baylor College of Medicine was now open and we set up working in one of the most lavish laboratory environments of the 20th century. So generous were the funds available that we were able to buy any equipment we thought might be needed. Strangely, the two and a half years in the Houston laboratory were among the least scientifically productive of my lifetime. There were many reasons for this, not least, the frequent visits to JPL and the long summers back in England, but I do believe that a surfeit of equipment is a handicap, not a benefit, to a scientist like me. It stifles invention and instead of devising new instruments with which to ask questions of Nature I was playing with the instruments we had bought.

I greatly enjoyed the time in Houston. I thrive in hot weather and like the ant seem to move faster and work harder when warm—and it could be very warm in Houston. However, my family, in spite of the air-conditioned comfort of our home, rapidly grew to dislike it. Helen did not drive and so was trapped in the house, and although the neighbourhood was quiet and there were sidewalks and an easy walk of a mile to the shops, it was too much for her when the temperature exceeded 85° F and was humid as well. She loved gardening in an environment where lemons and bananas grew outdoors but there is more to life than gardening. My daughters enrolled at the University of Houston. They allowed Christine to enrol in the English Department but Jane, lacking a High School Diploma was only allowed to audit, that is, attend lectures but receive no credits for having done so. This was a cruel blow for Jane who was seriously studious and given a chance would have proceeded to a degree. Christine, who could have graduated, had other ambitions. They seemed to spend most of their time in the Cougar Den of the student's union, where they met and consorted with a fine group of Arab students. One of them was Wallid Sharib, with whom Christine became engaged to be married. Wallid wanted her to return with him at the end of his studies to the Gaza Strip where his family owned and farmed orange groves. They were both in love but in the end sadly chose to part. The cultural differences and the lot of a woman in traditional Arab society, they both realized, made a life together too difficult to undertake.

One consequence of the girls' love of Arabs was that we met few of the local Texan boys or their families. I made up for this by forming a close friendship with Haskell Lilley, a salesman for the engineering firm Barber–Coleman. He was a true Texan, with an accent that was delightful to hear. He, like many Texans I met, was well read and familiar with European history, and our conversations were often political. I noticed that Haskell and other Texans put on a country bumpkin persona when faced by smart but less intelligent Americans from the North. It could be achingly funny when these Northerners were unaware of what was happening. By the end of our stay in Houston I found myself doing it, and on one occasion it nearly led to my undoing. I was having a sandwich and a coke in a bar at La Guardia Airport in New York, while waiting for a plane to Washington. When I opened my wallet to pay, I found that I had nothing smaller than a $100 bill that I kept as emergency credit. The barman, when I gave it to him, sniffed and said, 'Don't you carry anything smaller than this?' Without thought, I replied, 'We don't use anything smaller in Texas.' Almost instantly, the other customers and the barman became threatening, and it was only my English accent that saved me from a beating or worse.

My work for JPL required me to commute by air once a month from Houston to Los Angeles, a journey of about 1,700 miles, but taking only a few hours. A few times the whole family took the journey and we then travelled by car. Driving in Texas was easy after densely crowded England; we would travel for hundreds of miles along straight, wide roads that seemed to vanish thirty or more miles ahead. When crossing the wide flat plains of the desert landscape the distant mountain ranges had a beckoning beauty that enthralled me. Only occasionally did another car or truck appear in the far distance, and in these conditions it was no more arduous to travel 700 miles a day than it is in Europe to travel 200 miles. The journey from Houston to Los Angeles by car took two and a half days and we usually stayed at motels just before El Paso and at Yuma in Arizona. Sometimes we would take a holiday and stop for a day at one of the National Parks along the Mexican border—the Grand Canyon, the Meteor Crater, and the Petrified Forest.

At JPL the first year and a half was not as exciting as I had expected. Most of my time there was spent in technical discussion on the design of the chromatograph to be used for analysing the lunar surface. It was good to know that the purpose behind our work was to ensure that the moon was safe for astronauts to walk on, but after a while the discussions themselves became repetitive and to me boring. Towards the end of our stay in Houston, JPL became more interested in Mars than the Moon, and discussions on the JPL space instruments now had Mars as the target. I felt that I had made all the contribution I could to the chemical side of the design and gravitated towards the space engineers who translated our ideas for instruments into space-worthy hardware. They found me useful as an interpreter who could translate their thoughts and ideas into the language of the biologists and planetary scientists. For those of you who can remember the 1960s, scientific electronic equipment, and indeed domestic electronics like televisions and tape recorders, were fallible. We almost expected our televisions to break down once or more times in a year. The hardware that was to make its long journey to Mars had not only to endure the shocks of being lifted by rocket—a shattering and vibrating experience—but also had to endure exposure to the hard vacuum of space for a period approaching a year, and then survive atmospheric re-entry and the stress of landing on that inhospitable planet, Mars. And even when there, the stress was not over, for on Mars the temperature cycles daily between near $20°$ C in equatorial sunshine to night-time temperatures cold enough to freeze carbon dioxide from the air, and if this were not enough, the surface of Mars is acid and oxidizing and everywhere there is abrasive, windblown dust. For these reasons, the engineering required to build instruments for space vehicles and landers was of an order quite different to that used to make the 1960s car or television. It was as different indeed as was 1960s engineering from that of Roman times. I consider that the opportunity I had to mix freely, talk, and discuss problems with these competent engineers at JPL was the greatest of my rewards for working there.

I often felt like young apprenticed artists must have felt to be welcomed into the studios of a Leonardo or a Holbein. On one occasion, a scientist I worked with was demonstrating his version of a gas chromatograph for Mars. From the point of view of Earth engineering, it was a well-made portable instrument suitable to take into the field, as they call it, to analyse the soil at any place on the Earth. The space engineers then told us what they would do to such an instrument to make it space-worthy. First, we would need to think about the power needed to run the apparatus. The total power available on Mars would be about 100 watts and this would be shared amongst all of the experiments and all of the necessary housekeeping of the spacecraft itself. The energy-hungry part of our Earth-type gas chromatograph was the oven used to keep the chromatograph column and the detector at its operating temperature, usually in the region of 200° C. We were using about ten to twenty watts to heat the oven and this was too large a drain on the spacecraft power supply. The space engineers told us to aim instead at a power consumption of not more than two watts for the entire operation of the chromatograph. It seemed at first impossible to design a chromatograph that would run on as little power as that required to light a flashlight bulb. But it was done.

One of the most difficult problems faced by the spacecraft engineers was how to transmit back to Earth the data gathered by our instruments. A distinguished electronic physicist wrote an article during the 1960s on the impossibility of making radio or television transmissions from a place as far away as Mars. He calculated that the power required to transmit useful information over such vast distances would be in the region of hundreds of kilowatts and he doubted if we could ever send a transmitter this powerful to Mars. Yet, here I was a few years later, sitting in a room with sensible engineers who were talking confidently about how and when we would be sending messages from Mars. They would broadcast from Mars not only the data from the instruments, but also colour pictures of the Martian surface. They would do it with 100 watts of power, using a transmitter no more powerful than a ham radio transceiver—more than one thousand times less than the distinguished physicist calculated that we would need.

Being given the challenge to invent was what spurred these engineers to find a way to avoid the apparently unbreakable rules of science. If anyone ever asks what was the use of the space programme technologically, forget about the non-stick frying pan and other trivia hyped by NASA's publicists. Think instead of the technology that we take for granted. The users of today's ubiquitous mobile phones and personal computers are the beneficiaries of those pioneering space engineers and these are the true harvests of space technology. Another harvest that may turn out to be of greater importance was the discovery of Gaia.

Conrad Josias, a dark young man from New York, and Howard Marshall, a youthful patrician and graduate of CalTech, were two of the electronics engineers I talked with. They later left JPL to found their own firm, Analogue Technology, carrying on as private enterprise the same kind of work that they had been doing at JPL. One morning I was discussing with them the transmission of a gas chromatograph signal from Mars to the Earth. The chemists and biologists were insistent that we needed the whole chromatogram to characterize any of the chemicals of life present in the Martian soil. The output of a gas chromatograph is a long, wide strip of paper bearing a single inked line. This line moves from its normal position called the base line and rises to a peak and then falls back again. It does this every time a substance emerges from the column. The complete chromatogram is a set of tent-shaped peaks, each by its height showing the amount of each individual chemical. Howard Marshall looked at one of these chromatograph charts, which showed thirty compounds from a sample of soil, and said, 'This will take at least 100,000 bits of information; we can do it but there will be a lot of arguments from the other experimenters on whether or not that much channel space can be spared.' I then asked, 'Why do you need so many bits to transmit this simple analysis? All we need to know is that there are thirty compounds, how much of each, and when they appeared. Surely, the information content is a lot less than that.' Howard then went into an explanation of how many samples per second he would need to accurately describe the chromatogram. I realized that we were in one of those so typical confusions between the disciplines of science. The engineers did not know that a chromatogram has very low information content. Instead of 2,000 samples per second to describe it, two per second would be quite generous. So, by combining our expertise, we were able to send the data at a thousandth the information cost. JPL reminded me of my days in making instruments in the Second World War. Contraptions conceived in the lab were no use aboard aircraft that had to fly missions during wartime. The sheer vibration would shake almost any laboratory equipment to pieces in a matter of seconds and we needed something much tougher and better engineered. It was all very familiar. It made me wonder how much we need the urgency and sense of purpose that comes with war or a sense of mission to do our best.

An important step towards my practice of independent science took place in Houston, and that was the forming with Al Zlatkis of a small company called Ionics Research. By operating as a company we were able to offer advice and supply prototype detectors to any of the firms in the instrument industry who needed them. As ordinary consultants, we would have found it hard to act for more than one firm at a time. Soon after returning to England I formed my own company—Brazzos Limited—and resigned from Ionics Research.

6

The Independent Practice of Science

The start of an independent practice is more than a single step. Let me tell you how it happened for me. In the spring of 1963 we felt that we had had enough of living in North America. This is no criticism of the American way of life as it was then. From the viewpoint of suburban Europeans, we lived in a paradise. Houston was a pleasant, medium-sized city far more cultured than our New England friends ever realized and our gross income was approaching $40,000 a year—sufficient in those days to count us rich. We could, for example, as a whole family—two adults and four children—cross the Atlantic for a holiday in England by ship or by plane without thought of the cost. So why were we all restless for England? At that time, although less so now, England had an ethos so strong that no amount of riches could compensate for the lack of it. There were three parts to it: first, a benign authority and a people who were law-abiding and non-violent, second, a homogeneous society with few tribal divisions and where racial problems were as yet unnoticed; and third, it was still easy to live in a village, and that included the city villages of London where each adjacent built-up area still had some of the quality of the village it used to be.

What distinguishes village from suburban life is the random juxta-position of rich and poor, clever and stupid, wise and wooden, kind and cruel. A village is a self-contained microcosm of human life, with its pub, school, and shop, its village hall and cricket team in the country, and, of course, football team for the cities. Because we were homogeneous, the village could cope with the odd criminal family. We knew each other in the village by our Christian names, yet the villagers respected our privacy. Children could play safely and a woman could walk without fear along the unlit village road at night. There was too much hard work to do and too much happening ever to be bored in a village. All this and around the village we loved, Bowerchalke, was the glorious countryside of the small and medium-sized farms run by villagers, verging onto the unspoilt downs and wild woods of Wiltshire and Dorset. Southern England, up until agribusiness destroyed the countryside and the car-led battalions of sub-urban-minded people invaded it, was the most civilized and beautiful place I have ever known. In those halcyon days I guess the same must have been true of much of Europe; the hilltop towns of Tuscany and Umbria had a similar seemliness and so did those of the French and German countryside. England of the early 1960s had other plus values; there was the BBC—admittedly there were only three radio and two television channels, but after Houston they seemed to possess such quality that we needed nothing more. I wish that it were so still. Then there was the climate: gentle enough to enjoy walking at almost any time of year. The health service was then in its prime and it took away the fear of ruin from prolonged illness, something that hovered over life in the USA. Therefore, in early June 1963 I responded to an advertisement in *Nature* for the post of Director of the Medical Research Council's Radiation Laboratory, then based at Harwell, near Oxford. To my surprise, I promptly received a reply telling me that I was shortlisted for the post, and asking me to come for an interview when back in England in July.

We left Houston in early June, travelled by car north through Huntsville and Palestine, and stayed the night at a motel in the pleasant town of Sulphur Springs. The countryside of east Texas is flat but made beautiful by the green verges of its roads that are rich with wild flowers, and free of the billboards which spoil so much of the rural roads of other states. We went on through Arkansas and into the woody country of Missouri and crossed the Mississippi at St Louis and then on past Chicago to Lansing, Michigan, a huge university town where I was to give a paper at a meeting on radiation biology. We moved from there into Canada staying, out of curiosity, at a motel in London, Ontario. The next day we were in Montreal and ready to join the *Carmania*, the ship on which we were to travel the Atlantic to Britain. This ship had brought us back from England the previous

September and we were delighted as we joined it to be recognized and welcomed by our names. We went to our spacious rooms on the upper deck and settled in. To travel by ocean liner to England from Montreal was one of those great journeys of the world. The ship sailed nearly a thousand miles down the St Lawrence River, passing Quebec with its unusual gothic city and the many smaller communities of that French-speaking province.

On the way to Quebec, I could not help wondering about a strange tale told me by Mel Schachter, a Canadian scientist who had worked at Mill Hill. He and his wife had escaped from Lithuania just before the Second World War by crossing Russia on the Trans-Siberian Railway to Vladivostok. From there, they took a ship to Vancouver and intended to take the same route from Canada that we were taking. On the way from Montreal Mrs Schachter said to her husband, 'Mel, the ship will collide with that island ahead in the river if the Captain does not change course.' Mel replied, 'Don't be silly, they know what they are doing, leave it to them to sail the ship.' Like most men, Mel was reluctant to face the polite derision of the ship's officers so he did nothing. Minutes later, and with no change of course, Mrs Schachter pleaded with her husband, 'Mel, please go and tell them or we will crash.' By now, it was too late for Mel to alert the officers on the bridge, and moments later the crash came. No one was badly hurt but the ship was holed and their luggage was lost. We all watched as the island came in view and were relieved to see it pass. Family discussions dominated the return journey and they were about our decision to return to live in England. I already had made the first move by applying for a job. Now we had to decide where to live in Bowerchalke. There was a farm up for sale in the hamlet of Woodminton just south of the village; the Barter family who we knew well owned it. We would have bought it, although it was large—about 600 acres—but a couple that we had befriended overheard our conversation and they earnestly warned us about the harsh and hard life of a farmer and how unwise it would be for us to have anything to do with it. Their words fell on receptive ears, for already I knew enough about farms from my experiences as a student in Manchester. I knew just how tough it could be. Our shipboard friends had owned a farm near Bristol and had hoped for years to make enough money to relieve them from their drudgery so that they could retire. Quite unexpectedly, the local council had declared their farmland a building site. The value of their land increased tenfold and they became millionaires at the stroke of a pen. They were a likeable and intelligent couple and genuinely concerned that we did not make the mistake of taking on farming as a living, especially as we had not grown up with it. It was a fortunate encounter for us and one made possible by the eight days' travel and the leisured comfort of the ship.

We disembarked at Southampton and then drove through the bright resplendent countryside we had so much missed. Great full-bosomed trees overhung the road as we drove on through Cadnam and across the New Forest to Salisbury and from there to Harvard Hospital where the director, the distinguished virologist, David Tyrell, made us welcome. He had kindly arranged for us to stay in an unoccupied flat during the period that we were back in England. I went to the job interview at Harwell, still curious to see how they would receive me but sure that I would not get the job. I was more concerned, in fact, that they might offer it to me and I would have to refuse. My application for the job was a cry for help, dictated by the unconscious part of my mind. We all wanted to return home but this way I could let my past employers know without losing face. The interview was wonderfully friendly and courteous, and the interviewers sensed my hidden agenda and let me down as gently as a perfectly managed hot air balloon.

My stratagem worked. Within a week, there was a letter from my old boss, Sir Charles Harington, of Mill Hill, asking if I would call to see him at the Medical Research Council's headquarters in London. Sir Charles had retired from directing the National Institute but still worked as an administrator at the Medical Research Council's headquarters near Regent's Park. He was as direct as ever and said, 'I am so glad to hear that you are coming back from the USA. We would be very pleased if you would take the job at Mill Hill as head of the Biophysics Division. MacFarlane, the present head, will be retiring this year. What do you think?' It was quite an enticement but I knew that I was unsuited to administrative jobs of any kind. I had decided that I would never have anyone work for me. If I did, I would become so concerned for their welfare that concentration, which I need for creative work, would no longer be possible; being a boss is fine for some, but I was not one of them. I explained this to Sir Charles, and I think he understood, although he did not approve. I offered to come to work as a single scientist at Harvard Hospital just as I had done during the time I had worked at the Common Cold Unit. He grew enthusiastic about that and said he would speak to Sir Harold Himsworth who was then the Secretary of the MRC. Himsworth rejected my proposal immediately. He was one of those administrators who cannot understand that some individual scientists do best when working alone. He subscribed to that common belief that groups, or teams, of talented people spark ideas off each other. Reasonable as this seems, I doubt if it works for pioneering research. One strong and not always intelligent person among the team usually dominates. This is fine and is necessary with the team work needed to take a laboratory breakthrough and turn it into a public benefit. On the other hand, significant scientific advances come mostly from individuals, not from teams. Of course, the individuals who make the advances are sometimes team members, but when they make breakthroughs they are thinking for themselves and not according to the team agenda. The administrator who ignores this and tries to use talent manipulatively will find his teams left recycling old ideas. Sir Charles told me, with obvious regret, of Himsworth's decision but said, 'I hope that you will find what you want.' That he was concerned for me was confirmed the following week when I received a letter from Lord Rothschild. He just wrote, 'Will you come to see me on Thursday at 11 o'clock at Shell Centre on the South Bank to discuss something to your interest?' I had met Rothschild before when I visited him at his home in Cambridge. At the time, he, Chris Polge, and I were amongst the very few scientists in the United Kingdom who used spermatozoa as their experimental animals, so to speak. My interest was in their membranes and their resistance to freezing; his was in the mechanism they used for swimming. I liked his direct manner and we got on well, so his invitation intrigued me. Victor, the Lord Rothschild, was then the senior member of the English branch of that famous Jewish family and, unusually for aristocrats, both he and his sister Miriam were distinguished biologists and Fellows of the Royal Society.

Shell Centre is just by Waterloo Station in London and there is a direct walkway to the Centre. I took it to the main entrance where, in the large reception area, full of people and uniformed guards, I showed my letter of invitation and was taken immediately to the lifts and put on one for the 24th floor. On arrival Lord Rothschild's secretary, Miss Page, met me and took me to his room. As befitted his rank, the office was deeply carpeted and had a stunning view of Parliament and the river flowing under Westminster Bridge. Rothschild welcomed me and said he had heard from Harington that I was coming back to England but wanted to work independently. To my reply, 'Yes', he then asked, 'Would you like to be one of my advisors on scientific matters of interest to Shell?' He then went on to say that I could work from home and for the yearly fee of £1,500. It would require a visit to Shell Centre about once a month and a few visits to their laboratories at Thornton, near Chester, and Sittingbourne in Kent. 'You will find many of your friends in Shell: Cornforth and Popják are at Sittingbourne and Maurice Sugden will be at Thornton quite soon.' My delight must have lit up my face; this was just what I needed to go independent. I already had $6,000 a year from the Jet Propulsion Labs for my advice during three or four visits a year. That, together with the £1,500 a year from Shell, would provide an income of more than £3,500 per annum, just right for the start of work as an independent scientist. Rothschild said some flattering things in response to my question 'How do you know that I will be of use to Shell? I'm completely unfamiliar with the oil industry and the research it does.' He said that he had followed my researches at Mill Hill and agreed with Harington that I was a scientist very like the physicist Leo Szilard—someone who did best outside the team, someone who was best left to think. He said that he had anticipated my need to learn more about the industry and had already arranged for me to see the Wood River Laboratory of Shell in the United States.

I left Shell Centre in a happy daze and my mind was full, on the journey back to Harvard Hospital, with the prospects of this new life that was opening before me. The thought that the move would mean a drop in income of seventy-five per cent hardly entered my mind. We returned to Southampton and took our last journey on the *Carmania* to Montreal at the end of September with a future secured. We made the journey back to Houston driving across Canada to the small border town of Sault-Sainte-Marie and entered the state of Michigan there. It was a delightful journey back through the middle of the USA, one rarely experienced by tourists or visitors, yet it had much to offer. We made first for the small town of Marquette on the southern shore of Lake Superior and spent an afternoon on the clean sandy beaches, bathing and watching the large fresh-water waves breaking on the shore of, what seemed to us, a vast ocean. From Marquette we travelled south through western Minnesota and South Dakota, and on into Iowa and Nebraska. I had imagined this western region to be entirely flat and an endless ocean of grain. Some of it was, but there were long stretches also of rolling hill country, quite like the Wiltshire downs. We passed through Grand Island, Nebraska, stayed a night at Dodge City, the alleged centre of the US, and visited the tourist shrine at Boot Hill, and then went down through Oklahoma into Texas, with a fine view of a tornado on the way. As always, crossing the border into Texas seemed like entering a different and a more civilized country. Soon after returning, I resigned my post at Baylor College of Medicine and arranged to leave just before Christmas 1963.

Shell

I made my visit to the Shell Wood River station in November 1963. The industrial science world of an oil company was not new to me. I had visited many such laboratories in Houston to talk to the analysts who used my electron capture detector, and other instruments that I had invented, in their daily work. But I had never before dealt with the main business, what they called oil products—in other words, the outputs from the refineries that took in crude oil and turned it into gasoline, kerosene, diesel fuel, fuel oil and lubricating oils, and asphalt for the roads. They showed me their work on anti-knock additives for gasoline and the high-class physical chemistry of combustion that trying to invent better ones involved. We also discussed the strange series of chemicals added to base oils to make them into better lubricants. When I left Wood River, I had much to think about on the problems of this rather new kind of scientific world into which Rothschild had led me.

One of the most intriguing problems that arose during the thirty years I worked with Shell was the giant airship project. In the 1960s, Shell considered the possibility of a vast stainless-steel airship that would use natural gas, methane, as the lift gas to support it on its journey from the Middle East to Europe. This airship, twice the length and twice the diameter of the ill-fated German airship *Hindenburg*, would carry 2,000 tons of natural gas, would travel at over 100 miles per hour, and could carry several hundred tons of cargo in addition to the methane. Steam would be the lift gas for the return journey from Europe and it would transport in a year as much methane as a much larger ocean-going tanker. I loved the idea and hoped to see it develop into a passenger-carrying airship. How wonderful to cross the Atlantic on it; surely if the methane cargo version succeeded, it would not be long before a passenger airship flew. A transatlantic airship kept aloft by steam and with a hull made of two durable layers of stainless steel sheet enclosing two inches of insulating foam, sounded to me a safe and sound way of travelling. How much better, I thought, to cross the Atlantic in twenty-four hours on such a craft with a proper bunk to sleep in and dining rooms, than the cramped seats of a jet. But, as you know, it never happened.

They never let on what killed the project, but I suspected that no one in the ranks of Shell middle management would risk having his name attached to such a project. Their hands were stayed, perhaps, by visions of the obloquy of being remembered as the men responsible for the first of these to be stranded prominently on some peak in the Alps. The incredible business of the Brent Spar well illustrates this process. Here was an old, disused oil-storage platform that Shell had emptied and then decided to sink in moderately deep waters of the ocean. The way they presented their intentions to the public gave Greenpeace a fine opportunity for a stunt to picture Shell as a villain of the environment, contaminating the pure pristine waters of the Atlantic. So successful were they in conveying this impression that in Germany there was a near hysterical response and violence was done to Shell filling stations. Senior management had no option but to accept that they had lost this battle. The real marine biological evidence is that to bury a platform such as Brent Spar in the ocean is a gift for marine life. Iron is one of the most nutritious elements and the algae, the prime producers of marine life, need it. It is welcome; more than this, the iron network of the platforms before it finally rusts away as food provides a habitat where fish are protected against the nets of trawlers. The German Greens should have remembered that during the two world wars the opposing forces deposited a vastly greater quantity of steel in the Atlantic Ocean. No long-term harm to marine life has come from it.

I know that these thoughts of mine excusing the actions of a multinational oil and chemical company are considered by the Greens at best as misguided loyalty to friends and colleagues in the industry, or at worst, misinformation put out by me and paid for by the industry. I entreat them to reconsider their old-fashioned radical views about the industrial world. Multinationals exist to provide the products we demand, and they do so with impressive efficiency. So much so, that in some dry parts of the world gasoline is cheaper than water. We share equally with these companies the blame for corrupting the air. How many Green activists walk or cycle rather than drive their cars? My experiences with Shell left me firmly with the impression that they are neither stupid nor villains. On the contrary, I know of no other human agency that plans as far ahead or considers the environment more closely. The world twenty years from now is a serious subject of consideration by Shell and the other oil companies, and they are wise enough to worry about a reduction in the number of their customers through environmental degradation. Governments and the United Nations have a much shorter time constraint, caring only about a few years ahead—perhaps to the next election, perhaps not. What impressed me much more than these general facts was the objective personal view I had of the human pyramid of the multi-national. My role as an independent scientist gave me the opportunity to meet employees at all levels. Many of the senior management were scientists or engineers and they were aware of and concerned about environmental problems. I will not forget the extent to which Rothschild, a biologist, was disturbed by the revelations of Rachel Carson in her book *Silent Spring*. Shell were manufacturers of halogenated pesticides like dieldrin and aldrin, and DDT. They made them in response to the demand from farmers for better pest destruction. They were not out deliberately to poison the world; they were filling an industrial niche and receiving a reasonable profit for so doing. When the public think of chemicals as evil, poisonous products of a malign industry, they are reflecting the distorted thoughts of those who in their student days railed against capitalism. We all too easily forget how we hailed DDT as a lifesaver in the 1940s and early 1950s—according to the late Kenneth Mellanby it saved more lives than any other synthesized substance. We honoured its inventor, Paul Müller, with a Nobel Prize and he used all of the prize money to support young scientists. Shell stopped making dieldrin and aldrin well before it was illegal to do so. What a different picture is this from that painted by the environmentalists.

In the late 1960s, Rothschild asked me if I would prepare for him an essay on the prospects for Shell in the year 2000. He was due to lecture on this topic in Israel and wanted to make a speech based on the views of his advisers. My thirty-year-old essay has stood the test of time well. In brief, it said that by 2000 Shell and other industrial companies would be so concerned with global pollution problems that the only way they would profit was by selling products that alleviated, not worsened, pollution.

Shell was engaged in making chemicals as well as oil products, and their Research Centre at Sittingbourne in Kent was particularly concerned with chemicals for agriculture, including pesticides and herbicides. Here Goulden and his colleagues had first used my electron capture detector in pesticide analysis. Politically inclined environmentalists too conveniently forget that it was not some ideologue in academia that first found halogenated pesticides everywhere in the world; it was scientists at Shell and at the Food and Drug Administration of the USA. Shell funded and encouraged this work and did it in their own laboratory here in the UK. To my regret, I visited Sittingbourne only a few times. Cornforth and Popják worked there and, like me, were among those who had left Mill Hill in the early 1960s. It was a joy to discuss difficult problems of science with them. Kappa Cornforth was very deaf but he could read the lips of his wife Rita who had worked with him in the Chemistry Department at Mill Hill. I think that he was one of the most able of all the scientists at Mill Hill and I was so pleased when his work was recognized by a Nobel Prize in 1975. I recall fondly a happy two days at Sittingbourne and staying with the Cornforths in their small mansion nearby. We even played croquet on their lawn—something that evoked memories of lunchtime breaks in wartime days at the old Institute in Hampstead.

Shell's Research Centre at Thornton in Cheshire is a kind of industrial village made up of brick units which look a bit like houses. There are shrubs around them and lawns in front of them and small roads linking one building to another. It would be more pleasing but for the refinery of Stanlow that looms over its western edge. I was in a small conference room in one of these brick buildings talking to a group of senior engineers when one of them grinned, and with a rich Scouse accent, burst out, 'Hey, whacker, go down to Lewis's and buy us some acid.' I had forgotten that engineers do not much care for academic science-speak. I was discussing with them the peculiar problem of extreme pressure additives for lubricants. These are an odd family of chemicals which, when added to the oil used in the gearbox of your car, prevent the teeth of the gears from tearing metal from each other as they rotate under power. The engineers had discovered empirically that a peculiar set of chemicals, when added to the oil, could stop the unfortunate process that caused the car rapidly to come to a stop. But they had no explanation of how they worked. I caused the comment and the burst of laughter from the other engineers by saying, when I looked at their list of effective additives, 'They look to me like a list of Lewis acids.'

Now, GN Lewis was one of the century's truly great physical chemists and one of his contributions was to explain the true nature of acids. We all know about vinegar and lemon juice and the taste of acidity, and we know that it would be unwise to taste the much stronger sulphuric and nitric acids. But what are acids? What have they in common? An early Swedish chemist, Johannes Nicolaus Brönsted, recognized that they all, when dissolved in water, increase the abundance of protons, which are hydrogen atoms with a positive charge; protons exist in water, not as bare hydrogen nuclei, but in close association with one or more water molecules. So Brönsted said, 'Acids are proton donors, and the strength of an acid can be measured by the abundance of protons in its solution in water.' The pH scale measures acidity and alkalinity and this is a scale expressed in multiples of ten. An acid solution with a pH of 0 is very strong, one with a pH of 3 is one thousandth as strong, and pure water, which has a pH of 7.4 is no acid at all. Alkali solutions, which are proton acceptors, go from 8, weak alkali, to 14, a very strong one. GN Lewis enriched our imagination on just what an acid is by concentrating not on the proton, the hydrogen atom, but on its positive electrical charge. He proposed that an acid is more than just a proton donor: it is an electron acceptor. In other words, a substance with a hunger for negative electrical charges, that is to say, free electrons, is an acid. Now, having played for years with electron capture detectors, I knew all about substances that liked electrons, and it was this that led me to see the list of extreme pressure lubricant additives as Lewis acids. They included substances like tetrachloro phthalic anhydride and other halogenated compounds such as iodine and certain sulphur compounds, all of which I knew were electron attracting. It made me wonder if the avidity of these additives for electrons had something to do with their effectiveness. We all know that when two pieces of metal make contact, an electric current—a flow of electrons—is enabled. Could it be that under the extreme conditions of gear wheels, when the film of an ordinary lubricant is squeezed apart, the metal makes contact in the same way as it does at an electrical contact? And the electron flow across between the two pieces of metal in effect welds them together. The addition of highly electron-attracting compounds to the oil could have the effect of preventing this fusion of the two pieces of metal when they work in juxtaposition. I never discovered whether they followed up this idea, nor whether it proved to be a fruitful source of even better EP additives.

A fair part of my work with Shell was on ways to produce energy that were less environmentally damaging. We all, early on, agreed that burning methane instead of coal or crude oil was a good temporary measure. The burning of methane puts into the atmosphere only half as much carbon dioxide per unit of energy produced as does coal. In the 1960s, when North Sea gas was first made available, Shell and the UK itself was frustrated from using this clean fuel as the source of electric power by the inept legislation of those days. Lawyers with no understanding of science drafted the constitutions of the gas and electricity boards formed by the government after the Second World War. They denied any collaboration between the two boards—electricity and gas. Consequently, we continued to support dirty coal-burning power stations, far beyond their justification. We delayed the burning of North Sea gas for power until the 1990s. The most exciting of all alternative energy sources that Shell considered was the possibility of extracting the energy released when a fresh water river mingles with the salty ocean. I was astonished to learn that this is the equivalent of a 600-foot waterfall at every estuary. We tried, but failed, to harness this source.

Rothschild had the reputation of a tough and difficult man. I arrived at Shell Centre one day to find Miss Page, his secretary, in tears and Rothschild in a black mood. Because I could easily be the next victim of his hangover, I marched straight in to the urgent problem then facing Shell. In the previous week, a large tanker had been lost in the southern oceans as it was returning empty to the Middle East for its next cargo. It was the second such incident and we faced a problem very much like that of the TWA 747 that exploded in 1997 over the Atlantic as it climbed from New York to its cruising altitude. In both events, at the time little was known of the cause of their destruction. Everyone had guesses ranging from sabotage to a coherent wave pattern in the sea that flexed the ships until they broke, but guesses without evidence are not worth much. My contribution was to be sceptical about wilder hypotheses, such as that the spontaneously inflammable phosphine gas was produced from dead fish trapped in the tanks.

The correct explanation came weeks later. I do not recall who was the wise one who thought of it, but it was bizarre and as follows. A standard practice during the return journey of supertankers is to clean the tanks with high-pressure water sprays. This is done automatically with the tank sealed and the crude oil washed from the tank walls; the small amount of oil washed off is collected and stored in a separate small tank. There are nearly always volatile hydrocarbons present, such as propane, butane, and the pentanes in the crude oil, so that the gas mixture in the near-empty tanks is often potentially explosive. We all knew this, but where were the sparks to ignite the mixture? There were no faulty electrical currents to blame. How could a spark develop in the highly conducting spray of seawater? The answer was simple; just like in a thunderstorm. The huge volume of the empty tank, perhaps 50,000 to 100,000 cubic metres, was enough for a process of static electrification like that in a lightning storm to take place in the seawater spray and so ignite the mixture. The explosion of a 100,000-cubic metre tank of air and hydrocarbon vapours is the equivalent of forty tons of high explosive—more than enough to destroy the tanker. It was easy enough to prevent further accidents by inerting the gas atmosphere of these empty tanks, and this was done using the cooled exhaust gases from the ship's engines. The oxygen had been taken out in the course of the burning of the fuel that drove the engines. But no one had imagined such a need beforehand. This, and the result of the recent 747 accident, should warn us that it is not a good idea to have large tanks filled with explosive mixtures of gas and air anywhere. Because no one can imagine them exploding does not mean that they are safe. The investigation of the 747 accident showed that a spark with energy of only a few millijoules was enough—not more than would be caused by walking across a carpeted room on a dry winter day.

The tactic of getting straight down to the problem seemed to work and Rothschild recovered his composure. It is only fair to say that I never was a victim of his temper; he was always, to me, considerate and helpful. He would often ask if I were succeeding as an independent and approved when he discovered that my gross income was somewhat more than that of the Shell directors. He had the aristocrat's disdain for employees. Maurice Sugden, Director of the Shell Research Centre and a most distinguished scientist from Cambridge, told me that Rothschild once turned up at his Cambridge home, mid-morning on Christmas, to discuss a non-urgent work problem. He would call his employees at unsociable hours, but never did he do any of this to me. Perhaps he sensed that our relationship would have ended had he done so. After one session at Shell Centre Rothschild turned to me and said, 'Lovelock, do you pay income tax?' 'Yes, of course I do,' I replied. 'Why do you ask?' His answer was, 'How unfortunate for you. You know, I have never paid tax. It is quite simple. You see, I have no income.' I wish I had seen the value of this priceless piece of financial wisdom from a rich man. At the time, I was just surprised and did not use it as he had intended, as a guide for my own affairs. Sometime towards the end of our association he grumbled one morning and said, 'I have Margaret Thatcher coming to see me next week.' She was then Minister for Education, and he did not seem to look forward to the visit. A month later, however, he told me enthusiastically of his talk with our future Prime Minister and said he considered her one of the most intelligent people he had met. Coming from a misogynist this was praise indeed.

I lost touch with Rothschild in the 1970s when he left Shell to run a governmental advisory service, a so-called 'think tank'. My last encounter with him was a longish letter, for him, on my book, *Gaia: A New Look at Life on Earth*, after its publication in 1979. In it he said how much he enjoyed reading it and how it had reminded him of the days we spent together talking about environmental affairs during the Shell period. I owe a debt to Shell, and to Lord Rothschild in particular, for having been the only agency I associated with that actively supported my scientific work on Gaia. I owe a special debt to Sidney Epton of Shell, who did so much to help me with the early writing of articles on the subject. Sidney became a close friend and I'm proud that he joined with me in the first presentation of Gaia in the journal *New Scientist*. Anyone foolish enough to say of Shell in this respect, 'Well, they would, wouldn't they? Gaia was there to clean up the mess for them,' should read the article in *New Scientist* of 'The Quest for Gaia' that we then wrote. There is nothing in it that would justify such a statement. When I think of Shell I remember with affection my friends, Ted Adlard, Colin Quinn, and the others, who did so much to make my visits to Thornton memorable. Towards the end of his life, Rothschild suffered scurrilous allegations that he had been one of the Cambridge traitors that included Philby, Burgess, Maclean, and Blunt. It was a cruel injustice and no way to treat a man who had proved himself brave and a patriot. The King awarded him a George Medal during the Second World War for courageously dismantling a bomb. Allegations of treachery are easy to make but most difficult to refute. I know from my own contacts with him on security affairs that had he been as alleged, a Soviet mole, then events would have moved differently from what they did. To me he was a brave man, and one of our treasured eccentrics.

The Security Services

In early 1965 Sandy Lipsky, a friend and professor in the department of internal medicine at Yale University, rang one evening. 'I've just been asked,' he said, 'if there is any way to find people hiding in dense tropical forests.' Did I think people emitted some characteristic odour detectable by sensitive instruments at a distance? I had some ideas but did not want to iterate them across the transatlantic telephone. They were too ill defined and needed some careful thought, so I just said, 'I'll think about it and let you know.' The next day I did my sums. In those days there was not even a hand calculator to assist, it was all done by mental or pen-and-paper arithmetic, or by using the slide rule. How quickly we forget that scientists of the early space and nuclear ages did nearly all their work without the convenient computer at their fingertips. There were a few vast machines whose memories were made of magnetic beads strung out along the interstices of a web of wires, almost like the embodiment of a miniature abacus; or other clever but cumbersome devices. Their total capacity was no more than that of the better pocket calculators of today, and their cost and the number of acolytes needed to keep them working were far beyond my finances, or indeed those of most universities and institutes. It is eerie to think that even a digital watch would have amazed Buzz Aldrin and the astronauts who first walked on the moon. The computer that landed their lunar module had no more capacity than that of the tiny chip that now oversees the operation of your washing machine. So I did my sums by hand and concluded that no existing device could detect at a distance of, say, a hundred yards the specific odours of people living in a jungle. But, it occurred to me, if the people in the jungle were covertly labelled with something detectable by electron capture then it would be easily possible to detect them at 100 yards or more away. By now, I was familiar enough with American science where, unlike England, money was the main arbiter and I knew the importance of putting my ideas down as a provisional patent proposal.

I was due to visit JPL in a few days, and while there I took the precaution of having my proposal notarized by a notary public, who was on the JPL staff. On this visit I first met Dian Hitchcock and Gordon Thomas, inspectors sent by NASA to assess the space experiments, and I discussed my remote-sensing idea with them. They both saw the military potential of the idea and urged me, when I went to

Washington with them the following week, to get in touch with the CIA. Spy thrillers were amongst my bedtime light reading and the thought of meeting agents of the CIA personally intrigued me. I think it was Dian, through one of her many contacts in Washington, who arranged for me to meet representatives of the CIA. I recall taking a taxi to a part of Washington I did not know, walking down a street about two blocks, and finding a shop that sold antiques. I went in through a perfectly ordinary door and was met and taken to a room behind the shop. I was a little disappointed after the build-up, good enough for any of the thrillers I'd read, that the representatives of the CIA seemed so ordinary, just run-of-the-mill scientists like me. One, indeed, was bespectacled, but they were both courteous and polite and we went through the details of my proposal. Looking back, I suspect that they, like civil servants anywhere, were concerned that the strange foreigner might be trying to operate a scam using a completely bogus piece of science. After all, few at that time had used an electron capture detector and they were unaware how sensitive it was. My story must have sounded far-fetched. I, of course, was doing my best to stress its exquisite sensitivity and this made matters worse. It was so far beyond that of any rival instruments, ten thousand times more sensitive than the mass spectrometer or the flame ionization detectors of those days, as to be unbelievable. They continued to be polite but I heard nothing more from them. I now know that the CIA and other American agencies did not make use of my idea until many years later.

Dian was furious at the lack of response and urged me to see other agencies, one of which involved a visit to the Pentagon to see a General there. I expected the Pentagon to be a difficult place to enter. The Jet Propulsion Laboratories, which I knew well, were never easy to enter: so obsessive was their concern about security that I was once ushered from the JPL library by an armed guard because I did not have the necessary clearance to read the textbooks on the shelves. To my surprise, the Pentagon seemed wide open and insecure. I took a taxi, which entered through the underpass into the open centre of that vast building, and the cab drew up beside a curb. I walked along what seemed like a shopping mall and tried to find an entrance to the building. Eventually I came to an office labelled 'Information', entered, and explained that I had an appointment with General X. After a telephone call, they told me where to go. It was a complex set of instructions, which I wrote down in my diary. I was to report to another office where they would take me to the general's room. The way through the corridors was long and tedious, so long that the inhabitants of the Pentagon often used golf-carts for their inter-office journeys. The endless stream of humming vehicles reminded me of a mass raid by Daleks. No one asked me what I was doing there, and eventually I found my destination. Here again a quiet, middle-aged man took me along another corridor to the General's room. It was a decent-sized, comfortable den with bookshelves on the walls, their contents more academic than military. This time the cross-purpose was even more marked. I talked of sensitivities and feasibilities; he talked of their inability to give me a contract to develop the device. Plaintively, I remember saying, 'But aren't you interested in its possibilities?' Again, he misunderstood and suggested that I should go back and put in my proposal for a contract through proper channels. Here was a classic example of British–American misunderstanding. Here was I, brought up in the middle-class tradition of public service, where personal reward was not expected, in conflict with the General, raised in a different—capitalist—society, that of America, where getting ahead and getting rich were the things that really counted.

My last attempt was with the Advanced Research Projects Agency, ARPA. Here in a skyscraper building I met three very pleasant academics. They listened to me, half believed what I had to say, but clearly had a whole pile of ideas to sift through and this was another one of them. Not surprisingly, I heard nothing more from them. After three attempts to interest the American authorities in my idea, I returned home. A week later, I was due to visit Lord Rothschild at the Shell Centre in London. After talking about Shell problems with him in his top-floor office, I told him of my experiences in Washington. I was concerned that, as a British subject, I should have raised the issue first here in the United Kingdom and not tried to pass on what might be useful military information to what was, in fact, a foreign government. I sought Rothschild's advice, both as a friend and because it was rumoured that he had worked with the security services during the Second World War. He just said, 'Leave it to me.' A few days later, one of Rothschild's brief letters arrived. It simply gave a telephone number and a name to call. His letters were a joy to receive, so different from the prolixity of my scientist colleagues. I remember one that said merely, 'Lovelock, you have deserted me. R'; this was enough to remind me that a visit abroad had prevented our monthly meeting and Rothschild had missed it. I telephoned the number in the letter and spoke to Dr Walters, who asked if he and two colleagues could visit my Bowerchalke laboratory the following week.

Frank Pitson, then a senior scientist at the Atomic Weapons Research Establishment, AWRE, Hugh English, and another man, whose name I cannot recall, came to see me. Unlike the Americans, they believed me and liked my idea quite a bit. They told me they had a problem of intercepting arms smugglers who used Arab tribesmen to carry their weapons on camels in the Emirates. Did I think that labelled arms or ammunition would be detectable weeks later after crossing up to a thousand miles of hot desert? We then discussed how much tracer substance would be needed, what range of detection was possible, and worked out on sheets of paper, there in my office overlooking the Chalke Valley, that it could indeed be done. What a difference it was from the responses in Washington. To be fair, a distinguished person, Rothschild, had trickled me in, and we shared the same culture. Perhaps, most of all, I was on my own ground and they were visiting me. They asked some searching questions about the toxicity of the tracer substances I had proposed, and insisted that they must be harmless. This was very strange to me, for my fiction reading of clandestine operations suggested that the least thing of concern would be the health of the enemy. Nevertheless, they insisted. When they left, I realized, in the comfortable glow of a pleasant afternoon's work, that I had probably started something.

Sure enough, Hugh English telephoned and asked me to go to Waterloo Station where someone would meet me. As I moved from the Salisbury train onto the crowded concourse at Waterloo, I wondered how I would be recognized. Then, from the crowd the familiar face of Hugh English appeared. He smiled and led me to the stairs that went down onto the road that led to the street market just alongside the station. We walked past the stalls selling everything from fresh fruit and vegetables to cheap clothing and used tin trays. We walked on until we encountered the high-rise and indecorous Century House. There was plenty of security there, but Hugh English vouched for me and signed me in. I took a pass and we went by lift to somewhere in the guts of the skyscraper and took a corridor to a large seminar room. It was full, to my surprise. Hugh introduced me and invited me to say my piece. I could have done with some slides or a blackboard but I did my best, and then the questions came. They were clearly fascinated. Here was a covert alternative to the radio beacon, a way to mark a person or a car without their knowing it and it dawned on me that the casual story they told about camels was a cover story; the real interest was in the KGB and its agents in London and other cities. Again came the question, 'Is it safe to use? Will the chemical harm the person labelled in any way?' I was baffled. I imagined that few would care about the health hazards of a KGB agent in London. Not so: it was almost as if they regarded the opposition as merely rival civil servants and that they at least deserved the care needed to ensure a long and well-earned retirement at pension time. I now understood their reluctance to use radioactive markers.

A remarkable advantage of the electron capture tracers is their total lack of toxicity. It is hard to conceive anything less toxic than water, yet the perfluorocarbons are. If you fell into a deep pool of water with concrete tied to your legs, you would soon die; not so in a pool of perfluorocarbons. A lung full of these strange substances may not be pleasant but it is not lethal and they carry oxygen almost as well as air does and are so inert as to be unnoticed by the delicate cells lining the lungs. Some perfluorocarbons are used as blood substitutes, replacing as much as thirty per cent of the blood in the body, such is their remarkable lack of toxicity. I was able to answer all of their concerns over toxicity with as near to certainty as any scientist can ever achieve. One scientist present at the meeting asked such searching and pointed questions that at first I thought him hostile, even though his questions were deep and thoughtful. By the time the conference was nearly over, I had developed a respect for him. He had helped me to clear my own mind. It is always the way with good critics: they are the most valuable friends a scientist can have. I wished that I could get to know him better. I returned to Bowerchalke thoughtfully: 'What have I let myself in for?' I wondered. I had caught a glimpse of a real and serious world and one very different from the fictional stories.

Before I left Century House, Hugh took me aside and said, 'I think it would be wise if sometime you did a demonstration of your apparatus, somewhere discreetly in the country in your part of the world. Would you mind if we sent down one of our people to observe?' A week later, a young man, Colin Place, drove up to our Bowerchalke home laboratory in a small sports car. He was someone who looked more like the fictional characters that I had enjoyed. He said, though, that he was a chemist. I had built in my lab a simple portable apparatus for detecting the gas, sulphur hexafluoride, down to levels of less than a part per trillion. We arranged to take it into the New Forest, where he would release a small quantity of this gas into a gentle westerly breeze at times of his choosing and I would sit 500 yards away, sampling the air. It was a successful trial and I was able to detect all but one of his releases. Honour was satisfied and Colin reported to London that it really did work.

Then came a long period, I've forgotten just how long, while they checked to see if I was a safe person to let know more about the potential uses of my inventions. In 1966 many of us were still deeply affected by the political theories of socialism and since this at times more or less merged into Marxism, which was of course the Soviet culture, there was a need for care. Many regarded the Cold War as bogus, even wrong. My mother was a highly intelligent woman and a Quaker, not a communist, but she was sure that all the accounts of the gulags in Russia and the cruelty of that truly evil man, Stalin, were capitalist propaganda and had no truth to them. Now, after the Thatcher years and the collapse of the Soviet State, it is difficult to imagine the moral certainty in the socialism of that time. I do not even now know whose opinions they sought about my character and history. I was glad that as a student I had rebelled by joining the Catholic Society at Manchester University and toyed with moral theology instead of Marxism. In any event, I was too much of a simple scientist to swallow the certainty of those with faith, whether Marxist or Christian. Their views on life, the universe, and human behaviour I always found unconvincing. Marxism and Catholic moral theology seemed to have more similarity than difference. One person I know they asked about my character was Chris Gulliver, the landlady of The Bell Inn at Bowerchalke. They told me she was an ideal character reference and one far more likely to know important details of my life than were the professionals of the village such as the vicar or the schoolmistress, who apparently most give as their preferred reference. Rothschild told me several months later that I had passed their tests well. From his smile, I suspect they discovered more about my private life as well as my security rating.

Then Hugh called, asking me to come to London again. This time my journey was to Leconsfield House in Curzon Street. The cab driver gave me an odd look when I gave him my destination. He knew at that time just what agency Leconsfield House housed, but in the peculiar secrecy of those days, I did not know and neither did the public generally. Here, after signing in again, I met Hugh, who took me to a small room in which sat, to my delight, the good critic of my meeting at Century House. He was David Pengrew and, as the years went by, became a real friend. The discussion now was much more practical. We need, they said, a base for you to establish your work and it will have to be at one of the Ministry of Defence establishments. I immediately thought of the Chemical Defence Experimental Establishment (CDEE) at Porton, which is conveniently near to Bowerchalke, being on the other side of Salisbury and about the same distance away. 'No,' said Hugh, 'You would not like it there. We think a better place would be the Admiralty Materials Research Establishment at Holton Heath in Dorset, and that is almost as close to you.'

Hugh and David came down and stayed the night with us at Bowerchalke. The next day we travelled to Holton Heath to see the director there and prepare a site to work on tracers. The establishment at Holton Heath was in the delightful heathland of Dorset. Here, the sandy soil favours conifers and heather, and it is where most of the United Kingdom's reptiles are found, including the rare smooth snake. In the First World War it was a munitions factory and later it became a research station for the Navy. The Director, Dr Morris, took us to an area surrounded by a close-knit high steel fence and entered by a single guarded roadway with a small brick office for the guard. Inside were a series of brick buildings that were chemical laboratories. We met the senior chemist, Dr Lithgrove, and went on to a temporary wooden building, converted into a small laboratory. 'This will do for a start,' they said. Up until then they had paid my travel and subsistence costs and consulting fees by cheques drawn on Coutts Bank. When I started to work at the laboratory at Holton Heath there was a generous supply of funds available and they provided a graduate scientist, Tony Vizard, and a senior technician, John Brophy, to help me. They then paid what was, in effect, a salary. From the beginning, I sensed that the administration at Holton Heath regarded our laboratory as an abscess in the body of an otherwise healthy civil service establishment. Because of the high classification of our work, no one was allowed to know what we were doing and there was a wonderful freedom from paperwork, form-filling, and administrative meetings. It was an almost ideal way to do research. We soon built samplers that were more sensitive and synthesized or had made better tracer chemicals.

While work at Holton Heath was progressing, Lester Machta approached me. He was head of the NOAA air resources laboratory at Silver Springs in Maryland, just outside Washington, and he had a grand experiment in mind. He wanted to label the air mass over the

West Coast of the United States and follow its motion across the whole continent. His interest was meteorological. His sponsors were keen to know how toxic or radioactive products of a disaster spread across whole regions. He was anticipating the real disaster that came much later at Chernobyl. He knew of my electron capture detector and needed advice on how to use it for such an experiment. Collaboration with NOAA scientists on tracer technology would bring benefits for our work at Holton Heath. At the same time, it was potentially a conflict of interest and a breach of security. Here, David gave a decision that helped immensely—I do not know whether it was his decision or from the service itself. It was that uses by the security services of the tracer technology were wholly secret, but that the technology itself was open. Thus, collaboration with NOAA on a technological basis was fine and could do nothing but benefit us, so long as we kept them in ignorance about our uses of the technology. It was a wise decision and one that was inevitable, for Rothschild had been keen to use the technology in the interest of Shell. Shell went as far as labelling gases passing along pipelines and arranging systems that would automatically switch from one pipeline to another when the tracer material heralded the approach of a different product.

It was also an excellent technique for leak detection. This use was potentially hazardous and I was once able to stop what might have been a disaster of considerable magnitude. Hearing of my technique from Shell, the Gas Board, without telling me, decided to label one of their major gas pipes on the eastern side of England with sulphur hexafluoride to detect leaks along the pipeline. The technique would have worked well; unfortunately, they did not know that SF6, unlike the perfluorocarbons, is active chemically. If mixed with a flammable gas like methane or hydrogen, it will explode on a spark almost as violently as the same mixture of hydrocarbon and oxygen. And here they were, about to let in two whole cylinders of liquid SF6 into the natural gas pipeline to label it. A single spark at the point of introduction could have produced a disastrous explosion, but fortunately we were able to warn them in time. Leak detection, air mass, and water labelling proceeded scientifically alongside the more secure work that the security services were doing, and this parallel development has continued for over twenty years.

The potential for chemical tracing was considerable, and soon the security services decided to build a proper new laboratory at Holton

Heath specifically for this need. At that time Hugh Jones, a scientist working for the Admiralty and cleared to know about the work we were doing, was appointed to take charge of the laboratory. He and I spent some happy times planning the layout of a pleasant and efficient purpose-built laboratory in a comfortable setting. I was then able to drop back to my preferred role of adviser rather than active worker on the scene. In the new lab, work was much easier and soon the staff increased. I persuaded Peter Simmonds, who had been with me at Mill Hill, Houston, and at the Jet Propulsion Laboratory to come back to England and work part time at Holton Heath whilst continuing his external connection with the JPL. The San Fernando Valley earthquake in 1971, I think, helped to disentangle him from his home in Tajunga near the Jet Propulsion Lab. He and his wife Tina had a tough time in that earthquake and were quite glad to come back to the more stable environment of England. In the same year, Brian Foulger took over the administration from Hugh Jones. With the increased staff, the Holton Heath lab began to prove itself.

Throughout history, we have regarded our custodians warily. We are wise to worry about their accountability: 'Quis custodiet ipsos custodes'. Fiction, lurid journalism, the old Left, Soviet disinformation, and Irish republicans—I doubt if these conspire to denigrate the security services. But without conspiring, they certainly had left me, as part of the public, with a strong impression that these services were too powerful and unaccountable and could even commit arbitrarily violent deeds. We often ignore the extent of Soviet disinformation that once went on. I used to listen occasionally to the broadcasts on the short waves from Moscow. I well remember the frequent insistence during the 1980s that the AIDS virus was a deliberate product of United States laboratories. I knew that this was a scientific impossibility, but did the other listeners? It is so easy to sow rumour and I'm sure that many of our views of the security services come from the flood of disinformation that journalists, who were much too uncritical, all too readily spread. I do not know what goes on at the sharp end, but from meetings to discuss the deployment of surveillance devices I have been struck by their friendly humour. The kind of exchange I encountered is, 'You don't expect me to believe, do you Doc, that that thing you're holding in your hand can detect which burrow the rabbit is in from a hundred yards?' They were to me mostly like a refined version of the policeman on the beat I had so often encountered as a child in Brixton. It was not so surprising to find that some of them were Labour supporters, some of them quite devoutly religious, and one was even a Quaker. They surely did not seem at all like their detractors would have us believe.

On the negative side, the one thing that bothered me about my work with civil service agencies was their failure to appreciate the value of the ideas and inventions that they generate and apply. In America, there is always a constant watch to see if any idea that comes up constitutes a patentable invention, from which the inventor or the organization can profit. In addition, of course, society itself profits. Wonderful ideas would spin off in Britain, and I have seen this happen throughout my scientific life, but no one would ever bother to patent them. We complain bitterly when others patent and profit from our ideas and we complain even more when we have to pay them royalties for our own intellectual property—penicillin being the most outrageous example of this. It's not anybody's fault really; it is just that there is no feedback. There is little direct benefit to a civil servant in patenting an idea, since he will gain nothing from it. It will also mean a lot of work dealing with lawyers and I do not underestimate just how much work is required to patent something. For this, the country or the organization may have a reward but not the individual civil servant. So it is small wonder that there were always more urgent things than the patenting of bright ideas, but we have all lost because of this. I do believe that things are now better, but the fact that they are legally better and rewards are available, does not immediately produce results. It will take time for the culture of reward to move in, and as things are now, I think we have no option but to take it on.

Our tribal nature affects science as much as any other human activity. I soon found that our work at Holton Heath was strictly limited to chemistry; I suppose we were fortunate enough to have so large a field to roam in. I knew, though, that there were better ways of achieving our practical aims by using other scientific methods, for example, those in the disciplines of physics or biology. For many years, the internal tribal barriers between the sciences successfully prevented us from using our brains and our skills to answer urgent practical problems in the best way, not just a chemical way. Reasons such as the 'need to know' and the avoidance of departmental friction were used to frustrate our efforts. All of this was to the disadvantage of the service itself. I cannot too strongly stress my belief that the best results do not come from setting physicists, chemists, and biologists in isolated competition. They come from allowing the best group to emerge from a free association of all of them. The organization of the civil and military services is such that there is little hope of achieving this scientific nirvana. We need to keep it in mind, though, as a counsel to perfection.

The belief that the employment of a hundred qualified scientists will always do a hundred times as much as the employment of one of them is foolish but persistent. Generals know that they can train and inspire a group of fit young men to become fine soldiers. Their success in war will depend on good leadership, plenty of ammunition, and preponderant numbers. It does not work like this in science. Most universities have become like the fast-food industry. They package products that are safe, consistent in taste, but rarely surprisingly good. One or two scientists with a true vocation, aided by some skilled and dedicated technicians, are worth hundreds of lumpen graduates or PhDs and they are far less expensive. There is not enough natural selection at work. The incompetent who would not have survived in the commercial world suffer no more than a lack of promotion, or sometimes even tactical promotion to a position where they are merely a nuisance and cannot do damage. On the other hand, the service showed an impressive concern that no device we proposed would adversely affect the health of those under surveillance. Cynics might say that this was from a fear of lawsuits, but whatever the reason, the message given by the press that they were violent and unaccountable just did not wash. Fortunately for all of us, our civil service is a benign institution. It is accountable, although indirectly. My strong impression is that security services as part of it are also accountable, but in a different way. The security services share with the health service a degree of professional dedication that to some extent offsets the indirect accountability of state-run enterprises. Perhaps a life spent close to the sharp end brings out the best in physicians and security agents. My work for the security services has rewarded me with some real friends and the wonderful consolation that at least I have done something to counter acts of terrorism, not just ground my teeth in frustration.

During my years with the Security Services I developed an instinct for discretion. This was invaluable in my work with multinational companies and other government agencies, where I discovered much more about their workings than I needed to know. Fiction and political activists usually portray these large and powerful entities as malign and acting against the public good in a conspiratorial way.

In all my years as an independent scientist, I never encountered a conspiracy, but cover-ups were ubiquitous. The most enduring human trait seems to me to be cronyism; as Benjamin Franklin said, 'We must all hang together or assuredly we shall hang separately.'

Hewlett Packard

Avondale in Pennsylvania is not far from the huge chemical industrial activity of Wilmington, the home city of Dupont. In 1962 the air of that region often carried a smell of chemistry, and the water tasted of things in addition to the chlorine used to disinfect it, but Avondale also had a rural air; there were fields and woods and many mushroom farms that used a great deal of fresh dung. This agricultural smell mingling with that of organic chemicals from Wilmington gave the region an unforgettable and evocative aroma, and the first time I smelt it was on a visit from Houston one morning in February 1962. I was there to discuss with F and M Scientific the use of the electron capture detector. F and M was a small but vigorous firm started a few years previously by three Dupont scientists with an entrepreneurial inkling, and they manufactured gas chromatographs. This is something that happens often in the United States and plays an important part in its economic success. Young men with ambition will leave the safe career status of a large organization like Dupont and seek their fortunes by starting their own business. Sadly, this is something that only rarely happens in the United Kingdom.

Jim Peters, who worked for F and M, met me at Philadelphia Airport. He was a tall young man with a strange accent, which soon resolved into a mixture of South Africa and Liverpool. To hear it made me feel homesick and from that visit on, we became firm friends. Jim was my technical contact for the visit that lasted two days and for many years afterwards. I often stayed with him and his wife, Chris, and he visited me in England. The efficiency and professionalism of F and M in 1962 impressed me. They understood and used my detector well. Al Zlatkis and I had formed a small firm called Ionics Research and we made a know-how agreement with F and M Scientific. Few outside industry seem to understand how important 'know-how' is. Possessing the patent of an invention is like having the seed of a fruit tree. You cannot harvest the fruit until the seed is planted, tended while growing, and unless there is the wisdom to wait until the fruit is ripe and ready to be picked. Know-how covers all these details and is just as valuable as the patent itself. Part of the agreement was that I should visit the firm twice a year to discuss problems and further developments. The owners of the firm took me to lunch at the Brown Derby restaurant in a nearby village. The restaurant was one of those dark wooden buildings so common in New England; and the food, which included their speciality, crab cakes, was edible and sufficient. This visit was to start a routine of visits there that was to last, for me, thirty-two years. To meet with a group of friends and enjoy a pleasant memorable routine in between mornings and afternoons of challenging practical problems is one of the delights of doing science independently.

I was not alone in thinking that this small firm was unusual in its competent efficiency. Hewlett Packard, the fast-growing and first-class electronic giant, was seeking to develop a chemical instrument stance and had looked at firms like F and M all over the United States. Within a year, they chose to take over F and M and make it a part of their empire. It was a benign take-over and they rewarded the owners well and the technical staff were retained, but the capacity of the company was infused and enhanced by the expertise of Hewlett Packard's powerful electronic divisions. I could not help comparing it with the slow sad destruction of the equivalent British firm of WG Pye. This firm also had built excellent gas chromatographs but when the European giant Phillips took it over, a promising small industry that could have served the UK well, vanished within a few years.

At the time of the takeover of F and M, the benign quest for excellence that had been the aim of Hewlett and Packard, the founders of the firm, was still a potent force. Creativity was encouraged, and with it there was a tolerance of eccentricity; this is something that makes a proper habitat for invention and for the talented craftsman. There were some able but very odd people working at Avondale. At one time, the plant had its own foxhunt. Workers on flexi-time, who started at some early hour of the morning, would finish work at lunch and then dress in their red coats and riding gear and take off across the open country of Pennsylvania. Because it was a bottom-up hunt, it was not seen as a symbol of class warfare, and there were no hunt saboteurs. Indeed, the notion that hunting was cruel never seemed to surface. In England, the hatred of the hunt is somewhat hypocritical, and its emotional drive comes more from class war than from compassion for the fox. Some, I think, see the red coat of the huntsman as a powerful symbol of the sempiternal British class war, with those on their horses the rampaging cavalry of the ruling classes. As I write this, it astonishes me that the British Parliament is wasting its time voting for a bill to abolish hunting with dogs. My mother's family, all avid Hardy readers, also hated hunting and hunters, and I grew up in an atmosphere strongly prejudiced against the hunt. It was relieved, however, because my father, a true countryman, knew that the cruelties of hunting, perceived by city people who knew nothing about it, was as nothing compared with the daily cruelty of farm life. This was true in his time and it was to worsen when animals were condemned to the Belsens of battery houses for chickens, cattle, and pigs. I am ambivalent about the hunt. The sight of it stirs me as a colourful spectacle and I would not vote for its abolition, but I would not join it. Often on visits to Jim Peters, I would discuss work problems as we took a country walk across the fields and through the woods. Jim and Chris Peters were both from an urban environment in Liverpool, but in their new life in Pennsylvania, they had their own horses, enjoyed riding them, and seemed to find nothing odd in doing it. To give the flavour of my many visits to HP over the years let me tell how I arrived in the USA for one of them.

Philadelphia is an easy airport to arrive at—quiet compared with the pressure of Kennedy in New York or London's Heathrow—and this was particularly true near the end of the 1980s. I was quickly through Customs and there was the minibus for my journey to the motel at Chadds Ford. Getting aboard it was like listening to a soap opera after missing a few episodes. The driver was a casually dressed grandpa and the service was a family business. Soon the minibus was full of passengers and we were on the busy road towards Wilmington—and almost immediately, we were part of the family saga. The radio link to Grandpa's home bore news of domestic disasters. The basement was flooded, why hadn't he returned to fix it? Grandpa yelled back, 'How can I fix it when I am driving the damned bus? Why doesn't your lazy nephew fix it?' By the time the bus dropped me at the Chadds Ford motel, I felt again that I was a part of real America. The girl at reception checked me in and asked me if I was having dinner that evening. 'No,' I said, 'It's midnight now for me; I most of all want to sleep.' She nodded, and added, 'If you dine tomorrow, eat only the appetizer and dessert, the entrées are terrible.' It was a good reminder, for a year earlier I had spent a night of severe indigestion following an unwise meal at the motel. The food was far too rich and spiced for me.

Next morning Bruce Quimby, a senior scientist at HP, came at 8 o'clock to take me to breakfast. He proposed that we go to Mc-Donald's. It was my first visit to that bastion of Imperial America and I was curious to see what it was like. We parked and walked across to the dining room where Bruce ordered a substantial meal, at least an Egg McMuffin, followed by something equally substantial. After a frantic search of the menu for something light enough, I gave up, and merely had an orange juice and a coffee. We then travelled the back roads of the Pennsylvania countryside and arrived at HP's Avondale plant at about 8.45 am. Good companies nearly always employ lively and helpful receptionists who do much to set the mood of a visit. HP was no exception and a warm and welcoming woman signed me in and gave me my stick-on label marking me as a visitor. We walked towards the research and development department passing and saying 'Hi' to Mason Byles, at that time Manager, and sitting at his open-plan desk like everyone else. Successful managers seem to understand the need for visibility and accessibility. Managers in closed rooms guarded by protective secretaries are sometimes the sign of a badly run organization.

The R & D department occupied a large hall, lit by discreetly hidden fluorescent lights and filled with parallel rows of workstations. Walls about six feet high enclosed each of these. Inside the walls were desks, bookshelves, seats and computer screens. Somehow, looking from above, it appeared like a patterned carpet spread across the floor. At intervals, longer low walls marked off conference areas furnished with one large table, a blackboard, and about ten chairs. We made for one of these, stopping en route to pick up some more coffee. Tea was available but I have found from bitter experience that when in the United States it is better to drink coffee. The tea is anaemic stuff that tastes as if recently they had exhumed it from the bags thrown into Boston Harbour all those years ago. Around the table was the detector group with whom my first discussions were to be. The problem today was with the flame photometric detector, a strange device that senses nitrogen-containing substances specifically. It is useful, even invaluable, for detecting illegal drugs. I was glad that I had not invented it. It is notoriously erratic.

After this session, I had a wonderful but all too brief encounter with my friend, Leon Blumberg, a small man but one with a presence. He is a scientist who emigrated from Russia with his wife Rita and they now live in the United States. He had grown up as a child in a

Siberian gulag and was in some ways like a character from Solzhenit-syn's *The Inner Circle*. Leon is one of the most intelligent people I know, someone who during a tussle with a challenging problem reveals their inner strength. There were several friends at HP who gave intellectually as much as, and sometimes more than, I did in an exchange of ideas, but to Leon alone I always left feeling indebted.

My next task was to give an update on Gaia to whoever at the plant was free and wanted to come and listen. In one of the larger conference rooms, holding fifty or more people, I talked and showed viewgraphs. This time it was about progress in that most tantalizing of climate feedbacks, the cloud algae affair. How microscopic algae in the oceans make sulphur compounds that escape to the air where they oxidize to form tiny nuclei. Without these nuclei, the product of ocean life, the Earth might have few clouds and perhaps be 10–20 degrees celsius hotter than it is now. It was a joy to talk to these receptive engineers and instrument scientists who fully understood feedback and control. After all, it was their livelihood designing such systems. I sometimes despair of ever explaining to biologists, no matter how eminent, the subtleties of feedback in natural systems: the Cartesian linear thinking of reductionism makes them reject anything that requires the circular logic of control systems.

After my lecture a small group of us lunched in the cafeteria. Mason Byles, the plant manager, joined us and we talked about the progress of a gas chromatograph for the developing world. This was a notion I had for a cheap, simple instrument, not much larger than a pocket calculator. My idea was that in the developing world almost no one could afford the large and expensive instruments that HP made. An affordable instrument was what they needed. It might also become a saleable product in the developed world. We do simple sums on our calculators and leave the more difficult tasks to our computers. In the same way a hand-held gas chromatograph would enable a chemist to check his mixtures without having to fire up the complex instruments of the lab. I still have a most encouraging letter from John Young, one of the senior managers of Hewlett Packard, about this idea. It also had the backing of the United Nations University but for reasons unknown to me it was never made. As I said in the Introduction, I would not wish to start such an enterprise myself, although I would enthusiastically give it moral support.

In the afternoon I happily spent time with Terry Berger talking about the possibilities of supercritical fluid chromatography and with

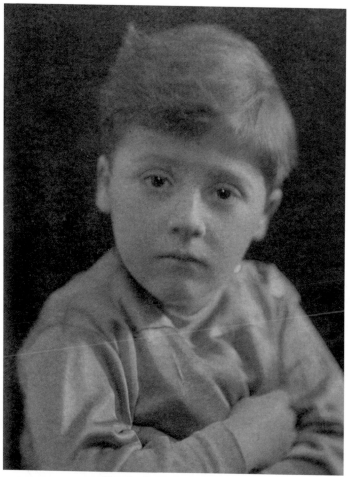

Plate 1. James Lovelock in 1924

Plate 2. My Father, Tom Lovelock, in 1893

Plate 3. The wedding of Tom Lovelock and Nell March, 1914
Standing: Ephraim March (grandfather) and Tom Lovelock (father). *Seated* Alice
March (grandmother) and Nell March (mother)

Plate 4. The March family at Deal, Kent, 1913

Left to right: Ephraim (grandfather), Ann, Alice (grandmother), Flo, Kit, and Frank

Plate 5. The National Institute for Medical Research, Holly Hill, Hampstead

Plate 6. James Lovelock, Owen Lidwell, and R. B. Bourdillon, 1943

Plate 7. A bullock with radio telemetering

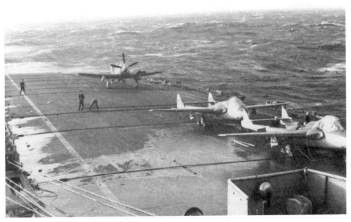

Plate 8. *HMS Vengeance* in Arctic waters

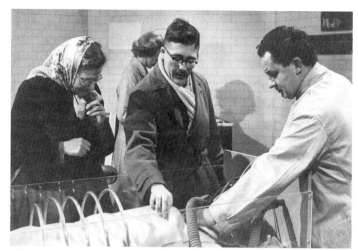

Plate 9. Audrey Smith, James Lovelock, and Leo McKern at the rehearsals of *The Critical Point* by Lorna Frazer

Plate 10. The experimental biology lab at the Mill Hill Institute

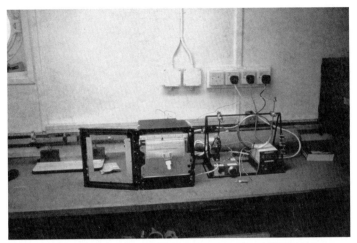

Plate 11. The apparatus for CFC measurements aboard *RV Shackleton*

Plate 12. The *RV Shackleton*

Plate 13. The Electron Capture Detector

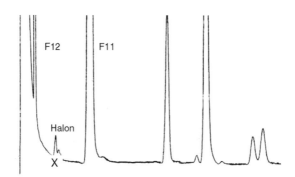

F12   F11

Halon

X

Figure 1. A chromatogram to illustrate the sensitivity of the ECD. The peak 'X' represents 1.1 parts per trillion of Halon in the air

Plate 14. Helen Lovelock at Bowerchalke, 1968

Plate 15. Andrew Lovelock at Bowerchalke, 1968

Plate 16. Christine and Jane Lovelock at Harvard Hospital, 1947

Plate 17. John Lovelock at Bowerchalke, 1960

Plate 18. The Bowerchalke laboratory, 1972

Plate 19. The Coombe Mill laboratory, 1985

Plate 20. *Left to right*: James Lovelock, Lynn Margulis, and Ricardo Guerrero

Plate 21. *Left to right*: Robert Charlson, Jim Lovelock, Andi Andreae, and Steven Warren

Plate 22. James Lovelock and Hideo Itokawa

Plate 23. James Lovelock and Tim Lenton

Plate 24. Robert Garrels and James Lovelock at Coombe Mill

Plate 25. Jim and Sandy at Portland Road, 1988

Plate 26. Sandy at Altarnun, 1999

Dick Kolthoff discussing the thermal conductivity detector. As the day's visit ended, I went to see Jim Sullivan and Bruce Hermann and talked with them about the electron capture detector, which is described in detail in Chapter 7, and its latest trials and tribulations. I learnt that the most recent complaint from customers was that the detector was too non-linear in its response to meet the stringent requirements of the Food and Drugs Administration's test for pesticide residues. We talked of ways of fixing this problem and about the use of fluorine gas to clean detectors. Leon drove me back to my motel in his huge ancient Lincoln town car. What is it about the United States that urges new arrivals to buy the largest and most uneconomical cars? Do they provide a sense of freedom or are they just insulation against an alien and incomprehensible New World?

I had a thirty-minute nap, a shower, and made ready for the real ordeal of my working day, the evening meal. This time it was a fish restaurant near the Ship Canal with an unusual ambience which allowed us, seated at a window table, to watch the cargo ships passing slowly by. It was a good and simple meal and we talked of other things than work problems. What I most dreaded on these visits were Italian restaurants. I like Italian food, especially as eaten in Italy, but the ultra-spiced super-fatted American version of Italian food often gives me a night of indigestion. This would make the next working day a nightmare. How can one have a clear flow of thoughtful ideas when one is dazed from lack of sleep? I would be condemned after one such meal to spend a day as if hung over, trying to see through gritty drooping eyelids the faces of my friends. Fortunately, this rarely happened on visits to HP, but it loomed as a hazard on all other journeys that I made across that great continent.

Often on visits to Avondale I stayed with Bill and Rosemary Buffington. Bill was in senior management and had been responsible for the development of the firm's most successful gas chromatograph. Rosemary was, among several things, a writer of manuals. Anyone who has tried to program a video recorder is likely to have experienced the frustrated confusion that a badly written manual can cause. From its earliest days, HP manuals excelled in the clear concise quality of their instructions but good writing never comes easily and Rosemary's was exceedingly good and did much to sustain HP's reputation for quality. On visits to the Buffingtons, conversation often turned to Gaia. Rosemary decided in the late 1980s to apply her writing talent to the publication of a Gaian Science Newsletter. It ran for four years and did more than I think she knew to break the ice jam that immobilized Gaian science at the time. Bill and Rosemary moved to Tokyo when Bill took on the task of managing a joint venture between HP and the Japanese firm Yokogawa.

I spent nearly all of my thirty-two years with HP at their Avondale division but I did occasionally go to the Corporate labs in Palo Alto in California. When I did, I sometimes stayed with Ellen and Harry Weaver; Harry was at the HP labs and Ellen a professor of biology at the nearby San Jose University and they paid a return visit to my home in England. Ellen was one of the few American biologists who saw Gaia in its early days as science not fantasy and introduced me to colleagues at the nearby NASA Ames laboratory. My visits to the corporate labs were usually on general topics such as the development of novel instruments for the growing biotechnology industry.

Soon after the Hewlett Packard takeover of F and M, in 1964, I moved on to a new working relationship. I resigned from Ionics Research, the company that Al Zlatkis and I had founded. HP took me on, used several of my inventions, and in return paid me what was in effect a retainer; it was adequate and kept pace with inflation. My last pay before I retired from working with them in 1994 amounted to a yearly fee of $32,000. I would grow anxious occasionally that few of my inventions were making money for HP. When I asked a senior executive of the company if I should continue to pass on patents, careless of their potential, he replied, 'This company already has too many lawyers. Patents and the legal affairs they generate keeps them busy. There is nothing worse for us than to have idle lawyers. They get up to mischief. So just keep those patents coming, even if they don't work it still does a lot of good.' It was a good and healthy relationship; it must have been to last as long as it did.

Inventions

To invent is to make useful practical things that did not previously exist, and what a misunderstood creative activity it is. The composition of music, the writing of verse and novels, the painting of pictures and sculpting of statues, all are recognized and praised as creative, but consider a wheel or a safety pin. They are hardly works of art but, without doubt, are creations and fine inventions, so why do we in England, although not Scotland, look on inventions as inferior? It may be a consequence of our obsession with class. The upper classes used to look on wealthy inventors who were from a lower stratum with disdain, and the lower classes envied them; this malign legacy of Victorian times persists. My father was a natural inventor and whenever we needed anything simple or mechanical or whenever anything broke, he would improvise a solution from whatever materials were to hand. The kitchen tap started leaking; it was Sunday and no shops were open. In no time, he had made a new washer from the sole of an old leather shoe. Greed, I think, makes many of us see inventions as a route to wealth but, in my experience, the truly inventive are rarely ever greedy; the satisfaction of solving a problem is their main reward. Inventors are often lazy and not motivated to acquire wealth—particularly if it means, as it often does, a long series of encounters with patent agents and lawyers and bureaucrats. Greed makes the uncreative steal inventions without a pang of guilt; the act of theft is often forgotten and soon the thief believes the novelty to be his own property. The decisive test for real inventors is to try stealing one of their inventions; if the inventor is genuine, he will hardly notice that it has gone, or if he does, he will give it freely and with his blessing. Good inventors invent all the time, and the loss of one of their inventions is trivial but if anyone is unwise enough to steal from another thief, his protests and denunciations will ring throughout the neighbourhood and beyond. This should not surprise: the first thief has lost the only invention he had and the one he cherished as his own. My mother was forever chiding my father for giving his ideas and inventions away; at times she would grow quite angry and call him an old fool. She never understood that to Tom Lovelock inventions were as prevalent as flies on a piece of decaying meat and, in his mind, of little more value. Towards the end of his life when he suffered an intractable kidney infection and was all but bedridden, he still had his inventiveness. The garden gate at the side of the house irritatingly banged in the wind, the noise repeated in a chaotic fashion and it kept my mother and father awake at night. Friends and neighbours had tried to fix it, always without success, but old Tom dragged himself from his bed, put on his dressing gown and wellies, and went out on a chill winter day and just looked at the offending gate. Then he went to his tool shed and within minutes had solved the problem and the gate never banged again for the two remaining months of his life. He died aged eighty-four. Creativity of the inventive kind does not diminish with age. I like to think I have inherited my father's inventiveness.

Inventing is a joy, but the driving force of invention is need, and it is difficult, perhaps impossible, to invent without it. Once the need is clear, the inventor soon finds an answer. Schoolteachers often have a strange notion about priority in inventions. When a child in their charge comes to them with an invention that he or she has made they will often dismiss it with scorn, saying, 'Oh, there's nothing new in that, my dear, it's been known about for years.' What they have not seen is that the child has retraced the steps of the first inventor and done so without prior knowledge. Therefore, that child has the potential to invent and needs encouragement, not putting down. Now that the sum total of human knowledge is so large as to be far beyond any individual understanding, re-invention grows ever more common. In addition, the wealth of new materials and devices makes re-invention novelty again. The use of a new alloy with superior qualities of strength and corrosion resistance can make a safety pin almost everlasting, and then it becomes a new invention. Some academics seem to enjoy diminishing the status of inventors. One of them referred to me as 'Not a scientist, merely an inventor who makes amateur equipment in his garage.' It compares well with the art critics who called John Singer Sargent 'Not an artist, merely a painter.' It must take a belly full of bile to hate and envy the creative so strongly.

A legend has established itself in England that I invented the microwave oven. It grew from some remarks I made during an interview by Sue Lawley for the BBC radio programme *Desert Island Discs*. I described how, in 1954, I had made several pieces of diathermy equipment to help my colleagues reanimate cold or frozen animals. One piece of equipment used a continuous wave magnetron as a source of microwaves for heating. Just for fun, I connected the output of the magnetron to a metal chamber in which I placed a potato. There was a timer, which turned on the power for the ten minutes needed to cook this part of my lunch. It worked just as any microwave oven does today and it may have been the first working microwave oven used to cook food that was then eaten. If it was, then I did indeed invent it. But I doubt if I did: surely some radar technician or scientist somewhere before this had trodden the same inventive path. If there is a real inventor of the microwave oven who feels anger or hurt at my appropriating the credit then I am truly sorry.

Let me tell you of one of my inventive experiences during the Second World War. I was sitting at a bench counting bacterial colonies growing on a blood agar culture plate; the colonies had grown from single bacteria-laden particles that I had collected from the air of a hospital ward. The patients of the ward were suffering wound infections caused by a rather unpleasant organism, a haemolytic streptococcus, which showed on the culture plate as clear circles against a dark red misty background. The bead-like colonies of bacteria were at the centre of each clear circle and the toxin emitted by the organisms, which gave them the name haemolytic, had lysed, that is, broken down the blood cells that were part of the culture medium. My boss, Robert Bourdillon, came in suddenly and apologized for interrupting my counting. 'Lovelock,' he said, 'I have a problem for you. Can you devise some means of detecting heat radiation under battle conditions? We need an accurate and clear indication of heat radiation sufficient to distinguish between that which would cause a first-, second-, or third-degree burn on exposed skin. I need your answer by tomorrow for an urgent meeting in Whitehall.' He dashed out as fast as he had arrived.

Now here was a straightforward need and there must be a simple answer. The obvious scientist's response would be to use a heat-sensing thermocouple and a meter. I dismissed this thought because it was neither simple nor suitable for a battlefield. Then I considered crystals of organic chemicals with different melting points stuck on a sheet of dark paper. The idea was that when the radiant heat reached a certain level, perhaps enough to cause a first-degree burn, some of the lower-melting-point crystals would melt. I knew the levels of heat radiation that would produce first-, second- or third-degree burns. Therefore, it was easy to test the idea. It worked after a fashion but was messy. It was hard to see if some crystals had melted, for they crystallized again as the paper cooled down. Then it occurred to me that if, instead of just dark paper, I used paper coated with gas-detector paint things might be easier. First, I must explain that gas-detector paint was a green paint applied to boards mounted horizontally all around London and its purpose was to reveal instantly use by the Germans of mustard gas or similar chemical warfare agents. Although called gases, these are usually sprayed as liquid, and when the droplets hit the gas-detector paint, they produce bright red circles, which show up clearly on the green background. This happens because the mustard gas liquid dissolves particles of a red pigment suspended in the green paint; the pigment particles are insoluble in the paint but soluble in the mustard liquid. There is nothing singular about mustard gas as a solvent and it occurred to me that any of the crystals I was using might serve as well when they melted. I tried sticking the crystals on paper painted with gas-detector paint and then exposing the paper to radiant heat. Whenever the crystals melted there was a bright red spot. Things were looking much better, but then I noticed that the crystals were not needed. When the heat flux was large enough to cause a first-degree burn, the paper itself went pink. At the flux that would cause a second-degree burn, it went bright red. At the flux that would produce a third-degree burn, it went yellow. Therefore, simply by painting a piece of paper with gas-detector paint, I had solved the problem. My boss, Robbie Bourdillon, was delighted and told me that it was just what they needed.

Much later, I heard from an Institute staff member, GL Brown, who had been present at the meeting in Whitehall, just what a gentleman Bourdillon was. It would have been so easy for him to go there and take credit for the radiation-detection paper, after all it was one of his staff that invented it, and leave it at that. Instead, he stood up and said, 'Gentlemen, thanks to the ingenuity of my young colleague, Mr Lovelock, I have a solution to your problem.' Working for men like this is a joy. There is that feeling of warmth and trust that no amount of payment or any other kind of reward can replace. I spent my formative years as an apprentice in this altruistic environment where my bosses were gentlemen in the old-fashioned usage of the word. Consequently, I spent a lifetime inventing without receiving more than a few per cent of the value of my inventions, indeed my belief in public service, inspired by the idealism of the Second World War, made the idea of profiting from my inventions abhorrent. The MRC paid me well, why should I expect more?

This attitude persisted even when I became independent and I patented personally only one of my inventions. Perhaps if I had been less successful and money had been short I would have tried harder to exploit my inventions. As it was, there always seemed to be enough for our needs and there were so many other things to think about.

7

The ECD

Perhaps the most important event in my life as a scientist was the moment in 1957 when, as a staff member of the National Institute for Medical Research, I stumbled on the electron capture detector (ECD). This simple device that fits easily into the palm of my hand was without doubt the midwife to the infant environmental movement. Without it we would not have discovered that chlorinated pesticides like DDT and dieldrin had spread everywhere in the world. The ECD was not limited to finding traces of pesticides; it soon found important trace quantities of other pollutants, notably the polychlorobiphenyls (PCBs), the chlorofluorocarbons (CFCs), and nitrous oxide. It made us aware for the first time of the global extent of pollution. Without the ECD, the appearance of environmentalism and green politics might have been delayed by as much as ten years.

Two things make the ECD special: first, its exquisite sensitivity—at least 1,000 times greater than that of other instruments at the time of its invention; and second, the fact that it is specifically sensitive to pollutants, poisons, and carcinogens. When I discovered the ECD I had no idea how much it would change the world, neither did I realize how much it would change my own life by enabling my independence and so setting me free to become aware of Gaia. It also led me to find how the CFCs were accumulating in the atmosphere—a discovery that culminated in the Montreal Protocol and the ban on the release of CFCs to the atmosphere. The simple and inexpensive nature of the ECD made it appealing to scientists in disciplines ranging from meteorology to geology. When I showed them how to use it to solve their problems it made it possible for me in return to discuss with them Gaia theory in the context of their own discipline. In this way the ECD was a passport that let me cross the frontiers of scientific disciplines which otherwise are guarded as jealously as national boundaries. In spite of its extraordinary influence on the course of both science and politics, the ECD was not seen as in the forefront of science. This was, I think, because it was seen as a mere invention and not as main-stream science. It was not until the 1990s, more than thirty years after its invention, that its significance was internationally recognized by the award of three environmental prizes: the Amsterdam Prize for the Environment in 1990, the Volvo Prize in 1996, and the Blue Planet Prize in 1997.

I will explain in more detail how the ECD works at the end of this chapter, but for now it is enough to know that when a gas like nitrogen is exposed to nuclear radiation, free electrons are torn from a few of its molecules, leaving positively charged nitrogen atoms behind. With pure nitrogen inside the ECD, it is easy to collect all of these electrons by making one of the ECD electrodes positive, and the flow of electrons registers as a small but easily measured electric current. When a trace of DDT vapour enters the ECD in a stream of nitrogen, close to one electron is removed for each molecule of DDT, and the current decreases. By this means as little as 200,000 molecules can be detected and this is equivalent to just over one tenth of a femtogram of DDT. A femtogram is an infinitesimal quantity; it is one thousand million times smaller than a microgram, which itself is a millionth of a gram.

In a way, I first became involved with the ECD in 1948, when I was working on the problem of the common cold. In those days, we knew precious little about the science of this subject, but, as often is the way in states of scientific ignorance, the man in the street knew all that there was to know about the common cold. To him it was quite simple: you caught colds in the winter by getting cold, hence the name. Now, the Medical Research Council was a government institution and therefore not immune to public opinion and political pressure. We thought it might be wise, therefore, to consider the possibility that we caught colds by getting cold. My job was to determine the extent of chilling objectively, and then compare it with clinical data on the frequency of colds. The three factors important in chilling are temperature, humidity, and air movement. The first two are easy to measure, but the air movements in a closed room—draughts, as the English call them—were so slight as to be undetectable by the simple anemometers then available. As usual, I had no option other than to invent a sensitive anemometer.

In those days, it was customary to build, not buy, instruments. Indeed, scientists were expected to invent, and I soon found myself with two novel anemometers. The first was an ultrasonic device that exploited the change in wavelength of sound due to air motion. It worked well, but was still too insensitive to detect the slight air motion we needed to measure. The second method I tried was an ion-drift anemometer. Positive ions move in air at a speed as slow as ten millimetres per second or, if you prefer the older units, about half an inch in a second, in a field of one volt per centimetre. Draughts easily perturb the drift of these slowly moving ions. It was great fun to make such an anemometer and to find that it worked even better than expected.

When I say 'make', I mean it literally. I had to make everything from the electronic amplifier to the sensor itself by hand. Remember also that in those days we used vacuum tubes, not solid-state electronics. I even made the radioactive source needed to ionize the air by scraping the dial paint from gauges taken from the flight deck of old wartime aircraft. These gauges provided a rich harvest of radium. I made the sources by ashing this paint, resuspending the ash in lacquer, and then painting this radioactive lacquer onto the anemometer ion source. It worked well and I was able to take it on my Arctic expedition in the winter of 1949. Its only drawback was that cigarette smoke perturbed its response; it was as sensitive to this as is a reformed smoker. To discover the cause of this disturbance by smoke and perhaps find a cure, I exposed the anemometer to a number of different gases and smokes and found that, in addition to smoke, CFCs disturbed its function. At the time, we did not need a device to detect low levels of halocarbons and so the electron capture detector was, in a sense, prematurely discovered.

In 1951, having by then found out little more about the cause of the common cold—other than that it was not chilling—I was moved back to our parent institute in London. My new task was to work on the preservation of life in the frozen state as described in Chapter 4. As I did my freezing experiments, I became aware that the fatty acid composition of cell membrane lipids was important in their sensitivity to freezing damage. Archer Martin and Tony James were in a lab one floor above me and I knew of their newly invented gas chromatograph. I asked them what chance there was of analysing the fatty acid composition of my cell lipids. At first, they were enthusiastic, but when they saw how small were my samples, just a few hundred micrograms, they advised me to extract larger samples. As an afterthought, Martin added that perhaps I could invent a more sensitive detector than his gas density balance. Larger-scale experiments with cell membranes would have required about two months' work. To go back to inventing seemed much more fun. I remembered the sensitive ionization anemometer I had made in 1949 and how easily the presence of CFCs disturbed it. I wondered how I could turn this disadvantage of the anemometer to advantage as the basis for an ionization detector.

At the National Institute it was the tradition of those days never to read the literature, especially textbooks. Senior scientists asserted that our job was to make the literature, not read it. This recipe worked well for me. Had I read the literature of ionization phenomena in gases before doing my experiments, I would have been hopelessly discouraged and confused. Instead, I just experimented. Fortunately, the excesses of the health and safety bureaucracy did not hamper us, like now. The Institute expected its scientists to be personally responsible when they used dangerous chemicals or radioactive materials. There was some risk, but I doubt if under the stifling restrictions of today I would have had the persistence to carry on with so uncertain a project as the infant ECD.

I modelled my first detector on the Dutch scientist H Boer's design of the ionization cross-section detector. The Boer detector was, in effect, a gas thickness gauge so that the denser the gas, the greater the numbers of ions, and consequently the larger the flow of current. I tried a detector made from a simple cylindrical ion chamber, about two millilitres in volume and which contained a twenty-millicurie strontium-90 beta-particle source.

I remember bending the stiff silver foil of this radioactive source behind a sheet of thick glass to protect me from its hard beta rays. Eventually its curvature was narrow enough to fit the detector cavity. I then joined the case of the detector to a source of negative electrical potential and the central electrode to a home-made electrometer. This used a pair of vacuum tubes in a balanced cathode follower circuit and I made the electrometer on our kitchen table at home. I purchased the electronic components from surplus equipment vendors in downtown London. The chromatograph itself consisted of a 1.2 metre-long straight glass column filled with a powder coated with a non-volatile hydrocarbon mixture called apiezon. I mounted the column vertically within a solid rod of aluminium, 2.5-centimetre in diameter and electrically heated. It ran at a temperature of about 100° C.

This ionization cross-section detector works best with light carrier gases such as helium or hydrogen; it is similar in this respect to the thermal conductivity detector in its performance. Helium was then expensive in Europe and hydrogen was unacceptable for use in a high-temperature apparatus expected to run overnight unattended. I was obliged, therefore, to use nitrogen as the carrier gas—as did Martin and James with their gas density balance. It was easy enough to confirm Boer's performance figures, but these were miserably insensitive when compared with those of Martin's gas density balance. The first ionization detector did not seem to be promising. Sometimes when confronted with a failed experiment or an unsatisfactory device, it is better to cut one's losses and move on to something else, but in this instance I remembered how well the ion anemometer worked and how its sensitivity was very dependent upon the applied potential. I thought it at least worth trying a few experiments to see if different ranges of applied potential would improve the performance of the ionization cross-section detector.

It was easiest to try low potentials first. I soon found that if I polarized the detector with less than thirty volts, the ion current in pure nitrogen became a little less, but that when other substances were present it became much less. Tony James had supplied me with a test mixture containing methyl propionate, methyl butyrate, methyl valerate and methyl caproate—these are pleasant smelling volatile liquids, chemicals like those that give fruit its flavour. With the detector operating at 100–300 V, one milligram of this mixture gave four small peaks. When I tried it with only ten volts and reversed the recorder connection in order to reveal negative peaks positively, the one-milligram sample gave what seemed to be a never-ceasing range of off-scale peaks. I thought that the search was over and that we now had a truly sensitive detector. I asked James and Martin to come and try it, which they did, bringing with them an allegedly pure sample of methyl caproate. I shall never forget the look of amazement on Tony James's face as peak after peak was drawn from a small sample of this substance. Worse, none of them had the retention time of methyl caproate or of any other fatty-acid ester. We now know that what we saw were traces of electron-absorbing impurities in the sample, but at that time, it seemed to be a useless and wholly anomalous device.

In spite of this disappointment, I continued to play with it whenever there was time, and by trying compounds chosen at random from the lab shelves, I discovered a certain sense in its behaviour. It seemed to respond to reactive compounds like ketones and alcohols but not to hydrocarbons and ethers. When I tried a mixture of compounds made up in the relatively unreactive solvent, carbon tetrachloride, the ion current fell to zero and remained there, resisting all attempts to restore normal operation. I did not realize that the ECD is so sensitive to compounds like carbon tetrachloride that mere traces evaporating from surfaces within the chromatograph were enough to overload it for a week.

For the ordinary gas chromatograph, we clearly needed something more sensitive than the original ionization detector, but less temperamental than the electron capture detector. Nevertheless, I continued to experiment with the ECD, and by 1959 I had reduced it to the practical form now used. It was then, and still is, the most sensitive, easily portable and inexpensive analytical device in existence. It is not easy to describe the exquisite sensitivity of the ECD. One way is to imagine that you had a wine bottle full of a rare perfluorocarbon liquid somewhere in Japan and that you poured this liquid onto a blanket and left it to dry in the air by itself. With a little effort, we could detect the vapour that had evaporated into the air from that blanket here in Devon a few weeks later. Within two years, it would be detectable by the ECD anywhere in the world.

I am often told that I must be rich because of the patent royalties accumulating from the ECD invention. It is true that my name is on the patent for the ECD, but royalties there have been none. The US Government seized the patent soon after its issue in 1964. What happened was this. In 1958 Dr Sandy Lipsky invited me to spend a sabbatical at Yale University in the Department of Internal Medicine where he was a professor. I travelled there with all my family and spent eight happy months in the small Connecticut community of Orange just outside New Haven. It was a wholly different experience from the difficult times in Boston three years earlier. While at Yale I reduced the ECD to practice and it worked well enough to justify a paper, which Sandy Lipsky and I published in the *Journal of the American Chemical Society*. Before publication, the Department suggested that it would be wise to apply for a patent. If the device was a success and the patent granted we agreed a three-way share between the University, a patent agency and me. I was happy with this proposal; a third share seemed better than no share at all. But when the patent was issued in 1964, I received a curt notice from the US Surgeon General's Department demanding that I assign the patent immediately to them. I refused equally curtly, saying that it was my invention, not theirs. Shortly after, a much more conciliatory letter came from the Dean of the School of Medicine of Yale asking me to reconsider and assign the patent to the US Government as requested by them. The reason given was that the Government was threatening to shut off grants to the Department unless I complied. The University told me that their agreement with the grant-funding agency included a clause that made all patents filed by the department I had worked in the property of the Surgeon-General. At the time I thought that the ECD was a minor invention and unlikely to be worth much. Certainly, I thought, not worth imposing hardship on my friends at Yale. Therefore, I assigned the patent. Looking back, I realize how naïve I was to comply without at least a minor battle.

The early ECD was an extraordinarily difficult device to use. It was prone to peculiar, even false results that frustrated scientists accused me of promoting a bogus device whose predictions were of no more use than those of a fortune teller. At times, I tended to agree with them, and it took several months to discover the cause of the ECD's mis-behaviour. It was, I found, due to the complex behaviour of the ionized gas inside the detector, complicated by the absorption of vapours on the detector surfaces. The cure for the electron capture detector's bad habits came from an encounter with Ken McAffee, a physicist at the Bell Telephone Laboratories. He had developed a way to observe the drift of electrons in a gas that involved applying brief pulses of electrical potential. It occurred to me that most of the difficulties with the ECD were due to the slow collection of the free electrons in a weak electrical field, and that I could resolve these difficulties by collecting the electrons using a brief high-voltage pulse. It worked well: the high-potential pulses overcame the all-too-frequent contact potentials and space charges that unpredictably either enhanced or opposed electron collection. Later, I found that by observing the frequency of pulses needed to sustain a constant electron population, the detector became even more stable and reliable. This method is now the one almost universally used. Its only drawback is a non-linear response to strongly electron-attaching compounds.

As I gained experience in the analysis of different molecular species by electron capture, I grew aware of an odd and interesting association between electron capture and biological activity. In 1960 and 1961, the last years of the Mill Hill apprenticeship, my experiments with the electron capture detector showed that a large proportion of the substances detected were in two main groups. The first group consisted of those important in metabolism, for example the alternate acids of the famous Krebs cycle, steroid and thyroid hormones, and other molecules important in the metabolism of living cells. The other group of substances the ECD detected were poisons, in particular, substances that interfered with metabolism, such as the nitro compounds, dinitrophenol or diodophenol, and all halogenated pesticides. The ECD also seemed to be uniquely sensitive to cancer-causing substances. Hydrocarbons, as oils or waxes, do not conduct electricity, nor do they react with electrons. But certain, special hydrocarbons, made of rings of carbon atoms fused together and called polycyclicaromatic hydrocarbons, capture electrons strongly. These unusual hydrocarbons included most of the carcinogenic ones. I could say that a tendency of a substance to capture electrons was all too often associated with carcinogenesis. Nowadays, whenever I come across a chemical substance that is strongly electron absorbing, I tend to regard it cautiously. I well recall critical scientists arguing that the apparent association between carcinogenesis and electron capture was illusory, since so many of the halocarbons were not carcinogenic. Vinyl chloride, chloroform, and trichloroethylene, they said, are substances safe enough for use as anaesthetics in surgery. Now, of course, we know them to be carcinogenic. I sometimes wonder about the phthalate esters. These ubiquitous plasticizers have long been a nuisance as electron-absorbing contaminants. We now suspect them to have a more sinister role as surrogate oestrogens.

It was tempting to speculate that the free electron might be a fundamental particle of biology as well as of chemistry and physics. It was a challenging coincidence that each alternate acid of the Krebs cycle (the major pathway for the oxidation of lipids and carbohydrates) was one of the few organic compounds that reacted vigorously with free electrons. These include pyruvate, oxaloacetate, fumarate, ketoglutarate, and cis-aconitate. It is still unclear whether this association is real or coincidental, but there is no doubt that a remarkably high proportion of electron absorbers are biologically active, which makes the electron capture detector so important a device in environmental science.

I tried at Mill Hill to use free electrons in equilibrium with molecules at room temperature as if they were a chemical reagent. To do this I borrowed a sewing needle from Janet Niven, a friend from my virology days. I placed the needle in a stream of mixed argon and methane gases and applied 10,000 volts of negative potential to it. There was a visible blue glow and a current of several microamperes flowed in the gas. The electrons released by the strong electric field near the needle point rapidly bounced among the gas molecules and became slowed to thermal energies. I let them flow towards substances like the acids of the Krebs cycle to see what happened. The experiments suggested that in nature a free electron is indeed a fundamental particle of biochemistry. But before I could complete these experiments, it was time to leave Mill Hill. I published the preliminaries in three papers, two in *Nature* and one as a Symposium record.

While I was just experimenting, serious scientists were applying the detector to the practical analysis of pesticide residues in foodstuffs. In the USA, Watts and Klein of the FDA, and in the UK Goulden and his colleagues at Shell, together established the base data on the global distribution of pesticides and soon we realized that pesticides like DDT and dieldrin were everywhere and in all living things. This was the information that led Rachel Carson to write her seminal book, *Silent Spring*, a book that warned the world of the ultimate consequences if these chemicals continued to be used by farmers against all forms of life that are not livestock or crops. This important book has changed the course of politics and, in many parts of the world, her gloomy forecast of a silent spring has come true. Although not, as she predicted, by pesticide poisoning, but simply by habitat destruction.

When I first heard of this use of the electron capture detector I was delighted. I shared with Rachel Carson a concern over damage to wildlife and to natural ecosystems. Some parts of the chemical industry reacted in a shameful and foolish way by trying to discredit her as a person. It did not work. Quite the reverse, it made Rachel Carson the first saint and martyr for the infant and innocent Green Movement.

As environmentalism evolved, Rachel Carson's vision and the data itself became corrupted. I do not mean that the data gathered was false, but so sensitive is the electron capture detector that it can detect utterly trivial quantities of pesticides and other chemicals. Before we used the ECD, it would have been quite easy and reasonable to set zero as the lower permissible limit of pesticide residues in foodstuff. In practice, zero means the least detectable amount. After the electron capture detector appeared, zero as a limit became so low that to apply it in full would cause the rejection of nearly everything that was edible. Even organically grown vegetables and fruit, even wild vegetation, contains measurable levels of pesticides, so sensitive is the device.

We needed common sense and the acceptance of the wisdom of the physician Paracelsus who said long ago, 'The poison is the dose'. Even water is poisonous in excess. Even the deadly nerve gases are harmless at the level of a picogram, easily detectable by an electron capture detector. Unfortunately, common sense is a rare commodity. I listened with astonishment to a recent radio broadcast by a Green who argued that Paracelsus's statement was no more than sophistry. Too many Greens are not just ignorant of science; they hate science. But despite this, they use the results gathered by the ECD and other instruments of science to support their crusades. The next intervention of the ECD into Green politics was in the relatively clear-cut problem of ozone depletion by halocarbons. I will describe my personal experiences in this 'Ozone War' in Chapter 8.

This is not the place to discuss the theory of the electron capture detector, but it is an opportunity to mention a few interesting theoretical aspects of the device which otherwise are rarely revealed. I find it helpful to think of the detector as a small reaction vessel like a test tube, holding a dilute mixture of free electrons in an inert gas, and I look on these dilute electrons as a chemical reagent. When an electron is in equilibrium with a gas at room temperature it behaves as if it were a very large particle, larger even than most of the molecules it encounters. Unlike the fast-moving electrons that physicists encounter, the cool electron is no tiny billiard ball or point charge, it is a sizeable wave packet with a wavelength of seven nanometres at room temperature. The large size of the cool electron makes encounters with molecules more probable and accounts for the great sensitivity of the ECD. The chemical reaction between electrons and molecules is what physical chemists call second-order, and some of the problems faced by analysts arise from this fact. If the electron capture detector were insensitive and the number of molecules present were vastly greater than the number of electrons, the device would be proportional and predictable in its response. Unfortunately, with the compounds it detects sensitively (those which the analyst seeks to measure), the numbers of molecules in the detector are comparable with the number of electrons. In such circumstances, as textbook physical chemistry would tell you, the response of the detector to varying sample size is unlikely to be either proportional or easily predictable. Lack of sensitivity was not a complaint levelled at the electron capture detector. Even so, once we realized the possibilities of electron-attaching tags or tracers, that ultimate of detecting single molecules was the new destination.

We are still far from taking a grab sample of air or water and finding in it one molecule of tracer. The best we can now do is to detect 100,000 molecules of tracer in a cubic centimetre of air. We have shown that certain fluorinated hydrocarbons can label air masses and let us follow their movement over thousands of miles. Andrew Watson has used the same technique to trace the movement of water masses in the oceans. We can now detect directly one part in 10^{14}, an improvement made possible by signal processing using gas-switching techniques. This improvement makes it feasible to detect and measure tracer at one part in 10^{16} after a modest 100-fold concentration. Every year of this odyssey I have expected to find this simple device that anyone could make superseded by some impressive flight of high technology. Instead, its use seems to be expanding into new territories.

8

The Ozone War

A dense haze that steals the sun's warmth and blurs vision so that half a mile is the limit of seeing sometimes spoils summer days in England. I was puzzled about this haze because I could not remember seeing it as a boy or even before about 1950. I suspected that the haze was some form of air pollution like smog, but smogs in England were wintertime phenomena, fed by the smoke from open fires. The disastrous smog of 1952 killed nearly 4000 people in one night, and is still in our memories, but since then smokeless fuel has replaced the sulphurous coal and the winter sky, even in London, is clear. So, what was the new miasma that spoilt the summer air? What puritan phenomenon stopped us from enriching our eyes on the full-bosomed and lush English countryside? My scientist friends had nothing to offer in explanation; they even doubted my memories of clean air before the Second World War. One person whose writing led me to suspect that he would listen with sympathy to my concern was Hubert Lamb. He was a staff member of the meteorological office in Bracknell and I went there to see if he could explain it.

In 1966 the Meteorological Office was in the new town of Bracknell. It was my first visit there and I was astonished to find that it was part of the Ministry of Defence. We English have always been paranoid about the weather but this seemed too much. Did we now see it as a national resource and treasure that needed the army to protect it? Intriguingly, the United States, then flexing its military muscles and obsessed with secrecy, put their weather bureau in the Department of Commerce. Perhaps they thought their weather good enough to sell. I propitiated the guards at this Ministry of Defence establishment, they gave me a pass for my visit and took me to Hubert Lamb's office. He welcomed me warmly, but seemed embarrassed by an office rule that required him to charge me for my talk with him. The fee was £5. To have a charge to make upon scientific visitors clearly upset him, but the bureaucrats imposed it and I did not see it as either a source of indignation or something that was a deterrent. We enjoyed a lively discussion on weather phenomena and I stayed for lunch and met others who seemed equally interested in my haze observations. What seemed to turn on their interest and make them take me seriously was my presentation of my observations as graphs. These compared the haze in Wiltshire, as it changed with the season, with that in Los Angeles. The smog in rural Wiltshire in the summer was almost as bad as that in urban Los Angeles.

By the late 1960s, it was a family ritual at Bowerchalke to measure the haze density using a sun photometer. We used a simple hand-held, battery-powered instrument that Robert McCormick, an NOAA meteorologist, had lent to me. Few such measurements were made in England and Hubert Lamb thought that visibility ranges, which had been observed daily at the meteorological stations throughout the British Isles, would have to do instead. They might provide some evidence on whether or not haziness had changed as time went by. My daughter, Christine, was as interested in this phenomenon as I was and had taken charge of the photometer readings. I arranged with Lamb for her to visit the Met office library and list the visibilities back to the start of the century. It was a disappointing exercise: no discernible trend was available from the records, but I am not the kind of scientist who is discouraged by one set of negative evidence. The haze of southern England looked to me like smog and I thought hard about gathering further evidence that would confirm or deny my ideas about its origin.

It occurred to me that a chemical analysis of both clean and hazy air might provide evidence of the origin of the haze. I could have collected haze particles that obscured the air by impacting them on sticky microscope slides or I could have analysed the air for sulphur dioxide and other products of combustion. I decided not to do either of these things, partly because the known analytical methods were not sensitive enough, but mainly because the presence of small amounts of haze-producing chemicals in the air does not tell us where the air came from. They could have come from natural or agricultural emissions as well as urban industrial sources. What would be proof would be to detect in the country air some substance that originated unequivocally in an urban industrial region and which had no, or a negligible, source in the countryside. One class of substance that fitted this specification well was CFCs, then used in aerosol cans and in refrigerators. By far the greatest release of these compounds occurs in large cities. Better still, I had in my lab at Bowerchalke an apparatus able to detect and measure them easily, even at extreme dilution.

So, in 1969 we started at Bowerchalke the simultaneous measurement of haze, wind direction, and the chlorofluorocarbon, FC11. Later the same year I took these measurements at Adrigole in far western Ireland. At both Adrigole and Bowerchalke the CFCs were more abundant when the air was hazy and it seemed that my notion that the haze was man-made was correct. I published the results in the *Journal of Atmospheric Environment*. I chose this journal because my friend, Jim Lodge, who was then on the staff of National Center for Atmospheric Research, was its editor. Having a friend as an editor eases the otherwise tedious process of satisfying the self-appointed tyranny of the peer-review system. The editor could at least select reviewers from a panel of reliable critics who would treat the paper reasonably and not from those who wanted a chance to vent their anger anonymously.

The *Atmospheric Environment* paper suggested that southern England, and indeed, western Ireland, was sometimes during the summer immersed in the same kind of smog that plagued Los Angeles, but nobody outside my small circle of scientific acquaintances showed any interest at the time. In 1973 I collaborated with atmospheric scientists from Harwell and we showed that even in far western Ireland, foul air from Europe had ozone levels in it that were above the American Environmental Protection Agency's safe limits. We published these findings in *Nature*, but again there was little interest from either environmental groups or the media. This small investigation might have ended, but I was curious about the fifty parts per trillion of one of the CFCs, FC11, in the clean Atlantic air. Had it drifted across the Atlantic from America? More excitingly, were the CFCs accumulating in the Earth's atmosphere without any means for their removal? To find out, the only thing to do would be to travel by ship to the southern hemisphere and measure the CFCs as the ship travelled across the world.

Although I was surviving as an independent, I welcomed the offer from Reading University of a Visiting Professorship. It made the publication of papers easier, and provided me with a respectable cover. It was an honorary arrangement and money never passed from me to the university or vice versa. It allowed postgraduate students interested in Gaia to work with me as research assistants. Andrew Watson, now a distinguished Professor at the University of East Anglia, and a friend, met me this way. Most of all I valued the chance it gave to discuss my science problems with Professor Peter Fellgett, chairman of the Department of Cybernetics. We would do so over lunch at his home, with his wife Mary, and at one of these working lunches, he suggested that I apply to the funding agencies, NERC (the Natural Environment Research Council) or the Scientific and Engineering Research Council, SERC, for support. He helped me to ask for a small grant to measure dimethyl sulphide, methyl iodide, and the CFCs aboard the research ship, *Shackleton*, which was due to make its voyage to Antarctica and back later the same year. After some months, we heard from NERC that the academic review committee had rejected my proposal, but they asked if an NERC senior staff member, Mrs Howells, could visit me. She came to tea one afternoon in the early summer of 1971. We sat in the large sitting room of our Bowerchalke house. Our architect had designed it to conform to the village and it sat, hidden from view, perched above the village high street. The room gave a god's eye view of the village and its pub. We were able to look down on the villagers, but the angle was too steep for them to see us. Double-glazing served to isolate us further.

Mrs Howells was a warm, pleasant woman, but she seemed embarrassed as she held her teacup and tried a piece of Helen's home-made cake. I had asked for modest support to travel by ship to the southern hemisphere to measure the CFCs in the atmosphere throughout the journey, but as a civil servant, Mrs Howells could not, by herself, approve my application. All proposals had to be examined and judged by a committee composed of scientific specialists from universities and government departments like the Meteorological Office. Her bad news was that this expert panel had rejected my proposal, and Peter Fellgett told me later that it was rejected unanimously. Not only this, but appended to their report was the complaint that bogus proposals such as mine should not in future be presented to the committee, it wasted their time. Their annoyance stemmed from the fact that the senior chemist of the committee was sure that no one could measure the chlorofluorocarbons at parts-per-trillion levels, as I had claimed I could do. He said the CFCs are amongst the most inert chemical compounds known and it would be difficult to measure their abundance in the atmosphere at the parts-per-million level; it was impossible to measure them at the parts-per-trillion level and therefore the proposal was bogus. Now this was a profoundly ignorant statement and could only have come from a narrow specialist, unaware of the advances in other branches of chemistry. Unfortunately, grant committees sometimes become cosy coteries of cronies who judge proposals from each other and each other's friends. It is a danger insufficiently watched by the community at large who pay the taxes, which ultimately go to fund the grants.

Mrs Howells mentioned none of this, but she did say the other staff members of the NERC thought my proposal was a good one and the purpose of her visit was twofold. First, to check that I really could measure CFCs at the parts-per-trillion level and, secondly, to offer me passage on the *Shackleton*, which was travelling down to Antarctica in the coming November. The ship was due to call at Montevideo in Uruguay and they thought that if I wished to return from there, NERC would pay my fare. As far as the expedition was concerned, I would have to supply the equipment and any personnel other than myself. Because the academic committee rejected my proposal, NERC could only offer this limited support. I was delighted: I could easily afford to make a simple gas chromatograph for the voyage. I would travel and do the measurement at least as far as Montevideo myself; I could afford that much time. My graduate student, Bob Maggs, was keen to do the return voyage from Montevideo back to Wales in 1972.

We were then taking daily measurements of the chlorofluorocarbons at Bowerchalke, so I was able to show Mrs Howells just how routine and easy was the procedure. I must have convinced her that I was a professional scientist and not a crooked outsider fraudulently seeking the welfare of a grant. She saw it as an exciting project and gave her approval. The apparatus I intended to take on the ship was so simple that I was able to make it in a few days. It ran without failure throughout the six-month voyage. The total cost of the research, including the apparatus, was a few hundred pounds, but the discoveries of the voyage led to the 'Ozone War' and to the international research programme on the links between marine algae, DMS, clouds, and climate. Taken together, these must have given employment to thousands of scientists.

The Voyage of the *Shackleton* in 1971–2

I spent much of my spare time in the next few months preparing for the voyage. The apparatus I took with me was simple. I arranged with the British Oxygen Company the purchase of four small cylinders filled with nitrogen gas. I used this carrier gas in my measurements and I decided on four small cylinders, not one large one, because I knew that leaks could all too easily develop in gas lines coming from cylinders, especially on a ship that is moving around all the time. The thought of finding myself half way to Antarctica with no gas for measurements was too embarrassing to contemplate. With four cylinders, at worst I would only lose a quarter of the total supply if a leak developed. In fact, no leaks developed throughout the course of the voyage. But it was good to have the backup.

I made sure that the boxes now filling for the voyage contained two or more of everything that I might need. To measure dimethyl sulphide was much more difficult a task than to measure the CFCs. I had a version of the flame photometric sulphur detector already working at Bowerchalke, but it was too insensitive and too cumbersome to contemplate using on the ship. I decided instead to extract the dimethyl sulphide from the seawater samples collected by the ship and then store them in the ship's refrigerator. We intended to analyse them on the ship's return. This worked well, and Bob Maggs did the analyses back in Bowerchalke in 1972.

In the early autumn, I made a journey to Barry Docks near Cardiff in Wales to see the *Shackleton* and negotiate the small amount of lab space I would need with the chief scientist of the expedition, Peter Barker of Birmingham University. Barry Docks are huge, dismal and all but deserted, like a theme park devoted to Britain's past industrial history. The presence of Butlins Holiday Camp at the edge of the near-deserted docks increased the theme park atmosphere. There were railway sidings full of rusting steam locomotives; some had shapes I had never before seen. There were a few banana ships moored at one dock so I suppose it was not entirely dead, but grass and yellow-flowered ragwort filled the gaps along the railway lines. I could find no one who knew where the *Shackleton* was moored, so I drove around this vast maze until I saw a small one-storey building with an NERC sign above it. They directed me to the mooring place, which they said was beyond a group of disused cranes. I looked for a ship's mast and funnel but could see nothing. I parked my car and walked to the edge of the dock. There below me, like a child's toy ship, was the small vessel. It was tiny compared with the banana ships, but soon it would take me to South America.

I climbed down and boarded. The *Shackleton* was a converted Baltic coaster of a few hundred tons displacement, powered by a diesel engine. Part of the conversion was a bow thruster, a propulsion mechanism in the ship's bows in addition to the main propeller, which made the ship unusually manoeuvrable and no doubt was required for the time it spent among the ice floes. The lab area was at the deck level and spacious. They gave me about twelve feet of bench with wooden drawers and cupboards beneath and a 230-volt electricity supply with normal three-pin plugs at the bench top. This was all fine by me. I never could see the point of bulky apparatus in science unless it was truly necessary. The ship was in the midst of preparation for the voyage and in an untidy and unwelcoming state, rather like a house full of builders and decorators. I returned to my car and drove back to Bowerchalke. As I drove through the Gloucestershire countryside, I could not help wondering what the voyage would be like. The view of the ship at Barry made it look uncomfortable. Almost, it seemed to me, like trying to do experimental science in a Tube train full of rush-hour passengers.

November came and I made my farewells to the family and travelled to stay the night at a small hotel in Barry, from which I boarded the ship next day. It was not due to sail until the evening tide and so there was plenty of time to set up the equipment and try it out. The ship had now been transformed since my previous visit and looked tidy and shipshape, and moving around was no longer an obstacle course strewn with large wooden crates and thick cables. The ship's mate Nigel Jonas took me to my cabin, which was far better than I had expected. It was at the level of the bridge and was where the ship's officers had their cabins. I was in the ship's sickbay, normally the home of the ship's doctor. It was a roomy and comfortable cabin, provided with a desk and all that I would need.

Lunch was in the ship's dining room just beneath the bridge. It was a cosy, pleasant room and gave me my first taste of the food we were to enjoy during the next three weeks. Like most English ships of those times, the quality of the food served was excellent. As a maritime nation, we understood well the need for an interesting and varied diet to relieve what to many sailors is the monotony of a long voyage. After lunch, I made a few measurements of the CFCs and other halocarbons in the air of Barry docks. The equipment was working well, but the air was rich with all kinds of chemicals that could be recognized by my ECD; not the background air that I wanted to measure.

Soon after dusk fell the gangway was detached, the moorings loosened, and, as we slipped away from the Barry docks, once again that most estimable of emotions overcame me—the sense of overwhelming contentment that fills me when I am on a ship that has just set sail. Sometimes on a plane, especially after a fraught and delayed departure, there is a feeling of relief as it leaves the runway, but that is a pale imitation of the joy of severing contact with the land which is the gift of a ship's departure. There is something good about becoming, even temporarily, part of a proper-sized human community. November in 1971 was a quiet, slightly foggy time and our passage down the Bristol Channel to the Atlantic was easy, just the gentle lively roll that came from the Atlantic swell. I think that I am immune to seasickness, so the ship's motion was always for me something to enjoy, to lull me to sleep when the time came to retire to my cabin.

At dinner that evening I met our captain, Shelby Smith, and the ship's officers. They had made sure that we had some good wine to drink with our meal. That night I retired early, replete and looking forward to an exciting and rewarding voyage amongst good companions. I rose early next day and took my first sea and air samples as we travelled somewhere near Cornwall. The wind was drifting from the east and the CFC levels were still high. I took my air sample at the ship's bows using one of the two large holes through which the anchor chains passed. A wind usually blew through these holes and made them an ideal place for taking clean air samples. Compared with other research vessels the *Shackleton* was free of chemicals but I had to keep in mind the ship's refrigerators that might be leaking CFCs. Moreover, some of my companions might be using aerosol cans of shaving soap or deodorant powered by CFCs. I drew the 5-ml sample of air into a clean glass hypodermic syringe with a needle attached. I did this several times to make sure that the sample was clean air and not some memory of past air residing on the glass surfaces of the syringe. I took my filled syringe back to the ship's laboratory, injected the air into my gas chromatograph, and watched the peaks appear. First, came the oxygen of the air, a large off-scale deflection; soon after came the peak for chlorofluorocarbon 11, then a tiny pair of peaks of methyl iodide and carbon disulphide, and finally a broader peak of carbon tetrachloride.

All was going well and I went in for breakfast. This was full English fare: cereals, porridge, all kinds of eggs, bacon, sausages, fried bread, and so on, followed by toast and marmalade and washed down with lots of tea or coffee. I rapidly decided that cereals and a slice of toast were all I needed on this comparatively sedentary voyage. At first, there had been a rush to set up and make sure that everything was working but now, after eating, I had time to look around the ship. I wandered over to the other occupants of the main laboratory, a party of scientists who were making a gravity survey in the southern oceans but were also taking measurements as we travelled down the Atlantic. Compared to mine, their apparatus and their team were substantial. I got to know them better when, in mid-voyage, the ship's technician and I discovered for them the source of mysterious and disturbing signals that appeared without warning in the middle of their charts and interfered with their measurements. It was the Morse code of the ship's radio transmitter picked up by their ultra-sensitive electronics. We cured it with some aluminium foil from the galley, which we used as shielding.

Another scientist on the ship occupied a sizeable lab closer to the bows; he was Hans Greese, a student of the German scientist, Wolfgang Seiler. His lab was festooned with a beautiful and intricate array of blown glass and in it he was measuring atmospheric carbon monoxide (CO). The student was from the Max Planck Institute at Mainz in Germany, a famous scientific centre for atmospheric research run by the distinguished scientist, Christian Jünge. Most of us think of carbon monoxide as a poisonous gas that comes from incomplete combustion and which is a favourite for suicides, since it is odourless and painless to breathe. Carbon monoxide, strangely, is a natural substance present in fresh air everywhere in the atmosphere of the Earth, but at an average level of only 80–90 parts per billion. It comes from the natural oxidation of methane gas in the atmosphere, and from the combustion of fossil fuels. Hans's apparatus collected, separated, and analysed this substance. His objective was to discover the difference in abundance of CO between the northern and southern hemispheres, just as I was doing for the CFCs, but his work was hard and unremitting, and only rarely had he time to leave his laboratory. I felt almost ashamed by the ease of my measurements and the way they allowed me time to wander around the ship and wonder about the ever-changing scene.

By mid-morning, it was time to take the first water samples. A research ship like the *Shackleton* has a pump to draw in fresh seawater from the bows so that the scientists aboard have a continuous sample of the sea the ship passes through. My first sample of this water was so laden with chlorine and sulphur compounds that it overloaded the chromatograph and I could make no analysis. I was sure that these substances were not in the sea itself but were contaminants coming from the pump or the pipes through which the water flowed. I could see no way to get a truly clean water sample from this source, so I tried collecting sea water by tying a small bucket to a rope and dropping it over the side of the ship. This was foolish, for the fierce pull of the rope nearly dragged me overboard, and I should have calculated that a bucket dropped into water flowing past at 14 mph exerts a pull of over 100 pounds. Contritely, I asked the ship's technician if he had a smaller vessel I could use. Lab vessels such as beakers were much too fragile; saucepans too difficult to manoeuvre on our rope. Then suddenly we wondered whether we could use a teapot? Sure enough, the galley had an old aluminium teapot now retired from use. This we tied to our rope, and everything was easy from then on. Every day we lowered it into the sea and used it as a source of surface water samples.

The sight of our teapot sampling stirred the serious-minded company of scientists; some were derisive of such low technology, others were appalled. One of them, who was not experimenting until the ship reached Antarctica, said to me, 'You know, the ship has proper Nansen bottles for water sampling and I'm sure the captain will stop to let you sample down to lower depths.' Captain Shelby Smith was more than willing to do this, and at frequent intervals we stopped to lower ships' bottles by cable down to depths as low as several hundred metres. Again, I was frustrated in my measurements, this time by the rubber closures of these bottles. The rubber absorbed and later released any volatile chemicals in the air around it. This memory of past atmospheres contaminated the water samples from these Nansen bottles. We tried several tricks. Taking the rubber and boiling it in water for hours helped, so did leaving the bottles exposed open to the sun and air on the deck before use. In the end, we used bottles without the rubber closures. They leaked, but not enough to prevent them serving my needs. Up until this voyage, marine scientists had been interested only in the inorganic constituents of seawater—things like salt, acidity, and other minerals. The rubber-sealed Nansen bottles were fine for this need. No one had anticipated the need to collect volatile organic vapours like the CFCs and DMS, and so they never designed bottles for this purpose.

It stayed cool as we passed the African coast. We pulled into a deserted harbour in Mauritania for some ship's repairs, but otherwise saw little of the land until we passed the Canary Islands. The captain told me that for much of the voyage we would be following the track of the *Beagle* that took Charles Darwin on his journey of discovery 120 years earlier. It was a thought that inspired us all to make this voyage significant in some scientific way.

The next day dawned hot, a sudden transition from the mild oceanic air we knew so well at home in England to tropical heat and humidity; the air temperature rose from 18° C to 27° C and the sea-water from 18° C to 25° C. Shortly after this, a younger member of the ship's crew had a fall that left him in pain and with restricted movement. The Captain came to me and said, 'You are a doctor. Can you have a look at him and tell us what we should do?' 'I'm not a proper doctor,' I said, 'I'm not qualified to practice or treat people.' Shelby Smith replied, 'You are the nearest we have to a physician on the ship and you will just have to do for now. After all, you have a PhD in medicine; surely you can do better than I can.' We had the boy carefully taken to my bed in the sickbay. He was conscious and his breathing rate and pulse were normal but he had back pain and found it difficult to move. Two things I remembered from my Medical Research Council years were: first, there are only three real medical emergencies—asphyxia, haemorrhage, and cardiac arrest. Secondly, when in doubt, do nothing and seek expert advice. This I did via the ship's radio. We called Portishead in England and they connected me to the physician on duty. He spoke with an accent, which was difficult to understand over the crackling and fading short-wave radio link, but I gave him an account of the accident and the boy's symptoms. He replied, 'It sounds like a spinal column injury. He must go to the nearest hospital as soon as possible. He certainly should not travel the rest of the voyage with its danger of rough seas and further damage.' Captain Shelby Smith immediately changed course for the nearest port, which was Dacca in Senegal. Here, an English-speaking, French physician examined the boy and then treated his injured back. The captain and the boy returned to the ship and I was able to return to my cabin for the rest of the voyage. The stay in Dacca was brief, but we did enrich our supplies of fruit and fish from the boats that flocked around us in the port.

We started towards the Cape Verde Islands. That evening at dinner the mate warned us not to wander on the ship's decks without using sun block. He said there was plenty of it in the ship's stores. Sunburn is a serious problem in tropical waters. Typically, we took little notice of this warning and, as we sailed further south, still in the northern hemisphere, nothing in the way of sunburn seemed to happen. Then one day after rising, I noticed that the air seemed different, the parallel streets of cumulus clouds now projected, it seemed, to infinity. The air had, in spite of its warmth, a fresh cleanliness we had not previously experienced. In the night, we had crossed the intertropical convergence that separates the air of the northern hemisphere from that of the southern hemisphere. The southern air is clean and unpolluted; the northern hemisphere is always, to some extent, hazy. As if to punctuate this change, suddenly two flying fish landed on the deck behind me as I took my air sample, and I was entranced. These were living things as strange to me almost as dinosaurs. Many others came on to the ship as we sailed along and we had fresh flying fish for dinner that night.

After breakfast, while collecting water samples, I found my skin burning—that warning sign that sunburn is happening. I went to my cabin and applied the sun block that the ship provided. It worked for me, but some of the others suffered a crop of blisters before adapting to the intense ultraviolet of the southern hemisphere. This incident and the incredible clarity of the night sky with its, unknown to me, constellations and brilliantly defined Milky Way, made real how hazy is the air in which we live in the north. My CFC readings were now down from seventy to forty parts per trillion and they confirmed it. However, the presence of forty parts per trillion of F11 in the southern hemisphere supported my speculation that these substances were distributed throughout the Earth's atmosphere and were accumulating ineluctably.

Near the coast of Brazil, we met our first Atlantic storm. The ship rode it well and I continued my sampling routine, just as if it were still calm. When I took my morning samples at the bow on the second day of the storm the sea was bursting over in a delicious warm shower. As I turned, after collecting my sample of air, I was surprised to find the bosun standing just behind me. I realized that he was there to catch me should a wave threaten to take me overboard. He smiled, but said nothing as we moved back to the lab. I was touched by this unsought but thoughtful gesture from the bosun and from the ship's company, who cared enough for me to make it, and do it without ostentation.

All too soon, the shoreline of the River Plate came in view and we docked at Montevideo in Uruguay. During the last day of the voyage, I had shown Roger Wade, one of the travelling but then not working scientists, how to use my gas chromatograph and he promised to continue the daily sampling for the next five months in Antarctica. In fact, his measurements were so diligent that I had complete confidence when later we came to analyse the charts. Roger's own programme was biological and part of the ship's Antarctic research. By now I dearly wished that I could have gone on, at least to the Falklands, the next port of call, but sadly there was no way for me to return in time for my own commitments. I was due to attend a meeting in the United States the next week. I reluctantly said my goodbyes to my shipmates. Captain Shelby Smith said enigmatically to me as we parted, 'This will be remembered as one of the key research voyages.' He was prescient, for at the time I did not know just how important the CFC and DMS measurements were to be. We gathered so much important scientific information on the *Shackleton*, and at so little cost.

I climbed down the gangway to the shore of Montevideo. As always, it was the land that seemed to be moving, so used was I to the ship's comfortable motion. A pleasant man from the British Consulate met me and guided me through the Uruguayan Customs and Immigration. He and I stood in front of a bench, behind which stood six formidable armed men. My consular friend said, 'Leave it entirely to me. Say nothing whatever.' He gave them my passport for inspection and then began to pass banknotes to the leader of the immigration team until the leader raised his other hand to show that he was satisfied. We moved on to his car. Curious, I asked, 'What would have happened had I landed here alone?' He replied, 'You might well have tried to bribe a junior Customs man, not the leader, and you would have landed in gaol on a corruption charge.' We drove through Montevideo, my first sight of a Latin American town, and then on to the airport. Here, another disquieting ritual of paying the export tax took place, and I was very glad that I had the friendly aid of the man from the Consulate. I then checked in at the Scandinavian Airlines desk for my flight home.

We stopped at Sao Paulo, which in those days was a small green airport, and then at Rio before crossing the Atlantic to Lisbon, where I caught my plane for London. The tantalizing glimpse of that southern American continent by air travel seemed so feeble after the full sensory experience and joy of three weeks on a ship. I published the *Shackleton* voyage results as a paper in *Nature* with the title, 'Halomethanes in and over the Atlantic' and it provided the incident that led to the Ozone War. Foolishly, I stated in the paper that the CFCs represented no conceivable hazard. This gratuitous blunder was due to my concern that politically minded Greens would seize on the paper as proof that the air we breathed was loaded with chlorine-containing chemicals produced by the multinational chemical industry, and that we would all be poisoned as a consequence. I should have said 'no conceivable *toxic* hazard', because at a few parts per trillion the CFCs were in no way poisonous to people or animals.

On my return from the Atlantic, scientists working for the chemical industry inadvertently drew me onto their side of the forces gathering for the Ozone War. A year later, in November 1972, Ray McCarthy and Frank Bower of Dupont held a meeting at a school in Andover in New Hampshire. There were industry scientists and academics at the conference and it was organized like a Gordon Conference (see Chapter 9 for a full description of these unusual conferences), but as far as I know, none of those present at the Andover meeting had any idea of the conflict soon to start. The meeting was a quiet but interesting account of the real and potential toxic hazards of the CFCs. We only touched briefly on the large-scale effects consequent upon their atmospheric abundance. The meeting was billed as the ecology of the CFCs. Much of it was devoted to the tendency of the CFCs, at high concentration, to cause ventricular fibrillation, a fatal chaotic confusion of the beat of the heart. Children, in their search for thrills, would fill plastic bags with CFC gas from an aerosol can and then breathe it in. Sometimes they died. Pathologists presented evidence to show that the deaths were specific poisoning by some of the CFCs and not caused by simple asphyxiation. Curiously, it seemed that fear or excitement enhanced the toxicity. We all agreed that, apart from this extreme effect at very high concentrations, these materials were free of human toxicity and safe in their normal domestic use. In my talk, mainly about the prevalence of the CFCs in the air, I did raise the possibility of large-scale atmospheric effects. I commented that when these gases accumulated above the parts-per-billion levels they might act as potent greenhouse gases and add their effect to that of carbon dioxide. This we all saw was a danger to keep in mind but of no concern now that these gases were present at levels ten times lower than those likely to cause perceptible global warming. In no way were the scientists gathered at this meeting in Andover trying to cover up known dangers or deny the public knowledge of potential hazards. Quite the reverse: they were openly concerned to consider the possibilities of danger.

I do not know if stratospheric chemists were invited to the meeting, and it was not until 1974 that the Molina–Rowland paper appeared. This well-written and finely argued text raised for the first time the possibility that the continued emission of CFCs was a danger to stratospheric ozone. It provided the environmental cause of the rest of the century. Its scientific importance was rightly recognized by the award of the Nobel Prize for Chemistry to Molina, Rowland, and Crutzen in 1996.

The Molina–Rowland theory predicted that the CFCs would decompose in the stratosphere and there release their burden of chlorine, and that this would deplete stratospheric ozone. The 'sink', as the chemists called the depletion process, was oddly above our heads and had been postulated earlier by Ralph Cicerone and Richard Stolarski. The bond-breaking short-wave UV from the sun split the molecules of the CFCs in the upper reaches of the air. I do believe that I had advance notice of the contents of this historic paper and, in early 1974, because no one had confirmed this hypothesis by direct measurement, I thought that it would be useful to make a trip into the stratosphere and find out if the CFCs declined in abundance there as the theory predicted. I tried asking Adrian Tuck, a friendly scientist at the Meteorological Office, if there was a chance for me to take air samples during one of their stratospheric flights. He liked my idea and made enquiries about its feasibility. He soon found that it would take two years at least for me to have permission for such a flight. Any modifications to the aircraft, such as the insertion of a sampling port, would require careful safety surveys and this took time. I then asked friends working for the Ministry of Defence if they knew of any RAF flight that I could use to sample the stratospheric air. They were much more helpful and soon I was at Lyneham airfield talking to the pilot and flight engineer of a Hercules (C130) aircraft. Lyneham is in Wiltshire and was then only about forty miles north of my home in Bowerchalke. The pilot said that he was due to fly the aircraft on a test flight in a week's time. I would be welcome to make my measurements as they went to the aircraft's ceiling at about 45,000 feet altitude. At that time of year the tropopause, the height at which the cloudy, well-mixed lower atmosphere separates from the clear, dry, upper air, was at 30,000 feet. This gave nearly three miles up into the stratosphere for me to take my samples. I arranged with the flight engineer my modest needs and started preparing for the flight the following week.

It was all amazingly easy. There was no charge for the flight and no papers to be completed. They warned me that officially I was not on the aircraft, and that if we were unfortunate enough to crash there could be no compensation. We took off early one afternoon and made towards Northern Ireland, climbing as we went. I sat on the flight deck with the flight engineer and took my air samples in stainless steel cylinders. I compressed the samples of thin outside air to about two atmospheres to make it easier for me to analyse them on returning home. After we reached the ceiling of 45,000 feet, the pilot turned the plane back towards Lyneham but, during the return flight, he made some interesting manoeuvres to test the aircraft and the crew. One of these was to make a recovery from a stall and I asked what would happen if the plane went into a spin. The confident reply was, ' No worry at all. This aircraft would make no more than half a turn before the wings came off.' And after that, I kept quiet. We also went through the motions of landing on small grass fields without actually touching down. All too soon, we were back at the airfield and I made my farewells to the crew. I analysed the samples immediately I reached home. They showed a steady level of CFCs and carbon tetrachloride in the troposphere and a decline, as theory required, in the stratosphere. I published these findings in *Nature* in 1974.

I had always suspected that there were natural halocarbons in the air. I had found traces of methyl iodide and it seemed likely that there would also be methyl bromide and methyl chloride from natural sources. When I suggested this at scientific meetings on CFCs, I found the idea unpopular with scientists. Many seemed to have accepted uncritically the 'Green' notion that organisms rejected chlorine from their metabolism, and they saw chlorine compounds as the toxic products of industry. To me this was fanaticism, not science, and I prepared a chromatograph specifically for methyl chloride analysis. During September 1976, I made a series of measurements at Bowerchalke and found methyl chloride present at a level close to one part per billion. This was nearly ten times more than the abundance of fluorocarbon 11 at that time. It is true that FC11 carries three times as much chlorine per molecule and releases it specifically in the stratosphere. Even so, the natural chlorine from methyl chloride was comparable as a source of chlorine with the CFCs. Industry scientists told me that there was no significant industrial leakage of methyl chloride and that the abundance together with its short half-life in the air suggested a large natural source. Later, scientists found that methyl chloride came from forest fires, from the ocean, and from fungi living on rotting wood. Nature, it seemed, was also in the business of ozone depletion. I published these findings in a *Nature* Letter in 1977.

Apart from personal enquiries from Peter Liss, Adrian Tuck, and Bob Murgatroyd, other UK scientists expressed little or no interest in the atmospheric abundance of halomethanes. With the exception of the Meteorological Office, the establishment, led by the Royal Society, was clearly interested in the Molina–Rowland theory but disdained my somewhat downmarket researches in rural Wiltshire. The financial support for my work in Wiltshire and for the running of the Adrigole station came solely from the Chemical Manufacturers Association (CMA). This is a trade association of the world's chemical manufacturers and it has a research funding committee staffed by academics and industry scientists. Greens and the Left tend to assume that this was tainted money and the beneficiaries of it were corrupted scientists. In fact, most of the funds from the CMA grants went to supporters of the Molina–Rowland theory. The only contact I had had with the stratospheric chemists on the other side, so to speak, was a letter from Ralph Cicerone sent on 7 October 1974. He invited me to a meeting of the American Geophysical Union in San Francisco on 12 December; here there would be a chance to meet Rowland and the stratospheric chemists. I should have gone, but I was weary from too much long-distance travel and it was not until 1980, when I received an invitation from Tony Broderick of the Federal Aviation Administration to attend their Stratospheric Advisory Committee that I began to meet and hear the scientific arguments of the other side. The FAA committee was not like any other that I had known—it provided a meeting place for the best of stratospheric scientists.

Looking back, I wish that there had been more free and open discussion of the science of the Ozone War. As it was, industrial and environmental scientists fought like opposing lawyers in a never-ending courtroom drama. After ten years surviving as an independent, I was becoming a fair judge of character. As I grew to know the principal scientists on both sides, I felt I could trust them, and time has proven this judgement true. Unfortunately, my first encounter with Sherry Rowland was in a courtroom, at a congressional hearing of the US government. Dupont had called me as a witness to a hearing on the future of the chlorofluorocarbons. This was in 1974, when environmentalists were crusading for an immediate ban on the use of the CFCs. The early models of stratospheric ozone destruction suggested a dangerously large depletion if CFCs continued to be released to the air. Sherry Rowland was the environmentalists' champion, and I was in the odd position of being the principal witness for the industry's defence. They chose me because, at the time, I knew more about the abundance of chlorine and fluorine compounds in the atmosphere than did anyone else. Had the stratospheric scientists approached me first, I would probably have appeared on Sherry Rowland's side. More important, he and I would have had a chance to discuss the science before appearing in court. I did not ask for a fee for appearing as a witness, nor did Dupont offer one. Someone paid my travel and hotel expenses for the hearing; I do not know who.

It was not long after this hearing that environmental scientists, according to the journalist Nigel Hawkes, now science editor for the London *Times*, were calling me someone 'in the pockets of the aerosol industry'. Reading University wrote asking if they should sue the newspaper because the article suggesting that I was a corrupted scientist was libellous. Sherry Rowland and Mario Molina, I think, suffered from similar character denigration by journalists who listened uncritically to the less reputable spokesmen of the chlorofluorocarbon industry. Happily, none of us felt that lawsuits would solve anything, but there is a need for a proper ethical structure in environmental affairs. It is wrong to accuse scientists of corruption when they appear as witnesses on behalf of industry. If I had solid evidence to show that a man on trial for a crime was innocent, should I stand aside and let him be punished merely because I knew him to be a criminal? We are civilized enough to have laws that are clear about one's duty in such an event. Environmental affairs are in danger of acquiring the cruel hysteria more characteristic of lynch law. We forget too easily that we as individuals are the principal agents of pollution. It is our home heating and our car that adds to the greenhouse burden of carbon dioxide, not the oil or coal industries alone.

We all were polarized and, like two opposing tribes at war, were prepared to think the worst of each other. This is no way to do science. The adversarial approach of the law court may have evolved to settle differences between people and between them and the law. It is wholly out of place as a way to advance scientific knowledge. During the early years, up until 1977, there was great ignorance, little solid evidence, and a flood of wild speculation about ozone depletion. The rocks on which this edifice was built were sound enough—the Molina–Rowland theory and my own measurements of the CFCs. The theory was universally respected; only its quantitative aspects were questioned. The CFC measurements were qualitatively approved; only their quantitative reliability was in doubt. The greatest exaggeration and the most nonsense was over the effects of ultraviolet radiation on living organisms. The stratospheric chemists were, frankly, ignorant about biology. They knew that the DNA of the cells absorbed ultraviolet radiation and that the DNA molecules were damaged. Some of them even knew that the damage occurred at the nucleoside base, thymine. This was enough knowledge for them. If ultraviolet damages DNA, the key molecule of life, then it is wholly bad and any depletion of the ozone layer, which increases ultraviolet exposure, must be equally bad. In the real world things are not so simple.

A few biologists had experimented with the effects of UV on organisms in their natural state but their voice was not heard during the Ozone War. If it had been they would have warned that, apart from light-skinned humans, considerable increases in ultraviolet intensity seem to have little adverse effect on the biosphere at large. Going from northern Europe to the equatorial highlands of Kenya increases ultraviolet exposure eight times; this is forty times more than the modellers predicted the UV would increase through ozone depletion in the 1970s. Nowhere on Earth is there a UV desert, a place where life does not survive because the UV is too strong for it. There are hot deserts, cold deserts, and salt deserts, but nowhere is there a UV desert. Organisms, even tiny bacteria with the thinnest of membranes, find it easy to avoid damage from ultraviolet. They make pigments that absorb the UV harmlessly. They have evolved subtle repair systems for damaged DNA. Much of my own scepticism came because, in the Second World War, my colleagues at the Medical Research Council had tried to kill potentially harmful bacteria using ultraviolet radiation. What they found was that UV equivalent to sunlight unfiltered by ozone had little effect on many organisms in their natural state. It was easy to kill by UV the same organisms growing in transparent quartz vessels, but this is not evidence about the natural world. In their natural state organisms are protected by a thin film of secretion that absorbs the radiation. Lynn Margulis and M Rambler tried exposing algae to the ultraviolet intensity of unfiltered sunlight. The algae grew in spite of a daylong flux of this potentially lethal radiation. Even in Kenya, where the ultraviolet would burn light-skinned Europeans in minutes, there are no sunburned trees or grasses. In short, the widely held belief that life could never have existed on the land before ozone appeared in the atmosphere is a legend based on faith, not science.

Life is tough and enterprising. The evolution of ultraviolet protection is easy; far less difficult than evolving ways to live in saturated salt or at temperatures near boiling. The main point of those concerned with ozone depletion was that sunlight harms people—especially light-skinned people. We suffer sunburn and skin cancers because of exposure to ultraviolet. They speculated about damage to the biota as if they were reporting facts of observation. I admit to being a finicky scientist, but I found offensive the claims that rabbits and sheep in the southern hemisphere were made blind by increased ultraviolet caused by the ozone hole. Equally, I scorned the stories of algal destruction by ultraviolet in the southern oceans. Many of these claims came from anecdotes, not from scientific observations. Like zealots of warring tribes, both sides used their speculations like atrocity fiction, not caring about the truth.

The nadir of this affair for me was a meeting at Logan, Utah, in September 1976. Here were gathered the faithful among the strato-spheric scientists, together with environmental lawyers, politicians, and a small defensive party from the chemical industry. When, during a session on UV-induced cancer, I showed a slide illustrating the physical and biological changes that vary with latitude on the Earth, the chairman, Dr Kauffman, interrupted. He glared at me and said, 'You are not medically qualified; you cannot speak on these matters.' In spite of my PhD in medicine, I sat down, realizing I might as well be trying to plead for contraception at the Vatican. All this followed an uncritical paper linking the incidence of melanoma, a fatal skin cancer, to latitude. The further south, the higher is the incidence of melanoma in the United States of America. My slide showed that not just UV intensity but skin temperature and the atmospheric abun-dance of free radicals also increased with movement south. No one wanted to know. This was not a scientific debate, it was not even a courtroom—it was a place where industry could be publicly judged guilty and not allowed a defence. All that was lacking was punishment.

One person who understood my difficulties was the science writer, Lydia Dotto. Here is an account of her interview with me from her book, *The Ozone War*, published in 1978, and written jointly with the Canadian atmospheric scientist, Harold Schiff.

In a way, Mrs Lovelock started it all. Back in 1970 when her husband, Jim, decided he wanted to measure fluorocarbons in the Earth's Atmosphere, no one was much interested—certainly not the people who supplied funds for scientific research in his native England. So Mrs Lovelock, the family business manager, broke out the grocery money, and with it her husband built a sensitive instrument that soon detected minute amounts of fluorocarbons in the atmosphere. These chemicals did not come from nature; they were man-made, and it was not hard to figure out where they did come from. What Jim Lovelock was measuring was largely the accumulation of several decade's worth of hair spray and deodorant propellants, with perhaps a small amount of refrigerant and air-conditioning coolants thrown in. Though neither he nor his wife could know it at the time, their modest investment in pure scientific research would threaten the billion dollar refrigerant and spray can industry and touch off one of the major environmental rows of the decade.

But Lovelock was no environmental crusader. He is an unassuming Englishman with modishly long greying hair and a soft almost hushed voice. There is a gentleness about him that provides a striking contrast to the rather high-powered American scientists who dominate the ozone controversy.

When I returned home from Logan, I was surprised to find a letter waiting for me from Dr Kauffman. It was a friendly letter and mainly to ask for help with a problem involving the electron capture detector. It was not an apology for having denied me my chance to speak, but reading between the lines, I sensed his need to make amends.

It was not long afterwards that Frank Bower and Ray McCarthy asked me whether I thought it feasible to set up a global monitoring network to measure CFCs in the atmosphere. Their reason for asking was that they had seen a proposal to the Chemical Manufacturers Association, the academic grant-funding agency of the industry, from Professor Ronald Prinn of the MIT. He proposed calculating the atmospheric residence times of the chlorofluorocarbons from accurate measurements of their atmospheric abundances in both hemispheres. Knowledge of the residence times was important for calculating whether CFCs were as dangerous as the stratospheric chemists feared. My reply was, yes, that four stations, two in the northern hemisphere and two in the southern hemisphere, should be sufficient to monitor long-lived gases like CFCs. I was less certain, however, that the required accuracy, better than five per cent, could easily be achieved. I offered to install immediately a new gas chromatograph at my monitoring station in Adrigole in Ireland. I would run it continuously for a year to check its reliability and accuracy. Here was an example of the value of independent science. If I had asked the CMA for money to buy the GC and funds to test it for a year they would have provided it, but I would have had to wait a year for their decision, and longer for the money. As it was, I purchased immediately from my own pocket a new gas chromatograph from Hewlett Packard and expected that the CMA would reimburse me sometime later. In fact, they never did. The year's trial at Adrigole showed that an unattended gas chromatograph could make as many as six automatic measurements a day. Moreover, the accuracy of the measurements appeared to be sufficient. Prinn's proposals were then accepted and funded. The Adrigole station was included within the atmospheric long-range experiment (ALE). The other stations were in Barbados, Samoa in the Pacific, Cape Grim in Tasmania, and Cape Mears in Oregon, USA. They were all set up exactly according to my instructions, using the same equipment that I had tested in Adrigole. Prinn's proposal was justified and we now know the residence times of CFC gases. These stations, except Adrigole, still operate and provide valuable information on the abundance of CFCs and other halocarbons.

By 1978 I could no longer run the Adrigole station, and I passed the management of it to Peter Simmonds of the ALE experimental team. Helen's increasing disability from multiple sclerosis made this decision unavoidable, since she was no longer able to travel with me to Ireland. Sadly, my departure from Adrigole led to the closure of the station. Within a few years, the politics of big science was used to justify moving the measurements to another Irish station, Mace Head, in Galway. This was a bad move scientifically: it lost two years' observations. At least ten atmospheric scientists—including Michael Prather, Michael McElroy, Steven Wofsy, Gary Russell, and David Rind—opposed in public the closing of the Adrigole station. It was not just bad science, it also deprived my friend and neighbour, Michael O'Sullivan, of the chance to participate in, what was for him, fulfilling work. When we moved to Adrigole in 1965, Michael O'Sullivan was working as a small farmer scraping a bare living from the well-named

Hungry Hill. Our presence opened a new world for him and his family and, although he had no scientific training whatever, he became, working with me, a skilled and diligent technician. He kept the apparatus running throughout the years of its use at Adrigole and he kept a record, using a sun photometer, of atmospheric turbidity. Michael and Teresa O'Sullivan's unstinted help and friendship made possible the Adrigole station. Without it, we might not have discovered the accumulation of CFCs for as much as another decade. The closure of the station was untimely, unnecessary, and brutally done. At the time, I was fighting my own battles with illness and could not help. It was a shameful affair, for in the late 1980s I discovered that UK grant-funding agencies were generously funding the monitoring of CFCs at Mace Head. I had assumed that their earlier disdain for my own efforts was a price I had to pay for pioneering and for independence. Now I felt chagrin because, among those who now received grants, were members of the grant committees. I was a fool to feel this way: cronyism is everywhere, why should I think science was different? I do not regret following Rothschild's advice to keep away from committees. Grants are a form of welfare and I did not need it. Even so, I feel incensed that I had no say in the closing of the Adrigole site. I would have been glad to recommend compensation to Michael O'Sullivan for his long service keeping the Adrigole station running.

My last work for the Ozone War was to develop a method of calibrating the monitoring instruments. It all began when I was preparing for the *Shackleton* voyage in 1971. It was easy enough to detect CFCs in the air using a gas chromatograph equipped with an electron capture detector, but I did not know how accurate my measurements would be. There were two ways to calibrate the instrument. First, I could take a minute but accurately known amount of pure CFC, dilute it in a large volume of air, and then use a sample of the dilute CFC to calibrate my gas chromatograph. This was not a good method for CFCs: they were everywhere, so where could I find fifty cubic metres of air uncontaminated by CFCs? Some chemists tried diluting CFCs in pure gases such as nitrogen to a few parts per million. Then they further diluted the few parts per million to a few parts per billion, and finally to a few parts per trillion. I was too much of a hands-on chemist to have any trust in such a serial dilution procedure. I happily acknowledge the skill of Ray Weiss, who pioneered the direct dilution technique to make calibration at the parts-per-trillion level possible, but this was not available until the mid-1980s.

My Green friends, many of whom believe in homeopathy and other kinds of alternative medicine, may be interested in my views on this kind of dilution. Homeopathic practitioners regularly serially dilute their drugs to levels trillions of times lower than parts per trillion. My experiences showed how difficult it is to dilute simple inert chemicals like CFCs. They made me deeply sceptical about the extreme dilutions of homeopathy. On the other hand, there can be few things as harmless as a drug applied homoeopathically, and there would be no side effects.

The other way to calibrate the *Shackleton* chromatograph was to make an absolute detector. This is an old trick of instrument scientists. It is simple to do, but it requires a theory of how the detector works. I assumed that the reaction between free electrons that were floating inside the detector and chlorofluorocarbon molecules led to their mutual removal from the detector. Each electron lost this way was then equivalent to one CFC molecule. I knew the average numbers of electrons in the detector quite accurately from the current flowing in it. A typical detector current of a hundredth of a microampere is exactly equivalent to 62.415 billion electrons per second. So if CFCs at a flow of ten billion molecules per second were passed into the detector, ideally they should remove ten billion electrons per second and hence decrease the current flow by 1.602 nanoamperes. From the simple arithmetic it was not difficult to calculate, from the area of a chromatograph peak, how many electrons were removed and hence how many CFC molecules had reacted. Reality is more complicated. Some of the CFC molecules could escape reaction and fail to be counted. To answer this, I joined two detectors in series and detected the amount of CFC that escaped through the first detector. It turned out that forty per cent of the CFC escaped the detector I was using. Therefore, I had to correct my first estimate by this amount. There were other more recondite doubts, mainly about other reactions of the CFC molecules in the detector. Nevertheless, I chose to use this absolute procedure to quantify my measurements made on the *Shackleton* expedition. This was both foolhardy and brave. First measurements have no predecessors to compare with. If I were badly wrong about absolute detection, I could not have chosen a better way to advertise my error than the first paper on the global distribution of chlorofluorocarbons that was published in *Nature* in 1973.

The first time that this procedure was called to account was at a meeting of the United States National Academy of Sciences' panel on ozone depletion. It was at the ski resort of Snowmass in Colorado, which is a beautiful place, at about 8000 feet up in the Rocky Mountains. One of the panel scientists asked, 'How accurate are your chlorofluorocarbon measurements?' 'About twenty per cent,' I replied. Twenty per cent accuracy implies that a quoted value of 100 parts per trillion represents a true value in the range 80–120. The errors start when the air sample is taken. How close in volume is the air sample to the 5 cc marked on the syringe used to collect it? They end with the estimate of the peak area of the chromatogram. On the *Shackleton*, I did it using a pencil and ruler. These errors added up, I calculated, to make an uncertainty of about twenty per cent. The true error may have been less but I had learnt in a lifetime of measurements that it is best use the worst estimate when trying to guess errors. Almost immediately, an American analyst present at the meeting jumped up and said, 'Oh, I can measure the CFCs to a one per cent accuracy.' I was impressed; I knew that my home-made apparatus and dubious syringe method of sampling were less professional than I would have wished. I had not realized how far ahead the high technology of the United States had gone. The panel was equally impressed and in its published report categorized my measurements on the *Shackleton* as inaccurate. It took me five years to discover that the claim of one-per cent accuracy from the young man who jumped up at Snowmass was false. The claimant, I discovered, was hazy in his mind over the difference between accuracy and precision. He meant one-per cent precision, not one-per cent accuracy. The difference is this: a badly inaccurate but precise weighing machine will record your weight as 90 lbs, never varying from 89 to 91, when in fact your weight is 150 lbs. An accurate but imprecise weighing machine will give weights between 130 and 170 lbs, and if you weigh yourself often enough will provide an average close to your true weight.

A professional body, the US Bureau of Standards, also grew suspicious of the analyst's ability to measure CFCs with such astonishing accuracy. Ernest Hughes, William Dorko, and John Taylor of the Bureau designed an experiment to find out the truth about these claims. They filled one set of small gas cylinders with clean air and another set of cylinders from a batch of the same clean air with some pure nitrogen added to it. They sent one each of these cylinders to the principal analysts measuring CFCs in the atmosphere, and asked them to report their findings. When they returned their measurements, the National Bureau of Standards plotted the two measurements from each analyst on what statisticians call a Youdon plot. This is a graph where the value of one measurement is marked by its position on the horizontal axis and the other measurement by its position on the vertical axis. If all the measurements were accurate to one per cent then all the reported values would have centred within a small circle—like the throws of a champion darts player, all in the bull's eye. In fact, the FC11 results were scattered over a range going from less than half to more than twice the true value and the FC12 results were worse even than this. My twenty per cent did not look so bad compared with this. Their report, which revealed inaccuracy throughout the community, brought me sharply back to my student encounter with Professor Todd, and the time when he could not believe the accuracy of my student exercise, not knowing about my professional training. Scientists working at universities, and using unfamiliar techniques, often make inaccurate measurements because they rarely have the time to become proficient.

The National Bureau of Standards report in 1978 renewed my trust in absolute detection. I decided to validate it as a method. This I did by building a fifty-cubic-metre chamber, hermetically sealed, within an old barn deep in the Devon countryside. The idea I had was to prepare accurately small volumes of chlorofluorocarbon gas by a vacuum line procedure. Graham Milne, an ICI scientist, gave me the apparatus needed for this and generously gave his time teaching me how to use it. First, I prepared an accurately known volume of chlorofluorocarbon gas in a sealed glass ampoule and then took the ampoule to the barn and placed it before a powerful fan. I then left the chamber and set my instruments running, taking samples of the background air of the chamber, and then I broke the ampoule by an electrically driven crusher. The chamber air was continuously refreshed by air from outside at a rate of two air changes an hour. At intervals, samples of the chamber air were taken and measured. I checked the accuracy of this dilution method by also releasing hydrogen gas into the chamber, and following its dilution using a well-calibrated thermal-conductivity detector. Whilst I was doing these experiments, a family of barn owls took residence in the space above the chamber. The barn programme kept me busy for nearly three years, and it was some of the most exacting and least rewarding financially of my life's work as a scientist. It was worthwhile because it did make honest the atmospheric CFC measurements, and it did confirm that the ECD could be an absolute detector for the chlorofluorocarbons. Most of all, for me, it justified my estimate of the accuracy of the *Shackleton* data. The paper describing these experiments in the barn appeared in *Geophysical Reviews* in 1984. For reasons I never understood, the ALE management team insisted that it appear as a joint paper with Rai Rasmussen, a member of the ALE team, as the lead author. Nevertheless, I did the barn experiments unaided by anyone.

During the time of the barn experiments my friend, Brian Foulger, and I made a series of measurements of the atmospheric abundance of halons, the bromine-rich compounds used as fire extinguishers. We made them here at Coombe Mill and in the southern hemisphere at Cape Town and in New Zealand. We found about 1.5 parts per trillion in the northern hemisphere and 0.6 in the southern hemisphere. The chemical company, ICI, funded the work. Unusually, but as was their right, they persistently refused us permission to publish these findings. This was the only time in my life as an independent scientist that a company or a government department blocked the publication of important scientific information.

The Ozone War was curiously involved with low-budget science done by British scientists in or near Antarctica. The voyage of the *Shackleton* to Antarctica in 1971 first drew attention to the global distribution of CFCs. The discovery by Joe Farman and Brian Gardiner of the thinning of ozone above the Antarctic landmass made us realize how serious it was. These were quiet, inexpensive researches inspired by a sense of wonder, and we were all inspired by the theory of Molina and Rowland in California, which was a modestly funded research. We need big science to complete our understanding of the intricate chemistry of the stratosphere, but we must never forget that pioneering small-scale research is just as necessary. I started the CFC ozone affair as small science, but by 1982 it seemed that I was on an accelerating bandwagon, and now was the time to jump off. At the end of that year, I fell ill and was unable to travel. I was glad that illness gave me the chance to escape what was now big science. I have never returned to it.

The Voyage of the *Meteor* in 1973

On the voyage of the *Shackleton* I had as a companion in the next laboratory on the ship a striking and friendly young German student, Hans Greese. His task on the voyage was the difficult one of measuring atmospheric carbon monoxide. Like me, he wanted to know how it varied between the northern and southern hemispheres. My equipment was simple, home-made and occupied no more than four square feet of bench space. His was intricate and filled the whole of the front laboratory of the ship. I was fortunate to have the electron capture detector, which is specifically sensitive to the chlorofluorocarbons that I sought. Hans had to do it the hard way by extracting the tiny proportion of carbon monoxide, less than a part per million, from the air by standard chemical methods, and then measuring it by chemical quantitative analysis. Just as I was impressed with his professionalism and craftsmanship, he was impressed with the simplicity and sensitivity of my chlorofluorocarbon measurements. In some ways, it typified the different approaches of our two nations: the German as painstaking and professional and the English as opportunistic but effective amateurs. He must have talked with his colleagues and his supervisor, Dr Wolfgang Seiler, when he returned to Germany. The distinguished scientist, Christian Jünge, was director of the Max Planck Institute of Atmospheric Science at Mainz in Germany. He wrote to me inviting me to Mainz to tell them of the discoveries made during my voyage on the *Shackleton*.

I travelled to Mainz sometime in the autumn of 1972. Dr JH Hahn met me at Frankfurt Airport and drove me by car to Mainz. They let me stay in the Institute guesthouse and Dr Hahn arranged to meet me there at 9 o'clock the next morning. After a good night's sleep, I awoke hungry and ready for breakfast, and then a good day of talks about the atmosphere. I wandered around the guesthouse but seemed to be the only one there. There was no dining room and I could not smell coffee brewing or breakfast cooking. Hahn appeared sharp at 9 and I asked, 'Are we going to have breakfast?' 'Breakfast?,' he said with a grin, 'you must have a German breakfast: a cup of coffee at the lab and a cigarette.' This was a culture shock for me. Breakfast is the most important meal of the day for the English. I don't go in for the whole thing: grapefruit and porridge, followed by egg, bacon, fried potatoes, tomatoes, and finished off by rounds of buttered toast and marmalade, all washed down with a large quantity of good strong tea. But to start the day on an empty stomach and no cup of tea was too much. I asked if there was a shop that sold something light. Jürgen Hahn kindly, sensing my lack of food, took me to a café where there were cakes and beer available. I settled for the cake and then returned with him to the Institute, where there was coffee brewing all of the time.

I was much impressed with the atmosphere and quality of the scientists there. Christian Jünge reminded me of Sir Charles Harington. He was a quiet, strong, and authoritative man with a towering intellect. We had a happy morning discussing the significance of the *Shackleton* analyses. Jünge had proposed in an earlier paper a way to estimate the atmospheric lifetime of a gas. He guessed that long-lived gases such as oxygen and nitrogen would not vary in abundance by a detectable amount, whereas short-lived gases like methane or carbon monoxide, with residence times of a few years or months, would fluctuate considerably in abundance. This approach suggested that the chlorofluorocarbons, in the southern hemisphere at least, had a long lifetime, which later we found to be over a hundred years.

Almost all of the Germans I met spoke good English and I felt ashamed at my lack of language. It was a pleasant stay and towards the end, Christian Jünge invited me to make another sea voyage, this time on the German research ship, *Meteor*. It was due to sail from Hamburg to Santo Domingo in the Caribbean in late 1973. What a wonderful ending for my visit: the prospect of another sea voyage filled me with joy and I now had something to look forward to and prepare for during the next year.

I flew to Hamburg in 1973 and a scientist from the ship met me, and took me to a pension near the port where many of the ship's company were staying. I was deeply aware that in the Second World War Hamburg had suffered the greatest civilian casualties of any bombing raid during the whole of that war, even more than were caused by the atom bombs in Japan. Close to 250,000 died in one night of intensive bombing, far beyond anything we had suffered in London. I was amazed at the extent to which they had rebuilt the city. No scars were visible to me in my journeys across it, nor did I detect any personal animosity towards me as a representative of the tribe that had so barbarously executed the terror bombing.

The next day, after breakfast, we climbed into a station wagon with our suitcases full of personal belongings and clothes to wear on the voyage. I had some spare old clothes, one good jacket in case of need, and some books to read. The journey to the dock was short, and soon we were wending our way past port cranes hunched mournfully against the morning sky, and past warehouses full of boxes and men with forklift trucks. Of all the working scenes, none has quite the capacity to move me like that of a dock area. The foreplay of preparation for a sea voyage has an excitement more than that of any other journey. Air travel is a dull thing by comparison; mostly a set of encounters with officials and bureaucrats in a peculiar kind of air-conditioned office called an airport. If all one's papers satisfy them they dispatch you down a pipe like one of those pneumatic account carriers that added mystery to the old-fashioned department store.

We left the car and looked at the sizeable bulk of the *Meteor*, not at all like the tiny *Shackleton*. Here was a shipshape floating palace full of laboratories. One of the ship's officers took me up the gangway and to a spacious top deck cabin, and here I met Dr Rai Rasmussen, an American scientist who was to share the cabin with me for the voyage. I was somewhat dismayed to be sharing a cabin. I am a private person and do not like sharing living quarters with strangers, but there was little I could do about it. As it happened, I soon found that Rai Rasmussen was a quiet and courteous person at close quarters. We soon, as the only two foreigners aboard the ship, were driven together and spent the voyage amicably. After settling in I went down to the lab assigned to me where I found the box with all of my equipment waiting. I spent the rest of the morning connecting it up, and by lunchtime my gas chromatograph was running. There was a spacious bench for me, and an excellent drawer and cupboard space below it. A friendly German graduate student who, like so many Germans, spoke English better than many of my countrymen, occupied the other half of the lab.

There was a spacious and well-equipped dining room on the *Meteor* and I looked forward to an encounter here with the German scientists who were to travel with me down the Atlantic to Santo Domingo. I had hoped to improve my German during the voyage to the point of colloquial conversation. It was not to be. Not even the sailors on deck would speak to me in anything but English. They always replied to my halting German phrases with a rejoinder in near perfect English, not rudely, but because life was too short to waste time over a mismatch in language. Lunch, indeed all lunches on the *Meteor*, were substantial German meals. To my taste, they were disappointing and too rich, but they were more than adequate for health. I missed the near gourmet food of the *Shackleton* and of the Navy ships. Breakfast, thankfully, was no continental breakfast of coffee and rolls. There was more, and it was adequate. The other meal, high tea at 5 o'clock, was the hardest to cope with: just quantities of bread and butter and a variety of cold sausages. I longed for some fresh fruit and vegetables, but there were none. Food is very much a cultural affair, and no doubt Hans, my companion on the *Shackleton*, would have found something to complain about with our food. There was a shop on the ship where Rasmussen and I bought chocolate to satisfy our craving for something sweet.

We set sail soon after we had boarded the ship, and in the afternoon I saw something of the flat landscape that bordered the Elbe estuary. It was a clear day and a wide sky, so beloved of Flemish painters, illuminated the smooth movement of the ship. The open decks were spacious and there was plenty of room to walk and to explore. In the evening I made the first chlorofluorocarbon measurements and found them to be well over 300 parts per trillion. This was unbelievable, for we were already out in the North Sea and the wind was off the sea, not the land. I soon discovered that the CFC level in the ship itself was so high, approaching one part per million, that measurement of CFCs in the lab on the *Meteor* was all but impossible with the equipment I had brought with me. The heavy halocarbon contamination came from several sources: some meteorologists aboard the ship had filled Dewar flasks with chlorofluorocarbons, from which CFCs vented to the ship's air. Other scientists were using carbon tetrachloride as a solvent for Vaseline, which they coated on glass slides. The sticky slides were then used to collect aerosol particles in the air the ship passed through. Most of the ship's company also used aerosol sprays powered by chlorofluorocarbons as deodorants and for shaving soap. The tightly closed and air-conditioned quarters of the ship kept the air inside and these rich sources caused the *Meteor* to have the highest concentration of halocarbons in any air I have ever measured. It was not the place to monitor atmospheric CFCs.

I had looked forward to seeing the Straits of Dover as we passed through that narrow part of the Channel, but it was dark and all that I could see were faint lights on shore. The ship moved comfortably in the Atlantic swell that came up the Channel. It was a more stable platform to work on than the *Shackleton* had been. I noticed no one seasick, even on the first day, and the whole voyage seemed to be one of unusually calm weather. Rai Rasmussen was busy measuring hydrocarbons in the air and in the water. He used a far more expensive and complicated commercial gas chromatograph. He was curious about my simple gas chromatograph and astonished to find it over a thousand times more sensitive than the equipment that he was using. It may have been his first encounter with electron capture gas chromatography. The ECD was so sensitive, so unpredictable, and so little understood that analysts regarded it with suspicion.

Science to me has always been something to wonder about and to have the daily ration of curiosity satisfied by successful experiments: to speculate then experiment, measure, or calculate. To my travel companion, science was a battleground, with castle walls to be breached or clambered over. He looked like his name, Rasmussen, a Viking. He had the Viking's untamed ambition and desire to win whatever the cost. When I said I would abandon my chlorofluorocarbon study because of the ship's excessive contamination, his response was to urge me to demand immediately the banning of aerosols by the crew and scientists aboard. Fortunately for both of us, I knew how easy it is to upset a ship's company. It would not be a good idea to interfere with the daily routine of life unless the cause was truly serious; moreover, we were guests on a German ship. When I said, 'No, I'm going to find some other project to occupy me on this voyage and forget the CFCs', I think Rai Rasmussen regarded me as a wimp, albeit a talented one.

What makes me an unusual scientist is a capacious and immediately accessible memory. Anything I read, or hear, or see that interests me stays with me and is available. I have never used card indexes or computer databanks. I try to keep it all in my head. It says something of the deficiencies of my character that this memory is not available for people's names, which I forget within seconds of hearing them. My memory, and some forethought during packing at Bowerchalke before the voyage, gave me a second project. I had included in the box sent to the ship several gas chromatograph columns that were suited to the analysis of other compounds than the chlorofluorocarbons. I did this because I expected to find on the voyage some other interesting substances in the air or the sea. The speed with which substances pass through a gas chromatograph column and appear at the detector is characteristic of their nature and can help to identify them. With several different columns, each of which has a different speed of passage for any given substance, the identification becomes more certain.

I noticed that after standing on the deck my skin and my shirt had a strong chlorine-like odour and I remembered that the notorious air pollutant called PAN smelt like chlorine. This is a peculiar substance, discovered as a major component of Los Angeles smog by the American scientist, ER Stephens in 1956. The pure substance is so dangerous that experimenters usually handle it as a dilute concentration in air or some inert gas. Pure PAN explodes violently at any number of pretexts, which include contact with rough surfaces, exposure to bright lights or sudden warmth. Therefore, we avoid ever using it. For those interested, the letters PAN are the initials of the word peroxy-acetyl-nitrate.

It so happened that I had brought with me a column just right for the analysis of PAN. It was filled with a powder coated with polyethylene glycol. I joined it up in place of the CFC column of my gas chromatograph, went on deck, and collected a few air samples. Sure enough, when I applied them to the chromatograph a peak appeared on the recorder at the time that I expected PAN to appear from the column. There were also three other peaks whose identity I did not know. I tried the same measurement a few more times and with the same result. I speculated that if this were PAN then it was in an air mass that had drifted from Europe into the air above the Atlantic. Here was a simple project for me. I could take daily measurements and follow the ship's passage through and out of the polluted air mass. I wished that I could have measured chlorofluorocarbons as well, to confirm the urban origins of the PAN, but it was not to be.

As the days went by, we moved west and south, ever further out into the Atlantic. To my surprise, the PAN in the air increased rather than decreased and was present even when the air was obviously clear, sparkling, and free of smog. My guess that it came from some distant pollution source looked to be wrong. Where could it have come from, so far out over the ocean? As we sailed further south, the sunlight increased, and it became warm enough on deck for open shirts and shorts. The PAN increased still more in abundance, although we were further than ever from land. It could not have come from a maritime industrial source, such as a fleet of fishing vessels and factory ships, for we were now in the notorious Bermuda Triangle, where few ships ever go. I asked permission to go out far away from the *Meteor* in a rubber boat and collect just a few CFC samples to confirm that we were truly away from urban industrial air masses. Permission was given and a German sailor took me in a zodiac-type craft about a mile away from the ship, which was at the time stationary. It was quite eerie to be in this boat and look back across a mile of empty ocean towards the small image of the *Meteor* waiting there. I felt as the astronauts must have done on seeing the Earth from the Moon, so small it was and so far away. I hastily gathered my clean air samples and the German sailor grinned and pointed to the *Meteor*. He was glad, like me, to be returning to our home.

When I analysed the clean air samples they showed the expected northern hemispheric background level of CFCs, about sixty parts per trillion: this was no smoggy air mass. I began to collect PAN samples throughout the day and soon found that the level varied with the position of the sun. There was little at dawn or dusk and the maximum in the early afternoon. So the photochemistry that made it must be local; the sea must be emitting hydrocarbons and nitrogen compounds. Rasmussen confirmed that the sea was a source of hydrocarbons and I now know from the work of my friend, Peter Liss, that it is also a source of amines. These nitrogen compounds would oxidize in the atmosphere to give the nitrogen dioxide from which PAN can form.

We were now well into the Sargasso Sea; everywhere were fronds of seaweed, Fucus-like, with bladders to keep them afloat. They were not dense and entangling but sprinkled over the waters of a clear blue sea. Nature has a way of leading scientists up the garden path and then suddenly removing the garden. For reasons I now forget, I sampled the air the next day with a polypropylene syringe, instead of the glass ones I usually used. To my dismay, the PAN had vanished. I tried again with the glass syringe, and there it was back again. Was the polypropylene surface destroying PAN? Unlikely, I thought. I would have expected the reverse, for PAN decomposes on glass surfaces but is stable towards polypropylene. I then tried incorporating a piece of glass wool into the polypropylene syringe and the PAN came back again in full quantity. It looked as if what I had thought was PAN in the air was in fact PAN coming from the reaction of something in the air with a glass surface. This was even more mysterious. What could be in the air out over the ocean that reacted so rapidly on the surface to make PAN? I could only guess that it was a mixture of nitrogen dioxide and a free radical precursor such as the acetyl peroxy radical. I knew that the methyl peroxy radical was a common product of methane oxidation, which goes on everywhere. Was the product of its reaction with nitrogen oxide also present? There was certainly always a peak well before PAN which, like PAN, was present only when the sun shone. Having no means of proving it or its precursor's presence, I can only guess that methyl peroxy nitrate was also there, forming on surfaces in this clear remote place. This odd phenomenon kept me occupied until we reached our destination, Santo Domingo.

The results of these preliminary investigations appeared in a *Nature* Letter, called 'PAN over the Atlantic and the smell of clean linen' in 1974.

I had many lively discussions with the German students working on the *Meteor*. One that recurred was about the Nazi period and the Holocaust. These young men felt strongly that it was inappropriate and unjust for the world continuously to remind them of the wrongs done in the Second World War. It was not that they wanted to bury the history or pretend that there was no evil. It was that they felt the injustice of being held personally responsible for deeds done before they were born. I strongly sympathized, and remembered my own angst when spiteful Irish republicans visited me with their synthetic tribal rage over the Irish famine those years long ago. We wondered if any nation is so free of the taint of genocide that it can cast a stone. We wondered, too, if the constant reminders of past atrocities are themselves driven by racial hatred.

Ten days after we entered the Sargasso Sea, there was a strange encounter with another ship, the USSR intelligence-gathering vessel, the *Gregyor Ushikov*. It seemed large compared with the *Meteor*, and kept station with us about a few hundred yards away. Antennae of all kinds festooned it, and we discovered through an exchange of visits that it had drifted along the whole length of the American coastline from Canada. The crew had been at sea for months since leaving their Black Sea port and were glad to exchange visits with us on the *Meteor*. Their hospitality was vigorous, and the Germans who went to the Russian ship had difficulty staying sober. There were no convenient flowerpots in which to pour the vodka that was plied to them. I had a nagging feeling that it would be unwise for me, in those Cold War times, to visit the *Gregyor Ushikov*. I was well aware of the many secrets in my mind that I might inadvertently reveal in the vodka-rich environment. So I kept a low profile and stayed on the *Meteor*, using work as an excuse. Now that the Cold War is long past, I doubt I would have been at risk on the Russian ship, but those were difficult times.

Soon we were at our destination, Santo Domingo. The *Meteor* was due to leave in three days, so on the first day I stayed aboard, using it as a floating hotel. And the last day before flying home, I planned to stay at a seashore hotel in Santo Domingo. With Rai Rasmussen and a few German friends, we left the ship the next morning for a walk into town. As we descended the gangway a group of young black boys, aged between about eight and fourteen, came to us and offered to show us the town. They were friendly and seemed so innocent in the way they took us by the hand that we all went with them. Our first port of call was a bank to change our money into local currency. In those days the British Pound was a weak coinage based on an always-unstable economy, and my companions expected that the bank would accept only Marks and Dollars. To my astonishment and delight, in fact, only Pounds and Dollars were acceptable. Marks were not wanted. The Caribbean, it seemed, operated as if it were still in a British sphere of influence. I doubt if this is still true twenty-five years on. We bought a few trinkets and postcards, had some coffee with the boys at a café, and then returned to the ship for lunch. We rewarded the boys for their guidance and they were quietly grateful. Their dignity was impressive.

When I returned to my cabin on the ship, a letter waiting on my desk surprised me. It was an invitation to dinner that evening at the German Embassy where the guest of honour would be the President of the Santo Domingo Republic. Panic-struck, I was still young enough to care that I had not even a work suit with me, just a blazer, a clean pair of trousers, some bright red socks, and some comfortable casual shoes. The car to take us to the Embassy arrived at seven. The other guest was to be the German Chief Scientist. To add to my feelings of inferiority, induced by my odd attire, they all wore good quality dark suits and everyone spoke perfect English; not just grammatically perfect, but that kind of English that reveals instantly an education at a good public school. My discomfort soon vanished in the euphoria of the good wine served with the meal, and in the warmth of interest shown by the President and his Chief of Staff in marine biology. They seemed to be scientists and were keen to build an institute like the Marine Biology Laboratory at Plymouth. They wanted to build it on the seacoast not far from Santo Domingo. The only jarring moment of the evening was before dinner when I crossed my legs and revealed the vivid scarlet socks I wore. 'My God,' said a German diplomat, 'red socks.' He added, 'My mother told me never to trust a man who wore red socks.' Everyone laughed. I just wore a sickly grin that clashed with the socks. However, the moment soon passed, and it was a very pleasant evening.

The next day I saw another side of Santo Domingo. The Ambassador had recommended a hotel a short distance along the coast, and I intended to spend my last night there with my German scientist companions. In the morning, we hired a taxi and told the driver where we wanted to go. Halfway there the taxi broke down and the driver explained that he would have to walk back to the city to get spare parts. 'However,' he smiled and said, 'you could, of course, stay at the hotel just here, just down that road there. It's just as good as the one you were going to.' From the outside, it looked good—a modern building in a scenic setting by the sea. Therefore, we chose to stay, not realizing that the driver had probably dropped us there deliberately. We went in, registered, and were shown to our rooms. The Germans discovered long before I did that it was not merely a hotel, but also a brothel. We sat at the tables outside by the sea and had soft drinks in the shade of palms. Young girls, perhaps the sisters of the boys who met us the previous day at the ship, came and joined us at the table. The notion of casual sex with a prostitute has never appealed to me, no matter how attractive the girl might be. To be turned on to a strong desire requires for me a loving relationship. Also, there was the high probability of infection with one of the many organisms that opportunistically use the tight coupling of sex as part of their life cycle. I returned to my room, collected my swimsuit and towel, and went down to the sea to bathe. Here I had another shock. I went to put my towel on the beach and nearly put it on a wasp's nest. To my dismay, there were nests at frequent intervals along the sandy beach. I have a fear of wasps which is very strong, and the thought of stumbling, shortsighted and naked but for swimming trunks, onto a nest quite spoilt the thought of bathing. I chose a spot near the sea, dashed into the shallow warm water, and tried to swim. It was not at all like the visions I had had of a tropical island. I seemed to have to walk forever to get any depth of water. Soon I was back in my room at the hotel and reading a novel. When darkness came at 6 pm, I discovered there was no electric light at this brothel that pretended to be a hotel. I suppose the normal customers did not need it. Worse, there was no water. When I complained they gave me a jug of water and a candle. It was a miserable night; too hot to sleep with the windows closed, and too many mosquitoes with them open, and I longed for dawn. When it came, I dressed, packed, and went downstairs. There was no breakfast, only coffee. I took the first available taxi to the airport, anxious that it would get there and not to some unscheduled tourist trap, with which the cab driver had a private contract.

We arrived at the airport and I checked in at the airline desk. The plane left on time and after a short flight, stopped at Port au Prince in Haiti, which, of course, is a country sharing the same island as Santo

Domingo. This was the closest I would be to the notorious Papa Doc, his family, and the Ton Ton Macoute. I was thankful when we took off for Miami, where there would be the British Airways connection to London and home. I often try to fly the airline of the nation to which it is flying. The pilot and crew have a personal stake in getting there, so it is less likely to over-fly to some unwanted city.

9

The Quest for Gaia

An eminent scientist recently spoke of me as 'a holy fool'. He may of course have meant 'wholly', but I like to think he saw me spending my life in a quest for Gaia as if it were the Holy Grail. In recent years I have grown fond of Wagner's operas, especially *Parsifal*, so that whatever was meant by it, to be called a holy fool is for me an accolade. Can there have been any more inspiring vision this century than that of the Earth from space? We saw for the first time what a gem of a planet we live on. The astronauts who saw the whole Earth from Apollo 8 gave us an icon that has become as powerful as the scimitar or the cross. In the years leading up to this mission in 1968, I had worked with the American National Aeronautical and Space Administration (NASA) and had seen behind the scenes. The meaning of that cloud-speckled ocean-blue sphere was made real to me by their newly won scientific information about the Earth and its sibling planets Mars and Venus. Suddenly, as a revelation, I saw the Earth as a living planet. The quest to know and understand our planet as one that behaves like something alive, and which has kept a home for us, has been the Grail that beckoned me ever since. Moments of intuition do not come from an empty mind; they require the gathering together of many apparently unconnected facts. The intuition that the Earth controls its surface and atmosphere to keep the environment always benign for life came to me one afternoon in September 1965 at the Jet Propulsion Laboratory (JPL) in California and it was here that most of these facts were gathered. Let me tell you more about those early days in California and how they led me to the Gaia theory.

I first visited JPL in April 1961, and in those days it had the hasty air of a temporary airport, with prefabricated cabins dotted over the hillside above the dry river bed of Arroyo Seco. I was sitting at a table in one of these cabins with about a dozen scientists and engineers. We might have been discussing the design of a new hospital or a farm tractor, but in fact we were talking about the surface of the Moon and what the proposed lander, the Surveyor, might find there. We talked in the most matter-of-fact way about how to collect samples of the lunar surface. I learnt that they needed me for my expertise as an inventor of exceedingly sensitive devices that they could use aboard their spacecraft. Every few minutes I had to pinch myself to make sure I was there with these other ordinary humans discussing such an extraordinary project. Even a few years previously, it would have been inconceivable. I made many more visits to JPL during the next twelve years up to just before the Viking spacecraft went to Mars in 1975. These visits were rarely more than three weeks long, and I usually stayed at the Huntington Sheraton Hotel in Pasadena. It was a rather unusual hotel for America. A grand brick-built building, almost like a stately home, standing in its own extensive beautifully landscaped grounds. It was unusual to have a brick-built building in an earthquake-prone area like Los Angeles, but there it was and it seemed to have stood up to the lesser shocks quite as well as anything else around. It had a comfortable old-fashioned air to it; such a change from cold unfeeling modern hotels with their clinical reception areas—no chairs to sit on and just a battery of lifts to take the guests to their various rooms. At the Huntington Sheraton, there were porters, a huge lounge, and quite a few old people sitting around. It seemed more like Bournemouth than Pasadena.

On one visit, a kindly giant of a man, George Hobby, came to take me to the JPL, and when they said that he understudied Tarzan at the nearby Hollywood studios, I could well believe it. We travelled the short distance to the laboratory in his small European sports car. George, a biologist, wanted me to sit in on a meeting of potential experimenters for the mission to Mars to find life there. He and others had the view that space biology was perhaps losing its way, getting out of hand. He was right, for as I listened to the experimenters describing the equipment they would use to find Martian life I doubted their capability. There was, for example, the Wolf trap. Not, I might add, a device to catch wolves, but a device named after its inventor, Wolf Visniak, and designed to collect and grow micro-organisms from the

Martian soil. A chemist, Vance Oyama wanted to collect soil from the Mars surface and analyse it for what he and others called life-characteristic substances. The flaw in their thinking was their assumption that they already knew what Martian life was like. From them, I gathered the distinct impression that they saw it as like life in the Mojave Desert, to the east of Los Angeles. This was convenient, for the Mojave Desert was close by and the experimenters could go there to test their equipment. Perhaps Mars was like this, but no one seemed to ask, what if it is different? Will its organisms grow on our culture media? What happens if the spacecraft lands at a barren place? Even on the Earth, a spacecraft might land on polar ice or on a sand dune in the desert.

Towards the end of the day I said, 'I think we need a general experiment, something that could look for life itself, not the familiar attributes of life that we have here on Earth.' This seemed to annoy many of those present, and my comment must have been repeated to one of the more senior laboratory chiefs. The next day Dr Meghreblian, a tough character held somewhat in awe by the staff there, asked me to come to his office. He asked, courteously, what I thought of the biological experiments. I replied that I did not think they justified the cost of sending them to Mars. His next question was the obvious one. 'Well, what would you send instead?' With some hesitation I said, 'I would send an experiment that looked for an entropy reduction.' He smiled, knowing that entropy is one of the most confusing topics and the bane of students, and said, 'That would be fine, but how could you do it?' At this point, I was not ready to reply and asked for a day or two to think about it. 'Okay,' said he, 'Come back on Friday afternoon and tell me how we're going to send an entropy reduction experiment to Mars.' Challenges like this have that quality observed by Dr Johnson in his famous remark, 'There's nothing like the prospect of hanging to concentrate the mind.' And so it was with me. Forced to think of ways to measure entropy reduction led me to read Schrödinger's famous little book, *What is Life?* I owe a great deal to Schrödinger and that book: it set me on the right track. I was mainly concerned to find out if the entropy reduction characteristic of life was easily distinguishable from the small entropy reduction of a lifeless planet illuminated by the Sun. Anyone who wants to know what entropy is could not do better than read the Oxford physical chemist, Professor PW Atkins's splendid book, *The Second Law*. Entropy, like temperature, can be measured precisely, and it indicates the degree of disorganization of a system.

This book confirmed my intuitive feeling that we could recognize life elsewhere by the signature of its low entropy. I returned on Friday to Meghreblian's office and gave him a set of experiments that would use entropy reduction as an indicator of planetary life. The first and best of these was simply to analyse the chemical composition of the Martian atmosphere. The argument behind it was quite simple. If there were no life on Mars, the atmosphere would be close to the chemical equilibrium state, which is one of high entropy. If there were life on Mars, it would be obliged to use the atmosphere as a source of its raw materials and a place to deposit its waste products, just as we do. When I say waste products here I am not thinking of junk or pollution, I am thinking of the carbon dioxide we exhale which is to us a waste product. Plants breathe out oxygen, which is to them a waste product and the exchange between producers and consumers is what keeps life going. I knew that these processes would change the composition of a planet's atmosphere, whether it's Mars or the Earth, in such a way as to lower its entropy. This would make it recognizably different chemically from the atmosphere of a dead high-entropy planet. This was my fundamental life-detection experiment.

Other experiments in my list included one where instead of looking for life-characteristic substances in the soil of Mars, we should look for ordered sequence amongst the substances that we found. If we picked up a trace of a hydrocarbon mixture on Mars and it was of inorganic origin, perhaps from a meteorite, the length or size of the molecules it contained would be randomly distributed. If, on the other hand, it had come from a biological source, the hydrocarbon mixture might show an ordered sequence of the numbers of carbon atoms in each hydrocarbon molecule. For example, the hydrocarbons made by living organisms contain evenly spaced numbers of carbon atoms. This is quite characteristic, and the presence of biogenic hydrocarbons can be distinguished even when diluted ten thousand times by inorganic hydrocarbons. Then there were other intriguing possibilities on a lively planet like the Earth. We could listen for ordered sequences of sounds. Bird song, even rock music, is quite different from mere noise. A fish swimming upstream against the flow of a river shows off the fact it is alive. These experiments would work even with life based on some other element than carbon, and they all were inspired by a Gaian view of the planets, which at the time was little more than a nebulosity of intuition deep within my mind.

These ideas excited that serious man, Meghreblian, especially the atmospheric analysis experiment. He was much more receptive than the biologist experimenters had been and he was prescient, for now NASA rates highly atmospheric analysis as a way to recognize life on extra solar planets. He knew that I was returning to England the next day and asked me to write a report on my ideas as soon as I got home. 'When you come back we'll take it further.' I was also excited and could think of little else on the long journey home. Even then, it was my extravagant custom always to travel first class. As a frequent traveller, I could not afford the days lost by the stress of economy travel over such a distance. I found that the long journey, up to fourteen hours by air from Los Angeles to London, was so debilitating in economy seats that concentrated thought was impossible for two or three days afterwards. Travelling in the comfort of first class, and sleeping for much of the journey, was for me worth the cost, and our kindly government did allow me to deduct the fares from my company's tax bill.

Soon after returning home, I walked over the Downs to Cranborne Chase Woods—a good ten miles around. I was then able to think about a paper on the entropy reduction method of life detection. I wrote it within about ten days and gave it the title 'A physical basis for life- detection experiments' and I submitted it to JPL and to *Nature*. Now this was my first submission to that famous journal since becoming an independent. To my chagrin, the paper came straight back to me with a rather curt note from the editor saying, 'We don't take papers from private addresses.' I heard afterwards that he had said to someone, 'They usually come from cranks.' This was a valuable experience. During the twenty years I worked at Mill Hill, *Nature* had always published my papers without any criticism other than mild editorial correction. The *Lancet* and other well-known journals also took anything I wrote without demur. It was a shock, and a necessary one, for me to discover that they published my papers not because of my bright ideas, or my reputation, but because of the quality of the Institute from which they came. The editors knew that nothing shoddy would come from a place like Mill Hill, run by a man like Harington. It was quite true; he did read every paper published from the Institute. I knew this from the pencilled editorial comments that were always upon them after they had passed through his office. When I explained to the editor of *Nature* that I was more than a science-fiction addict writing from a country cottage, that I was a scientist who had paid his dues by many years of work, they published the paper. Indeed, it was a lot easier to get a paper published in those days than now.

On my next visit to the Jet Propulsion Laboratory, about two months later, George Hobby met me as usual in the lobby of the Huntingdon Sheraton Hotel, but he was excited and warned me that things had changed at JPL. Two inspectors had arrived from NASA headquarters to look at, and to report on the quality of the experiments proposed for the Mars Mission. JPL felt like a bank under scrutiny by auditors. There was apprehension in the air. Some hostility had always seemed to exist between the Jet Propulsion Lab and NASA. This is a common experience for those working in institutions that are government supported. There is always a need to check accountability and I think civil servants do tend to be curious about what is going on in their out-stations. I first met these inspectors in the JPL cafeteria and we lunched together. At first sight, they did not seem to be that formidable or frightening. There was Dian Hitchcock, young and attractive but with a no-nonsense air, and her companion Gordon Thomas, a brisk and down-to-earth man who I liked immediately. To my pleasure, they both warmed to my idea of the top-down entropy reduction experiment. Interestingly enough, neither of them was a scientist. Dian was a philosopher who had graduated with singular honours from that good university, Stanford, and Gordon was a highly qualified statistician, but despite their lack of science, they made a powerful team. Dian was amongst the most intelligent of people I had met, and she had that formidable power of philosophers—the power to make me watch carefully my words and their meanings, even in casual conversation. They did not seem handicapped by their lack of a scientific background and were able to analyse, dissect, and judge well the type of experiments that JPL were sending to Mars.

Dian Hitchcock and Gordon Thomas sent their report on the JPL experiments to NASA headquarters, and soon I received a letter from a senior NASA scientist, the physiologist Orr Reynolds, inviting me to Washington. I checked in at the reception desk of the NASA Washington office, and Dian came to meet me. We went straight away to Reynolds's office where I found he shared our view that the proposed reductionist life-detection experiments, such as those that sought specific bacteria on the Martian surface, were unlikely to succeed and that a top-down approach had a better chance. He told us that after lunch there was a meeting on life-detection experiments in the conference room. Here scientists and administrators would be able to discuss the general problem of planetary life detection. He hoped that we would both be there to say our piece. On arrival, I was surprised to find copies of the draft of my *Nature* paper, 'The physical basis for life-detection experiments', at everyone's place. After the meeting began, one scientist, or administrator, I've forgotten which, asked, 'Who wrote this?' I admitted authorship and prepared myself for the same kind of destructive criticisms that I had encountered from the JPL biologists. To my delight, they treated Dian and me like explorers who had returned with news of a new and more promising land just over the horizon. From then on, life was heady and exciting, and I found myself taken seriously by senior administrators and scientists. I would not have missed it for anything. It was so different from the backseat advisory role that I had had until then. Looking back, I recognize now how much I owed to Dian Hitchcock. Her powerful intellect illuminated my intuition and not too well constructed arguments. She was also an American and knew instinctively, which I did not, how to frame a proposal so that it convinced the listeners. We all know Oscar Wilde's famous saying about the two cultures divided by a common language. Few of us, especially scientists, realize how different are the meanings of words used by the British and the Americans, and how easily a misunderstanding can arise.

Within a short time, I was astonished to find myself in the position of acting chief scientist for the physical life-detection experiments of the next Mars mission, then named Voyager. Dian and Gordon were part of the management of this project. Shortly after this meeting in Washington, I returned home to England. This was late in March of that year. Looking back, I realize that I must have been a great trial to my wife, Helen. Excitement over my promotion by NASA and the work of preparing proposals so filled my mind, that there was little time to be concerned with the pressing family matters that were coming fast upon us at that time. We did not know it then, but Helen was already well into the disease multiple sclerosis that was to blight her and all the family's lives for the next twenty-four years. The physicians in our part of Wiltshire, which was then deep in the English countryside, were not very experienced. Obvious signs, such as episodes of walking with one foot dragging, or partial one-sided blindness, were passed off as something that would get better by itself. Of course, in the nature of that miserable disease, MS, there are remissions, which tended to confirm the physician's diagnosis. To add to her problems, she was also in the midst of an early menopause. Then, as now, medicine was unduly influenced by an obsessive fear of cancer, and the slight possibility that treatment might cause cancer prevented physicians from using oestrogens, or oestrogen-progesterone mixes, now called hormone replacement therapy (HRT) for those suffering the miseries of the menopause. Many years passed before it became generally recognized that even if the gloomy prognostications of cancer were true, the general misery caused by denying those who suffered badly from the menopause the benefits of treatment were not worth it. Medicine in those days was still too concerned with diagnosis, and treatment was rarely the prime objective. To be fair, medicine before the 1940s had developed a relationship with patients which was little different from that of the alternative practitioners of today. Lewis Thomas describes it so well in his book, *The Youngest Profession*. Lewis tells of travelling with his father, a physician, on his rounds and discovering there were really only three medicines that worked at all: morphine, quinine, and insulin.

In late March 1965 I returned to California for a period of six weeks and travelled the whole continent. There were meetings with subcontractors, like Perkin Elmer, chosen by NASA to submit proposals for building the apparatus for the Voyager mission. We drafted a proposal to build an infrared telescope on top of White Mountain in California, specifically designed and built for planetary atmospheric analysis. At this time scientists still seemed to think that life flourished on Mars. I recall Carl Sagan enthusing over the wave of darkness that crosses Mars when winter ends. He and many others saw this phenomenon as indicative of the growth of vegetation, something similar to the springtime greening of the northern hemisphere of the Earth. This image of Mars sustained their belief in biological life-detection techniques.

There were visits to my friends, Sandy Lipsky at Yale University, who had first introduced me to NASA, and to Ab Zlatkis and Juan Oro in Houston. These university scientists saw my apparent preferment in NASA as a great opportunity for them and for their departments. Much of the time between these trips I spent as the guest of Dian Hitchcock at her home in Farmington, Connecticut. She, Gordon Thomas, and I worked daily putting everything into the design of our physical and chemical methods for detecting life on Mars. I had never before worked from immediately after breakfast right through until nearly midnight, but the pressure was on. In addition to this, we were also preparing a longer and more explicit scientific paper on life detection by atmospheric analysis. Dian helped me turn my partly digested intuitions into a firm and clear statement of why the analysis of the Martian atmosphere was the best way to look for life on the surface. On Bastille Day 1965 the Mariner spacecraft orbiting Mars sent back clear, high definition images of the Martian surface and showed it was all rock or desert. Far from causing the biologists to lose enthusiasm, this dismal news of a dead planet seemed to intensify their wish to seek life there.

This work for NASA so occupied my time that I had none left to continue working for my customers in England, who provided the bulk of my income. These were Shell, where I worked as an adviser to Victor Rothschild who was then science co-ordinator for the company, and to Pye Unicam in Cambridge, where I also offered advice on designs for laboratory gas chromatographs. Both companies were astonishingly generous. Pye offered to keep me on at half the £3,000-a-year retainer they had previously paid until the NASA work was completed. I did not expect it to continue indefinitely. Shell was even more generous, and Victor Rothschild said that as far as he was concerned I could work for NASA as long as I liked: it was a valuable service, and they would continue to pay my retainer in full. My formal connections with NASA were very vague; all I had was a yearly consultancy with JPL, and Dian paid my travelling expenses and hotel bills during the trips around America from her contract with NASA. If all of the contracts were added together, the proposals were seeking many millions of dollars of funds. In spite of the responsibility, I had no formal agreement with or payment from NASA headquarters itself. It did not seem to matter somehow.

Dian and I found time to write a paper on our proposed atmospheric life-detection experiment. Although neither of us realized it, the paper was a necessary step on the road to Gaia. Our paper so excited Victor Rothschild that he offered to edit it and then submit it to the Royal Society for publication in their *Proceedings*, and he duly did this. Predictably, the abominable no-men of the peer-review system rejected Lord Rothschild's submission just as disdainfully as they have most papers on Gaian topics. Those who rejected our paper took no trouble to read or understand it. They merely gave their own narrow views with that discourtesy typical of academics allowed to write as anonymous critics. Victor Rothschild swore, literally, and said that he would never submit another paper to the Royal Society. It was strangely comforting to me that Carl Sagan, who at that time shared an office with me at JPL, and who disagreed with almost everything in our paper, nevertheless offered to publish it in his journal *Icarus*, and this is where it appeared.

Looking back I can understand that the very idea of detecting life on a planet by atmospheric analysis must have seemed outrageous to the conventional astronomers and biologists who reviewed our paper. Conventional biology and planetary science held the false assumption that organisms merely adapt to their environment. My ideas for life detection acknowledged that organisms change their environment—this is an important part of Gaia theory but I did not think of it in that way then. Neither my critics nor I were aware of this fundamental difference of viewpoint. We argued from instinct, both feeling sure that the other was wrong. Peer review normally works well, but in these circumstances it was bound to fail.

In September 1965 these exciting but terrifying days as a space entrepreneur ended. Orr Reynolds asked me to meet him and Dian in New York. Over dinner that evening, he broke the news that Congress had withdrawn its support for the Voyager Mission. Dian and Reynolds were obviously disappointed, but it was not easy for me to hide my feeling of relief when I realized that I was no longer a manager and could go back to science. There was to be a Mars mission called Viking, using the life-detection experiments designed by the biologists. I guessed that some lobbying on behalf of conventional biology had taken place. Looking back, it was foolish to expect to overcome the opposition of the whole tribe of biologists; as in real war, having the right cause matters less than the size and equipment of your army.

I fully expected to hear from JPL that they no longer required my advice on instrument design, but they still welcomed my visits. My battles with the biologists and my fall from high managerial responsibility were of no consequence to the space engineers who needed me. They offered me contracts to develop breadboard instruments, and I willingly accepted. It vexed me a little to see the excellence of the engineers and instrument scientists wasted on what I thought were the wrong experiments—the search for living organisms or their products in the Martian regolith. I could not complain that not a single experiment on the Viking landers in 1975 incorporated any of my holistic life-detection ideas; it was not my personal spacecraft and I could have been wrong. A more serious complaint about the Viking Mission was that the scientific community lost a wonderful opportunity to find out more about Mars. Instead of looking pointlessly for 'life-characteristic substances' in the soil, they could have made an unbiased analysis of the Martian soil and atmosphere. In particular, the mass spectrometer that sat in the desert could have done much more than merely look for organic chemicals. It is true that some atmospheric analyses were made during the lander's descent, but these were not enough to answer important questions about the physics and chemistry of Mars's atmosphere. In science, as in warfare, strategy tends to conform to the national legend and consequently, the power and intelligence of the two Viking spacecraft were squandered on the search for life on a dead planet. Even today, NASA and its equivalent, the European Space Agency (ESA), seem to place the discovery of life in the solar system above the proper understanding of the system itself. Odder still, NASA scientists now propose using my holistic atmospheric life-detection method as the basis of their search for life on planets elsewhere in the galaxy, even though they reject its conclusions about the solar system.

The idea of using atmospheric analysis as a way to detect life on planets of the solar system is even more appropriate for detecting life on extra solar planets orbiting other stars. Indeed, apart from the rare event of life revealing itself by the emission of coherent radiation, there is no other practical way of detecting life on planets beyond the reach of landing spacecraft. A long-base interferometer mounted in space could, in principle, resolve a planet like the Earth from its star and provide a spectroscopic analysis of the planet's atmosphere. If we saw on some distant world abundant oxygen and water vapour, this would be good but not conclusive evidence of life. However, if we saw an incompatible gas mixture such as methane and oxygen it would be strong evidence of life. This would also be true if methane were the dominant gas, for it would suggest a planet with life at a stage like the Archean on the Earth when oxygen was only a minor constituent.

Gaia theory was born during my next visit to JPL. I arrived at LA airport at about 4 pm local time, midnight by my own time. Air travel encourages drinking, and an incipient hangover nibbled at the edge of my jet lag. No longer was the JPL helicopter waiting to take me to Pasadena. This time it was a taxi, and the journey through the heat and the smog and the creeping traffic of rush hour completed the discomfort. At least I could go straight to bed at the comfortable Huntington Sheraton in Pasadena and catch up my lost sleep during the long night ahead.

When I arrived at JPL the next morning, I was intrigued to find it easy to enter that security-conscious establishment in my new role as a contractor. Contractors were real people who understood the value of money, and in that wonderfully capitalist society, they seemed to be much more respected than mere scientists are. My work for the Jet Propulsion Labs was now almost wholly concerned with instrument design. They gave my company, Brazzos Limited, specific tasks to fulfil during the time that I was back in England, but they still invited me to participate in discussions about the life-detection experiments for Mars, and I regard this as a most generous gesture on their part. Much more than this, JPL gave me a second chance to be part of the Viking science team. Gerry Soffen, a senior figure at the laboratory, came to me one afternoon and asked if I would like to be the lead experimenter on the Viking atmospheric analysis experiment. Sadly, I had to refuse, for the post would have required me to move to California, or to make monthly visits, for the next six years. I could not do either of these things because Helen was now badly disabled by multiple sclerosis and she needed me near at hand for most of the time. Toby Owen, a first rank atmospheric scientist from Stoneybrook University in New York, took on the post.

One afternoon in September 1965, I was in the Space Science Building of JPL in a small office that looked out towards the mountains. The astronomer, Lou Kaplan, had brought in the infrared spectrum charts of the latest sightings from the Pic de Midi Observatory in France. They provided a detailed analysis of the chemical composition of the atmospheres of Mars and Venus and for the first time we saw that both planets had atmospheres dominated by carbon dioxide, with only traces of other gases present. As I had suspected, the cratered, moonlike Mars had an atmosphere close to chemical equilibrium, and it was profoundly different from the rich and anomalous atmosphere of Earth. Our sibling planets had atmospheres as barren and lifeless as the regolith of the Moon, but here our own air has oxygen mixed with methane, and carbon dioxide is a mere trace at only 300 parts per million. Even nitrogen, the dominant gas of the air, makes no sense. The stable form of the element nitrogen is not the gas in the air but the nitrate ion dissolved in the ocean. The distinguished American physical chemist, GN Lewis had proved this in the 1920s. Nitrogen in the air is always reacting with oxygen to form nitric acid, which dissolves in the sea to form the stable nitrates, and they would stay there but for the ceaseless activity of bacteria, which return the nitrogen to the air. Looked at as a whole, our atmosphere is a combustible mixture. More than this, it is in a sense continuously burning. This is because the shorter wavelength of sunlight, the far ultraviolet that illuminates the upper part of the atmosphere, can in effect ignite the combustion of gases such as methane and oxygen. It is what the chemists call a cool flame, and it has been burning for hundreds of millions of years. The combustion of the air is no mere metaphor—it really happens—and distinguished physical chemists like Sir David Bates of Queen's University, Belfast and Marcel Nicolet, in Brussels, were then wondering about its nature and significance.

Until that afternoon, my thoughts on planetary atmospheres had been wholly concerned with atmospheric analysis as a method of life detection and nothing more. Now that I knew the composition of the Martian atmosphere was so different from that of our own, my mind filled with wonderings about the nature of the Earth. If the air is burning, what sustains it at a constant composition? I also wondered about the supply of fuel and the removal of the products of combustion. It came to me suddenly, just like a flash of enlightenment, that to persist and keep stable, something must be regulating the atmosphere and so keeping it at its constant composition. Moreover, if most of the gases came from living organisms, then life at the surface must be doing the regulation. I blurted out my intuition to my colleague Dian Hitchcock and to the cosmologist Carl Sagan. There was little comment at the time. Afterwards Carl told me about the paradox of the cool Sun. Our star has not always been as bright as it is now, and in the beginning, it was thought to be some twenty-five to thirty per cent less luminous. The puzzle was, if this was so, how is it that the geological record suggests that, apart from a few brief ice ages, the Earth has always been warm. A twenty-five per cent drop in luminosity with our present atmosphere would freeze much of the Earth's surface and oceans. As Pasteur and others have said, 'Chance favours the prepared mind.' My mind was well prepared emotionally and scientifically and it dawned on me that somehow life was regulating climate as well as chemistry. Suddenly the image of the Earth as a living organism able to regulate its temperature and chemistry at a comfortable steady state emerged in my mind. At such moments, there is no time or place for such niceties as the qualification 'of course it is not alive—it merely behaves as if it were'.

By this time the distinguished biologist, Norman Horowitz, had taken charge of JPL biology; he was also Professor of Biology at that famous university, Cal Tech, which was not far from JPL. Norman was an amiable man who reminded me of the playwright Arthur Miller. He was open-minded, and although he disagreed with my views about the Earth and its atmosphere, he thought, as the good scientist he was, that they should be heard. Two years later, in 1967, he arranged for me to present the first paper on my idea of a self-regulating Earth system at a meeting of the American Astronautical Society in Lansing, Michigan. The space scientists and engineers who were there received my account of the Earth as a quasi-living system enthusiastically. This is not so surprising because engineers understand the concept of feedback and the way systems work; they share this understanding with physiologists. Norman Horowitz and I shared the opinion that there was no need to sterilize the Martian landers. The concept of contaminating a virginal Mars with earth-type life seemed the stuff of fanatics, not scientists, and the act of sterilization hazarded the delicate and intricate instruments we wanted to send to Mars.

In the next year, 1968, Princeton University hosted a more academically significant meeting, and here I met for the first time Lynn Margulis and the Norwegian scientist, Lars Sillen. This distinguished geochemist was the first Earth scientist I had met who was prepared to listen to my thoughts on a self-regulating Earth and consider them as science. Also present were some of the most prominent members of the United States geological community, and Philip Handler, who was later to become President of the National Academy of Sciences, chaired the meeting together with Norman Horowitz. Lynn Margulis, as the youngest member present, had the job of rapporteur, and she published her account as a book in the series, The Origins of Life. Perhaps the task of reporting everything we said was onerous and she had no time or opportunity to think about it. Certainly, I had no contact or discussion with her at the meeting. My fruitful collaboration with Lynn was not to begin until some time later. For me the meeting was fascinating, but frustrating because senior American scientists were then heavily authoritative. These eminent professors expected young scientists like Lynn and me to be seen but not heard; we were there to be used, not to have opinions.

Consequently, whenever I raised my strange views about the atmosphere they either ignored them or brushed them aside as irrelevant. Towards the end of the meeting, when I asked somewhat plaintively for a chance to get a word in edgeways, Norman Horowitz and Lars Sillen came to my rescue. There are a few of my words about our strange and anomalous atmosphere reported in *Proceedings of the Second Conference on Origins of Life* and published in 1971 by Gordon and Breach of New York.

Around about this time I started my first visits to the National Center for Atmospheric Research at Boulder in Colorado (NCAR) and it soon became a regular stopping place on my visits to JPL. It is probably the most beautiful scientific institute in the world and sited on Table Mesa well above the small city of Boulder, its shapely natural stone edifice is like a cathedral. On most visits there I would ask the directors, who included Walter Orr Roberts and Will Kellog, when they would open a department of biology at NCAR. Although I meant it seriously, it was good for a laugh in those days, but now there are biologists there and among them Lee Klinger who has pioneered the role of peat bogs as an ecosystem of global significance. Boulder is also the home of NOAA laboratories and the University of Colorado. It is a science city where my friends Robert Sievers and Adrian Tuck also live. Bob Sievers and I share a long history of instrument development and Adrian Tuck was my constant contact at the Meteorological Office in England before he left for Boulder.

The novelist, William Golding, suggested the name Gaia for my notions about a self-regulating Earth. He and his wife Ann were friends who lived in a large thatched house near where the river Ebble sprang from the chalk at the lowest part of the village of Bowerchalke. Bill had taught history at the Bishop Wordsworth school in Salisbury but the success of his novel *Lord of the Flies* enabled an independent life. He had the comfortable air and casual way of dress that justly earned him, when he was a schoolmaster, the nickname Scruffy. We would often meet in the Bell, the village pub, and exchanged visits to talk on some particular subject of mutual interest such as science fiction or space research. One morning when walking up the village road, I overtook Bill who was on his way to the post office. We began talking and he asked me about my latest trip to JPL. Bill had had a scientific, as well as a classical education, and he was warmly appreciative of my tale about a self-regulating planet. After we had walked and talked well beyond the post office, Bill turned to me and said, 'If you want to propagate a large theory about the Earth you had better give it a proper name. I suggest that you call it Gaia.' We walked on and continued talking for some time, but at cross-purposes: I thought that he had suggested calling the theory 'Gyre' after one of the great whirls of the atmosphere and the ocean. When he put me right by explaining that he meant the Gaia of mythology, the Greek goddess of the Earth, I was deeply grateful. Few scientists have had their theories named by so competent a wordsmith.

Biologists have attacked the name Gaia and the metaphor of a living Earth as if I intended them as fact. I now think they did this from an instinctive dislike of holistic ideas, not because they were greedy over metaphors. I never begrudged them 'The Selfish Gene', 'The Red Queen', or the 'The Blind Watchmaker'. Nor do I pedantically argue that to be selfish a gene would have to take thought and have purpose. Their attack on the metaphor of Gaia, the living Earth, was not a proper scientific criticism: it was a gut reaction to an unwelcome theory. Not all biologists were hostile. There was the friendly scepticism of that most eminent scientist EO Wilson, whose recent book *Consilience* reveals the breadth of his wisdom. The Nobel Laureate, Christian de Duve, in his book *Vital Dust*, gave Gaia a fair hearing and Norman Myers, when he edited the famous *Gaia Atlas of Planetary Management*, did homage to the name Gaia.

My first correspondence with Lynn Margulis on the science of Gaia was in the summer of 1970. Lynn had begun to wonder about the significance of oxygen in the atmosphere and had asked Carl Sagan, her former husband, who would be his first choice of scientist to ask about atmospheric oxygen. Strangely, Carl recommended me: had I been him I would have named either GE Hutchinson, the founder of biogeochemistry or LV Berkner who, with LC Marshall, had recently written a monograph on atmospheric oxygen. Soon after, I received a letter from Lynn inviting me to visit her lab on my next visit, but it was not until late in 1971 that I was able to accept. My memory of that first meeting is sketchy and mingled with numerous others in the years to come. I seem to recall Lynn meeting my flight at Boston's Logan airport in December 1971, and that we travelled to her lab at Boston University on a subway train. Our exchange there was enthusiastic and Lynn's deep understanding of microbial ecology impressed and influenced me; she was the first biologist I had met who had a feeling for the organism. After that, a bacterium ceased for me to be merely a membrane bag holding some genes and proteinaceous mechanisms which could reproduce itself, and nothing more. Lynn's empathy with microbial communities has greatly enriched our understanding of Gaia and of the importance of the microbial sector in the whole system. She explains it in a book written with her son Dorion Sagan, *Microcosmos*, and most recently in *Symbiotic Earth*.

It was a coming together of minds that led to many more visits and for several years, Boston was my first port of call on visits to the USA. So amiable were our meetings in the early 1970s that after one of them Lynn felt the need to set the ground rules for our continuing association. We sat in Logan airport waiting the call for my return flight and she turned to me and with great seriousness said that we must meet as scientific colleagues and nothing more. I agreed without any sense of regret; it is rare for close scientific collaborations to evolve into romances.

During those years, I enjoyed my visits to Boston. Lynn Margulis and her family always made me welcome at their home in Newton. She was then married to Nicholas Margulis and with four children in the house—Dorion and Jeremy, children of her first marriage to Carl Sagan, and Zach and Jenny from her marriage to Nicky Margulis—it was a lively family. The atmosphere was turbulent, warm, and familiar. Lynn and I worked closely and harmoniously together. We had a few arguments. The ones I remember most were about Vernadsky. I agreed with Lynn that he had anticipated some of our ideas, but I disagreed with her about his position in the pantheon of science. I could not see him as one of science's great figures, like Galileo or Darwin. His statement, 'Life is a geological force', certainly captured one part of Gaia theory, but I am unimpressed by those who merely talk or write about an idea without doing experiments or presenting models and theories that we can challenge. Moreover, like so many contemporary scientists, he did not seem to have a feeling for system science and the tight-coupled feedback between life and its environment. I did not understand Lynn's need to single out Vernadsky for special praise when there were so many others who had trodden the same path as we were on. I was sure that James Hutton, TH Huxley, Friederich Humbolt, Lawrence Henderson, AC Redfield, and most of all Eugene Odum, GE Hutchinson and Alfred Lotka were scientists as deserving of recognition as our predecessors. I suspect that we were arguing about legends, not science.

On most other things, Lynn and I supported and complemented each other wonderfully. Her broad experience and wisdom about living things, especially about micro-organisms, put flesh on the bare bones of my skeleton of Gaia. I shall never forget her welcome when I went to Boston University straight from the airport, and her enthusiasm as she told me about the snail in Brittany that lives in part by photosynthesis like a plant. What a metaphor: 'The solar-powered snail.' Lynn had her own battles with the ponderous scientific establishment, mainly over her support for the endosymbiont hypothesis. As with Gaia, they now take for granted that organelles, like mitochondria and chloroplasts, were once free-living organisms, and that at some step in evolution they entered a symbiotic relationship with their eukaryotic hosts. However, Lynn's contribution to this discovery is too rarely mentioned. William James was so right when he said that the fate of a new idea follows the pattern: at first absurd, then maybe true, and, finally, we knew it all along.

Lynn and I were strange opposites to be so closely connected by Gaia. Lynn was at her best in the centre of a group of good students, giving and taking. I was at my best alone and thinking. Together, we explored endlessly the possible systems involving the biota that could serve as Gaian regulators of climate and chemistry. Lynn opened for me the world of natural micro-organisms. I knew one end of a bacterium from the other, having spent my time doing clinical bacteriology, and I knew a little about the multitude of natural airborne organisms that have nothing to do with clinical bacteriology. I knew this from my days sampling the air of London, but I knew almost nothing of the great world of micro-organisms that has existed from 3.5 to 4 billion years ago until now. Through Lynn and through her scientist friends, like the micropaleontologist ES Barghoorn at Harvard, I learnt how important these are and have been since life began 3.7 billion years ago. Big things like trees, elephants, and whales, lesser ones like shrubs and humans, and tiny things like worms and insects, all are recent. During the period that we worked together, other scientists were glad to hear us tell our tale, but rarely ever would they take it seriously. It remained an entertainment, a flight of fancy.

In the early days, we were somewhat outrageous in our statements. We had to be. We were in a way like a neglected child who behaves badly if this is the only way for him to attract attention. I used the metaphor of a living Earth provocatively to make some humourless biologists think I really thought the Earth was alive and reproduces.

Of course, I did not. Our papers and my book allowed our critics to be more focused so that we could take them more seriously. For me, this led to model making, but Lynn, with that wonderful feeling for the organism that is the good heart of biology, had little time for abstract models and took a more direct approach.

An important step in the evolution of Gaia theory took place at a Gordon Conference on Atmospheric Chemistry in August 1971. These conferences are one of the best features of American science. During vacation time, the private boarding schools that spread across upper New England, mainly in New Hampshire, use their accommodation to host dozens of scientific conferences. The better ones are gatherings of actively working scientists who report their latest findings and ideas to an audience of their peers. There are rarely more than sixty present and their talks are not published, even as a conference report. Presentations take place in the mornings and evenings; the afternoons of the conferences from lunch until dinnertime are free for walks in the mountains or swimming in the lakes of that beautiful part of America or, of course, for quiet, intense debates, sitting on the terrace of the school.

As a frequent attender at Gordon Conferences I enjoyed the fringe benefits such as climbing one of the small granite mountains near New Hampton, the site of the 1971 conference. The guide who led us up Mount Cardigan was dubious about my capacity, at fifty-one years old, to keep up with younger men and women who had chosen to spend their afternoon this way. Having climbed Snowdon, a Welsh mountain of the same height, by the exciting Crib Goch the previous year, I told him that I thought I could manage. It was a glorious afternoon walk up a rocky pass, first through a pine forest and clear streams, and then up onto the smooth assembly of granite slabs, mostly bare, that led to the mountain top. As always, at the top there was a feeling of achievement and the reward of a grand view of the lakes and mountains of northern New England. I must admit to having misjudged the beauty of the New England countryside. New Hampshire, Vermont, and Maine were more attractive to me than the states further south.

The next afternoon I spent swimming in the lake and then walking along its beach with the German scientist Dieter Ehalt from NCAR. We talked about methane. Dieter was the acknowledged leader of research on the production and fate of this important atmospheric gas. I had long been interested in its significance as evidence for a self-regulated atmosphere and one of the props of Gaia theory. As we passed a small, slow-moving stream that flowed into the lake, Dieter took a stick and stirred the black detritus at the bottom of the stream. A burst of bubbles came forth. 'There's the methane,' he remarked. I had known that about 500,000,000 tons of the gas escaped from the ground into the air each year, but this simple demonstration fixed forever in my mind its reality. My long-time friend from Boulder, Jim Lodge, had organized this Gordon Conference on Atmospheric Chemistry and it was an outstanding success. The thirty years of important and exciting atmospheric science that followed owed their start to that meeting. We talked of future climates, the effect of greenhouse gases and the cooling by clouds and aerosols. We discussed at length the chemical cycles of the elements. Here, also, I presented my measurements of the atmospheric abundance of CFCs and DMS.

At this same meeting, Joe Prospero talked about atmospheric aerosols and the composition of dust collected at stations in Florida and even in Hawaii. I was amazed to hear that Sahara dust blew all the way across the Atlantic and even into the Pacific. We also argued over the super abundance of elements such as sulphur, selenium, iodine and zinc in the aerosol particles. I speculated that perhaps biological methylation rendered these elements volatile and carried an excess of them into the atmosphere. Here were the first steps towards the discovery years later with Bob Charlson, Andi Andreae, Steve Warren, and myself that clouds, dimethyl sulphide from algae living in the ocean, and climate, are all intimately linked in a great ocean atmospheric cycle. My report at this meeting on the prevalence of CFCs in the troposphere led Lester Machta later to alert Sherry Rowland to this source of chlorine in the atmosphere, and to the recognition that chlorine in the stratosphere might catalytically deplete the ozone there.

GD Robinson came to me one afternoon and said, 'Could you give us a ten to fifteen-minute talk on Gaia after dinner tonight?' He introduced me that evening as someone who would entertain them with a flight of fancy. It was my first talk on Gaia to an audience of atmospheric scientists and I published it in *Atmospheric Environment* two years later with the title 'Gaia as seen through the atmosphere'.

During the 1970s and until 1982, when I fell ill, Lynn Margulis and I spent as much of our time developing Gaia as we could. Neither of us received support for our work, and both of us were busy with other work. Lynn had her teaching and other duties at Boston University, and I had my customers, as well as the burgeoning ozone depletion research. We published two important joint papers. I wrote the first, 'Atmospheric homeostasis by and for the biosphere: the Gaia hypothesis', and it expresses Gaia as I then saw it. The second, 'Biological modulation of the Earth's atmosphere', Lynn wrote, and it expresses her view of Gaia. These titles reveal our ignorance then of the fact that regulation is a property of the whole system of life and its environment, not just life itself. A high spot in this period was an expedition organized by Lynn, who gathered the funds to enable a party of scientists to visit Baja California and do research on the algal mats there. She took us from San Diego to Laguna Figueroa, a place about 200 miles down the Baja California peninsula. Algal mats are the communities of micro-organisms whose ancestry dates back to the Earth's earliest history and may have played a huge part in regulating the Earth system over the whole of that time.

We met in a small hotel near the Scripps Institute at La Jolla, a cosy, wealthy institute, and so well sited on the shore of the Pacific. Almost as comfortable, I thought, as Coombe Mill. We travelled south in two people-carriers and passed across the border and through the dismal town of Tijuana, and then down the Baja peninsula itself. The real Mexico revealed itself as we travelled south. When we arrived at our destination, we found that we were booked into a small hotel. Having suffered from eating at American–Mexican restaurants, I rather dreaded a week of Mexican food. I could not have been more wrong. The food at our hotel was magnificent, and I found myself looking forward with anticipation to every meal. National cuisine gets a bad name from its restaurants in the capital cities of the western world.

Along the edges of the continents, earth movement and the drifting of sand and shingle forms lagoons that trap ocean water. In the warmer parts of the world, these lagoons lose more water by evaporation than they gain from rainfall or from sea water leaking in from the ocean. Consequently, the salt in the water concentrates until it crystallizes to form what the geologists call an evaporite deposit. This process has been going on since the beginning of time and we find evaporite beds buried under sediments all over the world. They form the huge salt deposits, like the one that runs across northern Europe a few hundred feet below the surface and is made notorious by the salt mines of Eastern Europe. The algal mats sit on top of these evaporite beds. Lynn, her student, Greg Hinkel, and I speculated about the role of these mats in sustaining salt in the beds, and so keeping the ocean below the critical salt level of 0.8 molar. Above this salinity, organisms find it hard to survive. I watched as Lynn cut out with a small spade a cube of the mat four inches in size. We looked at its banded structure: each band was a different community of micro-organisms segregated according to the flow of nutrients and oxygen. Lynn showed how similar was this banded structure to that of the fossil mats over two billion years old. I was convinced by her lucid explanations that micro-organisms are the heart of Gaia and always have been.

On one occasion, I went with Lynn, her daughter, Jenny, and a French au pair girl, to another Gordon Conference in New Hampshire. We gave our Gaia talks and soon discovered that we were not there as serious scientists but more as entertainment. The serious business of the conference, we discovered, focused on arcane topics dear to the timber industry. This allowed us plenty of time to explore the New Hampshire Mountains. We had just climbed one peak and were making our way down over the granite boulders and small shrubs, talking passionately about a Gaian problem, when suddenly we found ourselves deep in the forest. We were lost. Lynn gave a cry: 'There are thousands of miles of nothing between here and Canada and if we go the wrong way they will find our bodies in the spring.' We tried to retrace our path, and with luck, came upon a logger's trail, which we followed down to the road, but it was a scary moment. As time went by, Lynn and I saw less of each other, mainly because the forces of family life and work were dispersive not cohesive. It was the best of my lifetime collaborations and was a platonic relationship that kept in a lively steady state. The sad events in both our families conspired to separate us as active scientific colleagues in the 1980s but we both continued to develop Gaia in our own ways. My friendship with Lynn has grown with the years and it now includes my second wife Sandy, and embraces her own partner, the distinguished Catalan scientist, Ricardo Guerrero.

Well-disposed non-scientists seem to think that science is founded on impeccable measurements and based in certainty. Scientists sometimes act upon this myth and become as dogmatic as are the religious. Remember Einstein's famous denigration of the quantum theory, in a personal letter to Max Born, which is often summarized as: God does not play dice with the Universe. The radical French philosopher, Michel Foucault, said, 'The truth is not discovered: it is something produced by the elite.' He was talking of politics but his observation is true of science also. The truth at any time trickles down from the heights of the eminent. If senior biologists, respected by their peers, say life adapts to its environment, then this becomes the working dogma of biology. If senior geologists, similarly respected, say the presence of life is not needed to explain the evolution of the rocks, this also becomes a dogma. Together, these dogmatic beliefs become the conventional wisdom of science. It is in our nature to seek certainty. Because of their 'faith' in the conventional wisdom, most scientists rejected our life-detection experiments and Gaia theory when they were first proposed. They did so with that same certainty that the religious have when they reject the views of a rational atheist. They could not prove us wrong but they were sure in their hearts that we were. Lynn and I were astonished at what seemed to us a most unscientific attitude on the part of our peers, and by the scorn of their rejection. I was an innocent to expect Gaia's acceptance, and truly foolish to imagine that such a radical theory could succeed in such an environment. It had as little chance of success as would a proponent of market capitalism have had in Lenin's Russia.

The early 1970s were exciting yet frustrating. I read GE Hutchinson's wonderful chapter called 'The Biochemistry of the Earth' in a book on the solar system and found that he came quite close to my own views about the Earth. He seemed to draw back from seeing it as self-regulating and went no further than to say it was an interesting chemical anomaly. Sometime during this period, I tried to have a talk with him during a brief visit to Yale University. There was also present at the meeting the geochemist, Jim Walker, who strongly, but in a friendly way, disagreed with my views, and did not hesitate to speak out against them. Both Hutchinson and I were somewhat quiet speakers and needed time to digest our exchanges. The threesome did not work and we achieved little. Sadly, I was never to have another opportunity of meeting Hutchinson before he died. I regret not reading Eugene Odum's papers at this time for he alone understood that an ecosystem is a deterministic feedback system, which is how I saw Gaia: in many ways Gaia is the ecosystem of the Earth.

The first real stirrings of public interest in Gaia followed the publication of a paper written with my friend, Sidney Epton, of Shell. The title was 'The quest for Gaia' and it appeared in *New Scientist* in 1975. This paper did attract attention from the media. I received twenty-one letters and telegrams from publishers inviting me to write a book on

Gaia. I chose Oxford University Press mainly because they sent a most personable representative, Peter Janson Smith, someone I liked and could easily work with. The book took four years to write and appeared in 1979. Its publication completely changed my life and the fall of mail through my letterbox increased from a gentle patter to a downpour, and has remained high ever since. To my astonishment, the main interest in Gaia came from the general public, from philosophers and from the religious. Only a third of the letters were from scientists. I never intended the book as a science text for specialists, but I did expect them to read it. I have always thought that science should be accessible to any intelligent person. Science affects our lives and that of the Earth so much that it would be monstrous for it to retreat to a world of jargon accessible only to the denizens of cosy ivory towers. I wrote the book as if it were a long letter about Gaia to a lively intelligent woman.

Geologists rejected the Gaia book gently, but biologists ridiculed it. Ford Doolittle was the first to do so. His article 'Is Nature motherly?' in the New Age journal, *Co-Evolution Quarterly*, argued that self-regulation by organisms required them to have foresight and to plan, which was impossible. Then Richard Dawkins argued against it in his book, *The Extended Phenotype*. His robust criticism observed that a living Earth could never have evolved by natural selection. How could planets compete with one another? It took me until December 1981 to find the answer to these criticisms and it was in the form of a mathematical model, which I called Daisyworld. I never intended Daisyworld to be more than a caricature, and accept that it may turn out a poor likeness when we finally understand the world. Even so, I still see it as my proudest invention and its main value is as Andrew Watson called it, a parable about Gaia and Earth System Science.

I populated my model world with two species of plant, dark- and light-coloured daisies; their world was well watered and had a simple climate uncomplicated by clouds or greenhouse gases. Daisyworld was in orbit around a star like the Sun, one that increased its flux of heat as it grew older. The model showed that the natural selection of daisy species growing on this planet led to the self-regulation of climate at a temperature near optimal for plant growth, despite large variations in heat from the star. When the star was young and cool, dark daisies covered the planet and, by absorbing sunlight, made it 17° C, warmer than it would have been without them. As the star warmed, the lighter daisies began to grow and compete, and their reflection of sunlight cooled the planet and kept the temperature optimal as the star increased its output of heat. Eventually, the star became so hot that even a total cover with light daisies was insufficient to prevent overheating and the system failed. It showed definitively that Ford Doolittle's criticism that teleology would be required was wrong, as was Richard Dawkins's criticism that planets would have to compete to select for self-regulation.

Daisyworld is much more than an answer to these criticisms; it shows how self-regulation could be a property of a planetary system and result from the tight coupling of biological and physical evolution. Daisyworld also provides a tractable working model of the phenomenon of emergence, and is an illustration of that wonderful state when the whole is more than the sum of its parts. I presented the first account of Daisyworld at a conference in the Netherlands in 1982 hosted by the Dutch scientist, Peter Westbroek. It appeared in the conference proceedings, but this kind of publication only establishes priority in a legal sense. Scientists now accept only peer-reviewed papers. I knew that Daisyworld needed publication in a proper journal. My problem was that I could not write mathematical papers in a way the referees would accept. I therefore asked my friend, Andrew Watson, if he would join with me as co-author. Andrew writes well and, unlike me, in a way that other scientists like. He is also an accomplished mathematician. He agreed and we prepared our Daisyworld paper. We tried *Nature* first, but that journal would not even consider sending it to referees. We then submitted it to *Tellus*, the journal that had published my second paper on Gaia, the one written with Lynn Margulis in 1974. *Tellus* published Daisyworld in 1983.

Daisyworld is a synopsis of Gaia Theory. It shows how organisms evolving under the rules of natural selection are part of a system that is self-regulating. Daisyworld keeps its temperature close to the optimum for daisy growth. There is no teleology or foresight in it. Neither is there, as our critics persist in saying, any built-in prejudice in favour of regulation. The persistence of this inept criticism so irritated me, especially since it came from prejudice, not from thought, that I made a simple variant of Daisyworld where, at the start, the organisms were all grey daisies. Grey daisies have no effect on global temperature. I then allowed them a small chance to mutate at random either to slightly darker than grey or to slightly lighter than grey. This chance mutation is what would happen in nature, and biologists would see it as adaptation. Not surprisingly, when this new model Daisyworld was cold, the daisies that mutated to slightly darker than grey had a better chance of survival because they were warmer. In a short time, mutation had moved the average daisy colour almost to black. This is similar to the change of skin colour when white-skinned people are exposed to a few thousand years of tropical sun—the cumulative ill effects of sunburn reduces the family size of paler people. As Daisyworld warmed, so the average colour grew lighter, until at the hottest, it was close to white. This model was a better temperature regulator than the original Daisyworld. Tim Lenton has developed and expanded it. He demonstrated that adapting by mutation confers advantages not present in the original black-and-white Daisyworld.

Daisyworld can model the regulation of the chemical environment as well as the climate. In my book, *The Ages of Gaia*, written in the mid-1980s, are described models of bacterial ecosystems that simultaneously regulate climate, greenhouse gases, and oxygen. Daisyworld models are distinguished by their remarkable resilience and stability. Disasters can occur in the models that destroy up to eighty per cent of the organisms, but in spite of them, the system promptly recovers once the disaster is over. Stephan Harding, an ecologist working at the Schumacher College in Devon, has built complex ecosystems involving a wide range of food webs among plants, herbivores, and carnivores. He has taken advantage of Daisyworld's stability to show how more complex food webs give rise to greater climatic and ecosystem stability, and how this comes about due to tight coupling between organisms and their global climate. Stephan is a biologist who trained in Oxford in the Department of Zoology and had as mentors such luminaries as Richard Dawkins and William Hamilton. Stephan has been instrumental in building bridges between Gaian scientists and the evolutionary biologists. He and his partner, Julia Ponsonby, have become firm friends and we walk and work together regularly.

Daisyworld is the first mathematical model of a world that evolves by Darwinian natural selection, and on which the evolution of the environment, represented by temperature and the evolution of the organisms, is a single coupled process. The self-regulation of global climate emerges as the model evolves. It is both a simple climate model and a population biology model. Peter Saunders, Professor of Mathematics at King's College London, wrote a fine paper for the *Journal of Theoretical Biology* in 1994 analysing the mathematics of

Daisyworld and confirmed it as a valid evolutionary model. Few biologists seem to agree and some even refer to it as a mere computer game. There are fouls in science, just as in sport, and this foul criticism of Daisyworld is an own goal. No competent computer modeller would make the mistake of denigrating a computer game. However trivial the play, it can take the imagination of an artist and the skill of a wrangler to write the program for a game. A high moment in my quest for Gaia was a visit to Coombe Mill of a talented game programmer, Will Wright, who was at that time with the firm Maxis, and who had developed the popular game SimCity. He asked me if I would collaborate with them to produce a game about the Earth called SimEarth, which would include versions of Daisyworld. It was a thrill and enlightenment for me to work for a while with so competent a computer programmer. Maxis, without my asking, paid royalties from the sales of SimEarth to our charity, Gaia, that sustained our research during a difficult time.

The years between 1979 and 1984 were difficult. No matter how I tried to persuade scientists that they should take Gaia seriously, I rarely succeeded. Through the 1980s, Gaia was treated more as science fiction than science, and it became almost impossible to publish a paper with Gaia in the title or even in the text, unless it was to denounce it. The New Age movement took Gaia to their bosom but, sadly, too many of their good intentions were neutralized by a lack of rigour. The rejection by some New Agers of science itself made my task even harder. It confirmed for many senior scientists that Gaia was not only wrong; it was dangerous. They saw it as a topic like astrology that masqueraded as a science but was nonsense. An outstanding exception to the loose thinking of the New Age was the journal *Co-Evolution Quarterly*, under the editorship of Stewart Brand. The journal published several articles from Lynn and from me and from scientists who criticized Gaia. Stewart and Patti, his wife, became good friends, and we have visited and corresponded over the years.

A great comfort during these bad times was the presence of Teddy Goldsmith at Withiel, not far from Coombe Mill. Teddy was much like my Uncle Hugo Leakey—wonderfully erudite, fast on his feet in argument and, like his famous brother Sir James Goldsmith, effective. He was a fine critic and needed to be, because there were many issues of Green politics on which we disagreed, notably my liking for nuclear power. Teddy had more influence on my thinking than I think he knew. His strength and consistency made him for me a touchstone on

Green affairs and his book on Green philosophy, *The Way*, is a power-ful statement of the philosophy behind Green thinking. Teddy and his wife Kathy lived in a manor house where they lived a life consistent with their principles, even to the extent of using earth closets inside the manor house. Few things vex me more than Green hypocrisy, such as the sight of a monstrous four-wheel-drive gas-guzzler with a sticker on the back bearing some trendy Green message.

The disappointment I felt over Gaia's rejection was intensified by my problems at home; Helen was slowly losing her battle with multiple sclerosis, and I seemed to spend too much of my time in hospital for surgery. The 1980s were a decade of pain and long discomfort. Of course, there were good moments: visits to and from Bob and Cynthia Garrels were joyful events. And looking back, I think I was too depressed by my personal problems to notice that the work I did with Andrew Watson and Michael Whitfield at the Marine Biology Laboratory in Plymouth, was key to the establishment of Gaia theory in science. I had long thought that the observation that CO_2 in the soil throughout the world was concentrated between ten and thirty times more than in the atmosphere was important evidence for Gaia. Biogeochemists accepted the evidence and agreed that it was due to the metabolism of soil micro-organisms, but they failed to see its significance globally. I saw the high concentration of soil CO_2 linked with faster rock weathering and a greater rate of removal of CO_2 from the air, which in turn leads to a cooler global climate. We proposed that the weathering of the rocks by carbon dioxide and rainwater was part of a self-regulating process, which involved the living organisms in the soil. When it was warm, growth was faster, more carbon dioxide was pumped from the air, and any tendency to excessive heat or carbon dioxide was resisted. By this and other means the Earth was kept always at a comfortable level for life. We argued that rock weathering was more than just a geochemical activity, because the rocks were always in contact with organisms ranging from bac-teria, through lichens, to plants, and we suggested that weathering took place at least ten times faster as a result. Not only this, but because plant growth is temperature-sensitive, the presence of organ-isms coupled climate to weathering, and to the rate of removal of carbon dioxide from the air. This long-term geological process has kept the Earth at a favourable temperature as the Sun has warmed up. We published these ideas in two papers in the early 1980s and the American scientists, David Schwartzman and Tyler Volk confirmed them by experiment in 1989. They are now part of the wisdom of Earth System Science.

I was always seeking possible mechanisms for the self-regulation of climate, and the work of Glenn Shaw, an aeronomist working at the University of Alaska, intrigued me. He proposed that the biological emission of sulphur compounds from ocean sources was the source of the sulphate aerosol in the stratosphere. This aerosol reflects sunlight back to space and makes the earth cooler. It occasionally increases in density when volcanoes inject sulphur dioxide into the stratosphere, and consequently several years of cold weather follow the eruption. Glenn Shaw suggested that the biological emission of sulphur gases from the ocean might be part of a climate-regulating mechanism. It might have been in the Earth's past, but it seemed that at present the climatic effect of the background stratospheric aerosol was small.

The event that was to lift Gaia theory from its mid-life doldrums came unexpectedly. In 1986 the ocean scientist, Dr Murray, of the University of Washington in Seattle, invited me to be a Walker Ames Visiting Professor. This involved a month's visit to lecture and to interact with students and scientists of the university. Following a lecture in the Chemistry department, I had a fruitful discussion with Robert Charlson, a distinguished atmospheric scientist interested in clouds. Bob Charlson belied the name of his calling, he was no light ethereal being, but one with feet firmly anchored to the ground. He is a dark-haired sturdy man with the look of a sailor, and he would have fitted naturally on the quayside of my nearest fishing village, Port Isaac. I am proud to have him as a friend.

Bob told me that there was an unanswered question about clouds over the ocean. What is the source of the tiny particles, the nuclei of water-soluble substances, from which clouds form? Without these nuclei, there can be no clouds. When Bob said this, I was surprised. Surely, the water that evaporates from the warm sea will condense into droplets as it rises into the cold air. 'Yes,' he said, 'it will. But the droplets will be large because there are few nuclei for them to condense on. They will not be cloud droplets, which are so small that they almost float in the air. They will be large drops that fall from a clear blue sky.' He went on to say that over the land there are always particles for clouds to form on, such as the sulphuric droplets of air pollution; over the oceans, apart from a few volcanoes on islands, there are no sources of these nuclei. We used to think that sea-salt crystals blown and dried by the winds from the sea were the condensation nuclei. We have sampled the air over the Pacific Ocean far from land and we find a few sea salt crystals, but we always find abundant nuclei in the form of droplets of sulphuric acid and ammonium sulphate. Bob finished with the question 'Where does this sulphuric acid and ammonium sulphate come from?' It was one of those important moments in science. I had lectured the previous day on the regulation of the sulphur and other chemical cycles through the emission of dimethyl sulphide from ocean algae, and suddenly it occurred to us both that the oxidation of dimethyl sulphide could make the cloud-nucleating sulphuric acid droplets. We went on to wonder if this was part of some large-scale climate self-regulation. By coming to Seattle and talking about Gaia, Bob and I had been able to share two essential pieces of information that solved the puzzle: where do the clouds over the ocean come from? Here perhaps was the most important scientific discovery that either of us had made. Without the clouds over the ocean, life as we know it would not exist. This is because oceans cover seventy per cent of the surface of the Earth, and they are dark, and absorb sunlight strongly, whereas clouds are white and reflect sunlight. Bob told me that without clouds the Earth would be about twenty degrees Celsius hotter and that a cloudless Earth would have a surface temperature near 35° C, which would make the world inhospitable for our kind of life. There are other sources of nuclei for cloud formation, but we did think it reasonable to speculate about the link between climate, clouds, DMS, and algae as part of Gaia's self-regulation. There was little doubt that the microscopic algae of the oceans were the principal source of DMS.

We decided to put our ideas in print as an article in *Nature*. We sought the help of Bob's graduate student, Steven Warren, and the eminent geochemist, Andi Andreae, who knew more than anyone else about the DMS emissions from the oceans. Moreover, the editor of *Nature* at that time, John Maddox, had written to me to express his regret that *Nature* had turned down the Daisyworld paper. He invited me to send the next Gaia paper to him personally. I sent our paper to *Nature* with a covering letter to the editor marked 'Personal'. True to his word, after a proper round of peer review, the journal published our paper as a lead article. I consider it one of the most important scientific papers I have participated in. So did the scientific community, for two years later, they awarded the four of us the Norbert Gerbier Prize of the World Meteorological Organization (WMO). This paper was the turning point for Gaian fortunes, and has started a scientific enterprise linking algae to the climate and chemistry of the atmosphere that must now employ hundreds, if not thousands, of scientists worldwide.

It was natural for me to think that the success of the cloud algae research would make Gaia a respectable name in science, but the conference held in San Diego in March 1988 by the American Geophysical Union soon dispelled this illusion. The distinguished climatologist, Stephen Schneider, and the MIT professor, Penelope Boston organized this meeting on Gaia against considerable opposition from conventionally minded geophysicists who thought that to hold such a meeting would bring disrepute to the society. Naïvely, I saw their conference as a wonderful opportunity to establish the scientific respectability of Gaia. I spent many weeks putting all I knew, as succinctly as possible, into my paper 'Geophysiology—the Science of Gaia' and was given the opportunity to open the meeting. They heard my paper almost without comment. Lynn and Greg Hinkel followed it with a paper entitled 'The biota and Gaia: 150 years of support for environmental science'. Lynn and I had by now established a double act in which she argued from biology and I argued from physical chemistry. The audience listened politely but said little. Then came David Abraham's moving philosophical paper, and a long run of papers which had little to do with Gaia directly. There were some good sound criticisms by Ken Caldiera and Dick Holland, but most speakers chose a topic connected with their own work.

One delegate, my friend Ann Henderson-Sellers commented: 'This meeting is like the parable of the three monkeys. One sees no Gaia, one hears no Gaia, and one says no Gaia.' This went on until the session on Wednesday evening when a young physicist, James Kirchner, gave his talk 'The Gaia Hypotheses: are they testable? Are they useful?' In the manner of a skilled barrister he took selected quotes from my early papers and from my first book. He ignored their context and used the quotes to ridicule and diminish Gaia theory. He ignored entirely the paper I had just given at the meeting. I listened with growing chagrin as he proceeded with forensic skill to dissect, sterilize and destroy the separated parts of Gaia. I should have risen and replied vigorously, by arguing that Kirchner's arguments were sophistry, not science, and that Gaia can only be considered as a whole system, but I am not a natural debater. All I could do when I went to the lectern to reply was to congratulate him on his skill and ask for time to think before I replied. James Kirchner's was by far the best presented speech, and so strongly influenced the meeting that, from then on, few took Gaia seriously. Richard Kerr, writing in *Science*, shared Penelope Boston's view that the jury was still out, but D Lindley, a staff writer for *Nature*, confirmed my own opinion that Kirchner's speech carried the meeting. The organizers invited me to speak after the conference dinner and, sensing the mood, I asked, 'Is Gaia just a spoof?', and received a burst of laughter. I went on to say that I would be proud if one day Gaia was described as Popper had described the Theory of Evolution: merely a research programme in metaphysics. My after-dinner speech won a standing ovation, but it was for me as a good loser, sadly not for Gaia who I thought I had betrayed. You will find our speeches in the book of the meeting edited by Stephen Schneider and Penelope Boston: *Scientists on Gaia*. From then on scientists rarely ever spoke of Gaia, but the science of Gaia— the understanding of the Earth through geophysiology, flourished. It was the Gaia legend that languished. My memories of the San Diego meeting are sad and were made more so by a telephone call from Cynthia Garrels to tell me that her husband and my friend and supporter Bob Garrels had died.

One reason why Gaia has had a hard time is that few scientists have a proper grasp of self-regulating systems; these are often transdisciplinary and modern scientists are most often specialists. There are notable exceptions, and the first to come to mind is Christian de Duve, the Belgian biologist whose enthralling book *Vital Dust* presents the most convincing account I have read of the events in the evolution of life starting from Earth's primeval surface chemistry. Inventors intuitively understand self-regulation but such understanding is denied to some of our most competent analytical mathematicians. One of the first successful self-regulating devices was James Watt's steam-engine governor. This simple device regulates the speed of an engine by means of a pair of spinning balls mounted on a vertical shaft. The rotation of the shaft causes the balls to spin out and move a lever that partially closed the valve supplying steam to the engine. If the engine went too fast, the balls swung further out and shut off the steam, if too slow they fell inwards and increased the supply of steam. It worked wonderfully well and was demonstrated at a Royal Society Conversazione in London during the 19th century. Among the audience was James Clerk Maxwell, perhaps the greatest physicist of his time. He is reported to have said three days later that he was kept awake trying to analyse mathematically Watt's invention; he had no doubt that it worked but analysis eluded him. If it was too difficult for Maxwell to analyse then it is hardly surprising that the more complex system Gaia is not immediately obvious to most scientists.

In October 1988 Sandy and I were in New York for the launch of my second book, *The Ages of Gaia*. Ed Barber of the distinguished American publishers, WW Norton, was our host, and the Commonwealth Fund, who supported me while I wrote the book, had arranged a party to celebrate its publication. Among the guests was the United Kingdom's permanent representative on the UN Security Council, Sir Crispin Tickell. I was delighted to meet him, for I recalled with pleasure the kind letter he had written after the publication of my first book. We tried to talk, but were frustrated by the noise of the reception and the effort of eating while trying to hold in one hand canapés and a glass of wine. We arranged to talk under quieter conditions over breakfast. Sandy and I were staying at the Algonquin, and next morning, in a quiet alcove chosen by the head waiter, we enthusiastically exchanged our ideas on climate change and Gaia. From our meeting came a lasting friendship. Sir Crispin has done more than anyone to make the idea of Gaia acceptable, especially among the powerful and influential circles in which he moves. As I mentioned earlier, TH Huxley, who did so much to establish Darwin's science, was his great-great-grandfather. I am deeply grateful to have so staunch a friend. He told us that he would be retiring from his Ambassadorial post in the autumn and would be returning to England to become the Warden of Green College, Oxford. As Warden, he founded the Green College Centre, and so gave Oxford a global presence in environmental affairs. He also endorsed the College's invitation to me to become an Honorary Visiting Fellow. My battles for Gaia have taught me the value of an elevated position in the very human affair of science. For this I shall always be grateful to him and to Sir John Hanson, his successor as Warden, for sustaining my Fellowship.

In the summer of 1988, the publishers Jos and David Pearson of Gaia Books asked me if I would write a book on Gaia for them. I gladly accepted their offer as the chance to put on paper my ideas about planetary medicine. It would be a book about the Earth that saw it as sufficiently alive to suffer disease and then try to understand the Earth system through the perturbations of its maladies. I gave the book the title *The Practical Science of Planetary Medicine*. Not an exciting title but alternatives such as 'Earth Medicine' all seemed even more misleading. Gaia Books published it in the United Kingdom in 1991 and it is the book that I think best expresses the practical science of Gaia. The American publishers Harmony Books issued it in the United States under the title *Healing Gaia* because they were sure that my choice of name was wrong. It turned out that they were even more wrong and booksellers put the book on their New Age shelves along with books on astrology, aromatherapy, and the usual range of New Age topics, where it languished.

A Norwegian gentleman, Knut Kloster, gave Gaia the best chance of decent development as a unifying theory. He made a gift of £75,000, which I used to fund three international scientific meetings on Gaia in Oxford. He made the gift in unusual circumstances, and so unconditionally that I give an account of it, together with my proper thanks, in the Preface and Acknowledgements.

Sandy and I discuss plans for action in bed after a cup of tea at about 6 o'clock in the morning or sometimes we do so on a walk in the Devon countryside. It was in one of these discussions that we decided on the best way to achieve his, and our, objective of achieving scientific credibility for Gaia. We must organize and then hold a special kind of scientific meeting in a recognized scientific venue. I asked Sir Crispin Tickell, the Warden of Green College, if we could hold our meeting there. He gave enthusiastic support to the idea, but warned that we should need to share the meeting with St Anne's College. They were close by and had ample accommodation for the delegates and a larger lecture theatre than Green College. It seemed there could be no better place to invite distinguished scientists to talk about Gaia. Among Sandy's many talents, that of meeting organizer is supreme, and in this, the Green College Centre members, Rachel Duncan and later Susan Canney, gave their unstinted help and advice. This left me free to think of a topic and the participants for our first Oxford meeting. The topic we chose was 'The self-regulating Earth'. This was not so Gaian as to frighten the horses, so to speak. But all of those who chose to come to it would know that it was a Gaian meeting. The model for our meeting was that of a Gordon or its German equivalent a Dahlem conference: a small, tight gathering of active scientists working in the Earth science field. We were able to gather together fifty of the world's best scientists in this area, prepared to talk in an open way about the Earth as a self-regulating entity. It was not to be one of those cosy gatherings of the faithful; we included sceptics as well as supporters of Gaia. To our surprise and pleasure, almost all of those we asked said they would come, and did. Knut's gift, and an additional grant of £5,000 from Shell Research Limited, covered the cost of the meeting.

We had a strong sense that the conference had achieved its purpose. It enlightened scientists whose horizons had until then been limited by the walls of their disciplines. Many came to us afterwards and said that it had been quite different from the so-called interdisciplinary conferences where experts speak each in his own arcane jargon but no one hears, and the conference concludes with an anodyne plenary statement. Our conference did not end with an anodyne plenary session, but in the lecture hall at Green College in a heated debate. The subject was 'Who owns Gaia: the scientists or the public?' We had as a guest debater the eminent environmentalist Jonathon Porritt. He strongly opposed the notion that Gaia should become the property of scientists only; he felt that its value as a unifying influence was far too great. When I said, tentatively, that perhaps we should talk about Geophysiology rather than Gaia to make it more acceptable to mainstream scientists, Mae-Wan Ho, one of the participants, challenged me. She was clearly distressed at the thought that the word Gaia should be so turned down. The science journalist, Fred Pearce, reported our meeting in *New Scientist*. The title of his article 'Gaia, Gaia don't go away' says what he and many at the meeting thought. The extraordinary range of its power to inspire confirms the importance of this larger influence Gaia has provided for artists, writers, poets, painters, sculptors and musicians. Few other theories have inspired the composition of a Mass.

Students and postgraduate scientists at Oxford and from elsewhere were present at the meeting and there was little doubt that it served to restore interest in Gaian science. In the letter we sent to Knut to account for our use of his gift we said, 'We left Oxford feeling that we had been privileged to participate in a rare event and one that would change us all and perhaps start the process of a better understanding of the Earth.'

The success of the first Oxford meeting encouraged us to organize another for April 1996. This time we hoped for a larger biological interest and chose for the title, 'The evolution of the superorganism'. We were fortunate to have John Maynard Smith as the opening speaker. John was until a year or so before the meeting a vehement critic of Gaia. He still thinks it 'an awful name for a theory' and wishes that I did not refer to the Earth as living, but he was prepared to treat it as a scientific topic and this is all we asked. John came to stay with us at Coombe Mill before the meeting and, as we talked, we realized that our differences were less about the science of Gaia than the semantics and the use of metaphor. Neo-Darwinist biologists had had their own difficult times fending off creationists, traditionalists and proponents of group selection. To John, Gaia had seemed at first just another of these false theories: the New Age religious faith in an Earth Mother was anathema to him. I am deeply grateful to John for having come and spoken at our meeting in Oxford and later for giving my successor Tim Lenton strong support in his battles with referees.

The theme of the meeting was the concept of a superorganism. Biologists recognize that the paper nests of social wasps and bees, and the concrete constructions of termites, are the expression of the plans encoded in the genes of the queens. There is strong evidence to show that these nests are in homeostasis. Not just the individual organisms, but the whole nest, material and living parts together, keeps its temperature constant when the external temperature rises or falls. In other words, the phenotype is the material boundary of the nest. Now the Earth is not the phenotype of any species of organism, but the coupling between all the individuals of the planet and their material environment results in a homeostasis similar to that of the nest. We hoped that these thoughts would stimulate discussion on the concept of biological self-regulation at all levels, from the individual organism, the nest, and the ecosystem, to Gaia.

It was a meeting where ideas flowed freely, and for the duration of the meeting, the scientific tribes had dismantled the barricades between their disciplines. We even had a fine talk from Herbert Girardet on the city as a superorganism. On the last afternoon, we enjoyed one of those exciting moments in science, when a new and what may be a crucial thought emerges. Dick Holland had talked on the environment of the Archean period, over two billion years ago. He told us that the evidence of the rocks suggested that the CO_2 content of the air must have been low, not more than one per cent by volume. If this was so, then how was the Earth warm enough to stay unfrozen when the Sun's output of heat was much less than now? Out of the meeting came the thought: there were no algae in the oceans then, so maybe there were fewer or no clouds. The geophysicists present knew that a cloudless Earth would be twenty or more degrees Celsius hotter and confirmed the speculation. It may turn out that this does not answer the problem of the Archean climate, but the exchange was valuable. It is rare to have scientists from all branches of science talking together as friendly collaborators on a topic that extends outside their expertise.

The second meeting ended with a small group of us gathering for the formal foundation of the Gaia Society. Sir Crispin Tickell is the President, and the University of East London generously offered the society space and funds for an executive secretary. He is Philip George and among his tasks was that of organizing the third Oxford Gaia meeting in April 1999. These conferences have succeeded in establishing Gaia theory as a serious scientific topic. The distinguished science journalist, Oliver Morton, who attended the 1999 conference, wrote in the American science magazine, *Discover*, 'The idea that organisms collaborated to keep the planet habitable was once dismissed as New Age earth science. Now even sceptics are taking a second look.'

As you now read, there are few scientists who doubt that the climate and chemical composition of the Earth's surface are coupled with the metabolism of the organisms that inhabit it, and the German systems scientist, John Schellnhuber, called it, in a *Nature* article, the new Copernican Revolution. No one now thinks seriously of oxygen as anything but a product of photosynthesis by plants and algae. It is easy to forget, though, that twenty to thirty years ago serious scientific papers suggested that oxygen came mainly from the photodissociation of water vapour in the upper atmosphere of the Earth and in the splendid book *Earth* written in 1973 by Frank Press and Raymond Siever there is no mention of life's interaction with the composition of our planet's surface. They shared the general view as expressed on page 489 of their book: 'Life depends on the environments in which it evolved and to which it has adapted.'

In those days, they had no inkling that without life our planet would be like Mars or Venus, a vast desert. They knew that life needed water, but failed to see that life has actively conserved water. In a similar way, the climate research centres of the world, which once scorned the idea of life affecting the climate, now know that they must include the organisms living on the land and in the ocean in their models. Geologists now accept that the weathering away of the continental rocks is as much a matter of bacterial and plant digestion as it is a physical and chemical process. In the thirty-five years of Gaia's existence as a theory, the view of the Earth has changed profoundly. Yet, so far only a tiny minority of scientists realize how much Gaia theory has helped to change their view. They have adopted my radical view of the Earth without recognizing where it came from, and they have forgotten the scorn with which most of them first greeted the idea of a self-regulating Earth.

The quest for Gaia has been a battle all the way. Our critics are beginning to admit they may have been mistaken, but still they find self-regulation and the phenomenon of emergence obscure. Yet both of these are crucial to an understanding of Gaia. They may not understand Gaia, but this does not stop them mining *The Ages of Gaia* for research projects in biogeochemistry or climatology. They are right to insist that a large and still unanswered question remains: if the Earth is indeed self-regulating by biological feedback, how has this come about through natural selection? I like to compare our inability yet to give an answer with Darwin's inability to satisfy those critics who saw the amazing perfection of the eye as something that also could never have arisen by chance natural selection.

Take the most intriguing piece of evidence for Gaia—the connection between ocean algae and climate. We still do not know how the links between climate, clouds, and the organisms evolved through natural selection. It almost certainly, when finally understood, will involve a series of small steps, not some sudden large evolutionary leap. William D Hamilton and Tim Lenton have recently proposed that algae, like most organisms, need to spread their spores from areas they have denuded of nutrients to fresh pastures. Perhaps their emission of DMS acts by stirring the wind. Sailors know that the updraft generated by condensation in a cloud can make a surface wind. Perhaps the algae have used this wind to carry their spores. Dandelions have evolved their complex micro-airships for seed dispersal. So why should not algae take the opportunity of wind raised by their own gas, DMS, to transport their spores to fresher pastures? Hamilton and Lenton published these ideas in 1998 in a paper called 'Spora and Gaia'. It helped to convince me that I could now retire from active Gaia science, the sceptics had at last come to listen, and this is all that I have ever wanted them to do.

It is thirty-five years since Gaia's inception, that startling afternoon at the Jet Propulsion Laboratories, when it flashed into my mind. Writing in 1999 I see that the theory of a self-regulating Earth, able to maintain climate and chemistry always tolerable for its inhabitants, is moving into acceptance as part of scientific conventional wisdom. If they must reject Gaia as the name of their new science I hope that they will choose 'Earth System Science' as a sensible alternative. Whatever they call it, if I am right about the Earth's capacity to regulate the planet, science must soon begin to take it seriously, or it may be the worse for all of us. As we discover processes by which life and the climate interact, many of them seem to act as amplifiers of global warming. Thoughtful Gaia theorists suggest that in the present inter-glacial warmth natural forces increase, rather than ameliorate the global warming that we have brought about.

In any creative act—whether painting a portrait, writing a book, or developing a theory of science—an important and difficult step is knowing when to stop. Writers and painters choose their own moment to finish their work, but with theories of science, there is no personal place for stopping; they are like cathedrals in the building, something to share and hand on. When in 1997 I knew that Tim Lenton's dedication to Gaia was as deep as my own, it was easy and joyful for me to pass it on to him. I had no doubt that the time had come for me to stop my work on Gaia science and leave its further development in the capable hands of Tim, Lynn and Stephan Harding. There is still Gaia work for me to do. I want to follow up the inspiration of that most estimable of men, Václav Havel, who saw in Gaia theory a moral prescription for the welfare of the planet itself, something for which we humans are accountable.

10

The Practical Side of Independent Science

Scientists are usually pictured as serious, middle-aged men in white coats, their surroundings filled with large and complex equipment. It could be anything from astronomical telescopes to view the beginnings of space and time to electron microscopes for disentangling the intricacies of the organelles within a cell. A lot of modern science is like this, but it would be as untrue to say that all of it is ultra high-tech as it would to say that all cooking is done in the expensively equipped kitchens of a large hotel or restaurant. Home cooking with simple saucepans can make delicious food. In the same simple way, I have discovered the delights of muddy boots ecology walking with my friend Stephan Harding and the joys of field geology with Robert Garrels. There is still a place for the amateur scientist, as the sight of the Hale–Bopp comet, which enlarged our skies in 1996, confirmed. A lone watcher of the desert sky first saw its fast approach, not professionals in their observatories.

My apprenticeship showed me that I could ask questions about the nature of things with simple and inexpensive equipment, and this knowledge gave me the confidence to set up my own laboratory in a thatched cottage in Bowerchalke. At the start, there was no need to buy more than was needed for the first research problems of my customers, and I started by setting up a small and modest workshop. In it were good quality hand-tools, a watchmaker's lathe and milling machine, soldering and brazing equipment, and the miscellaneous items needed for electronics. As the years went by, so the range of chemicals and other consumable items increased, until I reached that happy level where anything I needed was on the shelf. My customers were also generous in providing equipment more expensive than I could have afforded. Wisely, Pye and Hewlett Packard gave me their gas chromatographs so that in them I could more efficiently try out the new detectors I invented. JPL was a wonderful source of new high-tech electronic items. Four years after starting my lab in 1964, I was able to make my own scientific apparatus, and soon I was using it to explore the trace gases of the air. Before long, these explorations led me to discover such important trace gases as CFCs, and methyl halides and sulphides in the atmosphere, and to show that they were everywhere. The harvest of this research led to the recognition of ozone depletion, and it provided supporting evidence for Gaia theory. A modestly skilled amateur could have constructed any of the equipment I made and used.

A difficulty faced by an independent is competing with university scientists for funds. When academics bid for small contracts, they are seeking perquisites only, because their universities usually pay their apparatus and other costs, as well as their salaries. This represents a large subsidy, and their bids are always less than an independent could afford to place. The same kind of distortion of the market price occurs over attendance at commissions or giving advice to government departments. Usually, only travelling and subsistence expenses at civil service rates are payable. A visit of this kind to London from Coombe Mill, for example, always involves at least two days away with a zero income during the time of the visit. Like most professionals, I manage by never having less than three main customers and this is, in any event, essential if one is to retain independence. One large customer alone, no matter how good, is inconsistent with independence, and it would be no more than exchanging one form of employment for another. One of the joys of independence is the extent to which the needs of different customers are shared in common: work done for one agency, like NASA, often cross-fertilized the work I did for another, such as Shell. Over the first fifteen years as an independent, contracts from the American agencies NASA, NOAA, the Chemical Manufacturers Association (CMA), and from the UK Ministry of Defence (MOD), provided the bulk of my gross income. More importantly, good customers were interested in the science I did independently. Shell, Hewlett Packard, NASA, NOAA, and the MOD, all encouraged me in my work on Gaia theory and on the atmospheric abundance of trace gases.

American bureaucracy can be daunting, and in my first contracts with the Jet Propulsion Labs concerning the Viking mission to Mars, JPL employed an expediter. He was a man who took my contract and me through all of the offices whose signature and approval were needed. This would have been an almost impossible task for me to do unaided, but I soon found that an American agency that needed your services pushed aside bureaucratic barriers. The possession of a provisional patent was a strong incentive for them to help in this way, because they could then say that my contract bid represented a 'sole source' and they could legally avoid the slow and unfavourable process of putting the contract out for bids. Of all the United States agencies, none was so helpful as the National Oceanic and Atmospheric Administration, NOAA. I suspect that Lester Machta, the head of the section I dealt with, worked hard to ensure the smooth progress of my contracts with them.

To do science independently it is wise to form a company. Consider for a moment the difficulties of ordering from a home address, such as 15 Acacia Gardens, a few kilograms of potassium cyanide or a curie or two of a radioactive element. The police, not the van driver, would call on you the next day, but if you place a company order, they deliver it without fuss. I called my company Brazzos Limited after the river Brazos in Texas, near where we lived while in Houston, and formed it in 1964. I deliberately spelt it wrongly; the real river Brazos has only one z. My motive in choosing this devious name was not dishonest; to have a proposed company name compared with those already listed cost £25 in 1964. After two or three false tries, I resorted to Brazzos, a name I thought no one else could have chosen, and I was right. We have traded as Brazzos from then until now. Quite apart from easing the purchase of chemicals and radioactive substances, a company also helps in making contract bids. Agencies like NASA or NOAA would have had a much harder time giving a contract to a foreign individual than to a company like Brazzos Limited, since companies are internationally recognized. By the time a company is formed and provisional patents are filed, and contracts drawn up, the legal and accounting costs become a significant part of one's overheads. To keep these costs reasonable, I found it necessary to reverse that old showbiz tag where an unsuccessful applicant for a part in a film is brushed off with, 'Don't call us, we'll call you.' I took only contracts that were offered; I never sought them.

In the early days of my independent practice, I did not know how much to charge my customers and usually sold my services too cheaply. It did not matter much because the total returns were adequate for my needs and I gradually approached a fair price by adjusting the time spent on a customer's problem to the amount paid.

The most valued lessons of my apprenticeship at Hampstead and Mill Hill were those in experimental science. The outstanding difference between these MRC laboratories and others I have known was the willingness, even the eagerness, of the scientists to build their own apparatus. From Mill Hill came the huge advances in separation science that enabled molecular biology, and it was all done with equipment the scientists themselves had invented and had made in the Institute workshop. It was a laboratory for medical research, yet the products of individual scientists made for their own personal research are now as important as the research itself. The Wright Spirometer, a simple instrument to measure the peak-flow rate when breathing, finds wide use in diagnosing asthma, and I well remember Wright and his wonderful inventive capacity, and fruitful arguments about the best way to measure something. He was, in the 1950s disdainful of electronics and preferred a mechanical solution if possible, and he was not alone in this. I remember Archer Martin arguing in favour of nanotechnology—ultra-microscopic mechanisms. Martin proposed a Babbage-style computer built of minute mechanical parts and said it would be as fast and as reliable as an electronic computer. Oddly, though, it is from the need to make ultra-microscopic electronics—the computer silicon chips—that has come the means of making minute mechanisms. At these medical labs, I learnt to blow glass, to make simple chemical apparatus, to braze and weld metal, and to use lathes and milling machines. I wonder why this is so rarely, if ever, in the science student's curriculum. These skills, together with a set of tools, have given me the autarky I needed. I treasure most the small watchmaker's lathe which was made by a firm called Pultra. I bought it in 1964 and it, with its wide range of accessories, is still in use here at Coombe Mill in 1999.

I find that I think clearly when my hands, as well as my brain, are involved. I frequently wake at five in the morning when it is too early to rise, so instead I stay in bed and try to model in my mind the invention of the day. By breakfast time, the model has taken shape as a three-dimensional image, and after breakfast I go to my lab to translate the mental model into something solid, a construction of metal, quartz, or plastic. This act seems to refine the idea behind it, but the mental experiments done in bed ensure that usually it works first time. Seen from outside, techniques can appear impossibly difficult; how could I ever paint a portrait or play the violin? In those examples, there are no satisfactory states in between starting to learn and becoming proficient as an artist. Experimental science is different: if a customer such as the JPL needed from me a device or an instrument to go on a spacecraft, they needed me merely to make a working model, what they called a 'breadboard'. The name breadboard goes back to the days when they made electronic equipment, like radio receivers, by screwing down the components onto a kitchen bread-board. Neither they nor I expected to send crude homemade pieces of hardware like this into space or to a planet. Their engineers would use my crude working model as a solid sketch from which to model their own exquisitely perfect constructions, each as light and as strong as an Arctic Tern, a bird that migrates across half of the Earth's surface. So long as my home-made apparatus works and demonstrates its prin-ciple, that is all that is needed. I never minded when at the JPL or at the Hewlett Packard laboratories, engineers would look at my hand-crafted device and say, 'We can do better than that.' I knew that if my breadboard had been as good as their finished product, they would not have thanked me. Even if I could have done it, it would have been an absurd waste of my time. It also pays to think small: I find that the instrument companies who supply the present-day laboratory equip-ment tend to make their devices monstrously large. A gas chromato-graph or a spectrometer is likely to be far too heavy for one person to lift and will occupy most of a laboratory bench, but I see no reason why these two instruments should be so large and so heavy. The combined gas chromatograph and mass spectrometer sent to Mars on the Viking lander weighed only seven pounds, and that was twenty-five years ago. Is it necessary for such instruments still to fill a small room? A project close to my heart has been to make a gas chromatograph as small as a pocket calculator. It would enable anyone anywhere in the world to do the science now only possible in the wealthy first world, and I discuss this in more detail on page 184.

The everyday life of an independent scientist is wholly different from that of a typical scientist working in the laboratories of industry, the universities, or government service. To bring you this unusual flavour let me tell you how I invented one small component of the instruments carried to Mars in 1975 by the Viking landers. Sandy

Lipsky, then a professor at Yale University, had persuaded JPL that they needed a gas chromatograph/mass spectrometer (GCMS) combination to analyse the soil of Mars. It was a much more powerful instrument than either of these instruments used alone. The combined instrument would not merely separate the substances present in the soil, it would identify them. Now, it was not easy at that time, the 1960s, here on Earth to join a gas chromatograph to a mass spectrometer. A gas chromatograph column delivers the substances it separates greatly diluted in a stream of gas such as nitrogen. The mass spectrometer operates with its interior kept as close to a perfect vacuum as possible, and the sample to be analysed must be introduced without breaking this vacuum. We needed a way to isolate the substances emerging from the column from the large volume of the gas that carried them. Sandy Lipsky brought to JPL a Swedish scientist who had invented a useful device in which the lighter, smaller molecules of helium gas were separated from the larger and heavier molecules of the substances to be analysed. He did it ballistically. If you take a handful of sand and stones and throw the mixture, the stones will travel much further than the sand. This is because, lacking inertia, the sand is quickly slowed by air resistance. In the same way, the heavier molecules projected in the stream of helium went on in a straight path, whereas the much lighter helium molecules diffused out sideways. It worked well as a separator, but the space engineers were unhappy about its power needs, particularly its requirement for a powerful pump to clear away the excess of helium. They did not think it would work on Mars. One of them said to me after trying the ballistic separator, 'What we need is a separator that removes all of the carrier gas without needing a vacuum pump.'

I thought about this need for a perfect separator and it occurred to me that I could use the strange properties of the metal palladium. Palladium is a precious metal rather like platinum in colour and it does not easily corrode. It is one of the so-called noble metals, favoured by jewellers and others. When it is heated to moderate temperatures round about 200° C, palladium allows hydrogen gas to flow through it as if it were no more substantial than tissue paper. To all other gases and vapours, it remains a solid piece of metal. We could use a long tube of palladium, or some alloy of palladium, and use hydrogen as the carrier gas; the hydrogen would diffuse out through the walls and leave the substances behind. This could be the basis of a most effective separator. JPL provided me with a contract and some palladium alloy tubes and said, more or less, 'Go home and try these and see if you can make a separator.'

This contract gave me a year of fascinating experiments. In a proper laboratory, a scientist would have set up the palladium tube in an evacuated glass vessel, and then with notebook at hand, he would have measured the flow of hydrogen through the walls of the tube at different temperatures and pressures. After this, he would repeat the measurements with the substances he wanted to separate added to the hydrogen; it would be a project taking several months to complete. In my thatched cottage laboratory at Bowerchalke, I did not have much equipment. My vacuum pump, a somewhat ancient one, was in the loft of the cottage and I could not be bothered to get it down. I was impatient to have a go and I connected the palladium alloy tubing to a variable transformer so that I could heat it to 200° C by passing an electric current along it, just as if it were the heating element of an electric fire. Then I passed hydrogen at a known rate of flow into it, with no more in mind than to see what happened. From a proper scientist's point of view this was a terrible experiment, but I was encouraged to do it by earlier conversations with that distinguished scientist, Archer Martin. He and I agreed that it was a mistake ever to do the first experiments too carefully. One should just join up whatever one had to hand, do it, and learn from the experience before designing a proper scientific experiment. Therefore, I merely watched how much hydrogen escaped from the end of my palladium tube when it was cold and when it was hot. To do this I lit the gas escaping from the open end of the palladium tube and watched the height of the small flame of burning hydrogen. I had to use a trick here, for the flame of burning hydrogen is invisible. What I did was to make some smoke in the lab by igniting a small pile of sodium chlorate and sugar; the fine particles of sodium compounds present as smoke in the atmosphere made the flame bright yellow and clearly visible. I turned on the hydrogen with the palladium tube cold—the flow was about one cubic centimetre a second—and lit my tiny flame. Then I turned up the current through the tube until its temperature was about 200° C and, to my astonishment, the flame went completely out. The hydrogen was flowing into the tube but none was coming out, but I found that by turning up the hydrogen to 4 cubic centimetres a second I could now re-establish a tiny flame at the end of the tube. I turned off the heating current and slowly, as the tube cooled, hydrogen began to escape from the end of it and the flame grew in size to the expected height at a flow of 4 cubic centimetres a second. To make sure I was not being fooled, I joined a short length of silicon rubber tubing to the end of the palladium tube where the flame had been and dipped this into a beaker of water so that I could see the bubbles of hydrogen escaping. When I repeated the experiment, the results were even more astonishing. At a flow of 1 cc a second, when the palladium tube was at 200° C, the hydrogen flowed back into the tube and drew water up from the beaker into the silicone tubing as if there were a vacuum inside the palladium tube. Here was hydrogen flowing into both ends of it: where was it going? This was the stuff of magic. I knew that if the tube was merely permeable to hydrogen, a little would always have flowed from the far end, but it was behaving as if the solid palladium metal were a pump. Moments like this are what make the life of a scientist worthwhile. Here was a simple experiment that any schoolboy, or schoolmaster, for that matter, could do and, more importantly, just what was needed to solve the JPL problem. I had fulfilled my contract by the very first experiment.

It took me some time to realize why I could find no reports of this remarkable behaviour. The permeability of palladium to hydrogen was well known and discovered in the 19th century. In proper laboratories, no one would have heated a palladium tube in air. They would have placed it in a chamber and measured the leak of hydrogen gas through the walls of the tube. I tried doing this and found that the extraordinary permeability of my palladium tube vanished when another tube or vessel surrounded it. Even with a vacuum on the outside, it did not pass hydrogen anywhere near as efficiently as it did when it was simply heated in air. It dawned on me that what was happening was that the hydrogen passing through the walls of my tube encountered oxygen atoms at the surface of the palladium in the air. Now, palladium is a catalyst when hot and there must have been an instantaneous reaction between the hydrogen escaping to the surface and the oxygen of the air. This completely removed all hydrogen atoms and constituted the most powerful pump that one could imagine, and this was the explanation of its apparently magical properties. I had just what they wanted for Mars and, a few months later, with many more experiments behind me, I returned to JPL to show them what a splendid separator they had in the form of a palladium tube. When I told them my story, it was so strange that at first few believed me. They were well used to exaggeration from over-excited scientists or salesmen, and how could they tell that what I was saying was different from this? It did not help either to start talking about magic; there is nothing that puts off a scientist more than that. But they were prepared, like the good engineers that they were, to give it a trial by experiment.

The next morning when I came in from the hotel, I found that an engineer had connected one of my palladium tubes to an old mass spectrometer that was in operation and indicated an internal vacuum of 10^{-9} torr. This is an exceedingly good vacuum (a torr is a unit of pressure used by those who work with vacuums and equal to about one thousandth of an atmosphere). He had joined the other end of the tube to a pressure gauge, a flow regulator and a hydrogen cylinder. He heated the palladium tube to $250°$ C and turned on the hydrogen until the gauge said twenty torr. This was the inlet pressure to my palladium tube and it was 20 thousand million times greater than that inside the mass spectrometer, but the mass spectrometer happily kept its vacuum and said that no hydrogen was flowing into it. The engineer turned up the pressure until half an atmosphere, 400 torr, registered on his gauge. Still nothing happened, and the mass spectrometer showed no hydrogen at all coming through into it. The engineer turned to me and said, 'Your tube is blocked—there's no way that could happen otherwise.' So we disassembled the apparatus and tried blowing hydrogen through the cold tube but found no blockage whatever. Puzzled, the engineer joined it all up again, and repeated our test at 400 torr; with just the same result as before. Hydrogen was flowing fast into the inlet of the tube but none was coming out. The engineer was so surprised that he said, 'Wait a minute', and went to telephone his friends, asking them to come over and watch the experiment. Soon some scientists, space scientists, and space engineers were drifting in to the small lab to see the experiment. We next turned the pressure up to a full Earth's atmosphere, 760 torr, and the mass spectrometer gauge stayed obstinately at 10^{-9} torr; no hydrogen was flowing into it. It was pouring in at the other end of the metal tube and literally vanishing.

It was not until we raised the pressure at the input to a 1000 torr, well above atmospheric pressure, that suddenly the mass spectrometer vacuum failed and it failed catastrophically. Reducing the flow through the palladium tube re-established once more the high vacuum inside the mass spectrometer. There was a small cheer, and from that moment on, doubts vanished. The tube, which we called a transmodulator, was to be the means of joining the gas chromatograph to the mass spectrometer that six years later went to Mars on the Viking spacecraft. Sandy Lipsky's original idea of a gas chromato-graph/mass spectrometer combination as the ideal soil analysis experiment had been reduced to practice. We had some fun breaking the turgid rules of scientific paper writing when we described the separator in a paper in the *Journal of Chromatographic Science* in 1970. Here is the opening of the paper by JE Lovelock, PG Simmonds, GR Shoemake, and S Rich:

> Maxwell's sorting demon, which could segregate hot from cold molecules, has so far eluded discovery although some of its attributes are to be found in the vortex tube. Lower in the hierarchy of demons is one able to segregate molecules of different species. Such a demon, doorman at an orifice connecting two vessels filled with a gas mixture, could segregate them completely or, alternatively, if only one gas was present stand as a perfect barrier between high-pressure gas and a vacuum. This note reports an experiment performed at the Jet Propulsion Laboratory, the results of which may be used to design an apparatus in which the functions of this second demon are automatically performed. Our motivation in making the experiment was not the promotion of unemployment in the underworld but rather to gather design information for a separator...

The JPL took out a series of patents on the device. They gave me three awards for it and three plaques, which I proudly hang on the walls of my laboratory here at Coombe Mill. There has been no successful commercial exploitation of the transmodulator here on Earth. This was probably because the gas chromatograph soon evolved to use narrow-gauge columns through which a mere wisp of gas flowed and mass spectrometers evolved with much more powerful pumps. We no longer needed the palladium transmodulator, which had served as a kind of marriage broker to bring together these two powerful instruments.

My experiments with palladium and hydrogen gave me a clue as to what may have led astray those who thought that they had discovered 'cold fusion'. Palladium will store as much as sixty per cent of its inner atomic space with hydrogen, and this readily happens when palladium is made the negative electrode in a watery solution. A piece of palladium filled with hydrogen is stable for a while in air, but then there is often a surge of heat as the stored hydrogen reacts suddenly and catalytically with the oxygen of the air. It was this, I think, that led to the false conclusion that cold fusion had occurred.

Computers

The most important single item that has sustained me as an independent scientist is the computer. So important has it been that I would like to digress and tell you how these wonderful devices entered my life and then changed it.

The plane from Los Angeles arrived on time and, with my small carry-on bag, I was the first of the passengers to arrive at the Customs counter. In those days, the largest plane was a Boeing 707, and Heathrow was comparatively peaceful and quiet. When asked if I had anything to declare, I said, 'Yes, I have two small electronic items.' I showed the Customs officer two of the early integrated circuit amplifiers. They looked like a pair of frozen black beetles, with their stiff wire legs hanging beneath. When he asked me what they were and what they were worth, I replied, 'They are small amplifiers. They are research items given to me in America.' He then said, 'This is a matter for the supervisor. Hang on, I'll give him a call.' Within minutes, they escorted me to an office occupied by an amiable middle-aged civil servant. I showed him the chips and he asked, 'Do you mean to tell me that these things are amplifiers. You know, like I have with my hi-fi?' When I nodded, yes, he snorted and said, 'Their Lordships are pissing against the wind if they think I'll be able to stop people bringing these things in with them.' He then helped me to fill in some forms that gave what he called Treasury direction, so that there was no Customs duty payable. It was a pleasant encounter to start the day. The chips that I had imported were early operational amplifiers made by the Fairchild Company and called μA709. I needed them to control a palladium separator, which I was building for the Mars mission.

Without at the time realising it, JPL was providing me also with a priceless education in the new electronics, and not only amplifiers. Soon I was familiar with and bringing in silicon-chip electronics: logic gates, timers, and inverters. By 1970, I started one of the extravagances of my scientific life. I bought an early HP computer, a 9100B calculator. Although it was heavy, it sat easily enough on my desk. It cost over £2,000 with its peripherals, enough then to buy a small house. Its memory was made of ferrite beads strung out on a grid of wires, and it was less than one kilobyte. The programme language was only slightly removed from the fundamental binary talk of computers, but thanks to HP's well-composed manuals, I rapidly became fluent in it. Soon I was able to answer the problem that had plagued me over the past ten years: how does the electron capture detector work? The differential equations that describe electron capture and the behaviour of the detector were easy enough for me to write down, but they were far beyond my ability to solve analytically by ordinary mathematics. I have since childhood suffered a peculiar form of dyslexia. I cannot distinguish immediately between left and right and I reverse the order of letters in words I write. Worst of all, I have great difficulties with the manipulation of algebraic equations. I cannot instinctively tell which side is which. In spite of this, I love mathematics and have little difficulty with its concepts, only with the practical execution of them. Even this primitive computer, or calculator as they called it, was my liberation. Now I could leave it to the device to solve my equations numerically. Soon it was plotting graphs to show how and why the detector behaved so strangely. I was hooked, and as any teenager would do, I spent a sizeable proportion of what HP paid me for my advice, to buy their computers. Moore's Law meant that every two years the computers evolved to a new desirable level and I bought a new one. It still goes on, thirty years later; soon I will be buying yet another.

It would be no exaggeration to say that computers have transformed my life, and I do not mean that I would be a lot richer without them. They are the mental equivalent of a bicycle, something that lets me travel much faster using my own mental muscle. Without Hewlett Packard's wonderful but expensive devices, Gaia would never have risen from the debating level. I would never have written the program of the definitive model, Daisyworld. It showed that the self-regulation of climate could emerge on a simple planet populated by organisms living under the rules of natural selection. Having a personal computer on my desk enabled me to interact directly with my problems. This was a privilege available to few scientists anywhere in the 1970s and 1980s. In those decades universities and scientific institutions tended to frown on personal computers; they preferred a single large computer with terminals connected to it in every laboratory.

Composing computer programs to solve scientific problems is like writing poetry. You must choose every word with care and link it with the other words in perfect syntax. There is no place for verbosity or carelessness. To become fluent in a computer language demands almost the antithesis of modern loose thinking. It requires many interactive sessions, the hands-on use of the device. You do not learn a foreign language from a book, rather you have to live in the country for years to let the language become an automatic part of you, and the same is true of computer languages. There is little chance of this happening in most universities and institutes. All too often the scientists have to ask another group, the programmers, to draft the mathematical steps of their problem in the language the computer can understand. Often the languages chosen, like Fortran and C, are for the convenience of the programmers, not the scientists. This means that there is little chance of the scientists interacting directly with their computers and getting that feedback so essential in the development of the solution of a problem. To delegate a problem to a programmer is appropriate when the computer is merely performing a range of tedious calculations, far beyond any individual's patience and stamina, but when a scientist faces important steps in understanding, delegation is unwise. Long ago, I learned that whenever one of my programs did not work, the error was nearly always in my thoughts, not in the computer. The hands-on interaction, sitting at the keyboard, looking at the screen, was like talking to a fair and honest critic. Are you sure, it seemed to say, that you have asked the right questions? This invaluable advice is hopelessly lost when it goes through several hands.

At the JPL and at Hewlett Packard individual scientists used their bench top computers interactively in the design of instruments and space hardware and it was a hands-on, personal way of working. In the 1960s, there were few computer languages available and we had to communicate in the raw set of instructions, which were all the chips themselves could understand. It was hard and tedious work, but the rewards were such that few minded the task of learning. We had the same urge as a holiday traveller has to learn the language of a foreign country. By the 1970s, a number of so-called high-level languages evolved. They were ALGOL, FORTRAN, C, LISP, and PASCAL. HP had started with its own version of ALGOL that they called HPL, and this was my first high-level language. I loved it and grew fluent in it to the point of composing elegant and parsimonious code. In 1975 Professors JG Kemeney and TE Kurtz of Dartmouth College, New Hampshire, introduced a new language BASIC, the acronym of 'basic all-purpose symbolic instruction code'. They intended it as a clear and comprehensible language with which to teach computer science. However, like human languages in the streets, dialects of this popular language soon evolved. Each tribe spoke its own version. These dialects of BASIC were often almost impossible for anyone not of the tribe to read. Teachers in universities soon damned them and BASIC from which they had evolved. This was bad, for BASIC was the computer equivalent of English and therefore a flexible language. It was sad to see FORTRAN and PASCAL taught in its place. These languages are like French, kept inflexible by the dictates of an academy. Logical consistency was preserved, but at the cost of freezing evolution.

Hewlett Packard was unusual in that it sold its computers mainly to engineers and other professionals rather than to academics. And obstinately, but with wisdom insufficiently appreciated, they persisted in using their own version of BASIC for their computers. The computer language, HP BASIC, was every bit as thorough and professional as the other computer languages, but much easier to use. The popularity of BASIC led Hewlett Packard to discard their ALGOL-like HPL language and I was obliged to learn their version of BASIC, since it was the only language of their desktop computers. Since the late 1970s, I have worked solely in this although, as Microsoft grew more professional, it also chose to favour BASIC, and in the 1990s, their version, called VISUAL BASIC, has served me well. I envy the young scientist now with a personal computer, who can explore the sheer elegance of the language of Mathematica, which I think is the best of all computer languages for interactive use. Computers seduce and enchain the mind so that the communing with them becomes so large a part of life that the rest of it is in danger. Nothing else, apart from an affair, would keep me up past midnight, or neglecting food. Fortunately the normal mind has its own way of restoring balance—the obsession calms to become the state like that of a good marriage. What does matter is the near total failure of those who use computers to realize that the elegant charts and illusions that they produce are products of their own imaginations. The models, the simulations of the world that evolve on computer screens, enchant us, but it is all too easy to forget that they are Pygmalion constructions, Galateas, and not the real world.

The Ozone War, the environmental cause that drew attention to the threat to stratospheric ozone from CFCs, started from a scientific hypothesis produced by the American atmospheric chemists, MJ Molina and FS Rowland. My part in this environmental cause is described in Chapter 8; I mention it now because of the importance of computer models in its development. The arguments that led to the first legislation banning the use of CFCs were from these models and not from measurements in the real world. This weakness was recognized by the scientists concerned, and in the 1980s, they flew instruments to measure the fluctuations of the ozone layer on satellites orbiting the Earth. These instruments were accurate and reliable, but no one watched their measurements on a dial or a digital display and the measurements accumulated in the data banks of a computer. At intervals, the scientist instructed the computer to analyse and present this data as illustrated maps and summaries. The programmers of the computers that handled the data had to make allowances for the natural errors of the instruments. Even the best instruments generate noise—random signals that are not observations—and in the real world events such as solar flares produce transient changes in the ozone layer. Therefore, the programmers told their computers to ignore signals that were outside what the scientists thought was the reasonable range of ozone values. The scientists used values predicted by their models to set what this reasonable range should be. The satellite instruments observed ozone every day throughout the 1980s, when ozone was rapidly declining over the Poles, especially over Antarctica. The instruments saw this and sent their message to the Earth, but the computers on Earth, following their instructions, disregarded these low values as wrong. This was why the big and expensive science with satellites and computers failed to discover the ozone hole. Human observers, Joe Farman and Brian Gardiner, found it in Antarctica by looking up at the sky with a simple Dobson spectrometer.

The Royal Society

In 1972, Archer Martin and his wife, Julia, came to Bowerchalke to see me. I was happy with anticipation. A visit from the Martins was a rare treat and I wondered what was important enough for him to make the long journey to Bowerchalke. We had just had tea in our dining room and were chatting about nothing in particular when Archer turned to me and said, 'I would like to propose you for the Fellowship of the Royal Society. Is that acceptable to you?' I was astonished and delighted at the same time. I had thought that going solo, becoming a scientific maverick, put me outside all the perquisites and honours of the cosy scientific community. Yet, here was Archer proposing me for the Fellowship of that wonderful and historic society of scientists, the world's first scientific academy. Now I knew the purpose of his visit. 'I'd be honoured and so pleased,' I replied. 'You realize,' said Archer, 'you may have to wait years before they elect you, if ever. Almost no one is elected on the first round and very few on the second.' Privately, I thought what a kind thing Archer had done, but so low did I rate my chances that I dismissed thoughts of it from my mind.

Then, in March 1974, the telephone rang just after breakfast. I picked up the handset and heard Sir Christopher Andrewes's voice saying, 'Is that James Ephraim Lovelock?' No one uses my middle name and I wondered what my old friend, the sawfly catcher, was up to now. 'I just saw your name on a short list that came by post this morning, new Fellows of the Royal Society. You mustn't tell anyone until you hear from them; it's very private you know.' I was dazed and the happy daze lasted a whole week. Then came the purple cardboard tube with a Certificate of Fellowship and I knew it was really true and not one of Sir Christopher's jokes. The certificate is strange, written as a letter inviting one to attend the next meeting and it asked me to sign that historic book that bears the signatures of King Charles II and all the monarchs that followed him together in juxtaposition with the distinguished scientists elected each year. Names like Newton, Wren, Maxwell, Rutherford, Huxley, and Darwin, down to the present day. I went to London for the meeting in April. Together with the other new Fellows admitted that day we were shown the facilities of our National Academy: the press and travel agencies, the library and the small suite of rooms on the top floor that provide bed and breakfast for Fellows. The ceremony itself, when the President, Sir Alan Hodgkin, called the new Fellows to come forward and sign the book, was a moving occasion and has sustained me ever since.

In its charter of 1663 the Society chose as its motto 'Nullius in Verba', an expression of its determination to stand against dogma and verify all statements by an appeal to facts. 'Nullius in Verba' translates as 'take nothing on authority'. It says something of the monarch, King Charles II, that he accepted it. Cynics have preferred to translate it as 'put nothing in writing'. I sometimes wonder if it should be emblazoned on every document that comes from the Society to remind us that we pledged ourselves to appeal to facts, and not to the consensus of chatterers.

Among the letters of congratulation that I received was one from Sir Stanley Hooker, the engineer who designed the Rolls Royce RB211 engines that powered so many jet aircraft. He said he had been Chairman of the Ad Hoc Committee that had recommended my election to the Council, and added, 'We need scientists like you who are also inventors.' The Ad Hoc Committee served to elect scientists outside the main divisions of science—chemistry, physics and biology. The Council of the Royal Society closed it shortly after my election. I doubt there was any connection between the two events, but its closure marked a change in the Society. It was not the Royal Society alone that was changing; science throughout the world was becoming a career employment instead of a vocation. Governments everywhere were funding and therefore assuming the right to interfere with the running of science. Science, like sport, was becoming less an international pursuit and more a matter of national interest. It may seem hard to believe now, but in the 1950s and earlier, society respected its scientists and paid them well. They were seen neither as threatening inventors of nuclear power and bombs, nor as makers of poisonous chemicals to destroy the environment. They suffered a mild disrespect, in that the public saw them as figures of fun, but they regarded their mad professors with affection; certainly never saw them as a threat. There were about ten times fewer graduate scientists in the United Kingdom then than now, yet nearly half of all the Nobel Prizes awarded came to the United Kingdom. Of the hundred or so scientists present during my time at the Mill Hill Institute, six were or were to become Nobel Laureates.

We scientists in those days ran our own affairs and we ran them well. I have never seen a satisfactory explanation of the decline of science in the United Kingdom. Few of us, indeed, will admit that it has declined. Scientists complain about their lack of recognition by poor pay, and about their bad image as portrayed by the media. They go on to say that government does not spend enough money on science. I suspect that we, as taxpayers, contribute in real terms at least ten times as much now to science as we did in the fecund 1950s. Why is there no proportional increase in scientific output? True enough, as our Chief Scientist, Sir Robert May, points out, we still do moderately well compared with the rest of the world. If papers published are anything to go by, we come second after the United States. But we have fallen relative to our past performance—in the 1950s and earlier we led the world. When I meet scientists employed in government service, in universities and in commercial enterprises, their conversation seems to have changed over the years. Now, there are fewer impassioned accounts of their new ideas and more mere talk, interspersed with complaints of bureaucratic interference and lack of funds. Many of the good scientists seem to have lost heart and talk wistfully of early retirement.

There may be many reasons for our decline but I would blame the perverse anti-elitism of our present culture. It led to the building of many new universities so that all could have the benefits of education. This push for numbers sounds good to the public, but what if scientific progress comes from a tiny group of truly creative scientists. What if they are born, not made by higher education? When I started science at the NIMR in the 1940s and 1950s, peer review hardly existed. Editors of journals like *Nature* were prepared to decide themselves whether or not a paper was good enough to publish, or, if in doubt, merely to telephone a few experts in the field and ask their opinion. The small number of scientists there were then helped it all; perhaps a tenth as many as there are now, and they tended to know one another. Also, there was no 'publish or perish' ethos. At good institutes like the NIMR, one good paper in three years was quite acceptable as evidence of a satisfactory career. Indeed, it was preferred over ten minor contributions.

Apart from a brief spell in the 1970s as a member of the Ad Hoc selection committee, the Royal Society has not asked me to participate in its administration. My dislike of committees and the society's preference for specialists ensured that we kept our distance but I think that we are consequently both losers.

The Marine Biological Association

Lord Rothschild had warned me early in my independence never to become a member of a committee, unless I wanted to run it and could. For most of my working years, I have followed his advice, but I ignored it in 1981 when I joined the Council of the Marine Biological Association (MBA). My love for ocean research, my many friends at the Plymouth laboratory of the MBA, and the kind persuasion of the lab's director, Eric Denton, made me accept the invitation to join this old and most distinguished association. I had come to know the MBA lab through a friendship with Michael Whitfield who lives only a few miles from Coombe Mill. Mike is a tallish, fair-haired man from Merseyside, and he is one of the most saintly men I have met. His researches on the distribution of the elements in the ocean led to his seminal paper 'Ocean chemistry, mechanism or machination?' (now reissued as a monograph). It was the stuff of Gaia and we have worked on Gaian topics ever since. Shortly after this, I persuaded Andrew Watson, recently returned from a postdoctoral visit to the USA, to take up a post at the MBA. Andrew is among the best of our scientists and I was lucky that he came to me as a postgraduate student in 1976. I remained a council member from 1981 until 1990, and during that time made voyages on the research ships *Challenger* and *Sir Frederick Russell*. Peter Liss, from the UEA at Norwich, and my son Andrew were with me on the first voyage, and Andrew Watson on the second.

In 1986 the telephone rang at about 6.30 in the evening and the caller was Eric Denton. He came straight to the point and said, 'Jim, we would like you to be President of the MBA when JZ Young retires next month.' I was so surprised that all I could say was 'Why me?' It was not that I did not appreciate the honour of the invitation but surely, I thought, there was someone better known and therefore more attractive to fund providers, someone who could drive the Council like a team of trained horses. Eric insisted that I was the best choice. He suggested that I call JZ Young and find out from him what the job involved. JZ persuaded me that the job was almost a sinecure and all that I needed to do was to chair the council meetings four times a year and sign the occasional document. Looking back, I think they chose me because I was the only one they knew who had no axe to grind, either on my own behalf or for some other organization. They knew, as I did not, that the MBA was due for a period of turbulence that could threaten its existence. This was the recommendation from the House of Lords scientific committee that the MBA be merged with another Plymouth laboratory, the Institute for Marine Environmental Research (IMER), which the Natural Environment Research Council (NERC) ran as a civil service institute. It was a short walk across Plymouth Hoe from the MBA lab, and the MBA council feared, justifiably, that their lab would lose its identity and be absorbed with IMER into a governmental conglomerate.

Decades spent working solo made me ill-equipped to handle the politics of the MBA takeover. Again, I wondered why they had chosen me as their President, but then I wondered how political parties choose their leaders, for they rarely choose wisely. I was sure that I would never take on such a task again but that, until the battle was over, I had to give of my best. It was easy for me to take sides with the MBA. It was a noble and distinguished English institution. Among its members had been several Presidents of the Royal Society, and even

Emperor Hirohito of Japan, in his role of marine biologist, had occupied a table at the Plymouth Laboratory. To make the problem worse, NERC management at that time seemed to see the taming of the MBA as a small but necessary part of their agenda. On the MBA side, we had a strong and single-minded team; Sir Eric Denton, who had just received a knighthood, and Sir John Gray, who had been chief executive of the Medical Research Council. The third member was the distinguished marine scientist, Eric Corner, and soon Professor Ann Warner, an eminent biologist from University College London, joined us. Pure as were our hearts and however strong the team, we had a lousy hand of cards to play.

The first battle was, I think, a pseudo battle. It was over the appointment of Mike Whitfield to succeed Eric Denton, due to retire as Director of the laboratory. I now think the NERC team had no quarrel with Michael Whitfield; they just wanted to show who was in charge. We spent too much time, I think, anticipating the objections they never made. We knew that Mike was a whole-hearted supporter of the lab and a first-rate scientist. We thought, wrongly, that his partisanship would be enough to make the NERC trio try to block the appointment. Early in my presidency, I confirmed my long suspicion about committees; namely that highly motivated small groups ran them. The MBA Council meetings were uncannily like a game of cards. There were the aces and the deuces, the kings and the queens sitting around the table, and some even dressed for their parts. We had to play them to win, or at least to make our opponents lose the war, even if not the present battle.

We were unable to prevent or put off the merger with the Institute for Marine Environmental Research, even though it was a crazy scheme that only liberal-minded peers could have thought of. We had one small triumph, thanks to Ann Warner's shrewd insistence; we renewed the lease of the laboratory on conditions that made it impossible for NERC to take it over. We also managed to establish a small independent nucleus within the MBA lab, which could carry on its old functions with a guaranteed support from the NERC. We all hoped that this could gradually grow until the lab restored itself to full independence again. In different times, this would have soon happened, but the ineluctable decline of England as a power in the world steadily eroded interest in science. Scientists, like other creative people, gravitate to the centre of power, which was the United States of America. The Plymouth lab was part of the Citadel, an army fort built in the 18th century at Plymouth and in the 19th century it was near the heart of power and benefited greatly from it.

The crucial meeting with the NERC was in November 1987. I had just travelled around the world, calling in at Hawaii to meet Lynn Margulis for a discussion. Whilst there I had caught a respiratory infection, and now that the meeting was due, it was at its height and I was feverish. I had to travel to Swindon, where the NERC head-quarters are. It was too long a car journey, over 300 miles there and back, and there was no direct train service. NERC therefore provided a limousine to meet me at Westbury Station on the mainline and take me from there to Swindon and back. I arrived at the Lego-style architecture of the NERC and SERC headquarters in the early after-noon and went straight to Sir Hugh Fish's office. He was the Chair-man of NERC and John Bowman and John Woods were his most senior staff members. With these three formidable NERC represen-tatives to deal with, the odds were not in my favour. One unexpected asset was my fever, which let me think more rapidly than usual. My briefing before the meeting made it clear what we could give away and what we must retain, but it was a poor hand to play. Thanks to Sir Hugh's courtesy, the bargaining was not abrasive, as I feared it might have been. We could not stop the merger but we held on to what we knew was ours, and to my delight and surprise we won support for the independent unit within the MBA lab.

Following the merger, predictably, the MBA, once a centre of excellence like Mill Hill, grew increasingly like a civil service labora-tory, where administrative convenience ruled and good science and common sense came second. To the scientific administrator, it seemed better to move the chemists and physicists from the MBA laboratory to the IMER institute and put all of the biologists into the marine biology labs building. Research is benefited by one-to-one encounters between scientists of different disciplines. To break this up for administrative convenience makes great sense to a civil servant, but it was a recipe for scientific decline—the unscheduled discussions between scientists of different disciplines could no longer take place. Let me illustrate, by an example from my time at Mill Hill, how useful such exchanges can be.

At Mill Hill the scientists' coffee room was the cradle of so many important steps. An eminent biochemist, soon to become a Nobel Laureate was talking with his colleagues after lunch about a problem he was having with rat liver cells. The failure of these cells to grow had stalled their research for weeks. Being biochemists, their attempts to resolve the problem were almost all biochemical. They were discussing such questions as was the pH right? And what about the ionic strength? Was the system critically dependent on its temperature? The eminent biochemist suddenly turned to me, sitting innocently in a chair nearby, and said, 'Jim, you have worked with all kinds of living cells. Would you have time to look at what we are doing and offer an opinion?' I was glad to help. We walked down the stairs to the third floor where his lab was, actually next to mine. He showed me the cell suspension they were using in its temperature-controlled environment. Everything looked most professional to me, and I doubted if I could suggest anything that they had not thought of long ago. Then, by chance, I noticed a bottle of buffer solution, a mixture used to keep the pH of the cell suspension near optimal. 'Is this the buffer you used for your cell suspension?' I asked. 'Yes,' replied the biochemist. TRIS is a useful compound; it is harmless to cells and does not affect the ionic strength of the suspension. I picked up the bottle and shook it. There were tiny refractile globules of some liquid present in it. 'What's that?' I asked. 'Oh, chloroform,' he replied. 'We always add a few drops of chloroform to our buffer solutions to stop moulds growing.' 'But surely that will kill your cells as well as the mould?' None of the biochemists, especially the one I was talking to, was stupid. It was just that the consequence of years of working with non-living systems, where chloroform-treated mould-free buffers are routine, had made them ignore the fact that the chloroform would kill their cells as well as the fungi. To add a drop of chloroform to the buffer solution was something done without thinking. This kind of error catches all of us when we move from one category to another; it has happened to me many times. Had Mill Hill been a lab where scientists worked in isolated sections and did not meet and talk to each other in the coffee room long past the hours of lunchtime, this small encounter would not have happened. The casual encounters between at most five scientists, usually one to one, are worth at least as much as the think-tanks or 'brainstorming' sessions so beloved of administrators.

By 1990 I felt I had done all I could for the MBA and put in my resignation as its President. It was accepted, but there was concern about who should be my successor. Happily, Sir Crispin Tickell agreed to take on the task. It was a felicitous move, for he would be in the post occupied by his ancestor, Thomas Henry Huxley, who was the first President of the MBA. I knew also that the civil servants would be more frightened of Sir Crispin than they ever were of me. He was, during the excitement of the Gulf War, our permanent representative on the Security Council at the UN in New York. He looked the part; indeed any director choosing an actor to play the part of our most distinguished ambassador would have chosen someone like him. Mike Whitfield recently gave me the good news that the MBA lab was on its way to its target of independence. It has also fathered the new National Marine Aquarium in Plymouth, an ecologically inspired museum where the visitor traces the path of moving water from an upland stream to the depths of the ocean.

Living in Ireland

It is difficult for us as inhabitants of the islands off the west coast of Europe to escape Irish politics. It was high on the agenda of family discussions when I was a child. My mother believed that the Irish were even more exploited than were the English working class, and she had sound personal reasons for this view. My grandfather's cousin, Samuel March, was a trade-union leader and had represented Irish Dockers working in London early in this century. I was aware, even as a young child, of the infamy of the Black and Tans. My father had come from an impoverished rural background and often argued against socialism in his gentle way—he resembled the horse in Orwell's *Animal Farm*. He had experienced more privation and abuse from the system than had any of the city-dwelling Marches, but was still a natural Tory. Even so, he accepted the family consensus about Ireland: he knew that the Irish suffered even more than the working class in England.

Anything learnt pre-puberty seems to become a permanent memory. We do not forget the things we learn in childhood, and somehow they are part of our powerful unconscious thinking. Because of this, I have deep within me empathy for Ireland and the Irish people. The cruel and wicked acts and words of Irish terrorists, both Unionist and Republican, have not changed this. I see the Irish war as a monstrous irrelevance; it has cost these islands dearly, has sustained hatred and suffering, and all quite unnecessarily. In spite of the malevolence of the fanatics, there is little hatred between the ordinary Irish and the English. They are both by nature peoples who respect individuals—we are polite and act to leave space for others. The truth of this is no more strongly revealed than in the statistics of traffic accidents. Ireland and England have almost the lowest death rate in the world; one-third that of continental Europe, and a similarly small fraction when compared with the United States. Only Japan, curiously, another island nation, and Norway match us. The same is true of violent crime. Belfast at the height of its tribal war in the 1980s was a far safer place, as far as violent death is concerned, than was New York or Washington, supposedly at peace. Moreover, it was safer even than most European cities.

My first encounter with the Irish war itself was in 1939, when the Irish Republican Army left a suitcase in the Left Luggage office of Tottenham Court Tube Station. It contained a small bomb and a timer-controlled detonator. At the time, I worked for a firm of consultants in Kinnerton Street, Knightsbridge and attended Birkbeck College as an evening-class student. I had ninety minutes to spare between the time I stopped work at 5.30 and the first lecture at Birkbeck at 7.00, and I would sometimes break the journey at Tottenham Court Road and walk the rest of the way to the college in Fetter Lane. I did so in February, but before the bomb exploded. Up until then, I had excused the Irish violence, as did most of the Left inclined, because we believed that they were victims of oppression and therefore had the right to protest. Suddenly, I realized that I might easily have been a victim of the protest. Nineteen years old, and full of testosterone, I was impatient for action myself. I sympathized with the Irish protest, but never thought of the consequences. I had even fantasized in simplistic socialist dreams a heroic suicide by taking a suitcase bomb into the Stock Exchange—a place I then saw as the temple of capitalist exploitation. It was not lack of knowledge about how to make explosives, and detonators, nor lack of practical experience in using them, that stopped me. What stayed my hand was the natural restraint of life as a subject of a civilized monarchy; in such a society to go this far was right over the top. It took the Tottenham Court Road bomb to make me realize the awesome responsibility placed on those who commit acts of terrorism. My bomb would not have killed the hated capitalists; it would have blasted the young clerks and people like me. Similar thoughts must have restrained the left-wing fervour of the poet John Betjeman when he wrote, 'Come friendly bombs and fall on Slough'. He pleaded with the bombers:

But spare the bald young clerks who add
The profits of the stinking cad;
It is not their fault that they are mad,
They've tasted Hell.

In 1939 most of us were marinated in socialism, and it was natural to think of profit as something unconditionally bad. We were certain that an industry run for the benefit of the people by the people would be just, kindly to the workers, and more efficient than private enterprise could ever be. As a young man, I believed in it wholeheartedly and it was not until I read Orwell's *Animal Farm* in 1948 that I understood its flaws. This simple faith in socialism still pervades in the north of these islands and it led that otherwise able man, Alan Bennett, to say that he could not understand how anyone intelligent could be other than a socialist. Do not assume that by doubting socialism, I see no good in it—I am passionate in my support for the Health Service, especially as it was until recently. Do not think that I have a similar simple enthusiasm for market forces, or some other political recipe. As a scientist, I have no faith, only a sense of wonder. I now look on socialism as a luxury, something that a rich and civilized nation can enjoy. I doubt if the poor can afford it.

I thought about Ireland again on a cold grey day in January 1965, when I heard the putter of a motorbike come to a stop, and the house door slam. My daughter Jane came in. She had travelled the thirty miles from Southampton on her small Honda bike and she was tired after her journey and her work as a trainee nurse. 'Dad,' she said, 'I have a week off. Can we go abroad for a holiday?' A holiday seemed a good idea and I could spare about a week. Charter flights to interesting destinations such as the Canaries and Seychelles were not an easy option in those days in the 1960s. I also knew that southern Europe and the Mediterranean could be bitterly cold in January so that going there was a gamble. It suddenly came to me, why not go to Ireland? I turned to Jane and said, 'Would Ireland do?' and at first she seemed disappointed. And then I said, 'Well, it is abroad, you know. We have to go there by ship if we're going to use our car over there.'

We all pored over the *Times Atlas* to see where to go in Ireland, and without hesitation, chose the far west; that is, the south-western part of Ireland where the mountain ranges, like five extended digits of a hand, point into the Atlantic, as if reaching for America. Rarely has political and physical geography so well concurred. We looked in our guide and found the Great Southern Hotel at Kenmare, which looked like the best in the region. Helen called the hotel and booked our rooms. I must admit to a fear of telephones so marked that I find it difficult to use them. Perversely, I feel exposed and vulnerable, trapped by the earpiece. I can only describe it as a feeling like the embarrassment of nakedness. Because of this, I cowardly welcome any offers to telephone on my behalf, and Helen, who in wartime had manned the National Institute for Medical Research telephone exchange, usually did. Perhaps my fear of telephony had something to do with the recent discovery that the disembodied voice is more revealing of a person's true intentions than a complete image: face, body, and voice. It is easier, apparently, to fool an audience by television than by radio. When they ask me by telephone to give a lecture or do something equally distasteful, I find it difficult to say no. Even when, in truth, I once told my tormentor: 'I am sorry but I can't do it. I have been invited to the South Pole on that date', it was clear from his voice that he did not believe me.

All that remained was to book a passage on the ship that travelled from Swansea to Cork. This done, we piled our luggage into the capacious boot of our Jaguar and set off for Swansea, which is about 200 miles from Bowerchalke. In those days, there was only one motorway in the United Kingdom, and that went north from London, the M1. There were no motorways in the south-west or Wales. We travelled along the small winding roads across England to the Welsh border just beyond Gloucester. The driving through south Wales was far from pleasant; it was an urban industrial scene of smoking chimneys and horrendous air pollution. We drove along seemingly endless terraced streets with barely a sight of a tree. The Welsh are a vocal, not a violent people, and they expressed their tribal hatred of the English by large crude graffiti expressions such as 'Kick the English out of Wales', scrawled in letters feet high on bridges and buildings. It did not augur well, we thought, for a visit to Ireland, where feelings ran even higher. I suppose the English must be high on the list of the world's most hated tribe; no doubt a legacy of our past imperial prowess and tendency to win wars. America, now the lead power, is experiencing this same dislike, but we will have to endure it for a long time yet. Individuals may be able to forgive and forget but tribes have memories lasting centuries or longer.

After six hours' driving, we reached the docks at Swansea. We took our hand luggage, watched our car driven on to a pallet, and then hoisted by a crane into the cargo hold of the *Innisfallen*, the ship we were to take to Ireland. We had a pleasant pair of cabins on the upper deck, where we stowed our baggage, and went down to the saloon for tea. These were the days before mass travel on passenger aircraft and roll on–roll off car ferries. Travel on ships, even small ones, was a pleasure. There was a sense of leisured dignity, and there was the quiet and courteous attention now only available to the seriously rich. In addition, ships in those days did not suffer the din and vibration from overpowered diesel engines that makes the car ferries so unpleasant. Nor were there cramped and noisy quarters and cafeteria feeding the masses. I never tried it, but I'm told that the old aeroplanes, like the flying boats and the stratocruisers, provided an almost marine standard of comfort. Lack of comfort is the high price we pay for cheap mass travel.

For once in January, our journey to Cork, about fifteen hours, was quiet and free of the Atlantic storms that so often savage the western approaches to these islands. Arrival in the morning was a delight. The ship sailed into the drowned valley that forms the estuary leading to Cork Harbour and passes Cobh, once the port where transatlantic liners stopped to take on Irish emigrants. Then it sailed on down the river, between the green fields of Ireland, to Cork itself. We enjoyed a leisurely breakfast on the ship whilst it docked and discharged cargo, including the few cars that it carried. There was a customs inspection, and then we were free to drive on through Cork into Ireland. The quiet roads and small towns we passed through on the way to Kenmare wholly delighted us. We went by Bandon, Bantry, and Glengarriff, and rejoiced in the mountain scenery.

The Great Southern Hotel was a graceful manor house in spacious grounds near the small market town of Kenmare. It was warm, comfortable, and wonderfully quiet. Not surprisingly, we were almost the only guests. Mid-January is hardly a time for holidays anywhere, especially in these islands. To give a measure of the style of the hotel, the other party choosing to holiday there were Lord Rank, the media magnate, and his friends. We explored two of the mountainous peninsulas that stuck out into the Atlantic. The Beara Peninsula to the south, and the larger mountain chain to the north, which contains the McGillicuddy Reeks—the highest mountains of Ireland. It is a region of enthralling landscapes and coastline. Imagine the mountains of Wales, somehow placed within Cornwall, and all of it uninhabited but for a sprinkling of farms, small fishing villages, and towns.

We fell in love with it there and then and prospected for a cottage to rent for a summer holiday later that year. We chose one on a mountainside just outside Kenmare.

In July we returned for two weeks and confirmed our January impressions. It was a wholly delightful place. We found the people of that part of Ireland courteous, friendly, and helpful. They remained so throughout the Troubles that were soon to start. A few of them were to become the staunchest of our friends. We so enjoyed the first week of our holiday that we looked for a house to buy so that we could come there and use it as a second home and place of work. The estate agent in Kenmare gave us a list of properties for sale and we travelled along the Beara Peninsula looking at them. All were inexpensive by English standards, ranging from £1,000 to £3,000 for small cottages, some even with acres of land. The choice suddenly narrowed to one cottage on the south coast of the Beara Peninsula, near the small village of Adrigole. There, on the slopes of the mountain Hungry Hill, made famous by Daphne DuMaurier in her novel, were three cottages, one of them a relatively modern-looking bungalow with a 'For Sale' sign outside. We stopped to look, when suddenly there was a knocking on the car window. I opened it to find a lady who asked if we could give her a lift into Castletown Bearhaven, about eight miles to the west. 'Yes', we said, and she then called out, 'Jimmy', and a small boy ran from the hedge to join her.

As we drove into the small town, we quizzed Mrs O'Sullivan about the cottage. Her husband, she said, had built it, and Miss Smith, who worked at Bantry Hospital as a pathologist, now owned it. It was a fine cottage, she said, and just the place for people like us. Her genuine enthusiasm confirmed the cognitive dissonance of our choice. The price asked was relatively high for Ireland, just over £3,000, but we bought it without bargaining. Extravagant by nature, I always believe that a little extra money paid for just what one wants is no waste at all, just an insurance against losing the chance to buy the place of one's dreams.

Ard Carrig, the Adrigole cottage, was to become a dream place for us for nearly twelve years. It is still in the family. I sold it to my Irish son-in-law, Michael Flynn, sometime in the 1980s. We spent two or three months there every summer until 1977. We frequently went to Ireland in the other seasons as well, and soon established firm friendships with our neighbours, the O'Sullivans. Michael O'Sullivan was a tall lean man who was as strong as an ox. He would lift a 200-pound gas cylinder onto his shoulder and stride up the slope to the cottage as if it were no heavier than a bunch of flowers. It took me weeks before I could understand him, so strong was his West Cork accent. Theresa O'Sullivan, his wife, was a well-built handsome woman and known as 'The Queen of Beara'. She knew everything and everyone on the peninsula, and far beyond as well. In those days, in what seemed to be an act of spite, the prosperous and growing European Economic Community denied the United Kingdom and Ireland membership. Consequently, both countries were still relatively poor. The O'Sullivans found it hard to make a living from their farm, which went from the shoreline to the slopes of Hungry Hill. Michael O'Sullivan welcomed the chance of winter work building a laboratory and an extra bedroom onto the small bungalow. He also, as a project, built a swimming pool one summer. Not so much as a luxury, but so that Helen could gain the exercise she needed to offset the enforced immobility of multiple sclerosis.

The easy informal life of western Ireland suited us as a family wonderfully well. Had it not been for the remoteness of the place and the difficulty for me of travelling elsewhere and keeping in touch with science, we would have moved there and kept only a foothold in England. I grew to love the wild slopes of Hungry Hill: warm slabs of bare, old, red sandstone piled up at an angle of forty-five degrees from the sea to the summit, some 2500 feet high. It was gloriously healthy walking and climbing country. There were a pair of lakes at about 1300 feet, overlooked by the precipitous mass of the mountain itself, and in the summer, the clear peaty water of these lakes was wonderfully warm for swimming. I used to sit on my favourite slab of rock overlooking Bantry Bay and the broad Atlantic. Here I would think through scientific problems that were my life's work and here I composed my first book, *Gaia: A New Look at Life on Earth*. I wrote it almost entirely in the cottage below.

As I sat in the warm sun on my ledge, high up on the sandstone slabs of Hungry Hill, it was not easy to think about the Earth in any way except romantically. I composed the book as if I were writing a long love letter to a woman I had never met. I saw her as someone intelligent, lively, and full of fun, but not a scientist. My imaginary partner was like someone the Irishman, Bernard Shaw, had in mind when he wrote his work, *An Intelligent Woman's Guide to Socialism, Sovietism and Capitalism*. My lady was not as serious, I think, as his. I sometimes wonder if my romantic style of writing was what offended my macho male critics of Gaia. If an excuse is needed, let's say it's the fault of the Irish, just as they say, when the weather is bad or they don't win at the lottery, it's the fault of the English. The extraordinary and wonderful thing that happened was that twelve years later, Sandy Orchard read the book as it was intended and written, and that is how and why we met.

Critics said that my first book, *Gaia*, was bad science. They were too serious-minded to notice that it was more a love letter than a textbook. It could have been written with less metaphor and made more acceptable for scientists, but it was not a carelessly written book; there is little in it that needs changing more than twenty years on. There was one mistaken statement, but that is the nature of all new theories in science. They are not born perfect; they evolve and their rough edges wear away under the grindstone of abrasive criticism. It can be painful at the time, but like good surgery is welcomed in retrospect. The problem with Gaia is the outrage I committed by putting forward so daring a theory in a book written for non-scientists. I compounded my error by writing 'life regulates the Earth'. I should have said Gaia is made of living organisms and the material Earth and she regulates herself. It was an easy mistake to make in the beginning, and looking back it seems a small error compared with the giant mistake of my critics. They stated, with a certainty that was near to dogma, that life had nothing to do with the Earth's apparent capacity to regulate its climate and chemistry.

About 200 yards in front of the cottage was the shoreline, reached by a narrow track that passed through the O'Sullivans' land. In the springtime, the path wandered through gorse bushes festooned with shining golden flowers, so abundant that their honey and coconut scent filled the air. The beach was a fairyland of rocks and rock pools, interspersed with small beaches and coves. It was ideal for swimming and there were small islands just a hundred yards or so from the shore, far enough to make swimming to them an adventure. Even in August, it was a private place for the O'Sullivan family and ourselves. Such places are almost impossible to find in England or in Europe—we are so densely populated, compared with Ireland. Like the Isles of Scilly, the far south-west of Ireland has a mild winter climate where frost and snow are rare and consequently the shoreline is more diverse and different in its wildlife. I once saw a shark head a shoal of mackerel into our cove, and the water boiled as the terrified fish sought to escape.

310

Most of all, for me, the coast was a place rich in varieties of the large algae or seaweed. I would wander with a book, identifying the many species that were there. Because I had a gas chromatograph in the cottage, I could collect the different species of algae in jam jars and analyse the volatile compounds they emitted. I soon found the two prize performers. The long straps of *Laminaria*, looking like old-fashioned razor strops, and the fuzzy red brushes of *Polysiphonia*, which grow as epiphytes on bladder wrack. The *Laminaria* gave forth an amazing suite of volatile bromine and iodine compounds. Methyl iodide was the most abundant among them. To me as a chemist this was extraordinary and fascinating. A toxic compound and known carcinogen, something that an organic chemist would normally lock away in the fume cupboard, was here in the most natural of scenes. I soon found that almost all seawater around Adrigole had easily measurable amounts of methyl iodide in it. Later, in 1972, I was to discover that this is true of the whole of the world's oceans. I soon found an evil-smelling chemical, something redolent of the bad side of the chemical industry, in the Adrigole seawater, namely carbon disulphide. This foul substance is a natural product and is in the oceans everywhere around the world. The most important thing I found was the copious emissions of dimethyl sulphide (DMS) from the fuzzy alga, *Polysiphonia*. It was not a new discovery—Challenger and others had noted it earlier—but for me the discovery was important because it marked the link between the life in the oceans and the great chemical and climate cycles of the atmosphere.

One of the several reasons why I regard the Green Movement with mixed vexation and affection is their obsession with the products of the chemical and nuclear industries. To many Greens, if a chemical like methyl iodide or carbon disulphide comes from some dark satanic mill, it is by nature evil, but if it comes from organically grown or natural seaweed, it must be good and healthy. To me, as a scientist, it does not matter where it comes from; I am poisoned if I eat too much of it. Strychnine or cyanide are no less poisonous if part of a plant grown naturally on an 'organic' farm and no more or less poisonous if synthesized in a laboratory. The most poisonous of all substances are the toxins of micro-organisms and plants: botulinus from bacteria, ricin from the castor-oil plant, and phalloidin from the toadstool, *Ammanita phalloides*, well-called the deathcap. Bruce Ames has wisely commented that in our normal diets, whether organically grown or from intensive agriculture, natural and just as toxic carcinogens and co-carcinogens are thousands of times more abundant than the products of the chemical industry. I do wish the Greens would grow up and forget the simplistic untruths of their student days. It is natural when young to distrust industry and the profit motive, but when we become consumers, we are all exploiting the Earth. Each one of us is as responsible for the damage done, as are the industries that supply our needs and wants. I wish that more among the Greens would turn their faces toward the real Green problem: how can we feed, house and clothe the abundant human race without destroying the habitats of the other creatures of the Earth?

Ireland in the 1970s and 1980s had tribal affairs, not environmental ones, at the top of its agenda. Despite this, we were never, while on the Beara Peninsula, subjected to dislike merely because we were English. I even recall queuing for the Sunday papers outside Murphy's in Castletown Bearhaven and chatting with the local IRA man. I noticed with amusement that he always bought the English *Sunday Times*, not the Irish Sunday papers. Had we chosen to buy a cottage in one of the eastern counties of Ireland near the Border, such as Monaghan or Armagh, I suspect that we would have been less welcome. There they brought up children to hate the English, even when sitting on their mother's knee.

The tribal instinct is so strong that young men will perform apoptosis for the love of their tribe. It must be the most powerful of instincts. It can make us embrace celibacy, it can drive us to starve ourselves to death, it destroys all feeling of compassion for our enemy. He or she is no longer human, like ourselves, but a thing to be eliminated utterly without pity. I wonder if the evolutionary biologists will assert that there is a genetic basis for tribalism. Did we evolve a trait of genocide in our ancestry? What better way to enhance our genes than to kill off all members, especially the women and children, of our opponents? Then their genes are gone forever. I find this thought hard to dismiss, awful though it is, and if true, it gives a grim slant to the religious concept of original sin. The distinguished biologist, EO Wilson, began an article in the *New York Times* in 1993 'Is humanity suicidal?' with the thought: what a pity the first intelligent animal on Earth was a tribal carnivore. My daughter Christine once brought home a foreign student from Oxford, a boring young man who had acquired anarchism as if it were an infection like measles. When we teased him, mostly for his lack of humour, by saying that we were anarchists ourselves, he replied with a sneer, 'You English are decadent; we are the only true anarchists.' I remember this exchange with affection as the epitome of tribal thinking.

I am an island person, and my view of the human scene is coloured by experiences in and on these British Isles. The people of these islands have seen a substantial decline in their status during my lifetime: the one-time superpower is now a small island group of separate and separating small nations on the edge of Europe. Strangely, over the same period, there has been an improvement in the standard of living of the people, and nowhere more than in Ireland. I must admit that today's 'wonderful' world of 'wow' does not fill me with enthusiasm, but I do see that people are now better off than they were when I grew up. What I dislike is the way we have traded good manners and a sense of personal responsibility for an uncritical belief in human rights and welfare. I do not whine about how much better things once were; instead, I give thanks for having lived through the most exciting and fulfilling century of human existence. In the main, things are not now worse or better, merely different.

A recent radio programme illustrated this difference. In it, a panel of critics reviewed some recently reissued classics. These included Evelyn Waugh's *Decline and Fall* and Apsley Cherry-Garrard's *The Worst Journey in the World*. These two books moved me deeply in my late teens. The critics praised them as good writing, but they puzzled over the world described. In particular, they could not see why Cherry-Garrard made and suffered his agonizing journey through the Antarctic winter. They found the English stiff upper lip difficult to understand and could see no place for it in their 'postmodern' world. I wonder if the difference between my world of the 1930s and theirs now reflects the changing role of women. The past was male-dominated; women were not treated fairly and their opinions less often heard, but now that women's place is recognized and most of the past injustices are remedied, there are unexpected adverse consequences. Most women, for excellent biological reasons, can never sympathize with the yearning for adventure that captures the minds of men between the ages of fifteen and twenty-five. They cannot understand that need of young men to pit themselves against the odds. Through their scorn at young men's behaviour, women have made adventure a pejorative, and cosseted safety desirable. On the other hand, the growing influence of women must lessen the chances of war. Sixty years ago, when I was twenty, there were few problems in the world but political ones. Today, our problems are global and environmental. Local tribal problems are still with us, but increasingly they grow irrelevant. Is this a consequence of women having a fairer say in national and global affairs?

Coombe Mill

In the hot summer of 1976 we were lucky to be in the relative cool of western Ireland. The summer provided near-perfect holiday weather, and a rare drought in that normally damp and misty region. There were even tankers delivering drinking water to farms around west Cork, something that probably had never happened before. We returned to a still hot, dusty, burnt, and burning England. Forest fires were frequent, and a pall of smoke seemed always to be drifting from the New Forest, south of Bowerchalke. Lester and Phyllis Machta had occupied our Bowerchalke house while we were in Ireland and had just returned to America. They said that it had seemed hotter in England than Washington that summer. Lester is a distinguished meteorologist, so I took this comment seriously. Not surprisingly, our garden had suffered from the heat. There was a ban on the use of hosepipes and remedial watering had been insufficient.

Early in September a visitor called. He was a tall active man who had retired to a village cottage in Bowerchalke, now converted to a level of comfort well above that its past owners could ever have anticipated. He wanted to ensure that Bowerchalke won the National Best Kept Village award. 'Lovelock,' he said, 'your garden is rather untidy. Do you think that you could make an effort to clear it up a bit? The judges come round next week and we do want Bowerchalke to win the competition this year.' I must have looked astonished; in fact, I was taken back to my school days, to the time when a master or a prefect would say, 'Lovelock, we expect you to play in the B team on Saturday. It is an important match for the school so see that you're there.' Quietly, we ushered Mr Bellringer out. We were enraged and had no intention whatever in meeting the newcomer's need to live in the village distinguished by the Best Kept Village Award. I realized that we were among the last representatives of Bowerchalke as it had been. Only five years earlier, it had been a village community with its own cricket team, good enough to beat that of the county Somerset. It had a good school, run by a competent teacher, and a well-run village pub. All these had gone, and now it was little more than a gentrified nest of middle-class strangers. It was time to move. A trip to Boston beckoned, so there was no time immediately to do it. Even so, I knew that I did not belong in the Wiltshire countryside any longer.

Helen and I decided to act after Christmas 1976. We did so by scanning the property section of our favourite Sunday paper, not then converted, as now, into a kind of up-market tabloid. There was a mill for sale on the North Devon coast, and after telephoning the agents we took off for Devon early in January. It was just what we had in mind—a big enough house with ten acres of land, about one mile from the coast. We made our offer immediately, waited, and then were disappointed to hear that the owners had decided not to sell after all. The agent was a friendly and intelligent young man from Fox's, an Exeter estate agency. He had made his own judgement about our characters and our needs and he said, 'Sad about Gooseham Mill but we have another one rather like it, twenty-five miles south of here. Would you care to see it?' We did; we liked Coombe Mill at once and offered to pay the full price and in cash. The owner, Mr Cheeseman, asked if we could buy it immediately and as I had no desire whatever to be driving 280 miles from Wiltshire to Devon and back looking at other possible properties, I said yes. To Mr Cheeseman we must have been the purchasers he dreamed of. We even bought his furniture so that we could move in whenever we wanted. He had tried, unsuccessfully, to convert the property into a water garden and make a living from it, and was desperately short of funds. He needed to settle his debts and we were the fairy prince and princess who had come to his rescue.

Helen was by now so disabled that our Bowerchalke house was difficult for her, still more was the climb from the village road to the house and, but for our immediate neighbour, Dorothy Golden, nearly all of her village friends had gone. The newcomers were not accessible, and she was as keen to move as I was. By April we had moved to Devon and we put our house in Bowerchalke in the hands of house agents. It soon sold, almost exactly at the price we had paid for Coombe Mill. The cottage in the garden sold separately for £12,000 and was a bonus. These seemed good prices to us but in two years, they doubled, such was the financial mismanagement of the Heath government.

In early December 1976 Helen and I went off to Ireland for ten days so that I could finish, in the peace and quiet of Ireland, the last chapter of my book, *Gaia*. We drove from Bowerchalke in a new large

Volvo car, a spacious and comfortable 164 model. As we drove into Wales to Swansea to catch the ferry for Cork, the weather worsened. Bursts of rain driven by gale-force southwesterly winds made driving difficult and we were glad to reach the port and drive onto the ferry. We had a small comfortable suite on the upper deck but we knew it was going to be a rough night ahead, and it was. We had little sleep as near hurricane-force wind and waves battered the ship, and the cold front passed just as we arrived in Cork. We drove across County Cork to Glengarrif, which is at the landward end of Bantry Bay. On the last ten miles before our cottage there was a high place on a narrow coastal road, and here a fierce gust from a line squall passing rapidly across the bay hit the car. It wrenched the steering wheel from my hand, and almost immediately, we hit a large rock head-on. Neither of us was hurt and our valuable IBM memory typewriter still sat on the backseat. The doors clicked open as usual and I went back to the road to seek help. A post office van stopped and offered to tow us back onto the road. I gratefully accepted, but when the driver looked at the front of the car, he said, 'You'll never drive that car again.' We looked down and saw one of the front wheels bent into the shape of a U and the front of the car looked squashed. He said he would call a taxi for us from the next post office, and he did. It was my first and only serious car accident. The Volvo advertisements telling of cars that could survive the most severe crashes were true. We had walked unharmed from a collision with a rock hard enough to wreck the car completely. In some ways, the crash was a blessing. It made me stay put in Adrigole and finish the writing, and by the time we left by taxi ten days later, the work was ready for the publisher.

The two years from 1977 to 1979 were the quietest in all my time as an independent. To travel anywhere was now much more difficult. It was an hour's journey by car to Exeter station and Plymouth airport, and then three or four hours to London. I still had my four sponsors: Shell, HP, MOD, and NOAA—but the settling in at Coombe Mill occupied most of my time. We had to build on to the house rooms for a lab and an office for Helen, and I had to decide what to do with the fourteen acres of land we had just purchased. In 1979 my book was published and my first warning of the way life would change came with a telephone call as we sat at lunch late in September. When I picked it up I heard an American voice say, 'I am Jim Morton, Dean of the Cathedral of St John the Divine in New York. I have just read your book and I like it. Would you care to address a small group here at the cathedral on it?' I was due in New York next month anyway, as part of the book promotion, and was glad to say yes. Meanwhile I checked on St John the Divine to make sure that it was what he claimed it to be, and found that it was indeed the largest Protestant cathedral in the world. It was part of the Episcopalian church in America, which is the equivalent of the Church of England here.

When I took the taxi to Amsterdam and 110th St one Saturday in late September, I saw how large it was, especially as I walked along its side on the way to the Deanery, which was a pleasant house in the gardens of the cathedral. I knocked, and soon Mrs Morton welcomed me, showed me to my room, and asked me to join the family at tea. Dean Morton, a tall handsome figure in clerical gear, came in. He had the air of someone who would perform miracles, someone who could charm the birds from the trees. My natural caution began to sound alarm bells and not without reason. 'Jim,' he said, 'I have arranged for you to give the sermon at tomorrow morning's service in the cathedral. It will all be properly done, and you'll be introduced by the Bishop.' I have wondered since if he saw me as terrified, like a rabbit before the fox, which he was. Wasps, the yellow-jacket kind, and giving lectures are the two things I most fear, and here was I condemned to giving a sermon in a WASP cathedral at the Sunday morning communion service. 'My talk is entirely secular,' I croaked, hoping that this might give me some means of escape. 'Oh that's of no consequence,' boomed the Dean. 'Tell it just as you did in your book and they will love it.' Saturday night passed in agony of anticipation and Mrs Morton sensed some of my anxiety and was wonderfully comforting to me at breakfast. It occurred to me that this kind of shock quite often happened in that household.

We all moved into the cathedral where the huge congregation was gathering. 'It's going to be a full house,' said the Dean, as he led me to the robing room. I was slightly relieved to be there, for my interest in what went on behind the scenes anywhere, especially a cathedral, took my mind off the ordeal ahead. They soon disguised me in flowing colourful robes, which helped quite a bit. Their anonymity made me feel less exposed. The Dean rehearsed me through my movements before stepping up to the pulpit. 'Just walk behind the Bishop and me down the nave and you will be directed to your seat. Then your cue to walk up to the pulpit will be the end of the hymn, "Morning has broken". Wait for the Bishop to introduce you and then off you go.' As always, the ambience of the cathedral moved me deeply, and I was interested to see that nearly half of the congregation was black. I did later discover that the cathedral was on the edge of Harlem. All too soon, we rose to sing that gorgeous hymn about the blackbird. As the organ sounded its closing chords, I felt a gentle push and I walked across to the pulpit and climbed the stairs. I was now above the congregation, and in a position that commanded, as well as detached one from, the surroundings. Never before had I realized what a well-chosen vantage point the clerics have for preaching. The Bishop, across from me in the other pulpit, began his welcome and introduction, smiled at me, and sat down. I was on. My sermon seemed to go well, and twenty minutes later, I was back in my seat. 'Just what I'd hoped you'd say,' said the Dean. 'You're a natural speaker.' I think he meant it, for this was the first of four occasions when he invited me to give sermons at the cathedral. The most terrifying of these was when he asked without warning one Sunday morning if I would appear in the pulpit with Father Thomas Berry to give a joint sermon on the subject of Jacob's ladder. Somehow, it worked, as I took a physical interpretation, with the ladder as the flow of photons bringing benefice from the sun to the Earth and Father Berry kept the theology right. I was so glad to have had the chance to meet this modern St Francis and to share his feeling for the Earth.

I had expected, even hoped, when I wrote Gaia that it would be criticized, even denounced, by the churches that would see the worship of the Earth as heresy. Yet, here was I giving a Gaia sermon at the morning communion service in a Protestant church. Soon I was to experience real denunciation as the fiery biologists castigated Gaia, and me, from their lecterns in the universities. The neo-Darwinists were like the Nonconformist hell raisers of Victorian times.

During the year following the publication of *Gaia*, I was astonished to receive twice as many letters from the religious and the philosophically interested as from scientists. Hugh Montefiore, then the Bishop of Birmingham, wrote to me asking which I thought came first: life on Earth or Gaia. This was not an easy question to answer. My attempt led to a friendship that has persisted. Hugh is President now of our charity, Gaia, and a welcome guest to Coombe Mill. His thoughtful question should have come from a biologist, but in recent times, leading biologists seem to be in a pseudo-religious phase, and churchmen are growing open minds. Hugh Montefiore published a book, *The Probability of God*, a title any physicist would have approved, and the book was for me refreshingly free of dogma. I have thought since childhood that there are no certainties; this, if you like, is a scientist's creed. I found it odd that the biological scientists who attacked Gaia spoke with near dogmatic certainty, something I had not heard since the days of the Sunday Schools where I was an unwilling pupil. Geological critics were better scientists, and argued from the interpretation of facts. I remember when I first lectured on Gaia at Mainz in Germany, the geologist Wally Broecker rose from the audience at the end of my talk to say, 'And there's not more than one chance in a hundred that your view of the Earth is right.' Now here were the words of a true scientist critic and I was proud that our work on Earth sciences, his and mine, were both recognized twenty-three and twenty-four years later by the award of the Japanese Blue Planet Prize. Perhaps the most rewarding letter about the book was from Crispin Tickell, then chef-de-cabinet to Roy Jenkins at the European Union in Brussels. Later, as Sir Crispin Tickell, he was our Ambassador to Mexico, and then our Permanent Representative to the United Nations in New York. I am glad that Gaia brought us together, and paved the way to a friendship with this remarkable man and his wife Penelope.

When Helen and I first moved to Coombe Mill in early 1977, we wondered how we could ever manage its fourteen acres of farmland. Helen loved gardening, but was disabled, and could not possibly cope with so large a garden. I was no gardener at all; indeed, I detest gardening. At first, we tried growing and selling the grass of the meadows. Local farmers were prepared to come and cut the grass and pay us a modest sum for it. This seemed a noticeable improvement on suburban life, where it may be necessary to pay to have the grass cut. Then in the autumn of 1977, a man with a tractor and a hedge-cutter appeared on the 250-yard road that led to Coombe Mill. He trimmed the hedges meticulously, backed round, and drove out, waving to us as he went. We asked our neighbour, then Dennis Fry, at Huntsdown Farm, who it could have been. 'Oh, Mr Rockey,' he said. 'He cuts the hedges every year.' This was even better. My worries about how to do it myself, what equipment to buy, were over. Only slight doubts remained about how was I to get in touch with Mr Rockey to pay him. Dennis said not to worry, he would turn up when he wanted paying—and he did, in January 1978, with his bill of £10.00. I wondered how it could be worth his while to do such good work for so little.

We were settling in to Coombe Mill and it was looking after us. I still had fanciful notions about using the land productively. I thought of growing lettuces and salad vegetables in hundred-yard lengths of polyethylene tubing. The field behind the house sloped gently down. My idea was to glue the seeds to a long string passing down each of these plastic tubes, inflate the tubes and feed the plants with a solution of nutrients pumped continuously. When fully grown I could seal the lettuces mechanically in their compartments and so provide sterile vegetables never touched by human hand or by the excrement normally applied as nutrient. Not pressed for money, as I still worked for my customers Hewlett Packard, Shell and NOAA, I did not become a lettuce farmer. I did try growing potatoes by simply pegging down a large sheet of black plastic on an area of grass. Then I cut crosses in the plastic in the form of a square matrix and placed seed potatoes beneath each cross. To my delight, it worked. Without light, the grass underneath the plastic died and formed mulch in which the potatoes grew. Months later, when the previously healthy looking plants above ground started to wilt, I lifted the plastic sheet, starting from one corner. Underneath were fine potatoes and I reached down to pick them. Hastily I backed away, for not only were there potatoes, there were adders, the one venomous snake we have in England, slithering around them. I lifted the whole sheet and left the reptiles to dissipate. My plastic sheet had provided a wonderful habitat for snakes. Field mice abounded in the grass around my plastic potato plot, and they would come to feast on the potatoes but instead fed the adders, who stayed warm, safe, and well fed.

So successful was this experiment in ecological farming that I planned to extend it in the next year 1979 but the winter of 1978/9 put paid to that ambition. Just before Christmas the north wind reached storm force and brought with it particles of snow so fine it was almost an aerosol. It was a full blizzard and impossible to walk against. It blew most of the night and we endured it without heat or electricity. The next morning brought blue skies and thick snow cover and was colder than I could ever remember. The outside thermometer registered $-19°$ C, and it was so cold that many plants and animals around died, and I never saw the adders and the grass snakes at Coombe Mill again. The worst of the cold for the humans at Coombe Mill were the burst pipes in the roof and the inch-thick layer of snow dust everywhere across the roof space. I had to sweep it into plastic bags using a dustpan and broom. The winters of the late

1970s and early 1980s were severe in our region. The snowfall one year was so heavy that the small lanes of Devon filled from hedge top to hedge top. The worst of the snowfall was about two miles to the east and north of Coombe Mill. We could just manage to drive to the village, but snowdrifts ten or more feet high blocked the roads to the north and the east.

The heating at Coombe Mill when we bought the house was primitive and inefficient and used open fires. I wondered about some 'Green' form of central heating, and was inspired by an article in the *Farmer's Weekly* that described a grass-burning boiler. We grew several tons of grass each year, and this seemed a fine and Green way of exploiting solar energy indirectly. We installed central heating, with radiators and copper pipes joined to one of these grass-burning boilers, which I had placed in an old stone building near the house. We had grown the grass the previous summer and it was stacked in a haystack covered with plastic. A friendly local farmer had baled it for me in return for a share of the bales. The hay bales were about four feet long and eighteen-inches square. They must have weighed forty or fifty pounds each. The idea was to put a bale into the boiler, ignite one end of it and let it burn like a cigarette. In practice, it rarely ever did and more often than not, it would go out, usually at some socially inconvenient time, when we needed warmth. When I opened the boiler a vast puff of toxic smoke emerged, and it seemed to me a health hazard worse than heavy smoking. I had to wear a gas mask to tend this stove, and it slowly dawned on me that this was a mad way to live. I gave up burning grass and bought logs instead from Mr Thomas, a local forester, who always seemed to have thinnings for sale. They burnt better than the grass, but the smoke, when the boiler was open, was almost as bad. At the end of 1981, after an accident with my tractor hauling logs, I at last saw sense. I replaced the wood-burning boiler with an efficient, carefree gas burner, which is still there.

I vented my annoyance with three years of frustrated misery with 'Green' methods of heating by writing, with Michael Allaby, an article called, 'Wood burning stoves, the trendy pollutant', which *New Scientist* published. This successful collaboration led to projects that were more ambitious. Mike wrote a book based on some ideas I had about the extinction of so many species from giant lizards to ocean organisms 65 million years ago. The finding by the Alvarez family of traces of iridium and other extra-terrestrial elements in the rocks contemporary with the extinction were what stimulated me. They argued, and I believed them, that a large planetesimal collided with the Earth, and the collision devastated the environment so that few living things survived. Inevitably, many biologists, who preferred to believe that inter-species competition caused the extinctions, scorned the collision theory. The book that we published, *The Great Extinction*, acted as a lightning conductor for their scathing criticism, and the reviews were among the worst we had experienced. Now, the collision theory is widely accepted, and the site of the impact thought to be close to the Yucatan Peninsula, but no one among our critics has admitted that they might have been wrong. Not daunted by our rough treatment by reviewers, Mike and I wrote a second joint book, *The Greening of Mars*. It was on the impropriety of terraforming and written as a novel. It has done well in Japan, but poorly elsewhere. From working together, Mike and his wife, Ailsa, became our close friends.

The illness of the 1980s and these experiences reduced me to practice. No longer did I attempt heroic acts of farming like the characters in *The Good Life*. We decided instead to let the Coombe Mill land go back to Gaia. We tried to help by planting two-thirds of the land with the sort of trees that would have been there before mankind appeared. The other third we kept as meadow, to indicate the kind of pleasant ecosystem which man in harmony with nature sustains. We did this by cutting half of each meadow once a year in July. Now, sixteen years later, we have increased the land area of Coombe Mill to thirty-five acres by the purchase of a long strip on the other side of the river. It is woodland with grassy glades and is wonderfully moving back to Gaia. Wildlife, both plants and animals, are beginning to appear in a habitat that they find congenial. Sandy and I, with the unstinted help of our friend and accountant, Godfrey Rehaag, have formed a charity called Gaia. Its purpose is to promote meetings and research on Gaian topics, and also to own and care for the house and land at Coombe Mill. Sandy and I have donated all of this property, including the house and outbuildings, to this charity, so that the habitat here will be as much as possible free from human intervention and remain a true refuge for wildlife. Soon after this Margaret Cooper who, with her husband, founded the charity Earthkind, asked me to serve as their president and I have happily done so ever since. Earthkind has aims close to my own and runs the small ship *Ocean Defender* that quietly does environmental good.

It would be wrong to give the impression that the inhabitants of Coombe Mill are entirely unsociable and live like hermits. On a typical day, the postman will call between 8 and 9 am, and often chats for a while as he delivers and takes our mail. Clifford Nosworthy and Geoff Francis have delivered our mail for over twenty years now, and are our friends. Later Margaret Sargent comes from the village to look after us, and my disabled son John, who lives in a cottage just near the house. Margaret is a farmer's daughter, a true country-woman, and is so much a part of Coombe Mill that to us she is a family member.

We have a small circle of local friends, among them John and Truda Lane, who live in a manor house near Beaford, about twenty miles away. John is a fair-haired, tall man with a wonderful sense of fun coupled with an erudition that makes him the perfect companion and guide. Truda's drawing has the delicacy of a fractal design in bone china, and she is one of the few women I know whose voice matches her trim elegance. They are among our most stimulating and amen-able friends. Sandy has a love for music, and we travel to Taunton for musical weekends at the Castle Hotel. Here those most estimable musicians, the Lindsays, entrance us, and here we meet our musical friends Monica and John Pethybridge, who, like us, come to listen. Music links us to Yvonne and Walter Reeves, who live nearby, and to my old friend and scientific colleague, Peter Fellgett, the inventor of ambisonics and fourier transform spectroscopy. All of us meet at what we think is the best restaurant in Britain, Percy's at Coombshead, just two miles from Coombe Mill, where Tina and Tony Bricknell-Webb care for us in style.

A remarkable friend is Satish Kumar. He was born in northern India, and as a child, he became a noviciate Jain monk. In his twenties he felt the call to protest against nuclear weapons, and chose to walk from India to the western side of Europe, and from there travel by ship to New York to the United Nations. He has vividly described his long walk, which included a large section of the then Soviet Union, in his book *No Destination*. He and his English wife, June, now live in the village of Hartland, some twenty-five miles away, where they edit and publish the journal, *Resurgence*. Satish was a key figure in the founding of Schumacher College in the grounds of Dartington. This alternative university is one of the first places to teach Gaia science and runs, in collaboration with Plymouth University, a Masters pro-gramme for Gaia scientists. The college is also prominent as a place for discussion about the philosophical and political consequences of Gaia theory.

Our pleasures are things we do together. One of them is walking on that grand mountain block of Dartmoor, or along the superbly rugged coastline of North Devon and Cornwall. Those places are not much more than twenty miles away at the furthest, and even in summertime, amazingly deserted. Few, it seems, wish to walk more than 100 yards from their parked car. The whole of Dartmoor is no larger than greater London, less than 1,000 square miles, and tiny compared with the vast national parks of the United States of America. Yet, once we have climbed the first 1,000 feet and we reach the open inland plateau of the moor, we seem to be in an infinite, never-ending space. We drove one morning the ten miles to Lydford, a village on the edge of the moor, and from there walked across the short turf to the rocky valley of the Lyd. Ahead lay the wall of the moor, rising in two steps of 600 feet each to the central mass, at 1,500 to 2,100 feet high. The first steps led from the valley to a small peak, Doe Tor, from which the panorama of West Devon, with its green and yet almost unspoilt fields and woods, lay before us. Eastwards, across a stretch of heather and bog, lay the next step up to Hare Tor. Past Hare Tor lay a stretch of almost featureless moorland, the central part of the moor, where it is so easy to get lost when the mist comes down. We set off on a course slightly east of north on the compass, and after a mile suddenly came upon the single boulder as large as a house that marks Chat Tor. From here, the going was easier and Great Lynx Tor, with its castle-like rock pillars, lay in view to the northwest. Our destination was no more than a map reference that marked the furthest point of a twelve-mile round walk. We reached it by crossing the bogs that surround the Rattle Brook. On the banks of the brook is the ruin of Bleak House, which is well named. The manager of the peat mine used it as his home fifty years earlier. We wondered if he was a married man. If he was, how had his wife endured the lonely existence of so remote and inaccessible a place? We sat in the sun on a slab above the brook with the house shielding us from the brisk northwest wind and ate our lunch— sandwiches filled with good strong cheddar cheese, slices of beetroot and onions, followed by an apple or a bar of chocolate, and a soft drink. There are few events in life so good for me as the feeling of contentment that a good walk to such a place brings. Sharing it with Sandy fills my cup to over-brimming.

It was now one o'clock and time to continue to the furthest point of our walk. Like some of the other elevations on Dartmoor, it has an animal name, Kitty Tor. It was more of a map reference than a place, but we had planned to reach it. We walked back across the heather to the wind-carved granite of Great Lynx Tor. We find its sculpted rocks, with their sense of ineffable purpose, the most enthralling of all places on Dartmoor. Looking north we see the high slopes of Yes Tor and Great Willhayes, and looking west the Tamar Valley and Bodmin Moor. From here, it was an easy run down to the Lyd valley and to our drive home. Such a day would end with some experiments, a swim, or a laze in the sun, followed by an evening meal and an evening of music on CD. Such are the freedoms that work as an independent brings.

Although we have no desire to live there, London beckons, with its wonderful theatres, concert halls, and museums. In 1988 Sandy and I purchased a small flat in St Mark's Road in North Kensington. It was a modest but comfortable place in a quiet road on the wrong side of the Westway, a monstrous piece of motorway that, like the angiogenesis of a cancer, keeps London's malignant traffic alive. We bought it so that we could enjoy London's unsurpassed supply of music and theatre. It soon turned out to be more expensive than we could afford, and in 1991 we sold it at a loss. We decided to sell when we found the Clearlake Hotel in that never failing source of good accommodation, the Consumer Association's *Which? Good Bed and Breakfast Guide*. Hotels in London are comfortable, but far beyond our price, or cramped, noisy, and not for us. The Clearlake in 1991 offered all that we needed, and at a price we could afford. There was no meal service of any kind, but the hotel provided its guests with either a small suite of rooms or a 'bedsit', including an en suite bathroom and a tiny kitchen equipped with a microwave cooker, refrigerator, china, cutlery, and all things needed to cook a light meal. It has theatrical associations, and they have decorated many of their rooms with posters of plays once performed in London. The price in 1991 was £50 to £60 a day. This we could afford and the hotel has been our home in London ever since. Situated in a small road, Prince of Wales Terrace, opposite the west end of Kensington Gardens, it is almost an ideal site for us. We can walk the three miles across the parks to Piccadilly or Whitehall free of the noise and fumes of traffic. The lift does not always work, but that is a small disadvantage in what is a family hotel. We have grown fond of the Herkovits family who run the Clearlake, especially of Nava who welcomes us so warmly. The Clearlake Hotel was once the home of a Victorian family, a house in a proud and comely terrace in a fashionable part of London. The Prince of Wales Terrace is now wonderfully restored to its Victorian excellence and in its new usage is every bit a source of pride for Londoners as it ever was.

We stole down the two flights of stairs from our room at the Clearlake at 7.45 am in 1996. We opened the street door as quietly as we could and glanced back at the reception desk, wondering if someone had noticed our furtive departure. We walked into Victoria Road and turned south, past the blossom-covered villas of the some-what rich. What had once been modest housing for the Victorian upper-working class or lower-middle class was now far up market. Soon we were in the Gloucester Road, with its vast array of terraced mansions; were any of them homes of a single family, I wondered? Most likely they were now flats or offices. Soon, as we walked on, that incredible bulk of the Natural History Museum loomed before us: a Victorian masterpiece of variegated marble and brick in a Gothic style—perhaps the unkind might say it had the look of a Lego con-struction. It was by now 8 am and we walked up the grand entrance steps to the doors of the museum. And once inside, the director, Neil Chalmers, welcomed us. He had invited us to attend a tour behind the scenes of the museum and a breakfast. It was a joyful event to be invited back to the Natural History Museum in these VIP circum-stances. In my childhood, seventy years ago, I spent so many happy Sunday afternoons here whilst my mother and father were visiting the Victoria and Albert Museum just opposite. They were there for the works of art, and I was here, or in the Science Museum, learning all the things that were to form my life as a scientist. Dr Chalmers then introduced the other guests and made a short speech as we all stood in the shadow of the *Diplodocus* skeleton that fills the great hall of the museum. After a satisfying breakfast, behind the scenes on the top floor, we met our guide, Sandy Knapp. She showed us some of the tens of millions of plant specimens in what seemed an unending row of polished wooden cabinets. She provided an impressive account of the expeditions to remote and wild places that they had made to collect the dried specimens before our eyes. The quest for Gaia has also rewarded us with enthralling visits to the great gardens of Kew and St Louis where the directors, Sir Ghillian Prance and Peter Raven, generously gave us their time.

11

Building Your Own Bypass

The flight was nearly half an hour late and, as we circled Salt Lake City preparing to land, I was anxious. Traffic had delayed the departure from Chicago and now there were only twenty minutes left to catch my flight to Idaho Falls. I suspected that Salt Lake City Airport was no different from many others in the United States; there would be the long walk with my heavy bag from the landing bay to the departure lounge of my next flight. We landed with fifteen minutes to spare. Somewhat relieved, I began a fast walk, and then a slow run to the concourse. As I ran, I felt an odd pain grow in my lower chest, which I attributed to muscular pains caused by the imbalance of carrying a heavy bag whilst running and dodging people on the way to the departure lounge. Soon I saw the sign, TransMagic, and the door leading to the TransMagic Airlines plane. This miraculous airline flew a one-way flight to Idaho Falls. I could not help wondering if they disassembled the plane in Idaho and sent it back by truck. I checked in and thought no more of the pain; it had gone away. I boarded the small plane and flew across the Magic Mountains to my destination.

My friends at the National Oceanic and Atmospheric Administration, NOAA, had booked me in for three weeks during September 1972 at a pleasant hotel near the Snake River. We were due to spend the time at the National Reactor Facility, a government institution sited in the lunar landscape of the lava fields of north Idaho. The facility itself was a remote place where strange nuclear reactors were tested; a place where an explosion or a meltdown would—they hoped—be less noticeable and less obtrusive. To my slight regret, my role there was in no way connected with these fascinating monsters: all that we had to do was conduct an experiment in air-mass labelling. So exquisite is the sensitivity of the electron capture detector that it is possible to detect as little as one part in 10^{16} of a tracer substance diluted in air. Our minds cannot deal with large numbers like this; we are not really much better than the apocryphal tribe whose number system was one, two, and many. One in 10^{16} means one part in 10,000 million million, or one with 16 noughts after it. This is too small a dilution for our imaginations to grasp; it is as scarce as three seconds out of the age of the Universe. Yet, by collecting and concentrating a few litres of air, the electron capture detector is sensitive enough to detect the tiny amount of tracer in it.

My friend, Lester Machta, was in charge of the Air Resources Laboratory of the agency, NOAA, in Washington. He wanted to label air masses on the West Coast of America and follow their motion across the whole of the American continent. I believed that my detector was sensitive enough for this ambitious project, and we were in Idaho to prove it. Among the substances it could detect at great sensitivity, were the perfluorocarbons. These are strange volatile odourless liquids. In some ways, they are similar to the hydrocarbons of petrol, but have fluorine, not hydrogen, attached to the carbon. These substances are so inert that they are neither flammable nor poisonous, nor for that matter do they react with other chemicals. As I mentioned earlier, they are so benign that they are less poisonous than water. They were thus ideal materials to release into the air as tracers. These were chemicals that even the most sensitive Green would find difficult to condemn. NOAA was to conduct its experiment in parallel with several from other US government departments. The others were intending to release much less safe materials than our perfluorocarbons: for example, one group was using methyl iodide labelled with the radioactive isotope 131 of iodine. The release of so dangerous a substance was possible only on this remote site in Idaho.

We made our first experiment on a crisp sunlit morning with frost on the ground and the warm sun fast rising over the dry lava desert. I set up my sampling equipment with the distant mountains as a backdrop. Solid though they were, they stood flat against the sky like the stage scenery of atmospheric theatre. Science can be a wonderful occupation when there is the chance to work in such a place.

I shared the fine food served at our motel with my NOAA companions: fresh fish from the Snake River and Idaho's tastiest baked potatoes. At weekends, we explored the Yellowstone National Park, the Teton Mountains, and the country around Jackson Hole. There are few other parts of the American scenery so splendid. We were fortunate that it was late September, well outside the tourist season, and when the trees were already putting on their red and gold to celebrate the fall. I most remember the companionship of the meteorologist, Bob List, with whom I worked, and of a Major in the US Army, whose name I cannot remember, but whose face is still clear before me. One Sunday we went to the waterfall in Yellowstone that roars down into what looks like a miniature Grand Canyon, and which is a favourite spot for visitors. A long flight of wooden stairs, perhaps 100 feet of them, leads to a platform at the very edge of the falls. A damp, deafening, but exciting place, with a breathtaking view and the thunder of the water. It filled me with exhilaration, and I challenged the Major to a race to the top of the stairs. We made it and I just won. We were both breathless, and my legs and thighs in such pain that a few more steps would have broken me, but I felt inordinately pleased. Here was a near sedentary scientist at fifty-two years matching the performance of a fit young Army officer.

In early November I was back again in the United States, this time to visit a firm in West Palm Beach, Florida, who were making ion drift instruments. These are devices similar to the electron capture detector, but lack its sensitivity. We use them because they are more convenient to handle than is the ECD. I was visiting this firm on behalf of UK departments that were interested in picking up small traces of explosive vapours that would reveal bombs in places they should not be. In the evening, after dark, I walked in the warm, humid, tropical air along the beach outside my motel. I might even have walked past Sandy Orchard, as she strolled along the beach from her home, not knowing that in eighteen years she would be my wife. From Florida, I was due at Andover in New Hampshire, some 1300 miles north, where there was to be a conference on the ecology of the chlorofluorocarbons. Indeed, I think it was the first conference ever held specifically on this topic, and some time before Rowland and Molina published their famous paper.

I flew from Miami to Boston, where my friend, Jim Lodge, a scientist from the National Center for Atmospheric Research, NCAR, met me. We waited outside Boston's Logan airport for a car that was to take us to Andover: it was bitterly cold and an astonishing contrast to the near tropical warmth of West Palm Beach. We were shivering, but soon the heat of the car warmed us as we drove north into the New England winter. The conference met in one of those pleasant timber buildings with spacious rooms and polished wooden floors that abound in New England, and we luxuriated in its warmth. If you want to be warm in the North American winter, go to Canada or the northern states. Whatever you do, do not go to California, where the indoor climate can be bitterly cold. Californians believe their climate to be so perfect that they need no heating, and they share this illusion with the inhabitants of the Mediterranean. We enjoyed a vast evening meal that ended with an emperor-sized hunk of cheesecake. I retired replete, slept well, and the next morning joined Jim Lodge and Ray McCarthy of Dupont and Camille Sandorfy of Montreal University for breakfast, which of course was ample. After breakfast, I collected my lecture notes from my room and started out into the cold air for the short walk to the conference hall, not more than 100 or 200 yards away. Two American scientists, who I did not know, walked and talked with me. About half-way through this brief journey, I experienced an increasing dull pain in my lower chest, just as I had at Salt Lake City Airport and I tried to suppress it, but it grew worse as we approached the hall. I began to fear I was having a coronary occlusion, but when I sat down in the hall, it passed away, and with it my apprehension. I gave my talk about the discovery of the chlorofluorocarbons in the atmosphere and I said that they were at present harmless, but might become a danger if ever they accumulated to the parts-per-billion level. This was because they absorbed infrared radiation intensely and, at those levels, would be adding significantly to the greenhouse effect of carbon dioxide and other gases.

As I walked back to lunch, the pain returned and I began to worry. In the evening, I experimented by walking the quiet road outside the conference hall; every time I walked over fifty yards the pain came on, but went away again if I stood still. I knew now that I was experiencing angina pectoris, but somehow I could not believe that such a thing could happen to me. It was outrageous: after all, I was fit.

Next day I travelled back to Boston and took a taxi from the airport to Lynn Margulis's laboratory at Boston University. I was due to stay with Lynn and her family that night in their house in Newton, a suburb of Boston. We took the tram outside the University to

Newton Station and began the uphill walk from there to Lynn's house, not more than a few hundred yards away. Soon the pain came on again and, as Lynn walked briskly on, it forced me to say, 'Slow up, I can't walk fast, I've a medical problem.' Lynn slowed down and the pain became bearable. When we reached the house I was walking like an old man, with leaden steps, and I turned to Lynn and said, 'I think I am having a heart attack, do you have a physician I could see?' Lynn was shocked and said, 'I am sorry; I thought you meant by a medical problem something trivial like an itch in the crotch.' She was about to telephone her doctor when Nicky, her husband, said, 'We can do better than that. We can take Jim to the local hospital in Wellesley where they have a programme for dealing with coronary emergencies.' He turned to me: 'It's only a short distance, let's go.' He was a marvellous comforter; calm, matter of fact, and just what I needed.

I remember travelling through the tree-lined streets of Newton to the hospital where I went straight to the desk of the nurse receptionist. Tongue-tied, I found myself blurting out, 'Can I see someone about chest pains?' In those days, coronaries were almost epidemic, especially in America, and they were prepared at every hospital for anyone who came in with such a statement. She told me to sit down and soon a young intern came out to see me. I went with him to his office, where he quizzed me and then arranged an ECG and X-rays for me. I returned to the waiting room and sat with Nicky Margulis. The young intern returned and said, 'We are admitting you at once. Your condition is serious and it requires immediate attention.' At this, the alarm bells began to ring in my mind. I was more worried about the cost to my family than about death or heart disease. I was uninsured and knew, having previously been a staff member of the Baylor College of Medicine, just how expensive uninsured medical treatment can be in America. I had no wish to put such a burden on my family. I said, 'I am sorry but I have to fly back to Britain tomorrow. Can you give me something to alleviate the pain of the condition?' The young intern shook his head and replied, 'You have three conditions sufficiently serious to require admission. Your blood pressure is too high, you have angina pectoris, and your ECG is not good.' Nicky Margulis broke in saying, 'It is his life isn't it? He wants to go home; it's a normal, natural thing to do.' Nicky was a wonderful friend: he supported me forcefully and effectively. In the end, the doctor gave up. He said, 'Oh, well, there's nothing

I can do, but you must promise me that the moment you get to London you will go to St Mary's Hospital, report your condition, and let them treat you.'

With great relief, I went back to the Margulis's house carrying with me a few trinitrin tablets given to me for the temporary relief of the pain of angina. I spent all the next day lying on their floor propped up with cushions. I was afraid to worsen my condition and I thought that just lying still was probably the safest thing to do. My flight was due to leave Boston Airport some time in the evening, I think about 7 or 8 o'clock. Lynn came home early with much concern and I remember travelling with her in her car to the airport, and a somewhat fraught departure. I remember most clearly the plane, a VC10 of British Airways, accelerating down the runway and taking off. As soon as it was airborne and committed to its flight, a sense of comfort came over me. The anxiety of the past few days evaporated. When the stewardess came round and offered refreshments, I said, unusually, 'Yes please, give me a double vodka and tomato juice.' I needed something to celebrate my escape. There is something wrong about being ill thousands of miles from home.

I recall little of the flight to Heathrow but I do remember rediscovering the pain of angina as I walked too fast along the long corridors of the airport to the customs and immigration. My baggage was carry-on only, and soon I was in a taxi and on my way to St Mary's Hospital. This old and dignified hospital is just by Paddington station in London. I marched in to the casualty department and tried to tell my story. The response I received was wholly different from that at Wellesley in Boston. The young physician who saw me showed cheerful lack of concern and asked why I had not gone to my GP. I replied, 'I'm doing what they told me to do at the Boston Hospital and, in any event, my GP is at least a hundred miles away.' 'Oh,' said he, 'Well, we will have a look at you. Are you in any pain now?' 'No,' I said, 'Only when I walk fifty yards or so.' He took me into a small room with a bed and the usual hospital furniture. He did the kind of things that physicians usually do, such as sounding my chest with his stethoscope. I never know whether this is to impress or soften up the patient, or whether it serves a useful purpose. Anyway, he did it, went away, and said, 'I'll arrange for you to have an ECG and an X-ray.' Shortly afterwards a young nurse came in and said, 'Are you the one with angina?' 'Yes,' I replied. 'Oh that is a terrible pain,' she said. 'Oh it's not so bad,' said I. 'Nowhere near as bad as toothache, just worrying.'

She was clearly disappointed. It was my first realization that some women choose nursing as a profession because suffering itself fascinates them. They are not necessarily worse nurses on this account, but it is a sobering thought. Many years later, I discovered that an ability to appeal to this spectator instinct in some nurses could be essential for survival in a busy hospital. They were thorough at St Mary's and repeated all that Boston had done and took some blood samples as well. At the end, the cheerful intern came in again and said to me, 'Yes, you have an angina but go home and see your GP some time next week.' I had been expecting immediate admission to the hospital and at least a little drama. I was also worried about having to telephone home with the bad news that I would not be returning but would be in hospital in London. Yet, here they told me to catch a train to Salisbury, in Wiltshire, as if nothing had happened. What an anticlimax.

This little episode highlights, I think, one essential difference between British and American medical practice. In America, when faced with a medical emergency, the response tends to be 'My God, we must do something'; in Britain, the response is 'Nature will take its course.' In fact, there was little that the medical services of those two nations could have done for me. At that time bypass surgery had only just started and was not nearly the routine and effective procedure that it was to become.

At home in Bowerchalke later that day, I faced the difficult problem of breaking the news to Helen. She was in the early stages of multiple sclerosis and this was hardly the most cheerful of news to give her. I think I just said, 'Oh, by the way, I had a heart attack when I was in Boston.' She found it difficult to accept. I looked fit and well and could move around. It must have seemed to her unreal. I recall going to my favourite medical textbook and looking up angina and coronary occlusion. It was a subject that was familiar to me for I had spent my last years at the National Institute for Medical Research working on the biochemistry of coronary artery disease—had even published papers on it. I had also worked for a few years in Houston in the same department as the famous surgeon, Michael DeBakey, but there is a large difference between scientific knowledge of a topic and personal experience. I was not one of those who read medical texts in order to titillate their hypochondria, but this time I read Davidson's *Principles and Practice of Medicine* with an unusual intensity; no longer the detached scientist. Here it was in clear print, 'The patient must be reassured, but some relative must be told that the future is unpredictable.'

I spent the rest of my weekend coming to terms with the idea that I might not have long to live. My body, with which I was on good terms, was also telling me that this was a serious matter. Later I discovered that the occlusion was in my left main coronary artery before it forks into the two branches that feed blood to the left ventricle. In the USA they call this particular lesion the widow-maker, since a complete blockage of the artery at this point is almost invariably fatal.

Monday morning I broke my usual custom of walking the two miles to see Dr Brown at his surgery in Broadchalke, the next village from us. This time I drove. He was the nicest of men, a general practitioner who brought comfort to those in need of him. He never stinted house calls at any time of the day or night, and he had a wonderful way with old ladies and gentlemen. However, the medicine he practised was more that of his student days than the conventional wisdom of 1972. I had tried during the previous years to persuade him to prescribe for my hypertension, but he would not. Insurance companies had twice turned down my applications for life insurance because of high blood pressure, but he just did not believe in medication for hypertension. He would tell me about old folk in Broadchalke who were in their eighties and who had had hypertension for years and seemed to thrive on it. When I told him my news of the heart attack in America he was contrite and arranged an appointment with a consultant cardiologist, Dr Mullen, in Salisbury, for the next day.

In 1972 Salisbury was a city in the early stages of traffic blight. Cars, with their incessant noise and never-ending demand for space and attention, were beginning to turn what had been a beautiful medieval city into a nightmare. Cars, like a pack of noisy smelly dogs, disturbed and fouled everywhere they went. The elegant plan of the old city was giving way to concrete car parks and shopping malls. It was a relief to enter the Close of Salisbury Cathedral—a quiet haven away from the roaring vehicles outside, where, apart from the cars of residents and occasional visitors, it was a place of peace—a place for walking, not driving. Today, with my problematic heart as an excuse, I drove in and parked near the consulting rooms of Dr Mullen, the cardiologist. His rooms were a few yards from the East Gate and near the greensward that surrounds the cathedral itself. It was a sunny day in late November and, in spite of it all, I felt cheerful and full of well-being. It is strange now to muse on the sad day, over twenty years later, when I was in the cathedral again. This time, free of my heart problems, but part of the congregation mourning my friend, Bill Golding. On that cold and bitter day, I was so much sadder.

Dr Mullen was plump and occupied a cosy set of rooms that complemented his comfortable Victorian manner. He arranged for me to visit the Salisbury Infirmary where they repeated the ECG and X-rays. I found it intriguing that the three different physicians who had examined me applied the same set of tests. I wondered if they distrusted the observations of their colleagues. It does not matter for most of the time, but it must waste resources and, where X-rays are repeatedly used, be undesirable for the patient. He confirmed the diagnosis of an angina and prescribed warfarin, the anticoagulant drug which is also an effective rat poison. He also prescribed Aldomet, an anti-hypertensive drug, and trinitrin for the immediate relief of anginal pain. He asked me to come back again in a month's time. He also advised me to walk slowly, not run, and to take it easy, and in particular to do nothing strenuous for at least a month. It was a great blow to me to have to walk gently instead of striding out heel and toe, as was my wont. I recall telling Helen on a gentle stroll around the village, 'Well, dear, at least we can now manage the same pace.' It made me realize also the extent of her disabilities through multiple sclerosis.

After a month of this sedentary life, I was deeply frustrated. Then I recalled the experience of that famous clinician, Sir Thomas Lewis. He suffered an angina like mine and came to terms with it by sawing wood each morning up to the limit of pain he could endure, but he went on to live out a full and rich life. If exercise was good enough for him, surely I could do something better than gentle walks to improve the state of my heart. There was no wood to saw, so instead I tried one of my favourite walks, which involved a 200-foot climb up a nearby hill, or as we in England called it, a down. Marleycombe down was a chalk hill covered with turf and it overlooked our village and it was quite a struggle to climb it; ten or twenty paces then a rest, breathless. The trinitrin tablets were effective in relieving the pain but at this stage did little to improve performance. Within a week of daily climbs, I could manage 100 feet up the steep slope without stopping and without angina, and within a month I could climb the whole 200 feet without having to stop. I was well on the way back to health. Soon

I found I could walk fast and climb fast, so long as I kept taking trinitrin tablets. Within six months, I felt fitter than I had been before the attack, although without the trinitrin the angina came on after a mere hundred yards of walking on the flat. With the trinitrin, I could do anything. What a miracle drug it is, yet how unsung. Nobel, the explosive maker, who used nitro-glycerine to invent dynamite and gelignite, should have awarded himself one of his own prizes for its outstanding benefit as a vasodilatory drug in medicine.

The whole episode made me realize the value of a brush with the threat of death and of the recognition of one's own mortality. Until then, I had squandered my time and failed to enjoy each day as it came. Now I knew how sweet was life and how foolish it was to waste a day in pointless work. I never smoked again, whereas before, like Mark Twain, I had given up smoking a hundred times, and no longer did I fool myself with the thought that I could put off the needed walk until next week. No matter how fit I became the angina never changed —without the aid of the trinitrin it came on at precisely the same distance walked—about a hundred yards, and this tolerable state went on without change for almost exactly ten years. It worked so well that often during summers spent on the Beara Peninsula in Ireland, I was able to walk and climb the twelve miles over the mountain tops from Glengarrif to Adrigole. My next battle with disease was at Coombe Mill and happened because of my own carelessness.

On New Year's morning 1982 a hazy sun shone from a milky sky and the air temperature was close to $-5°$ C. It seemed a good day to move a load of logs from the pile near the barn. For small jobs like this, I used a small farm tractor made by the Japanese firm, Iseki. I think they had built it for use in rice fields and it was unusual in having a 4-wheel drive. As I drove near the barn, the tractor suddenly slipped on a patch of ice and moved, crab-like, sideways. It fell over the edge of the track and out onto a steep down-going slope of grass and rocks. It turned over once, then again, and stopped precariously on the slope. I was pinned beneath the tractor by the steering-wheel. There was no roll-bar on this tiny tractor. I turned off the engine and with what seemed a vast effort, dragged myself from underneath the steering wheel. Later I found that the force transmitted through my abdomen to the ground bent the wheel itself. I had a feeling that something was wrong, and felt shocked, but I could still walk around and move without pain. I walked over to where Helen was sitting in her golf-cart. I asked if she could see anything wrong with me, anything out of place. 'Is my back all right?' I asked. 'What have you done?' she said, and I explained what had happened with the tractor. In her usual calm and unexcited way she commented, 'Your jacket is torn right through.'

I decided to telephone our GP and ask his advice, but I had reckoned without the British bank holiday on which days everything stops, even to a large extent the National Health Service. This is especially true of Christmas or New Year's Day. When I called, I reached a sleepy young doctor I did not know. I explained what had happened and told him that all seemed well but I felt odd and some-what shocked. He dismissed me, saying, 'You probably have a few bruises. Come and see me tomorrow if you have any further trouble.' Later that day, my thigh began to ache, enough to require relief from painkillers. I felt shivery and nauseous. A local schoolmaster who was visiting at the time said, foolishly, 'Ah, you have delayed shock.' Like an idiot, and perhaps because I was still dazed, I took his amateur diagnosis as correct. Certainly, the pain passed away in a few hours. Next day I felt well enough to carry on without bothering my GP again. I now know that the accident had so damaged my left kidney that it never functioned again. There is a wonderful redundancy in our body parts and, unless we are contemplating some extreme trial, like crossing the Sahara with a minimum water supply, we do not need two kidneys. One will do, as many people living now who have donated one will know, and it seems to be true even of the brain. There are many carrying on useful lives, even holding down demand-ing professional jobs, with a third of a brain or less. The loss of a kidney did not seem to bother me, but looking back, I realize that during the next few months I was less active.

The next mishap occurred in early April. I was then a member of the governing council of the Marine Biological Association (MBA), and I was attending the Annual General Meeting at their wonderful old building at Plymouth, part of a fort called the Citadel that stands overlooking the sea at the east end of the green that is the Hoe. The Director of the MBA, Sir Eric Denton, invited me to dinner at his home in St Germans, a few miles west of Plymouth, and after the afternoon session, I walked back to my hotel, the Duke of Cornwall, changed, and at 6 pm drove across the Tamar Bridge from Plymouth into Cornwall and St Germans. Eric and Nancy Denton lived in a beautiful old house, set back from the village road, and immersed in the shrubbery of their well-kept garden. The Dentons had that wonderful capacity to make their guests feel wanted and at home, and we met in their sitting room—a large and gracious room made comfortable by two vast settees placed on either side of the fireplace. It was so comfortable that I felt as if I were sitting tucked up with my friends in a giant feather bed. Dinner was the best that Devon could provide, which means plenty of cream, and I remember having a second helping of Nancy's trifle, which was very rich indeed. Normally I eat sparsely, but on special occasions such as this, I have always felt that one should enjoy treats and break the rules. It was a marvellous evening and we talked of everything, from cabbages to kings, until about 10.30, when we departed and I drove back to Plymouth and to the Duke of Cornwall Hotel in a warm and pleasant mood. I parked in the side street outside the hotel and began to walk back the few yards to the front entrance. As I climbed the first steps, my angina hit me extra hard. I felt in my pocket for trinitrin tablets and then realized that they were in my bedroom. To my dismay, the lift was out of action, and, as I slowly climbed the two floors to my bedroom, the pain grew worse and had a crushing intensity, something I had read about but never before felt. I began to fear that my coronary artery was now completely blocked, but somehow I reached my room, took a trinitrin tablet, and lay on the bed thinking 'If it doesn't ease in sixty seconds, I'll telephone for help.' I waited, and it went away. I was relieved, thinking that however bad, it was still an angina, not a blockage. I undressed and slept the night through.

I joined the other MBA Council Members for breakfast. It was difficult to believe as I chatted with them, my fears of the night before. After breakfast as I climbed the stairs to my room—the lift still did not work—the angina came back as it had the night before. This time the pain appeared after no more than a few steps, it seemed, but the blessed drug trinitrin worked its usual magic, and my mind turned to the morning ahead: the final stage of the MBA meeting. I remember sitting in the large dining room on the top floor of the MBA laboratory, with its fine view of Plymouth harbour, Drake's Island and beyond it the sea approaches to Plymouth. The Oxford physiologist, JZ Young, our President, effortlessly guided the meeting through its course. He was a great story-teller and extemporizer and he kept the meeting moving on, like some amiable dog herding us sheep, with instructive barks and little nudges, in his chosen direction. I was to wish for these powers when a few years later I took over as President. He, Sir Eric Denton, and Sir John Gray were essential figures of the

Plymouth laboratories of those days, and represented the strength and excellence of science in England.

I drove home through the greening lanes of spring in Devon, through Tavistock and up over the quiet hills near the extinct volcano of Brentor to Lifton and to Coombe Mill. As I drove I thought about my heart; something bad had happened to my coronary arteries. I decided, as before, that the only thing to do was diet and exercise, and on Monday following the meeting I went into Launceston and bought a bicycle; maybe the exercise of cycling along the less hilly roads around Coombe Mill was what I needed. I also started a strict, almost fat-free diet that would continue for the rest of 1982. Working alone means that long periods of inactivity due to illness bring a proportionate fall in income, the luxury of sick leave available to those in employment is not available to those of us who live by our wits. The very idea of sitting around and doing nothing was, in any event, to me repellent. It was like the concept of retirement—a sure path to disintegration and death. My personal guidance came from that simple phrase, 'Business as usual'.

Later in the month, I made the first of my trips that year to the United States to see my customers, Hewlett Packard and NOAA, and I visited Lynn Margulis at her lab in Boston. On the day before leaving for America, I gave a lecture at Dartington Hall, which is about sixty miles from Coombe Mill and on the other side of Devon. This was to fulfil a promise made somewhat reluctantly, in the previous year. I say reluctantly, because it grew ever more apparent that Gaia as science did not benefit from association with Gaia as an emblem of the New Age. I recognize the value of Gaia as a unifying symbol, but knew that scientists would never accept Gaia as a valid theory if they saw it as an alternative science like astrology. Even so, the Dartington meeting was a good one and the start of two key friendships for me. In the audience were Jonathon Porritt who, to me, is our most distinguished environmentalist, and Jenny Powys-Libbe a warm-hearted and pleasant woman attached to Dartington. Whatever—if any—scientific credibility I lost through mixing with the greener side of Gaia, these two friendships more than made up for it. I respect and admire Jonathon for his clear, incisive voice on Green affairs. He stands far above what is, to me, a confused and babbling community of Green politicians and philosophers. That we disagreed over many things—in particular the dangers of nuclear reactors as power sources—did not matter; we learnt so much from each other.

Jenny Powys-Libbe was powerful in a very different way: she gave me comfort during one of the more trying years of my life. She had written, inviting me to the meeting and had offered to put me up for the night after the meeting so that I could then travel directly to Heathrow and to my flight to Philadelphia.

As soon as I was back from the United States, I began walking and cycling the small roads around Coombe Mill, at least once each day. Sometimes the walk was a mere two-miles round trip—along our own road and then up to the nearby farm of Emsworthy—and it included a modest but steep climb of about a hundred feet. On better days, I would walk the four or five miles round the road and back to Coombe Mill that involved a climb of about 300 feet. My average walking speed for the whole walk was about four miles per hour and always, of course, during these walks I was popping trinitrin pills, one about every half mile or so. Several times during May and June I fainted, waking up a few minutes later to find myself lying on the road. In our part of Devon, there was almost no traffic other than the farmers' tractors and their Land Rovers, and because of this, never did anyone see me slumped unconscious on the road. My surgeon, Mr Keates, told me much later that these faints were a consequence of global ischaemia; in other words, the failure of the blood supply to the greater part of the muscle of my heart. However, the exercise regime seemed to work, and gradually I lost weight, and grew fitter in the sense that I could perform more without tiredness. The angina became like an old friend and would come on even when resting, although never when lying down.

I did not entirely believe in my own course of treatment, and therefore I visited my friends and physicians, the doctors Alan Edwards and Ian Barker, at their practice 'The Holsworthy Doctors'. Holsworthy is one of the last remaining small market towns of England—most of the others have been urbanized in one way or another. In Holsworthy Market Square, farmers and their wives still shop in their dungarees and wellies. Here, banks, building societies, and estate agents do not dominate. The quality of the six or so physicians who make up the Holsworthy Doctors is as genuine as the town itself, and one of them revealed it by the reply he gave when I asked his views on the Health Service: 'The practice of medicine is hard enough', he said, 'without the worry about whether my patients can afford it.' Alan Edwards was concerned about my condition and arranged for me to see the consultant cardiologist at Plymouth, Dr Marshall, and

I saw him at Plymouth one morning in July. He quizzed me about the symptoms and then asked his technician to take a resting electrocardiogram—ECG. Then he came through to me afterwards and told me not to worry, my electrocardiogram was quite normal, but to come back if my condition worsened. I complained a little and said surely my condition was worse than that, but he replied with, 'Oh no, there are people much worse off than you coming to see me. You have nothing to worry about,' and dismissed me. To be fair on Dr Marshall, I must have seemed an oddity—a fit, vigorous man for his early sixties, with a good complexion and colour and one who walked quickly along the corridor and into his consulting room. Not the picture expected of somebody with a left main coronary insufficiency, if not occlusion. Alan Edwards confirmed the next week that Dr Marshall had written to say that my problem was a mild one.

Whatever these physicians said, my body told me, and I half understood, that death was close, and it put me in a strange frame of mind. One part carried on business as usual; the other sought comfort and knowledge about how to prepare for dying. In this second area, Jenny satisfied my needs and gave of herself generously, but it must have been miserable for Helen. She could see that I was far from well and she would sometimes say, when I returned from my walks looking quite grey, 'Jim, you'll kill yourself if you keep doing that.' She needed me badly, for she was now approaching the immobile state of multiple sclerosis, and grew ever more dependent on me for comfort, and for strength to cope with her advancing disease. I remember telling Alan Edwards, our physician, who was concerned about us, 'We are three cripples who make up about one whole person, and that is how we run Coombe Mill.' The third person was my son John, disabled at birth by brain damage caused by anoxia. He was physically able and could function as the hands and arms of Helen, but he was epileptic and suffered in other ways. John and Helen would work and talk together during the day; Helen always in her electric vehicle. They did this winter and summer, gardening and doing the many small jobs that needed doing outside at Coombe Mill. I sustained the cash flow needed to keep it all going, and served in other ways, the hardest of these was acting as surrogate physician for Helen. At intervals, she would pass into a crisis that required some remedy immediately, and once this happened at a weekend when our physicians familiar with her problems were not available. They had earlier given her the drug ACTH: she became oedematous and incoherent, and when I called the doctor on duty, I found that he was one that neither of us knew, and I was unable to persuade him to make a house call. I knew enough to suspect that the nature of Helen's distress came from an electrolyte imbalance. She was taking diuretic pills as well as the ACTH injections, and it seemed possible that her troubles were iatrogenic. After some agonized thought and reading, I concluded that lack of potassium seemed a likely explanation of the incoherence and oedema. Cautiously, I gave her some potassium citrate dissolved in orange juice to drink. I say cautiously, because had I misdiagnosed and her condition been attributable to an excess of potassium, this would have been a most unwise thing to do. But the effects were near magical, and within a few minutes, she was no longer mumbling meaningless phrases like a drunkard. She became her old self again, and within an hour, she was able to get up from her chair and go to bed. Physicians rarely ever treat their own families. I now knew why. The option to try a remedy that could worsen rather than improve the condition of a loved one is too hard a decision to have to take personally, but this was to be my lot on occasions like this throughout the next six years before she died in 1989. Multiple sclerosis can be the most terrible of diseases, and not merely for the sufferer.

As spring spread into summer, Jenny became my guide and comforter, and she was representative of some who used Dartington in those days. For them it had become a legendary place where new thoughts and radical ideas flourished. It is an ancient manor house in hundreds of acres of its own land, rich in woodland, and watered by the river Dart. It is a place of eclecticism, where poets and politicians, scientists and composers and artists and intellectuals meet, and these were the golden years of the New Age. It was a chaotic time, almost entirely free of constraint, and by my own Gaian arguments, was unstable and could not last long. The New Age existed in a wholly unpredictable landscape fashioned from the self-similarity of its own ideas; it was the human social equivalent of chaotic mathematics. Their interest in me and in Gaia came from a misunderstanding of its rigour. They saw Gaia as the great Earth mother, embodiment of eastern religions, and comforter of feminists. They did not see the other side of Gaia, where she resembles her sister goddess, Kali, the stern grim figure who drank the blood of humans from a scull. Gaia stands above all for firm constraint—something the New Age never understood—but even so, these also were golden days for me. I seemed to live suspended a few inches above the ground, and I joined in enthusiastically with the entertainment of Dartington's New Age menu. What appealed especially was transpersonal psychology, with its imaginative games, rather like an intellectual version of dungeons and dragons. On the dark side were Jenny's own death workshops, where noviciates were led across an imaginary meadow dappled with spring flowers and sunshine, and led on to a green wood wherein dwelt their death. The object of the exercise was to meet and talk sensibly with the personification of one's personal death. For anyone fit and well, this must seem an absurd and extravagant nonsense, but for me then, those imaginary journeys seemed real. However, not then, nor at any time, have I felt as Philip Larkin wrote in Aubade.

> Waking at four to soundless dark, I stare.
> In time the curtain-edges will grow light.
> Till then I see what's really always there;
> Unresting death, a whole day nearer now,
> Making all thought impossible but how
> And where and when I shall myself die.

I suspect a part of me is still immature, still needing to grow, and death therefore seems part of the life's adventure. When it approaches and there is no escape, perhaps I will feel as he did, but Larkin's certainty is not yet for me, although I love his verse. Even at the height of the New Age Dartington was more famed for its concerts and exhibitions. Now under the Chairmanship of John Lane and with Satish Kumar's inspiration of the Schumacher College, it has become an alternative university as well as a distinguished centre for music and the arts.

Before 1982 and soon after in 1983, I had no place in my mind for the transcendental part of the New Age, but somehow my perception of the imminence of death put me in that mood for much of 1982. Once or twice a week I would take the one-hour journey along quiet country roads from Coombe Mill, across the northern edge of Dartmoor, through the small towns of Okehampton, Moretonhampstead, and Bovey Tracey to Abbotskerswell, where Jenny lived. That year I also took her son Christopher as an apprentice, and he came to live with us at Coombe Mill for the summer. He was a welcome guest, and his kindness to Helen was unstinted. He was a talented computer maker and user, and converted my crude Basic language Daisyworld programs into pure and fast Assembler. I agreed to pay him and provide, if the work were satisfactory, the strongest of references.

He had no quotable 'A' levels, but I hoped that a personal reference from an FRS would do as well. He wanted a career with one of the larger computer companies, and as it happened, this worked out extraordinarily well. In September my friend, Leslie Banks, and another senior executive of the British branch of IBM came to visit. They saw the product of Christopher's work running on my computer and were so impressed that they offered him a job on the spot, which put Christopher in on the ground floor of the PC revolution. He rose rapidly in his profession but sadly, a few years later he died in an untimely car crash.

By August 1982 Helen grew aware of my obsession with the attractions of Dartington. She said nothing, but I knew from the way she retired still further into her shell that she was unhappy. We had shared nearly forty years of good and bad and brought up our family as best we could. In recent years, the constraints of MS had put an end to any chance of a warm or loving marriage. I never realized how much Helen and I had missed in our marriage until the experience of the last ten glorious years with Sandy. These have been the happiest of my life. I do believe that for some of us marriage is incomplete unless the partners are in love. Helen needed a great deal from me, but the malign omnipresence of her disease conspired with her natural dislike of the demonstrative. She could not return the warmth needed to make our marriage more than just two people occupying a house. We had been, since the mid-1970s like a pair of friends sharing some common memories, and soon after we moved to Coombe Mill, the growing discomfort of Helen's illness kept her awake and reading for much of the night, and drove us to sleeping in separate rooms. I would get up at 6.00 in the morning, make tea for both of us, and climb into her bed, and we would drink it together. We talked then for an hour or so before rising to start the day. There are worse ways to start a day. For many years, this was a tolerable and often cheerful way of life; but for the strange events of 1982, it could have gone on for years more. My son Andrew once referred to his mother as a gentle tyrant and it well expresses her character. Helen was always cheerful and rarely ever complained about her condition, but as soon as I knew she was unhappy over my visits to Abbotskerswell, I had not the heart to continue them at the frequency that I had been doing, and my meetings with Jenny declined.

With the decline of this alternative medical treatment from Jenny and from her world, I began to seek conventional medical advice. In

October I asked friends from my days with the MRC who might be the best cardiologist for me to see. They replied unanimously that Dr Douglas Chamberlain was the one. I was about to arrange to visit him when an invitation came from the United Nations University in Tokyo. They offered travel costs and a fee for a lecture on Gaia. This was too good a chance to miss and it enabled me, by travelling on a round-the-world ticket, to fulfil my United States obligations to Hewlett Packard and NOAA. It also allowed me to make the whole journey in the kind of comfort that would be no stress. Soon after accepting the Tokyo invitation I arranged also to visit NCAR, which is one of my favourite United States laboratories, and is sited magnificently on the side of a mountain overlooking the town of Boulder in Colorado. There I looked forward to exchanging ideas with old friends on atmospheric science and, as always, seeking new discoveries that might point towards the self-regulation of the Earth and Gaia. I also accepted an invitation from my friend, Bill Thompson, the Irish-American historian and founder of the Lindisfarne Fellowship. The Fellows of Lindisfarne were an eclectic mix chosen, mainly by Bill himself, from a global elite. They meet annually and include Dean Morton of the Cathedral of St John the Divine in New York, the economist Hazel Henderson, Amory and Hunter Lovins, and John and Nancy Todd. I am a Fellow of Lindisfarne and so is Lynn Margulis. The organization has its base near Crestone in Colorado and the Lindisfarne house was up on the mountain slope. The Lindisfarne fellow and architect, Keith Critchlow, designed it according to the principles of sacred geometry, and it had the ambience of a sacred place. I can remember little of my visit to the Lindisfarne house, other than the warmth of Bill's greeting and a walk up the mountain one day with Christina Watkins, another young woman, and the poet Gary Snyder. It was a picnic: Christina Watkins and her friend carried wine and food for us in their rucksacks, and we climbed to a point just above the tree line, which in that part of the world was about 10,000 feet in height. I popped my trinitrin as we climbed and felt no distress in spite of the thinner air. Perhaps my American companions were walking and climbing more slowly than I was accustomed to do: anyway, it certainly did not seem stressful. It was good companionship, healthy exercise, and fine food, the flavour heightened by the picnic atmosphere and by our hunger. Bill Thompson retired in the mid-1990s and the Fellowship is now led by the author and physicist, Arthur Zajonc.

From Lindisfarne, I flew to San Francisco, and then took the long fourteen-hour flight to Tokyo on Northwest Airlines. There is no question that first-class travel by air greatly diminishes the stress of long-distance travel. It has little to do with the food, drink, and personal attention from the cabin staff; it is simply that in first class there is space to lie flat and sleep—something impossible in business or tourist class. I have often wondered if an airline might be courageous enough to put in bunks, perhaps stacked three high, and so provide the blessings of proper horizontal sleep to business, even tourist-class passengers. It was about 5 pm local time when my plane set down in Tokyo. I was anxious, for I had no words at all of Japanese and expected Tokyo to be the most alien place that I had yet visited. As I walked along the corridors linking the disembarkation point from the plane to customs and immigration, I felt a strong sense of the familiar. Suddenly, it came to me that Narita was just like Heathrow, and not at all like any American or European airport. What constituted this familiarity was hard to pin down. Partly it was the shape and layout of corridors, partly the voice of the lady speaking English-style English and Japanese instructing us on what we should do, and also perhaps the body language and movement of the Japanese themselves. Suddenly, whatever it was, I felt a sense of being at home. It was a feeling for Japan that was to persist and strengthen right through my most recent visit in October 1997.

When I returned home in mid-November I resumed my regular walking and had a few more of what my grandmother would have called, 'nasty turns'. This reminded me that it was time to get in touch with Dr Chamberlain. I wrote to explain my problem and tell him why my local medical specialists did not seem able to help me. He replied courteously and suggested that I go to see him the following week. A week later, I went to stay the night with my son Andrew at his home in Warminster, Wiltshire. He had kindly offered to take me to Brighton the next day. Andrew is a tall, good-looking, talented man shaped by the culture of the 1960s; he graduated in physics from Sussex University in the early 1970s and has subsequently worked as an independent computer consultant. Andrew and I find communication difficult, but it does not seem to matter too much. He and his partner took me by car next day to the cardiology department of Brighton General Hospital where, after a short wait in the outer office, Dr Chamberlain called me in. He had a large and comfortable room full of books, and filing boxes, with that air of mild untidiness characteristic of a busy and productive man. I sat down, went through my all too familiar tale, and wondered, after my experiences with Dr Marshall, the Plymouth cardiologist, if I were making too much fuss over an insoluble problem. Dr Chamberlain listened and made notes and then said, 'I have to do a ward round now.'

In English hospitals, the ward round is a ceremonial occasion, held every few days, when the consultant physician or surgeon makes his round of the ward and visits personally each of his patients. It is quite relaxed now, but I remember what an occasion it was when that stern figure, the matron, made sure that every bed was spotless, and every nurse was almost standing to attention, rather like a visiting General inspecting a regiment. It still has an air of ceremony attaching to it. Dr Chamberlain said as he stood up, 'While I am away, I would like you to have a few tests. After the round I'll return, and we can discuss the results.' He showed me into a room full of instruments and apparatus and went off on his round. The room was the sort of place in which I was entirely at home, although I can imagine many patients being fearful and intimidated by its hi-tech ambience. In all of my dealings with the physicians and surgeons of this affair, I have never had any apprehension or fear. Medicine and surgery had been so much a part of my MRC days that the sights and smells of clinical medicine did not disturb me. What I felt, indeed, was a sense of adventure, almost like the arrival at a long-anticipated holiday destination; the senses heightened and the mood receptive.

Dr Chamberlain had introduced me to the nurse and technician before he left. They asked me to stand on an exercise ECG, which was a short sloping path with handrails on either side. The surface of the path was a moving belt, so that as I walked I did not move forward. A bit like *Alice Through the Looking Glass* where the Red Queen says, 'Now, here, you see, it takes all the running you can do to keep in the same place. If you want to get somewhere else you must run twice as fast as that.' Soon they joined me to an amazing array of electrical leads, so that I must have looked like the prey of a giant cephalopod. First, I stood still, and they took their readings, watching the paper charts flow beneath their fast-moving pens. They asked me to walk at my normal pace, and I did, while the charts continued to pour from the recorders. Then, like an anticipated acquaintance that one meets every morning walking to work, the angina came back to me. Suddenly, the nurse who was watching the charts said to me, 'Stop', turned to the technician and asked him to go fetch Dr Chamberlain, then turned to me, took my arm, and sat me in a chair. She disconnected the leads and I sat waiting until Dr Chamberlain appeared. I knew that something must have happened, for consultants do not normally interrupt their clinical rounds. The nurse took me back to the waiting room, where Andrew and his partner were sitting. They asked me what was the news and I said, 'I don't know, but I'll soon be told by Dr Chamberlain.' Within a few minutes, I was back in his office. His first words to me were, 'Would you like your family with you, for I fear I have bad news.' 'No,' I said. 'It would probably upset them a lot more than it does me.' He then told me that the ECG suggested that my heart muscle was seriously deficient in blood supply, and that most probably I needed surgery at the earliest opportunity if I were to survive. This was the news I had been expecting all along, and perversely it was good news. My body told me that at last someone had heard its urgent messages, and the year's anxieties lifted. I felt so grateful to Dr Chamberlain: he was someone I knew that I could trust with my life. He went on to say, 'I will try to arrange a bypass operation in the next two weeks at the latest. Go home and if I have not called you within a week, call me.'

Andrew drove me back to Westbury Station and I travelled from there to Exeter by train and drove home. It was now early December, and the dark days of northern winter with a full gale blowing, as I travelled from the station along the old A30 road. There was little traffic, and the high beams of my headlights merely illuminated the raindrops and not travellers on the other side of the road. I arrived back at Coombe Mill about 7 o'clock in the evening. Helen was anxious and I told her the news as gently as I could. She saw that I was cheerful and looked on the coming operation as both an adventure and a cure; this helped, I think, to allay her fears. The next day, as I walked around our fields, which at that time were open grass, not the forest of trees now there, I wondered if these days would be my last. In spite of the dull skies and drizzling rain, I knew I loved this place, and how much there was to lose. I telephoned Alan Edwards, told him the news, and got his reassurance. Dr Chamberlain was, it turned out, his mentor as a student, and a man he greatly respected. I must declare here my passionate belief in our National Health Service—even if I could have afforded private medicine, I would not then have used it. I also knew enough about the practice of medicine to be aware that in large problems, such as heart surgery, the facilities available to private medicine rarely matched those of the National

Health Service. But excellent though it is, the Health Service is not free of drawbacks, as we shall now see.

After a few days, Dr Chamberlain called to tell me to go to King's College Hospital in London for an angiogram, and prepare for at least two days' stay. Jenny offered to come with me, and I met her at Exeter Station. We travelled together to Paddington, and from there took a taxi to King's College Hospital, where I was put into a pleasant single room with a bath attached, called Stork Side Ward. Jenny stayed a while as I settled in. I assured her that I had no fears, and soon after she had left, I started to read a novel, and then fell asleep.

The next day I was prepared for my angiogram by an intravenous injection of Valium. I did not really need it; I was calm enough anyway to cope with the minor procedure of an angiogram. This consists of inserting a narrow-bore catheter into the femoral artery and then feeding it up through the aorta and into the ventricles. They did it so expertly that I was unaware of the insertion of the catheter, or its passage up through my arterial system, and while they did it, I was lying on the table beneath a monitor that showed a live X-ray-image of my chest and heart. They then injected x-ray-opaque dye into the catheter: the screen showed my heart suddenly darkening, with its blood vessels outlined like black twisted wires. I understood little of what was happening, but I recognized that there was some excitement amongst those around me. 'Look at this,' one of them said. 'He's built his own bypass.' They gave me some trinitrin and took another set of pictures of my heart as the dye passed around it. I could now see on the monitor a line of black going transversely across my heart, from the right coronary to the left. They took me back to my room, doubly euphoric from the Valium injection and from the participation in so interesting a physiological experiment, and I soon fell asleep.

After breakfast, three distinguished visitors entered my room—the Professor of Medicine, Dr Jewitt, Dr Chamberlain, and Mr Keates, the surgeon. After a round of good mornings, Professor Jewitt said, 'I am afraid you have a left main block—the complete block of the coronary artery before it bifurcates. Hardly anyone survives this, but you are fortunate to have a small artery connecting the right coronary to the left main at a point below the blockage, so that blood is being supplied to the left ventricle, retrograde, along this artery.' He did not add, 'That is why you are here now and not long dead.' He went on, 'However, it is a precarious state to be in, and we are arranging for a bypass operation to be done at the earliest opportunity, which as it happens is in a week's time. We would like you to stay in hospital until then. We do not consider that it would be safe for you to leave before the operation.' 'That won't do,' said I. 'I must return home first. My wife is severely disabled by multiple sclerosis and it is too much to leave her alone unnecessarily next week worrying about me—especially since I clearly won't be home to see her during Christmas.' At first both Dr Jewitt and Dr Chamberlain were adamant. I could die at any moment, they said, and should not think of travelling. I felt sure they were wrong and said so. Why, only a month ago I travelled around the world—even climbed on a mountain from 8,000–10,000 feet without harm. If I could do that, surely I could go home for the week? They conferred among themselves and then the surgeon, Mr Keates, came away with a smile at me. He said, 'Okay, I think you'll be safe enough to go home, but you must take care and return here without fail on Sunday for the operation scheduled for Tuesday 21 December.' He then went on to give me some more practical advice such as taking the beta-blocker drug, Atenolol, in large doses every day for the week before I came in.

They left at about 11 am, and I dressed and packed my small bag and made my way to the hospital front door. Oddly, at King's College Hospital one climbs a flight of steps to the door to the street. As I was climbing up, aided by my trinitrin, I saw the startled look on Professor Jewitt's face as he came in the door and down the stairs. For a moment, I feared he might change his mind again and insist that I stay there the week before the operation. The moment passed and I was outside looking for a taxi.

Jenny travelled with me again on my way back to King's College the following Sunday afternoon. This was to be almost the last time that I saw her, although I did not know it then. The consequences of the surgery now imminent were to blight the social side of my life for several years. At the hospital, we went back to my room, the side ward of Stork, talked for a while, and then she left. I read my book and went to sleep. The next day there was a seemingly endless round of visits from technicians, nurses, and other professionals. They assigned me a nurse responsible for my personal care throughout my stay at the hospital, and soon she came to talk to me. This is a good and comforting feature of some hospitals in the health service, and as one patient, I can say how much I applaud it. Then there were the X-rays and blood samples, and I was amused to find that they would not allow me to walk to the X-ray room, but wheeled me there in a chair. They were taking no chances, it seemed. It was a pleasant and fully entertaining day and, to my surprise, the food was excellent. In the evening, just as I was dropping off to sleep, my nurse entered and offered me a sleeping tablet. I refused, and found that I could sleep the night through unassisted by drugs.

Next morning, I awoke fresh and ready for the operation. I knew that all my hair would have to be shaved off, and this caused me mild anxiety, because I was old-fashioned enough to have qualms about a young nurse shaving off my pubic hairs. Would I get an erection as she did it? What could I say other than something like, 'I'm afraid he's up early this morning', or something equally banal? But it did not happen like this. They gave me a razor and some shaving soap and asked me to get in the bath and shave myself completely. I had breakfast, but they warned me that there would be no lunch or indeed anything until after the operation. The round of visits went on, including one from Mr Keates, who explained in full detail what he would do, and then asked if I would like to see the intensive care recovery room, where I would be for the next day. I took him up on this offer, and the sister in charge showed me round. It was the only disturbing feature of the whole operation. Here I saw figures, wrapped like mummies, attached to a bewildering array of pipes and cables. Some carried air, some were intravenous drips, and others were drains leaking fluid away from damaged tissues; and then there were the electrical leads to the various instruments monitoring the patients. This long, quiet room filled my mind with the image of a mortuary full of corpses, and it was not what I needed just then. The Sister who was showing me round sensed my disquiet, and led me to the door and back to my room. It is not my nature to dwell on the unpleasant, and my mind soon turned to the less personally disturbing thought of the cost of the surgery. I started to calculate just how much I was to cost the health service, and how fortunate I was not to have to pay for it myself, and my mind was at ease again. Waiting for me in my room was a young assistant surgeon who told me that his job was to take out my saphenous vein, which goes from the thigh to the ankle, and would give the material for the bypasses between my aorta and the lower part of the left coronaries. I asked him, curiously, how they worked out the flow rates, and what diameters of vein would be needed. He looked startled at first, but then warmed, and began to explain his craft in full detail. Yes, of course they calculated the flow rates, and it was quite a business getting just the right-sized piece of vein or artery to do the job. Both he and Mr Keates were patient in explaining in full detail exactly what they would be doing. I did not dwell too deeply on the thought of my lifeblood circulating through a heart-and-lung machine for thirty minutes or so; the possibilities of things going wrong—like bubbles or clots—were all too familiar to me. The thought of my heart chilled and anaesthetized by potassium chloride, to stop its beat, was fascinating and brought back memories of the reanimation of frozen animals nearly thirty years previously.

In the course of conversation with the surgeon, I recall telling him that I had worked as a biochemist in that famous surgeon Michael DeBakey's department in Houston in the 1960s. He seemed impressed. 'DeBakey,' he said, 'is certainly the great pioneer of all that we do today in cardiology. Why, a sizeable number of the surgical instruments that I will be using in your operation are named after him.' I then recalled an odd conversation I had had with DeBakey when we were both members of the faculty of Baylor College of Medicine. It was during a rather boring faculty meeting, something that we had to attend at frequent intervals. Dr DeBakey turned to me and said, 'You know, I don't buy this notion that coronary disease is just a matter of biochemistry, that it just depends on what fats are in your diet, and so on.' I had my own doubts about the biochemistry, thinking it to be a typical crusading piece of pseudo-science and not based on verifiable facts. 'Go on,' I said. DeBakey replied, 'I have seen the inside of more arteries than most, and quite often I see what looks like an inflammatory process, something that might be caused by a virus or bacterial infection, and I wonder if this also is a part of coronary artery disease.' Time has shown that DeBakey's speculations in 1962 were correct.

Then I had another bath, and they put me in one of those gowns that do up at the back—irritating and awkward things to wear, and almost impossible to do up, but they do serve to mop up spilt blood. Back on my bed, my wrist and ankle were fitted with plastic tags bearing a number, and I was then, so to speak, trussed and ready for carving. Lunchtime passed. I telephoned Helen to tell her that all so far was well, and that my surgery was due at 5.30 that evening. Around about 4 pm I was given a pile of pills by the young surgeon, who explained what they were all for. One was cimetidine to stop my stomach digesting itself away during the long course of the operation, and the rest were premedication of various kinds: Valium I recognized but not the long, dark, dried-insect-like pills of some other preparation. He said that after taking these I would remember nothing until after the surgery; the last I do, indeed, remember is that they wheeled me on a trolley to the theatre. In the anteroom, they marked me in places with a felt tipped pen. I also remember the anaesthetist telling me that the only anaesthetic that I should receive for the whole operation would be morphine.

I awoke the next day in the intensive care room to find a breathing mask over my face. I tried to remove it, at which a young nurse appeared saying, 'Don't do that, your blood gases aren't right.' 'Well, I feel fine,' said I, 'are you sure there's nothing wrong with your instruments?' Startled by this liveliness from a patient, she turned to look behind her, and then returned and took off my mask. Soon after, they wheeled me along to Lonsdale Ward and a very different world from the high-tech, ultra-clean environment I had just been in. In the first hours and days of my stay in the ward, I was still under the spell of morphine, and I felt amazingly well, cheerful, and entirely free from pain. Having once damaged a rib in a fall, I remember well how long it was before I could breathe without feeling the pain of it. Yet, only a day ago they had cut open my ribcage and drawn it back to allow the surgeon to work on my heart. In spite of it, I could now breathe just as easily as if nothing had happened.

On that first day in the ward my brother-in-law Neil and his wife Pauline Hyslop came to visit. I think they were expecting to find a weak, feeble, and barely talking relative, instead of which they found a strange mummified figure that seemed full of life. I was so euphoric that I am sure that they left thinking that I was fine physically after the operation, but that my mind had become addled because of it. Looking back, I can understand the appeal of opiates to those who use them for pleasure. The first few days, when these powerful painkillers were still being administered, were in every way pleasant, but treatment involves a diminuendo, and by the fifth day we were down to ordinary codeine and paracetamol painkillers, and only if needed. The only time I felt pain during the first days was when they took out the catheter dwelling in my bladder. The insertion of an in-dwelling catheter is usual during long surgery, to allow the bladder to empty, and to provide a continuous supply of urine for biochemical analysis. When my nurse deflated the small internal balloon that holds the head of the catheter inside the bladder and prepared to pull it out, she said, 'Don't worry, you'll probably feel nothing at all.' She was wrong, and in spite of the opiates I was still receiving, withdrawal was acutely painful. The catheter came out covered in blood and dotted with shreds of adhering tissue. She was clearly concerned, and fetched the young surgeon who was on ward duty. They talked, but now my pains had gone again and I dozed. I did not know it then, but this small incident was the forerunner of years of pain and misery, something still present nearly twenty years later.

By the third day, I grew fully aware of the ward and my fellow inmates. Before the operation, I had always imagined that the best way to stay in hospital would be in a private room, separated from the problems of personal encounters at a time when one felt least like making the effort. In spite of its problems, Lonsdale Ward gave me my first lesson in the virtues of Florence Nightingale's plan of an open ward, a plan where rows of beds, side by side, faced each other across a wide space. This layout ensured space for hospital traffic to pass without disturbance or hold up, and made sure that the nursing staff and patients were visible to one another. These wards have some of the air of an army barracks. Normally, there is strong discipline exerted by the ward Sister over both the nurses and the patients. The physicians and surgeons occupy the roles of the officer class, and are less often seen; their uniform is also distinctive and different. There is blood and pain and suffering around, and death at times as well. It is an atmosphere where discipline overrides fear, where camaraderie cheers and overcomes the pain—an atmosphere that afterwards one remembers with affection.

I have made over forty separate visits to National Health Service hospitals for surgery during the last nineteen years. These experiences have convinced me that the open wards of the NHS are not just for the care and cure of the sick, but that they also serve to keep our society decent. A stay in a ward is like a lottery: in the next bed can be a tramp or a millionaire; a wise man or a fool; the kindly or the malign. The thing is, after ten days in such an environment, you cannot but get to know them well. In peace time there is nowhere else in our society that provides such a complete social education. If you have never been a patient in a ward, I can understand that you would regard such enforced acquaintance as intolerable, but you would be wrong. I am by nature a private person and choose to live with the nearest neighbour about one kilometre away, yet, when I go to hospital again, I would never willingly choose a private room over the open ward. It can be miserable lying in pain alone, wondering if ever someone will come; wondering if the pain warns of something serious about to happen or is just the normal state. In the open ward there are always those who had the operation a few days ago and who will cheerfully tell you, from their state of recovery, 'Oh, yes, the second day is the worst; you'll feel fine tomorrow.' Then there is the never-ending entertainment, the laughter to join in with, and the sadness; so much goes on in a ward that we need no other entertainment. I always take a novel intending to read it, or even some serious books, but rarely ever get beyond the first few pages.

Some people learn best to swim when thrown in at the deep end, and so it was for me in Lonsdale Ward. It was mostly for men who had had heart surgery. I remembered these wards from my childhood days at the Strand School, which had a connection with King's College Hospital. Each year they took some of us from the school to see a ward that the school supported by our donations. In those days of the 1930s, the wards were immaculately clean and tidy; they had to be because then there were no antibiotics and freedom from infection depended upon strict cleanliness and aseptic techniques. To us the nurses seemed powerful figures who ruled with calm authority. We knew about, although we never saw, that formidable authoritarian figure, the Matron, who presided over it all. Her firm rules and strong discipline set the environment in the way of her great predecessor, Florence Nightingale. Lonsdale Ward of December 1982 was an outrageous exception to this ordered scene and, I hope, to the National Health Service generally.

At the time of my admission, King's College Hospital was suffering its own illness. It was the site of a smouldering tribal war, aggravated by a trade union out to gain members from one of the tribes, and consequently taking sides in the conflict. I grew up in Brixton, which is part of the neighbourhood close to King's College Hospital. It has always been a comparatively poor area: the looming pile of Brixton Prison no doubt has something to do with it. Criminals tend to repeat their offences, and their families gravitate to the neighbourhood of the prison to make easier the journeys to visit their imprisoned relatives. Brixton in 1982 was a very different place from the Brixton where I had grown up. It was now the site of a West Indian settlement whose inhabitants were painfully adjusting to a wholly different culture from that of the sunny Caribbean. As my recovery progressed, it slowly dawned on me that the ward was in fact a battleground of a war between the West Indian ward staff and the hospital establishment, some of whom, but not all, were white. It was no simple racial contest, if there are any such. Here, Trinidadians, who seemed to dominate union membership, saw themselves as the most superior of all the black races, and bitterly resented having to take orders from black African nurses. I was astonished to hear a Trinidadian ward maid call my favourite night sister, a huge, warm and wonderful Nigerian woman, black African trash. Ordinarily the strong discipline of the hospital could have coped but not now.

We were in the midst of 'industrial action' by the trade union, NUPE (the National Union of Public Employees). The union had recruited the West Indian hospital staff, including the ward maids, whose normal task would have been to keep the ward clean, and, by their cheerfulness, raise the spirits, and hasten the recovery of the patients. But they were now going slow, and were far from cheerful. NUPE—or as it is now called Unison—claimed to take great care to ensure that if there was industrial action patients would not be harmed. My experience in Lonsdale ward showed me how false was this claim. At every level, from our comfort and feeling of security, to the risk to our lives, we were threatened. It was more than just a strike, because at that time, Brixton had passed through a series of racial disturbances. I do believe that the West Indians had real cause for complaint, but to make the ward of a hospital their battleground was no way to gain our sympathy. So blinded were these union members by their grievances that they seemed to see us, the mostly white patients, as enemies. It was an outrage—the ward sisters, who ordinarily would have kept order and an environment suitable for recovery, were wholly frustrated. The least reprimand to one of the ward maids brought the threat of an all-out strike. This blackmail did not merely undermine their authority; it also put our lives at risk.

The ward had two lavatories and, soon after I could move, I asked to use them and not the bedpan. When I reached these lavatories, dragging my intravenous drip and catheter bag behind me, I was sickened to see the floors of both smeared with faeces. On the door, where once there had been a hook to hang one's dressing gown, there were just the screw holes. It had been broken off and never replaced. My long experience researching problems of hospital cross-infection had never shown me anything so gross as this—not even in the Second World War. I felt that I was a casualty in a battlefield hospital somewhere in the developing world, and in many ways, this was the truth of it. I began to think that the greatest threat to our health service came not from the political right or from private medicine, but from the brutal abuse of trade-union power, perversely the power that enabled socialism itself.

My mother's family proudly remembered their famous relative, Samuel March. For a time, he was Mayor of Poplar, an activist who spent time in prison for a political offence. He was an early Labour Member of Parliament, and an early leader of what is now the Transport and General Workers Union. In those days, we needed the trade unions to fight the gross exploitation that was part, but not all, of Victorian industry. Great-uncle Sam March represented Poplar, and many of his constituents were Irish Dockers who suffered privation and appalling conditions of work. With such a background, I had always voted Labour. The events in Lonsdale Ward were to shake that simple loyalty.

The fourth day after surgery was Christmas. We were delighted by a traditional Christmas dinner, enhanced by having one of our surgeons personally carve the turkey and serve the meat to us, on a table set up in the ward. We were by then strong enough to sit at the table to enjoy our meal and a glass of wine. As the days went by, the reaction to the withdrawal of the opiates set in, and by the sixth day several of us behaved as if we were unhinged. We became exquisitely sensitive to the squalor of the ward, and the pervasive smell of a sticky disinfectant fluid spread on every horizontal surface. At about this time, a West Indian maintenance man came to replace a bulb in the reading lamp of a patient near me. He came, examined the bulb and pronounced it broken; he went away and did not return with a new bulb for about two hours. He looked at it and the lamp and said, 'I will have to fetch my ladder, to put it in.' Another two hours passed and he returned with the ladder but without the bulb. He went away and I do not think he ever returned. By now, we realized that we had watched a particularly creative act of 'going slow', the tactic unions use to force a bad firm to recognize their call for more wages or better conditions. Suitable in that context, but what possible justification did it have in our ward? We are foolish to allow our public servants, secure in their jobs, to behave in this uncivilized way. Surely crude and brutal 'industrial action' is no way to meet their genuine needs.

I have reason to believe that the 'go slow' at King's has harmed me grievously. I have been unable to uncover the whole story as, quite naturally, the hospital authorities are not happy about telling me everything that happened on the evening of 21 December 1982. I can well understand their caution: in these litigious times, there is too great a risk that their revelations might serve as the basis of a lawsuit. The facts, as I understand them, are these: when the time came for my surgery, the instruments needed were not available because of 'industrial action'. The surgical team therefore chose—quite reasonably—to proceed, after sterilizing the instruments used in the previous operation. The method used was to place them in an autoclave chamber and expose them to the gas, ethylene oxide, which is a powerful and effective method for sterilizing metal scalpels and forceps. The gas can also sterilize catheters and flexible airways but, unfortunately, unlike metal, the elastomers used to make catheters absorb the gas, and if the catheter is used soon after sterilizing this way, it slowly releases its burden of toxic and carcinogenic ethylene oxide into whatever tissue it touches. For me this was my urethra. The sequence of events may not have been exactly as described, but there is no doubt about the damage done, and had the hospital been running normally and free of industrial action there would have been no need for the emergency sterilization of equipment at the start of a major operation. I am telling this story because of my anger at the impropriety of overt trade-union activity in the health service and its hospitals. Accidents rarely come from a single cause; they are usually the consequence of a cascade of errors that culminates in disaster. Poor maintenance is a frequent cause of errors that lead to accidents—the chemical and aircraft industries know this well. Accidents in hospitals, I suspect, also arise through a sequence of errors in which poor maintenance plays a part. Because of this, the claim by health-service unions that their actions will not affect patients is cynical and disingenuous. In case you think this is just the complaint of a single patient, I know that I was not the only one in the hospital to suffer from the union's industrial action. However, the surgery itself was good, and by the ninth day, I was walking around the hospital, climbing stairs, and delighting in the absence of angina. On the tenth day, I walked again with my small bag up the stairs to the exit from King's College Hospital to meet my friendly car driver who was to take me the 250 miles to Coombe Mill.

My homecoming on 1 January 1983 marked the start of a new way of life—the feverish days of 1982 were over. Helen was joyous to have me home, and the first part of January was an unusually happy time. I soon found that I could do the five-mile round walk briskly and without pain or breathlessness, but in mid-January I grew aware that I had not yet escaped the consequences of 'industrial action' at

King's College Hospital: an abscess as large as an egg grew on the wound scar that ran down my chest. My physician arranged for me to have it drained at the North Devon Regional Hospital in Barnstaple and, in the mildly euphoric state engendered by the success of my bypass operation, I took this in my stride as a minor affair, and so it was. By the beginning of February, something more serious began to obtrude; I found that it took minutes to empty my bladder. I returned to Barnstaple hospital again for day surgery to enlarge what was assumed to be a small stricture—a side effect of the heart surgery— and I was not apprehensive, but when I came round from the anaesthetic I was aware of a great deal of pain. I imagined it was to be expected—the penis is a sensitive part, that is half its use. I thought it would soon pass, but it grew worse. A nurse appeared after an hour or so and gave me some tea to drink and said, 'Try to pass water as soon as you can.' I did try but nothing happened. I recall little from then until I found myself on a bed in a ward of the hospital in severe pain and the discomfort of retention. I tried to pee but it would not flow, and by 7 o'clock that evening, I was feeling desperate. I remember crouching on the floor next to my bed to ease the pain.

After a while, the nursing staff noticed my misery and fetched a pair of interns. I should add that I had not yet realized the necessity of whingeing to get attention. As an Englishman, I suffered unnecessarily because of my stiff upper lip. A white woman doctor and a black surgeon came to my help. The woman gave me a sizeable injection of intravenous Valium, but it was without effect on the discomfort and pain. They then tried unsuccessfully to pass a catheter into my bladder. The Valium must have been working to some extent, because the pain of doing this was not as great as I thought it would be. The young surgeon was most solicitous and said, 'I'll give you an operation to fit a supra-pubic catheter as soon as I can, but you might have to wait another two hours, because I've two operations now to do, and one of them is an emergency appendectomy that cannot wait.' They left me dazed, in pain and profound discomfort from an ever-extending bladder. Well meant but foolish offers of more tea from nurses I turned aside. Never can I recall time passing so slowly, and it was not until midnight that relief came. They took me to the operating theatre and the surgeon performed his work using a local anaesthetic. It seemed to take an age to cut through the layers of tissue over the bladder but at last he was through, cut a slit in the bladder wall, and inserted the catheter: the relief was incredible. In some ways,

I found the discomfort of retention worse than pain. I remember thanking this young man profusely and then falling into a deep sleep and not awakening until the following morning.

I was now in King George the Fifth ward. A modern form of open ward consisting of bays containing about six beds, three on each side, and dispersed along a corridor. It was better than single rooms, but nothing like the friendly atmosphere of the old Nightingale wards. Architects had fiddled again, and fiddled to no good, with Florence Nightingale's design. I now suffered no pain or discomfort, and the supra-pubic catheter, with its pipe emerging from my abdomen, was doing its job. A nurse came and attached a leg-bag for me so that I could walk around. Helen and Margaret soon appeared, bringing with them my dressing gown, slippers, and razor. As soon as I had changed from the gown lent to me on arrival, I went with them to the canteen, where I tried to tell them what had happened, but did not really know myself. Later that day I saw the surgeon responsible for the disastrous dilatation and asked, 'Whatever went wrong?' 'Nothing went wrong,' he said. 'You had the worst stricture I have ever seen. It went all the way from the glans to the neck of the bladder. I've no idea what caused it but you must have had a roaring urethritis.' Oddly, it did not occur to me then to connect this disaster with the catheter used at King's.

In a few days, the oedema surrounding my urethra subsided, and I found that I could pee at a reasonable rate. The supra-pubic catheter was removed, and I prepared to go home, thinking, 'This has been rough but now I can resume life again.' The surgeon warned me that it would close up and would need dilating again, but the after effects would not be so severe as those I had just experienced. Within three weeks, the flow declined again to a few cubic centimetres a second, and I was back at Barnstaple. Sure enough, the second time was not as bad as the first and after an hour or so I could pee, although painfully. Every three weeks I was back in Barnstaple for more dilatation, but now after each of them the pain was worse and more prolonged. Margaret Sargent came to collect me from the hospital, and each time the sixty-mile journey over country roads was agonizing. I seemed to be taking antibiotics and codeine painkillers almost continuously. The year before I had almost enjoyed the dreamy but quite bearable threat of imminent death, but I now faced a painful decline that filled me with despair. I knew that I could not go on like this, but even so, I kept up my daily walks, no matter how hard they were to do.

In between the painful excursions to Barnstaple, business kept on as usual. I travelled to London for meetings, and to America to maintain my obligations to my customers there. In April 1983 I visited New York at the invitation of the United Nations University and saw my friend, Walter Shearer, at the United Nations Building. There we discussed the plan for a meeting the following summer in Corsica. I vividly remember having to give a lecture on Gaia to the Sigma Xi Society, of which I am a member, in Washington. I was in severe pain during the introduction by the chairman of the meeting. When I rose to cross the floor, it intensified, and I fainted and fell on the floor. Within moments, I had staggered to my feet, and to the lectern. The audience seemed to think I had merely tripped on a cable. I looked at my lecture notes and saw only a dark blur with no words distinguishable. Somehow, on automatic pilot, I started my lecture, and after a few minutes could see my notes again. It seemed to go all right—audiences could be most tolerant. No one commented on the fraught beginning.

Life from February until June 1983 was a nightmare of pain and despair. What I had hoped would be a cure at King's College Hospital seemed to have worsened my affairs. Rescue came in a letter from a past colleague of my days with the Medical Research Council, David Pegg. He wrote asking if I would give an after-dinner speech at a conference in King's College Cambridge on cryobiology. It seemed an occasion on which I could reminisce and tell stories about the Mill Hill Institute in the 1950s; it also gave me the opportunity to cry for help. I replied, saying that I would love to come, but warned that, because of my frequent visits to Barnstaple, I might not be in a position to do so. I asked him to recommend a first-rate urologist who might be able to cure my affliction. He replied promptly, recommending the surgeon Michael Bishop, who operated from the City Hospital in Nottingham. The next day I had a sympathetic letter from Mr Bishop, inviting me to go there to have the next operation performed by him in July.

I took the train that goes cross-country from Exeter to Nottingham, and travelled from the station by taxi to the City Hospital—a large, multi-storey building occupying a sizeable area. Mr Bishop came to see me soon after I settled in the ward, and explained what he would try to do. It was surgery of the urethra—a urethrotomy—he said, and then explained that it was a careful and painstaking procedure, done using the magnified view of an endoscope, not the crude surgery done at Barnstaple. Here, blunt instruments had dilated my injured urethra—they had used thin stainless steel rods called bougies to expand the damaged tissue. I had my operation the next day, and learnt from Michael Bishop that the repeated attempts at dilatation in Barnstaple had produced a mess of broken tissues and blind passages. He had made some much-needed repair, but warned that I needed a great deal more before my urethra would function properly again. It would not be necessary for me to make repeated journeys to Nottingham, as a skilful surgeon, Mr PI O'Boyle, practised at Taunton, in Somerset, much closer to where I lived. He would write to him and explain what I needed when my urethra began to close again. As the train drew away from Nottingham and passed through the flat industrial landscape of the Midlands and on towards the West Country and Devon, I felt a great sense of thankfulness. At last, it seemed that I was safe again. Michael Bishop did such a good job that there was a wonderfully long interval of eight weeks before it was necessary for me to go to Taunton.

During that respite, I travelled to the United Nations University meeting on the island of Corsica. At Coombe Mill in early July 1983, the temperature rose, most unusually for England, into the nineties Fahrenheit and stayed there for most of the week. We were lucky to live in a mud-and-straw constructed house, a kind of English adobe—cob is the word Devonians use to describe it. The two-to-three-foot-thick walls keep a cool environment in hot weather and a warm one in winter. The heat capacity of all those tons of mud was such that its temperature could only slowly respond to that of the air at its surface, and it required weeks of torrid heat or freezing cold to change it from comfortable to unpleasant. The English climate, with its endless samples of weather—hot and cold, wet and dry—almost never tested it to its limit. Corsica, strangely, seemed cool after Devon, although the Mediterranean was heavenly to swim in, which I did on most days, from a rocky cove beneath the hotel where we were staying. The distinguished environmental scientist, William Clark, was my companion for much of the stay in Corsica, as well as my friend, Walter Shearer. As at all scientific meetings, the key things were said tête-à-tête at the restaurants in the evening, or during walks to and from the beach. I sometimes wonder why there are so many prepared talks at scientific meetings; we would do better to spend our time in private conversation.

Eventually, in September, I knew I had to go to Taunton for more surgery. I arrived at Musgrove Park Hospital and went to Ward 3. It was a familiar old-fashioned ward, part of a temporary wartime hospital built in the 1940s, a series of huts angling from a boardwalk—ugly and well beyond its anticipated lifetime. Perfect, I thought, for a propaganda film by American private medicine to show how awful was the National Health Service and socialized medicine. In fact, the quality of the surgery and nursing care I received during the twenty-five or so visits I was to make there over the next thirteen years, could not have been bettered anywhere in the world. It was comforting to see, on a recent visit to Ward 3, a party of surgeons from the distinguished Mayo Clinic who had come to Taunton to learn about the pioneering techniques that my surgeon had developed. Unlike King's College Hospital, the interior was warm, clean, and amazingly full of laughter. The domestics here were local women, and they seemed to know that they were an essential part of the hospital system. They took care of us and hastened our recovery; their friendly concern and help showed what should have been the conditions in Lonsdale ward.

I first met Paddy O'Boyle in Ward 3 one Thursday morning in September 1983. I had not expected an immediate operation when I arrived there, and so had breakfasted before leaving home. 'Never mind,' said Paddy, 'Over lunchtime I will have a look at your urethra by endoscopy and we'll use an epidural anaesthetic.' A cheery Australian anaesthetist did the epidural as I waited on the operating table. Then my legs were set up on a stand, similar to that used for women in labour, and a blanket was set up between the surgeon and me. I wondered if this was to spare my feelings, but not so. The blanket slipped off during the surgery and Paddy asked the nurse to put it back. I said, 'I don't mind,' to which he replied, 'But I do.' It was good to know that I had a sensitive surgeon. What he did was little more than endoscopy, to look at the extent of the damage and then decide on the repair that he would have to do. The endoscope, being somewhat large, automatically dilates the urethra anyway. Michael Bishop had done a fine job clearing up the worst of the ragged mess—the traumas of King's College and Barnstaple together—but there was still a great deal to do. Paddy warned me that the incidental dilatation now done would last only a few weeks. I must prepare myself for a prolonged spell of urethral surgery. He said, 'It will involve operations every week for quite a while. You will have to come here every Sunday afternoon and leave on the following Tuesday. Can you arrange your life to make this possible?' After the previous miseries this seemed no great problem, and he started the long series of operations that eventually led to a partial cure. There was pain, but nothing like the agonies I had experienced at Barnstaple. The only bad times were when I experienced a proctalgia: this is a nearly intolerable pain in the inguinal region and it came on when there was, simultaneously, inflammation of the urethra and the bowel. It seemed to be a consequence of taking antibiotics to keep bladder infections at bay. My physician, Alan Edwards, gave me Temgesic tablets to ease the pain; these are fast-acting, tiny sublingual tablets of a synthetic opiate. They certainly did the trick, although with a pleasant side effect of a day's excitement and euphoria. Not something to which I would want to become addicted but, again, it made me realize and understand better what appeals to the drug users whose daily lives are often bleak and cheerless. I have often wondered how much addiction is part of our personal programming: are those who lead normal lives in much danger of becoming addicted to drugs? After all, we rarely drink to excess when life is good. I was fortunate to be able to work in a laboratory attached to my home and I managed, during this period, my two visits a year to the United States and some to Europe.

There were about five more visits like this to Taunton, where Paddy O'Boyle diligently repaired blind holes and other problems caused by the crude dilatations with stainless steel rods at Barnstaple. He tidied up my urethra to make it again a pipe, rather than something like an inverted river delta, but there was still scar tissue from the damage done earlier. The problem with scar tissue is that it contracts, and I needed relatively frequent operations to keep my urethra open. A less serious side effect was that I now had a curved penis when it was erect. Then came the day when he said, 'I do not think there is much more I can do by urethrotomy, so we have to decide what the next option is. The main problem is the contraction of the scar tissue; it makes dilations every three weeks a necessity. After talking with my colleagues, I have decided that the most useful thing we can do is to make a short channel from your bladder to the inguinal region. In other words, to arrange for you an artificial urethra that would be similar in construction to that in most women. Next time you come to Taunton, prepare for a longer stay, perhaps ten days.' With the thought that my penis would soon be redundant, celibacy seemed now not to matter quite so much. I resigned myself to this next ordeal. I must admit that, during this period, I became quite obsessed about trade unions, and cheered when the union leader Arthur Scargill lost his long battle over the mines.

As I drove along the M5 on the way back to Musgrove Park Hospital, my mind was full of the consequences of my next operation. I nearly missed the turnoff, exit 26 for Wellington and Taunton. I do not much care for cars or driving them, but there is no other way to travel from Coombe Mill to Taunton. The welcome I received on arriving at Ward 3 was warmer than usual, and everyone there seemed to know that tomorrow's surgery had profound consequences for me. I had for some time regarded the ward staff as almost a second family, and knew most of them well. A great deal of this strength and cohesion came from those most closely associated with it, especially from Sister Chant and the surgeon, Paddy O'Boyle. Sister Chant wore the dark blue dress of a hospital Sister, with its belt and silver buckle, and she wore it with authority. She wore it in a way that Florence Nightingale would have approved. She was no mere senior nursing officer, although that may now be her title. Doctrinal egalitarianism does not allow for honourable vocations, like nursing. I cannot imagine her, whatever the provocation, joining in a strike. In all of the fourteen years of visits to Ward 3, I have heard her raise her voice only twice. She did not need to. Whether by choice or by accident, the staff appropriate for Ward 3 seemed to gravitate there and to stay. Prominent amongst them was Robert Conway, also a quiet and powerful figure, whose striking appearance was part of the ward's quality. The staff called it the grandfather's ward, since most of the patients were over sixty and having some or all of their prostate gland removed.

A strange incident occurred at this time. I had brought with me to read a book by the author, Richard Cowper, called *The Road to Corlay*, first published in 1978. I did not usually read books of this kind: it was science fantasy. To me, science was fantastic enough anyway, but Richard Cowper wrote so well that I have read and enjoyed immensely everything he has written. He had also written to me personally about a small story in my first book, *Gaia*. He was keen to use it after revision, and publish it as a short story, and sought my permission, which I gladly gave. I was looking forward to a good read, while I waited in the afternoon and evening before the next day, when I was to be partially converted in the female direction. I had reached page sixty when I was astonished to read:

> in the North Wing of the General Hospital. From its fourth floor windows those patients capable of looking out had a view westwards across the Vale of Taunton to the Brendon Hills and northwards to the Quantocks. Few took advantage of it, for in June 1986 the vista, which should have lifted their spirits, served only to depress them. Rachel Wylde was no exception. She gazed with blank eyes at the sodden landscape while the raindrops pattered against the windowpane of Ward 3 and trickled downwards in slow, interminable tears.

Not bad for a coincidence: the year and month were wrong and Ward 3 was on the ground floor, but what a surprise to read, while preparing my mind for major surgery. Every week someone wins the lottery at comparable odds against, so coincidences like this must happen every so often. But just as the winner is happily amazed at the news of the win, so was I by this coincidence at such a time.

Next morning, which was Monday, I woke earlier than usual, and shaved and showered before anyone else was up, which would be about 5.45 am. I helped to take the morning teacups around the ward, went back to bed, and read again for a while. The tall figure of Robert Conway came up to me and said, 'So you are for the big one this morning, Jim, and you are the first on the list and will be going along to the theatre at about 9 o'clock.' At about 8 they brought me two 10 mg Valium tablets as the favoured premedication of that time. Soon, it seemed, the porters came with their trolley, or what the Americans call a gurney, to take me to the theatre. They wheeled me along the short distance to the theatre, and in the anteroom the anaesthetist chatted to me as he prepared his intravenous cocktail of anaesthetic. He then inserted a cannula with a syringe port into a vein on my hand: this welcome invention saves repeated puncturing of veins to deliver doses of any drug or antibiotic. Soon, he injected his mixture into this device while we went on chatting and then suddenly I was away. I came to in the recovery room adjacent to the theatre, and soon I felt the familiar touch of tubing on my thigh and put my hand down to confirm it. Yes, there it was, a catheter tube leading from my penis. Strange, I thought, then Paddy came over and said in a matter-of-fact voice. 'We decided after all not to do the big operation and just completed the urethrotomy.' I should have sung my praises to him there and then. Where would I have been in five years' time with nothing to bring to my second marriage but a withered member?

From now on visits dropped back to four weeks or so, but another problem arose: that of repeated bladder and kidney infections. A kidney scan and a kidney function test using radioactive technetium, soon revealed the damage done to my left kidney by the tractor accident at the beginning of 1982, and it looked as if it needed removing. Sister Chant told me that Paddy was one of those surgeons who operated only when it was wholly necessary. I had good reason to believe this, and I could see that he was loath to remove the damaged kidney and preferred to try to coax it back to life.

One day, whilst busy preparing a lecture that I had agreed to give in Vienna in a few weeks' time, Dr Lightfoot, the pathologist at Taunton, called. 'Can you drop everything and come to Taunton at once?' he asked. 'What, now, this afternoon?' 'Yes, it is urgent that you do. Do you want us to send an ambulance to bring you in or can you drive?' 'Oh, I'll drive in, but what's the fuss?' said I. 'You have a *Pseudomonas* infection and it should be treated without delay.' Feeling as well as I was used to feeling, I chose to drive in to Taunton, having packed my pyjamas and dressing gown and other odds and ends.

Dr Lightfoot came to visit the ward as soon as I was in bed to explain the need for urgent action. *Pseudomonas aeruginosa*, a bacterium that I had previously regarded as a friendly benign inhabitant of the natural scene, was also, he said, a deadly pathogen. It could cause a septicaemia that could kill within hours. One disadvantage of a medical background is that they never spared me this kind of detail, nor would I want it otherwise. Even so, it was sobering in the way of Ogden Nash's verse:

This creature fills its mouth with venom and walks upon its duodenum.
He who attempts to tease the cobra, is soon a sadder he and sobra.

Dr Lightfoot took some blood from my arm and, shortly afterwards, injected me with the antibiotic tobramycin. He said I could go to lecture in Vienna but immediately afterwards I must return to Taunton to have my diseased kidney removed. I must also inject myself twice daily with the antibiotic. I wish that I had been well enough to enjoy my visit to Vienna. As it was I gave my Gaia talk to a receptive audience at Laxenberg Castle and then returned to Musgrove Park, where Paddy O'Boyle removed the offending kidney. During the ten-day stay in Ward 3 afterwards, my mind was filled with the thought that shortly after I returned home to Coombe Mill, a team would arrive from the BBC to film a *Horizon* programme on Gaia. This was, of course, a wonderful opportunity to put my case before a large, even global audience. I was concerned that I should be fit again and able to do it with vigour. For the ten days after the surgery, they gave me the antibiotic piperacillin by intravenous drip; at that time, it was the antibiotic of choice for *Pseudomonas* infections. Towards the end of my stay in Ward 3, Dr Lightfoot brought the good news that I was free of infection. A friendly local taxi driver, who provided blankets to keep me warm over the seventy-mile journey home, fetched me from Musgrove Park Hospital. Two days later, the *Horizon* producer, John Groom, arrived with his team of cameramen and sound technicians, and began to put me through my paces. They were considerate of my condition but, consummate technicians that they were, the film was what mattered, and these were still the days when the BBC's science flagship programme, *Horizon*, was elitist, and about science. The 1985 *Horizon* programme was fine and was shown worldwide. It did much to bring Gaia into perception as a scientific topic and it did so without denying the value of Gaia as a unifying sign and concept for a holistic view of the Earth.

I continued to visit Taunton, now at intervals of six months or so, for the fine-tuning by dilatation or urethrotomy of the strictures still left by those miserable events at King's College Hospital in 1982. In 1985 Robert Conway showed me how to dilate my urethra by inserting a catheter. Since then, I have dilated myself at intervals of two weeks, and Paddy tells me that I shall probably have to do this for the rest of my life. He also told me how fortunate I was to have no more than this to do. Many others who have suffered similarly are doomed to a restricted life with a permanent supra-pubic catheter. He did not say that my good fortune was due to his patient skill as a surgeon, but I know that it was. The philosopher Rousseau also had a stricture and needed to catheterize himself regularly. He, unfortunate man, had to use willow twigs, not smooth plastic tubing.

Institutions large and small can become recognizable as entities, and their names are memorable. They take on a quality that gives pride to those that serve them. Ward 3 at Musgrove Park Hospital, Taunton, is just such an entity, and had been for all of the years that I knew it. My strongest memory is of laughter. Extraordinary in a place where blood and pain are all too common, yet it exemplified the hospital wisdom that the happiest ward to be in is men's surgical.

Some time ago, when I visited my friend Henry Bentinck in his carpeted room at the Nuffield Private Hospital in Taunton, I was glad that my next stay was in Ward 3 not there. I do not think Henry minded, but not for me a lonely private room in a hotel for the sick.

I am aware that the nursing profession is changing fast. As the staff nurse at Taunton put it to me on my last visit there in 1995: 'Make the most of us now—next time you come here the nurses will all be graduates and they will not look after you as we do.' I hope that the consequences of this facet of women's liberation are not as dire as she predicted.

Had my urethral misfortune happened in America I would prob-ably have sued for damages. Why did I not sue here in the UK? My answer is that in America, the courts are the natural means of redress, and here they are not. In America, there was no health service. I would have been obliged to pay for the repair work done during those numerous hospital visits and my own resources would have vanished in the cost of the first few of them. There would have been no option but to sue, and even with adequate cover, the insurance company would have insisted on my suing. Here in the UK, the heart surgery and the repair of my urethra cost me nothing. As far as I could see, the damage was a result of 'industrial action' by the trade union, not negligence on the part of the surgeon or the hospital. As far as my heart is concerned, the surgeon truly gave me a new lease of life; what ingratitude it would have been to sue.

Lynn Margulis paid a visit later in the year and brought with her a wonderful gift. She came as a member of the committee of the Commonwealth Fund, a fund that had, as its chairman, the famous author and physician, Lewis Thomas. She brought from him the invitation to write a second book on Gaia and the offer of $50,000 for doing so, as a grant. This meant that I could set aside much of the next two years to write *The Ages of Gaia*. What other recompense did I need?

12

Three Score Years and Ten and then the Fun Begins

As I moved to the end of my sixty-ninth year, thoughts of the biblical life span of seventy years were much in my mind. The quest for Gaia seemed to have stalled at San Diego, Helen was now failing, and I was due for more corrective surgery at Taunton hospital. The prospect was grim, but then suddenly in April 1988, things changed and this is what this chapter is about. But the title is, I admit, outrageous. I chose it deliberately to cock a snoot at the dull grey pessimistic world I then seemed to inhabit. I am aware that some may see it as unkind and discourteous to Helen's memory, but this is not my intention. I want to show that life can indeed begin again at seventy, and this is how it happened.

In the autumn of 1987 Wilfrid Grenville-Grey wrote me to say that he and Mrs Orchard would like to visit and discuss my appearance at the Global Forum, due to be held in April the next year. This was a meeting that I had somewhat regretfully agreed to attend and to deliver a fifteen-minute speech. They never came, but I imagined them to be seriously Anglican, and these suspicions were confirmed when I read in their letter that they intended to visit me by travelling from Paddington to Liskeard in Cornwall. Nobody but liberal church people would take such a circuitous route to reach Coombe Mill. In my imagination, Wilfrid had the demeanour of at least a Dean; Mrs

Orchard, his companion, the church lady dressed neatly in twin set and pearls, and sensible shoes. Both of them I imagined to be officers of one of the flagships of what was then middle-class England, the Anglican Church.

I had more than three weeks after returning from San Diego to prepare my talk, and somehow the disappointment of the Gaia meeting there drove me to put my heart into it and give them their money's worth. On Sunday 10 April I arrived by train from Exeter to Reading, took the coach to Heathrow, and went on to the Post House Hotel where the delegates were. After checking in at the hotel desk, and before going to my room, I had to register for the conference and receive my badge and programme. A sprightly middle-aged woman, Margaret Rogers, greeted me. I did not know it then, but meeting her was the start of a complete change in my whole lifestyle. She was a smartly dressed English lady who could have understudied for Miss Marple, and she did nothing to dispel my image of the conference as comfortably Anglican.

Next morning after breakfast, along with other delegates, they whisked me away to Oxford on a set of buses. My seat companion was a young rabbi from Israel who I found easy to talk to, and I was surprised to discover that his wife had attended the Henrietta Barnett School in Hampstead Garden Suburb at the same time as my daughter, Christine—and later I found that they knew each other. The absurd familiarity of this link seemed to melt the jagged edges that separated our wholly different cultures, and I enjoyed talking with him all the way to Oxford. We soon arrived and were disembussed at Christ Church, an Oxford college founded as Cardinal College by Wolsey in 1525, but refounded as Christ Church in 1546 by Henry VIII, after Wolsey had fallen from royal favour. It is a splendid college with its vast quadrangle, its Tom Tower, and its own cathedral. Happily on this cool but sunny April morning, I stood by some steps in the quadrangle, soaking up the sun, and watched a woman walk diagonally across from some offices on the far side of the quadrangle. She came up to me and introduced herself. 'I am Sandy Orchard,' she said. Now, she was no middle-class Anglican churchwoman, she was an American; but she spoke softly with an accent that was more transatlantic than those of New York or Boston. Her trim figure put her in my mind as somewhere in her early forties. She read my name badge and immediately we began to talk about her interest in Gaia. I asked her whether she was free for lunch so that we could talk some more. She said, 'Yes, meet me here at 12.30.' But it was not to be: the surge of arriving delegates overwhelmed her wish. She shared with Wilfrid Grenville-Grey, of the London office, the task of arranging and running the conference. The New York organizers of the Global Forum, led by Akio Matsumura, Dean Morton, and Cecile Reyes, were in charge.

After lunch, I returned to the conference office and soon found that, as a speaker, I rated VIP treatment and was booked into a suite at the Randolph Hotel, about half a mile away. I walked out through the gateway under Tom Tower and onto St Aldate's where the traffic noise was almost physically painful after the quiet of the quadrangle. It remained so as I made my way through the thronged streets to Carfax, past the shops and buses to the Randolph on its corner facing the Ashmolean Museum. Oxford, like Calcutta, seems always overripe with human life, especially along that fecund axis linking Christ Church to the Randolph.

There was a conference reception that evening with the Great and the Good in attendance. These included: the Chancellor of Oxford University, Roy Jenkins, who came in his gown, and the Archbishop of Canterbury, Robert Runcie. I missed this colourful opening cere-mony but I joined the throng at the reception. Here, I spoke briefly to Mrs Orchard again, but retired to the Randolph early to be in good shape for my speech next day.

In the morning, I made my way the short distance up St Aldate's to Oxford Town Hall, a dreadful building for a city otherwise blessed with glorious architecture. I cannot think how the city fathers could have made so wretched a place their town hall. I sat, along with the other speakers, at one end of the large hall and, of course, public address systems were necessary, as few speakers had voices that could reach the far end of the building unaided. James Morton, Dean of the Cathedral of St John the Divine in New York, and the famous scien-tist, Carl Sagan, shared the platform with me. Hardly had I finished the first words of my speech when the public address system died. Dean Morton said, 'Go on and shout, you can be heard even if the public address system doesn't work.' I replied, 'With a voice like yours I could, but not with mine.' For a moment I felt utterly betrayed, then, after some seconds of agonized confusion, the sound system came on again. I should have started again at the beginning but I did not, and continued my speech as if the interruption had not occurred. I was surprised to find that it went over reasonably well. I sat down and listened to Carl Sagan's speech. They had allowed him forty-five minutes to speak and he thrilled them with a modern version of a hellfire sermon, with nuclear winters and atomic fire standing in for the devil and damnation. The gathering, being mostly of the religious, loved it, and were taking notes, no doubt to weave into their own sermons later. It was growing ever more clear to me that 1988 was continuing as a bad year for Gaia. Both the scientists and the clerics, it seemed to me, had lost the enthusiasm that had greeted Gaia's debut in 1979. Schooldays had taught me to emulate the stick insect when things are bad and to disappear into the background looking like a twig. There would be other opportunities, I thought, to fight for Gaia, but certainly not here. I had lunch with some of the delegates, and in the afternoon attended a few working groups, before retiring to the Randolph to change for dinner.

Dinner was again in the refectory at Christ Church, a room with all the splendour and certainty of its founders. Opposite me on the long table were the once Rector of the United Nations University, Soedjatmoko, and sitting next to him, Dean Morton of the Cathedral of St John the Divine. Sandy, that is to say, Mrs Orchard, was sitting next to me. I had been looking forward to having a talk with her, a continuation of our discussion in the quad, but again it was not to be. Soedjatmoko and Dean Morton, both exuberant extrovert characters, dominated the conversation in the liveliest of manners, and it was an enjoyable dinner, but not the one that I'd expected. After dinner, however, I took Sandy along the few short steps from the refectory to the cathedral at Christ Church, where an old friend of mine, another Lindisfarne Fellow, Paul Winter, was giving a small concert of his music. We sat on excruciatingly uncomfortable pews and although we had had no more than a few uninterrupted minutes together, I saw Sandy as a stunningly attractive woman and longed to hold her hand. I discovered later that she felt just the same urge, but during the concert we sat in our discomfort and listened to the music. Afterwards, with great relief, we stood and then went over to meet Paul Winter, who immediately embraced us both. He is the friendliest of men, and he gave us that feeling of being a part of his world as if we had a private invitation to meet him backstage. We walked from the cathedral; I had nothing planned, but hoped something pleasant would happen and then, as so often happens at conferences, a woman I had never before met, came up and started talking seriously and intensely about Gaia. I had to be polite and turn to her and, when I looked round, Sandy had gone. I discovered later that she felt she would be intruding if she stayed; if only she had known. After five or ten minutes, I pleaded the need to return to the hotel to do some writing, and went back to the Randolph.

Next morning I had breakfast with Academician Velikov of the Russian National Academy of Sciences. This was before the break-up of the Soviet Union, and the Academy had the backing of a superpower in addition to its distinction. We were together at a single table and able to discuss a number of topics; I was delighted to find that he was as sceptical about the efforts to find life on Mars as I was. We talked mostly about planetary science and the environment, and I wished that we had had more time.

At the Town Hall I listened to a few more talks and then went on to Christ Church for another all too brief meeting with Sandy in the quad. She reminded me to be sure to attend the dinner at Blenheim Palace, the great occasion of the conference—she added that I would be collected by a coach from my hotel. In the afternoon there were some workshops, but they were wholly humanist. I accept that people and their rights are important, but my interest was in our habitat, the Earth, and I was disappointed to find the participants so uninterested in anything to do with the Earth. I went back to the Randolph to sit and think, and I had not been there long before Carl Sagan tele-phoned and asked if he could talk with me. I was delighted and invited him to come to my suite, where we sat and talked over old times and new ideas. Carl had always been a friend and I had found him the most amiable of men; I felt sad that he and Lynn had failed to make a go of it. Then it was time for me to get dressed for the dinner at Blenheim Palace.

Soon the coach was waiting to pick us up. Everyone was decked in their finery: the Africans in their ceremonial costumes, the clerics in theirs, and the Western males in their dinner-jacket uniforms. We arrived to the sound of a military band and were led up the steps into the great reception hall and introduced to our host for the evening, Sir George Sinclair and his wife Mollie. Soon after the champagne reception, we went into the library at Blenheim, a grand room designed by Nicholas Hawksmoor. The dinner tables seemed to enhance, not disturb the ambience of that elegant room, and they were circular, each seating eight, spread across the library floor—an ideal arrangement. I was at the table with Sir George Sinclair and his wife and the publisher, Henry Luce; there were four others whose names I wish I could remember. It was a pleasant dinner, with splendid food and wine, and at the end of it, I was in a mellow and happy mood. I left the dinner table after the last toast and speech and made my way to the corridor, where I visited the magnificent Blenheim loos. I came back up into the corridor, now somewhat behind the rest of the crowd, and walked along at a comfortable pace aiming for the main hallway and staircase and the buses. My mind was in a cosy neutral state, mulling over the lively conversation and the splendid dinner, and then as I approached that part of the hall at Blenheim above the stairway to the entrance door, I saw Sandy straight ahead of me. She was in a small group that was talking animatedly, but suddenly she turned her head and looked towards me. Our eyes locked and we both moved as if drawn by a powerful force: we were in each other's arms wholly unaware of the throng around us. Saying nothing, I remember taking her hand and going down the stairs and out through the door, and into one of the waiting coaches. It seemed more like Cinderella's pumpkin coach, and I wondered if we failed to reach Oxford before midnight chimed on the many clocks of Oxford's colleges, would this wonderful, wonderful illusion just vanish? We sat close together saying little, holding each other's hands, until the coach arrived at the Randolph, my destination, and that was it. I remember Sandy asking me if I could stay until the Saturday, but regretfully I said no, I had to return to Devon.

The next morning, after breakfast, my mind was full of the previous night and I realized that this was no conference pick-up, no start of a one-night stand, and no casual liaison. Here was someone with whom at last I really could share the remainder of my life. I telephoned home to Coombe Mill and said I would not be back until Saturday lunchtime, and then wrote a brief note. 'Sandy, it's okay, I can stay over until Saturday morning.' The rational side of me questioned my impetuosity, but instinct insisted that I was right, and I passed the note to her during one of the talks at the Town Hall meeting. I quietly made my way out of the hall, and waited. When the talk was over she slipped out and joyfully we made our plans for the day to come. Later that morning, Mother Theresa gave a talk, and in it she chastened us over 'our concern for the Earth'. We needed, she said, 'to take care of the poor, the sick and the hungry and leave God to take care of the Earth.' This was more than I could take and, inspired by Sandy's acceptance of my proposal, so to speak, I waited for her speech to finish then rose and said, 'I must disagree with the reverend lady. If we as people do not respect and take care of the Earth, we can be sure that the Earth, in the role of Gaia, will take care of us and, if necessary, eliminate us.' Perhaps I should not have done so, but somehow I felt that there was a need to speak out for the Earth, and who better to address it to than that most humanist of people, Mother Theresa. She did not reply.

That lunchtime in the refectory, I sat at the high table at Wilfrid's invitation. There I met one of the benefactors of the conference, Mr Nomura. I sat opposite him but his English was limited and my Japanese, of course, negligible, and very little conversation actually took place. There were more workshops in the afternoon, and that evening I attended a reception in the library of Christ Church. I was somewhat dismayed to find that Sandy was not there, and my imagination worked overtime on dismal scenarios. Fortunately, I was distracted from these unproductive thoughts by Richard Harries, the Bishop of Oxford. I have long enjoyed his thoughtful and thought-provoking sermons, and I was so glad to receive from him the same wisdom in our conversation on environmentalism. I kept looking for Sandy around the room, but she was not there and, regretfully, when people were beginning to leave the room, I went on to the refectory for dinner. By then nearly all the seats were taken and I was obliged to sit between two people I didn't know—I spent a rather desultory and ineffectual dinner, alone in effect.

After dinner, we met on the steps of the hall and all was light again. Sandy said that an administrative problem had delayed her and stopped her attending the reception. We went together to the Junior Common Room, where there was a musical evening. Both of us thought of music in classical terms, but we soon found it was to be trendy, guitar-playing Evangelism. For reasons I do not understand, the Church, despite its heritage of some of the world's best music, now tolerates country and western, protest, and junk music, all assumed to appeal to the young. When a performer rose, strummed his guitar, and announced that he would sing a song about injustice, I turned to Sandy and asked, 'Do you like this?' She shook her head and said no. I replied, 'To me, it's just whingeing to music.' We took each other's hands, quietly left, and made our way to Sandy's room in the Peckwater Quad. I sat on the worn settee one expected of a student's room, and Sandy made me a cup of tea. The tea was Earl Grey, which I detest, but I was too much in love to notice at the time. We talked freely, without any hesitation, and we seemed wholly at ease with one another and suffered none of those awkward pauses searching for appropriate things to say. Even silences were comfortable in the way they are with old friends or partners of a good marriage. We hugged but no more, for we knew that the next day we could meet privately at the Randolph.

I spent the morning being filmed by Jean Parr and her cameraman for the Conference record, at a site near the river just south of Christ Church. I cannot remember whom I had lunch with, but afterwards there was more filming, after which I walked to a wine merchant and there bought a bottle of vintage Krug champagne and took it back to the Randolph, together with some cheese and grapes and a few things to eat. I was frustrated afterwards at Christ Church in the quad waiting for Sandy to finish all her duties. She and Wilfrid were the last to leave and, even though it was April, it was already dusk. Eventually we made our way back to the Randolph, and by then it was dark. Sandy went to her room and shortly afterwards, knocked on the door of mine. We sat on the settee of our suite, toasted each other in Krug, and exchanged our ceremonial gifts. Sandy had brought me a copy of VS Naipaul's *The Enigma of Arrival* and the book by Walter and Dorothy Schwarz entitled, *Breaking Through*, and I gave her an audiotape of Mozart's *Mass in C Minor*. We talked and nibbled at the cheese and grapes, but not for long. Soon we were in bed for a riotous night. Awake for most of the time, we repeated our love-making. In the intermissions, we told each other limericks and laughed . . . and laughed.

There was something wonderfully cosy about breakfast in the Randolph the next morning. We sat near the window, looking out on to the street as the early workers hustled by in the rain. We watched it pouring down the windows in between gazing at each other. We knew that in thirty minutes we would part, but it hardly seemed to matter. For the first time in a lifetime, I had fallen deeply in love and had it requited in full. I knew that this was real—not sex after the seminar for two hungry delegates: it was a total commitment and in our hearts and in our genes we knew that it was a perfect marriage. In haste, we packed and checked out. The taxi took us too fast to Oxford station and our tightly held hands tried to hold back time. There we parted full of sad euphoria, knowing that we would soon meet again, but not where.

I dozed in the train to Reading, the connecting station for the Great Western line, and slept from there to Exeter. Sadly, I drove the forty-five miles to Coombe Mill where Helen was facing, although neither of us knew it then, the last months of her long fight against multiple sclerosis. Our marriage had long since changed into a relationship more like that of brother and sister. I dreaded going home after any absence, even after a few days, for so often a further episode of MS had moved her remorselessly further into decline, and I feared what I should see. Somehow, always, I felt personally responsible and guilty for having been away when it happened. Now things were changed. For me, there was the possibility of a new and fulfilled life emerging, where previously in our sad, shared marriage time passing could only lead to the death of one of us, and a lonely old age for the other. I said nothing to Helen of Sandy, partly because it all seemed too good to be true, and partly because I did not have the heart to add further to her burdens.

I spent the weekend in a daze, and on Monday I called to speak to Sandy at her office in London. I was on edge, fearing to hear that 'Oh, well.' Now that she had been home with her husband I feared she had changed her mind. Not a bit of it, she was—as ever, full of joyful enthusiasm. After we had spoken I wrote a love letter and put in it a peacock's feather and some pictures of Coombe Mill. Now that I was home, I had time to wonder what it was about Sandy that made me love her so much. I knew that at this stage it was mostly intuition, for I had no idea how she was in other circumstances. She must, like me, have many faults, but so far the only one I had noticed was an overactive attention to detail. I thought then, and still do, that on the crack of doom Sandy would first make sure to turn off the gas, lock the house door, and feed the cats before going to meet her fate. Cognitive dissonance made me disregard this trait as utterly unimportant, and to me she was everything I had ever dreamed of in a woman. Time has proved my intuition right.

Work as an independent and at a site so remote as Coombe Mill has always involved me in much travelling, and it was not necessary for me to change things so that I could meet Sandy. The next week I was due to go to Liverpool University to visit Ann Henderson-Sellers, the Professor of Geography, in her department there. Ann was amongst the most eminent of the climatologists in the UK and, sadly for us but not for her, we were about to lose her to Australia. This was my last chance to talk before she left the United Kingdom. I drove to Exeter on that Monday, caught the London train, and by 12.30 had arrived near the ticket office on Westminster Underground Station, where

Sandy had arranged to meet me. I was facing the entrance from Westminster Bridge Road, and full of that extraordinary euphoria of courtship, when Sandy appeared. She was to me an image of delight as she came through the station entrance, and we walked arm-in-arm across the bridge that Wordsworth found so entrancing in his sonnet:

> Earth has not anything to show more fair:
> Dull would he be of soul who could pass by
> A sight so touching in its majesty.

His excitement could not have matched mine as I floated, not walked, to the International Maritime Organization's (IMO) building on the Thames embankment. Sandy and Wilfrid had well-equipped offices there, as was befitting their formidable task of managing so magnificent a conference as the Global Forum, and I began to appreciate what a talented woman she was. We lunched at the IMO canteen with Wilfrid, and afterwards spent a few moments in Sandy's office in as close an embrace as we could manage in that busy place. Our bodies cried out for each other, and we arranged to spend a night at the Randolph again on Thursday, when I returned from my travels in the north. Sandy came with me to the bus stop outside the IMO and I left to catch the train from Euston station.

Mary Benbow, one of Ann's postgraduate students, met me at Liverpool station, and took me in her car to a hotel near the university where Ann had booked me in. She was unusually adult, well dressed, and well spoken for a postgraduate student. I was to be the external supervisor for her PhD examination and we had a working dinner at a nearby restaurant, while Mary showed me the computer printouts of her thesis work. She had chosen as her subject 'Modelling the dimethyl sulphide feedback loop'. I thought she was brave, in view of Gaia's unpopularity with academics and because I would have been disappointed by anything less than competent. The next day I spent with Ann at the university, and on Wednesday morning, Mary Benbow's father took me from my hotel by car to my next appointment at the Thornton Research Centre of Shell, near Chester.

Immediately on arrival, I went to see the Director, Colin Quinn. He was a good friend and I knew him well from the twenty-four years of visits to Thornton. One topic of our conversation was the corrosion of the steel legs of platforms in the North Sea used for oil and gas extraction. It was beginning to look, according to the Shell scientists, as if algal growth on the steel was to blame. I was then President of the Marine Biological Association, and my mind turned to the possibility of a research contract for its beleaguered laboratory in Plymouth. Neither Colin nor I then knew how crucial is the element iron for algal growth, and how well received would be the gift of a steel platform to hungry marine life. It was interesting to think that many years later Greenpeace and the German Greens were foolish enough to protest against the burial of the old Brent Spar rig in the ocean—almost as foolish as to protest on vegetarian grounds against feeding meat to the lions at the zoo. I had many friends at Thornton Research Centre, especially Ted Adlard, with whom I looked forward to talking about separation science, and hearing the gossip about Thornton and Shell.

The next day, Thursday, I continued my discussions in the morning, and after lunch the Shell driver took me to Runcorn station to catch the train back to London and to Sandy. We met on Euston station and it was the first of many mainline train station meetings—shades of *Brief Encounter*. We flew into each other's arms on all of these, regardless of suitcases and other passengers. Soon we were at Paddington and on the Oxford train bound for the Randolph again. After a brief and light meal in our suite we went to bed for an orgy of lovemaking that lasted all night. We were so physical that early in the morning, Sandy cricked her back, and pain spoilt what should have been a cosy and slow breakfast. Deeply concerned, I took the train to London with her, and saw her into a taxi for her journey home to Putney—at moments like this separation was extra hard to take.

Back at Coombe Mill, there was time to think about the extraordinary events of the past few weeks. The year before, when life had been unusually bleak, my friend Ricardo Guerrero had sent to cheer me a translation of a Homeric verse. It said, more or less, 'the man who is true to Gaia will be rewarded with all manner of material things but most of all with the best of women with whom he will enjoy a long and prosperous life'. In the discomforts of the 1980s, it came as a warm and kindly thought from a good friend in Barcelona, and though I welcomed it, I thought no more about it than I would the predictions of a fairground gypsy fortune-teller. Now it seemed there was the probability of a new life with a light and comely woman, whose quality and virtues matched my model of a perfect mate, and who I was in love with as never before. Anyone meeting Sandy would have seen a slender, good-looking woman with a warm and pleasing manner and whose voice had that melodious quality of a professional singer. I saw and heard her then, and still do, through numinous effulgence that defies and deplores description. I knew that together we were more than the sum of our two persons. We were a domain: something so good that we must sustain it for the rest of our life together.

My calendar was empty of visits away until May, when I was due to attend a Lindisfarne meeting in Perugia in Italy. I wondered whether Sandy would be able to spend the week away with me; it would be our honeymoon. I hoped that the leader of Lindisfarne, Bill Thompson, and the other Fellows would welcome us. By now we were so committed that, in the words of that song *Haitian Divorce*, 'So in love the preacher's face turned red.' True, we had both experienced many years of celibacy, through no fault of our spouses, who through illness and for physical reasons, were unable to participate. We both knew that what we did was wrong, but we were sure that it was more than the mere sexual gratification of a brief affair. We knew we had a real and deep relationship, a rare event in any lifetime. Now, as I write this nearly twelve years later, we are as much in love as ever, and we like to think that our domain is good enough in itself to have inspired and heartened those who witnessed it. Christine and John, who were close to me and to Helen, were shocked, but understood. My other children, Jane and Andrew, who lived far away and saw less of the long and hideous years of Helen's decline, were more censorious. They seemed to see me as a betrayer of their mother in her time of trial. Time seems to have healed their hurt and anger, and these hard feelings were, in any event, limited to my own children. Helen's sister, Betty, and David Orchard's sister, Sheila, are, and have been throughout the years, our closest friends.

Two weeks later we were at the Randolph again, before our morning flight to Rome en route to Perugia, where we would have seven whole days together. The thought of it was so good that its inevitable ending in separation again seemed infinitely far away. After landing in Rome, we took a long journey through heavy rain to Perugia—a delightful small hilltop town in Umbria, with narrow streets unspoilt by tackiness. I was fearful that Sandy and I would evoke a censorious reception, because many of the Fellows knew Helen, but the warmth of their welcome said much for the quality of the Fellowship. They seemed to recognize that here was something special and that they could defer condemnation, if needed, until later. I will never forget the warm support from Lynn Margulis and Nancy Todd, both Fellows of Lindisfarne. These two women were as physical as we were, and they both, in their own words said that ritual faithfulness in a celibate marriage was more than should be asked.

We attended the daily meetings and outings by Lindisfarne and went to the nearby towns of Gubbio and Assisi. Then, through that enhanced sexuality that is the by-product of romantic love, we spent the rest of the time in bed. Our friends were wise indeed, and left us to ourselves for the evenings. We would buy a picnic meal of fruit and bread and cheese and wine and retire to bed early to eat and then to explore our bodies and all the pleasures that they could offer. So it went on for a whole week, and by the end of it, our bonding was complete. We travelled back in the plane to London in a fearful anticipation of the separation to come, and I shall never forget the wrench of it at Heathrow as we parted: it felt like surgery without an anaesthetic. I took a taxi to Windsor Castle, where there was a meeting at St George's House on the church and the environment. I remember sitting in the pews of St George's Chapel, entranced by the heavenly singing of the choir—the state of love is a wonderful amplifier of the senses and the emotions. Next day, there were discussions among bishops, civil servants, theologians, and politicians on the role of the church in environmental affairs. At the coffee break, Professor Sam Berry introduced me to the Duke of Edinburgh, and we talked briefly about Gaia. Sunday lunch marked the end of the discussions and was a good meal of English food in St George's House.

One day in June I drove to Westbury station, met Sandy there, and took her to Bowerchalke and the countryside of the Chalke Valley and Cranborne Chase. We endured yet another agonized parting at Tisbury station, and then I drove on to Poole to see my old friend and long-time colleague, Brian Foulger. Brian and his wife Barbara both come from the English countryside, and represent the people I most admire. I have seen their family—Rebecca, Thomas, and Stephanie—grow from childhood to young adults, and in a way that any parent would envy. They are our closest of friends, and indeed Brian and Barbara were witnesses at our marriage in 1991.

After eating with the Foulger family in their spacious detached house in Netherbury, Brian and I went for a walk along the beach promenade. It was a four-mile walk at about four miles an hour, finishing with a modest cliff climb to Brian's car. Ordinarily we would have discussed science and our work the next day at the Ministry of Defence laboratory which Brian now ran, and I had founded in 1966. This time I had to tell him about Sandy, and it says much about Brian that he was warmly supportive of my enthusiastic babble which went on for most of the walk.

The summer went on like this, and Sandy and I came together in London hotels during my trips away from Devon. I tried to compensate by extra care for Helen at Coombe Mill. I still had no notion that her months were few and that she would soon die: instead, I saw her as a tough, cheerful fighter who would survive for many years. Sandy and I decided, now that we were committed, to find a place of our own where we could come together. We both found distasteful the anonymous, inappropriate, and expensive venue of hotels. I knew that I would never leave Helen while she was so much in need of me. She had a room at Coombe Mill purposely built as an office, from which she managed the affairs of our company, Brazzos Ltd., and she dealt with the enquiries about Gaia from scientists, theologians, and others all over the world; indeed, like me, her interest in Gaia gave her something rewarding to live for. The only thing we did not share was knowledge of the domain that Sandy and I occupied. Helen's physical health and capacity to walk deteriorated during 1988, but Margaret Sargent, who came from the village to help us, and Christine, were always there when we needed help. A friend in the village, Frances Edwards, who had been a hospital sister and who still worked at a clinic, began to provide support well beyond the expectations of friendship and I am truly indebted to her for her unstinted help during the last months of Helen's life. I really do not know how I would have managed without her.

During the greater part of my time at Coombe Mill in the second half of that year, the nights were made hideous by the need to treat Helen's bedsores and deal with her failing physical functions. So many things tortured the body of this woman who was the mother of my children, and who, for many years in the past, had been a loving wife. Surely, there are few diseases more cruel or distressing than multiple sclerosis, both for the sufferer and for the family. My brief stays away with Sandy in 1988 gave me the strength to cope with it. Significantly, those angry at my behaviour rarely came when she was ill. It is as in wartime: the most bloodthirsty and tribal of the combatants are the middle-aged and elderly civilians, living in safe havens far from the battlefields. Soldiers often see the enemy as men like themselves.

Helen spoke these words while we had tea in bed on Wednesday 3 November 1988:

> I always knew as a girl that I was not physically strong. My only ambition was to travel and have adventures, not to work. I thought that Jim was the right man for me because I wanted with him to have a go at the impossible and make life one long adventure. I think Jim needed me because he had such a poor self-image and always under-rated his ability. I found Jim's obliviousness—self-absorption to the point of ignoring my own weaknesses—valuable. Multiple sclerosis was in my body from the beginning and the worst thing that could have happened to me was to marry someone who cosseted me and took charge of everything. Life for me has been an endless fight to hold the line against encroaching disability. I knew that I could never win—only hold on until the next attack. I compare my marriage with that of my sister Betty and her husband George. He is wonderfully solicitous, always unselfishly helping both Betty and me. He takes charge of every movement and always anticipates our needs; he is always there when we need him. I think it would have been disastrous for me to be married to George. I needed someone like Jim who never seemed to know I wanted him and who expected me to fend for myself. I would have died long ago if I had not had to fight. I think that Jim is just like me in that way and has fought as hard.

I knew that the wishes, expressed by family members and by our physicians, to move Helen to a nursing home were wrong, that come what may she ought to be able to live here at her beloved Coombe Mill. One of the great cruelties of modern societies is the wish to put old people away in places that are neat and hygienic and where they will be well looked after by professionals. This is, to my mind, an imprisonment because as one grows older, the sense of well-being depends on the familiar, comfortable things that one has known and has grown to love and to live with. I think it is far better to die in discomfort in one's own home than be 'cared for' in a perfect clinical environment. In any event, there were always John and Margaret at home, and Frances in the village in case of emergencies, and I would be there at least half the time.

Then, one evening in January, when I returned to Coombe Mill, Helen was in her downstairs room in her new adjustable bed, but in great distress. She was breathing with rapid sighing respiration, was feverish, and it looked to me as if she had pneumonia. I called our physician, Alan Edwards, who came immediately, examined her, and called for admission to the Plymouth Derriford Hospital. An ambulance came soon afterwards and we travelled in it to the hospital. The paramedic on the ambulance gave her oxygen, and she was much improved and even annoyed to be in hospital. They gave her antibiotics and slowly, over the weeks, she seemed to improve. Then there was a telephone call from the hospital to tell me that she was gravely ill and would I return at once to see her. I flew back from London to Plymouth Airport, which is conveniently almost opposite the hospital, and there I saw the physician in charge. He told me that they could do no more for Helen and that she would almost certainly die within a few days.

When I saw her she seemed so normal that it was hard for me to believe the physician's words, and I went back to speak with him. But he confirmed them and showed me an X-ray of her lungs. I still could not believe that she was dying, and asked if it wouldn't be better to have her transferred home, because even if she were to die she would be a lot happier there. His response was that she was so ill he doubted whether she would survive the transport back. I think I should have insisted on her return home; some hospitals are grim places to die in. But in four days, she did, although unconscious and therefore not uncomfortable. All of my children were there, around the bedside and, with the best of intentions, Christine called Sandy to come to Plymouth, although not to the hospital, because she saw me as so distressed as to need the comfort that only Sandy could give. Helen died at about 5 pm in the afternoon of 4 February. After this, my mind was in that kind of turmoil seen in chemistry when a reaction in a flask has started and the heat generated makes it go faster and faster, until the whole thing boils vigorously and sometimes bursts forth from the flask. Grief, relief, sadness, and guilt were all reacting together in my mind.

Next morning the cloudy grey skies of English winter matched our sadness, but the task of arranging the funeral, and dealing with the paperwork that comes after any death, gave us no time to concentrate on grieving. There is something therapeutic about the routine of recording and recognizing death. Sandy and I went first to the registrar's office, and then to an undertaker who had served when my mother died in 1981 in Plymouth. He was unusual: he had previously worked as a physicist, but said he preferred and found much more fulfilling the life of undertaking. He was amazingly good at his job, and knew exactly how to handle me and to keep a balance between a proper concern and the practical details. He was entirely free of sentimentality, something that I dreaded. I told him of Helen's wish for burial at Coombe Mill, and he was well informed and helpful about this unusual request. The Reverend Alan Brownridge, the Vicar of St Giles on the Heath, was wonderfully comforting and helpful to me although we were not his regular parishioners. It was a full day and I did not return to Coombe Mill until late in the afternoon.

The days before the funeral I stayed at Coombe Mill with Jane, my daughter, to keep me company. Helen's grave is at a high spot, where she often used to sit and look over the house and the land. There is a memorial seat nearby for both her and for David Orchard, Sandy's husband, who died of cancer at Coombe Mill a year later. Margaret and John tend the grave. From then on, Sandy and I were together. We flitted between St Mark's Road and Coombe Mill. In March, we felt a great need for a break away and took a week's holiday in the sunshine of Lanzarote. It did much to clear the miasma of bad grief that still seemed to linger over Helen's death. It must be rare to fall deeply in love and establish a new firm bond when both former partners are dying, yet we did rise, phoenix like, from those ashes and today eleven years later we are still flying. Love has been a great teacher, and has revealed the world of literature and music that previously I had been too busy to enter. We confirmed our commitment by marriage in February 1991 and, as a wholly unexpected consequence, I found myself a part of an American family. Sandy's sister Phyllis and her husband Tom live in the suburbs of St Louis, as does her brother Harley and his wife Vernell. During the five years I lived and worked in the United States I was no more than a resident alien and, although I paid my taxes, I never felt a part of the nation. But when I became Tom Hollman's brother-in-law, things changed. No more for me the long and lonely isolation of hotel rooms; together Sandy and I share the warmth of a good American family and we seem in our hearts, although not legally, to hold dual citizenship and be part of both our great nations. We applaud the good things we encounter on our visits and are concerned about the less than good.

Illness had made the 1980s a time of painful self-absorption, whose bounds were limited as if by the straitjacket of an insect's pupa. The 1990s set me free to soar like a dragonfly and I saw for the first time the political world, somewhere scientists rarely go. As an Englishman I always, even as a young socialist, regarded the aristocracy as part of the native scene and a favourite humorist, Osbert Lancaster, used to captivate me with his sketches of the fictional Lord and Lady Little-hampton. I have no idea why I found their world—one that PG Wodehouse occupied—so funny, but I did. The aristocracy was then, and even more now, like a species of endangered, brightly plumaged birds. I shall be sorry to see them go from the House of Lords, and cannot believe that either an elected or an appointed second chamber will be as fair and as representative as is our jury of hereditary peers. Biodiversity is a natural state and a better one than the featureless monoculture of egalitarianism.

I first met Henry Bentinck, the Earl of Portland, in 1991 when I was spending a few weeks at Schumacher College near Totnes in Devon. I was holding forth on Gaia. Henry had chosen to listen to what I had to say, and he quizzed me afterwards, wanting to know how such a view affected our vision of the future. He wanted to know if I had any practical suggestions about how to live with the Earth. It did not take me long to discover that he was someone I could talk to for, in spite of our different backgrounds, we shared in common a serious interest in Green affairs, and soon we became close friends. Henry was one of those rare men who had the courage to admit his mistakes and turn error to advantage, and this requires integrity not mere obstinate consistency. He thought it right on humanitarian grounds to be a conscientious objector at the start of the last world war, but saw the error of this choice when he came to understand that the Second World War was quite different from the First. He gave up his conscientious objection when he saw that our own hard-won civilization was in danger.

In the same way, the enthusiasm we shared for humanism, with its exclusive belief in human rights, changed in the 1960s when we realized that there was more to life on Earth than the welfare of people. Human rights were not enough. We knew that if our grand-children were to inherit an Earth worth living on, the relentless growth of population, and the unending exploitation of the natural world, must cease. I think the fact that he was soon due to take his place among his peers concentrated his mind. He was much con-cerned about his maiden speech and sought my advice on the science of it. He wanted it to mark a change in the attitude of the second chamber—a change towards a better understanding of the environ-ment. He delivered a radical speech that was refreshingly free of party political dogma. Before he gave it, only one other British politician had spoken clearly and seriously on global environmental affairs, and that was Margaret Thatcher. In her speeches to the Royal Society and to the United Nations Assembly, she was the first to warn of the dangers of global change that loomed in the next century. She predicted that the environment would eventually usurp the political agenda. John Prescott's splendid speech at the Kyoto conference, nearly ten years later, confirmed her prediction, and our record in environmental affairs. We have been fortunate to have some of the world's best environmental politicians and it is good to know that Henry was among them. We will always remember the way that he brought life into mere history. On one occasion, Henry told us of his aunt who lived in the Netherlands and who had had the Kaiser to tea one afternoon in 1918, when he was obliged to flee Germany. From his personal tales we began to see why England has such a struggle coming to terms with Europe.

It is unusual to make close friends in the seventh decade. Perhaps our unconscious recognition that it could not be for long made it the more worthwhile. Even so, I wish that we had met earlier. The few glimpses I had of his life in Tasmania and in advertising revealed a man who was much after my own heart in other ways than Green politics. Old-fashioned dogma of the Left makes us think of Earls as belted and presiding over thousands of acres of land. In fact, Henry and Jenny's home at Little Cudworthy was comparable with Coombe Mill. He had worked as a BBC producer and had enlivened the words of commercials; I can never now browse the shelves of a supermarket without thinking of Henry's campaign for 'Mr Kipling's exceedingly good cakes'. He had a true feeling for the natural world and was a wonderful companion to have on a walk through the countryside, someone with whom to share the pleasure of its beauty and the pain of its degradation. He was someone who knew how to be outrageous for a purpose. The Earl of Portland died in January 1997. Sandy and I take the gift of these last seven years' acquaintance with Henry and Jenny as something that has enriched our lives. We miss him sorely.

I have often walked along Whitehall from Trafalgar Square to Old Queen Street, where the Medical Research Council once had its head office. At the west end of Whitehall, not far from the Cenotaph, is Downing Street, that small street with the houses of the Prime Minister and the Chancellor of the Exchequer. One morning in the autumn of 1988, a letter arrived from Downing Street, inviting Helen and me to a dinner with the Prime Minister on the occasion of a visit by the President of Bangladesh. I suspect that this invitation came through the suggestion of Sir Crispin Tickell. He became an advisor to Prime Minister Margaret Thatcher on climate change, and through his introduction I had the chance to meet her on three occasions. Helen was too ill to travel, so in October 1988 I arrived alone by taxi at the Whitehall entrance to Downing Street. The policeman there checked my letter of invitation and pointed me towards another policeman at the door of Number 10. It seemed sad that not many years before I could have just walked up to the door and knocked, but terrorism has made this impossible. Once inside they directed me to the stairs that went to the reception room where the Prime Minister and her husband, Dennis Thatcher, received me, as did the President of Bangladesh and his wife. There were perhaps fifty in the reception room. Not knowing what lay ahead, I took an orange juice and chatted with a couple about the health service. Soon they led us to our places for dinner at the long table. The Prime Minister and her distinguished guests were at the head; I was somewhere half way down. Seated next to me was a senior civil servant from the Ministry of Health, and over dinner we talked more about the health service, a topic that you will have noticed is close to my heart. I began to think that this had been a wonderful experience, something to remember as a high point of my life. An invitation to No. 10 and a meeting, however brief, with that powerful lady who ran our country, was something to tell my grandchildren about.

Then we retired to the sitting room for coffee. I was standing alone against a wall taking in the faces of politicians and others I recognized but did not know. Then, suddenly the Prime Minister moved rapidly across the room and said, 'Professor Lovelock, I've been so looking forward to meeting you', and at once started a conversation that seemed to go on for at least fifteen minutes. It was mainly on the environment and she wanted to know what I thought should be done about it. I expressed my views as forcibly as I could. I was delighted to find that she had read my book and had questions on it. When she left, I found myself surrounded by other people. Her obvious interest in this otherwise unknown man stirred the gathering. They plied me with questions about what we had discussed. There were several consequences of this meeting; perhaps the most important was the invitation to a seminar at Downing Street hosted by the Prime Minister.

On 26 April 1989 I was back at No. 10 Downing Street, this time for the seminar on climate change. Margaret Thatcher is one of the few politicians with an informed scientific understanding of the natural environment. She had the advantage of training in science at Oxford, where she took an MA and BSc. Her subject, chemistry, is the most transdisciplinary of the sciences: to be a good chemist you need a working knowledge of both physics and biology. Most physicists and biologists can get by very well in the smaller world of their own discipline alone. Margaret Thatcher had the wisdom to see, as she put it, that the environment would usurp the political agenda in the next decade. When she said this in her speech before the Royal Society on 27 September 1988, few believed her. That she was right can be seen from the column inches of newsprint and the media time now spent on topics like pollution, Greenpeace, El Niño, fuel-efficient cars, the greenhouse effect, etc. No noticeable environmental disaster has yet happened, but it would be a brave forecaster who predicted that we would not have one in the next one hundred years.

Number 10 is just like that fictional time and space machine, the Tardis, created by Terry Nation in the television series, *Dr Who*. A small door with a constabulary presence opens into the vestibule, which itself leads to an endless series of connected rooms and corridors. I seem to recall on one occasion entering at No. 10 and leaving from part of the Cabinet offices in Whitehall. This time they took me to a conference room equipped with rows of chairs and a raised platform, on which the Prime Minister and a few members of the Cabinet sat. There was an overhead and a slide projector. It was, in fact, just like any other small, select, scientific meeting room. The familiar faces around me of British and American atmospheric scientists heightened the feeling of familiarity. Among them was Robert Watson, part of the American contingent, and I remember Sir Crispin Tickell and Sir John Houghton from our country. Margaret Thatcher handled the meeting as if she had spent her life in science. Robert Watson said to me afterwards that it seemed as though she had been running scientific meetings all her life. He added, 'Is there a head of state anywhere who could take on a group like this and make you feel that she knew what she was talking about?' There were about three set-piece lectures on the greenhouse problem, but we spent most of the time in a general discussion of the problems that lay ahead and what could be done about them. At the end of the meeting, Sir Martin Holgate made a concise and accurate summary.

The meeting closed at about 1 pm and we all went to lunch in one of the dining rooms of No. 10. This room was set out with a series of round tables, each seating about eight. There was a Cabinet minister or senior politician at each of them. I was lucky enough to be at the Prime Minister's table, along with Sir Crispin Tickell, Lord Marshall, Lord Porter and Sir James Goldsmith. During lunch Margaret Thatcher asked, 'Do any of you know if there is anything in cold fusion?' Without thinking, I answered promptly, 'Prime Minister, there is nothing in it. Pons and Fleischman have made a mistake, and I think I know what it was.' Lord Porter immediately intervened, 'You cannot say things like that, Lovelock. They are distinguished scientists. Fleischman is an FRS and they have both published peer-reviewed papers on cold fusion.' I think I replied, 'In ten years it will all be forgotten.' Then Margaret Thatcher added, 'Good, then we can ignore cold fusion.' (Those who want to know more about my reasons for doubting cold fusion should go back to the first section of Chapter 10.) The discussion moved on. Looking back, I am sorry that I was right, for cold fusion would have been a great boon. After lunch, there was an opportunity to chat with the other participants, and we left by yet another exit to avoid the press. It did not work: they quizzed me but I could say very little. The meeting was held under Chatham House rules; that is to say, we could quote what we had said ourselves, but not repeat anyone else's comments. The Prime Minister sent a hand-written letter of condolence when Helen died, and later that year a friendly postcard when she visited the Jet Propulsion Laboratories. For the brief time during the last months of her premiership, I enjoyed the warmth of her patronage.

Together with Professor Sam Berry and Lord Nathan, the Cabinet Office sent me to Brussels in 1989. We were the UK representatives at an EEC meeting on environmental ethics. We met and dined in an old Belgian palace in its own grounds, not the high-rise faceless monument of the Berlaymont. I think I contributed very little to the proceedings on ethics. I left the expression of our private discussions on the subject to Lord Nathan, a distinguished lawyer, and to Sam Berry, unusually both a theologian and a professor of biology. Gaia is not about human affairs, except where, like now, they impinge upon the health of the planet. Gaia requires us to live sensibly with the Earth, and this would require that we restored the natural habitats we have destroyed to feed people. This requires politically difficult choices, such as giving up meat eating or reducing our numbers to a third or less. I could not think of any way to introduce topics like these into the serious discussions in Brussels. They were wholly about human affairs, and when they did talk about the environment, it was in human terms, such as how to deal with urban pollution. At lunch at the palace, I sat opposite Jacques Delors, the formidable chief officer of the EEC. I had a strong impression, as he gazed across the table at me, that he was daring me to speak on Gaia. Sadly, I did not take the opportunity offered. After lunch, they took us back in VIP style to the Brussels airport and there the three of us shopped. Sam and I took back engraved glass figures of birds; mine was an owl. Sandy met me at the London City airport and we returned to our flat in St Mark's Road.

Following this turbulent start, my seventh decade has calmed into the happiest years of a lifetime. The highlights were the receipt of four International Prizes, several honorary degrees and four visits to Japan; I will conclude this chapter by telling you about them.

My relationship with academia has been an uneasy one. I was on the inside as a Professor in the 1960s at Baylor College of Medicine and loosely attached as a visiting professor for twenty-five years at Reading University and for shorter spells at the University of Houston and the University of Washington in Seattle, but I am too much a loner ever to feel a part of collegiate life. Therefore, I have been humbled and made grateful by the generosity of academics at the eight universities that awarded me honorary doctorates; Exeter, Kent, East Anglia, Edinburgh, Colorado, East London, Stockholm, and Plymouth. The most exciting of these was the high ceremony of the Doctor of Science degree I received from Stockholm University in 1991. The pageantry, the sounds of gunfire and trumpet calls, the award of the degree and the gold ring that I have worn ever since, made me aware that I was truly married to science. I remembered with affection my many friends among Swedish scientists and my visits to their country.

In the spring of 1990, a telephone call from the Royal Netherlands Academy of Arts and Sciences brought the stunningly joyful news that I was to receive the Amsterdam Prize for the Environment at a ceremony in The Hague in October of that year. My friend and colleague Sir John Cornforth had put my name forward several years previously but I had never expected the prize and it was the first intimation that the 1990s were to be the decade when my researches during the long years in the wilderness of independence were recognized. Following a letter of invitation from Mr. AH Heineken, chairman of the Amsterdam Foundation for the Environment, Sandy and I travelled to the Netherlands a week before the ceremonies. Professor Kuenen who represented the Academy and was our close friend and guide throughout our stay in the Netherlands met us at Schipol Airport. I lectured at universities at Groningen in the north and Rotterdam in the south, and I received the prize from Prince Claus of the Netherlands at an immaculate ceremony in the Knight's Hall of the Binnenhof at The Hague. Sandy and I enjoyed a private banquet afterwards with the winners of the other Amsterdam Prizes, hosted by Mr Heineken. My prize lecture was entitled 'In Search of the Superorganism' and given at a meeting of the Royal Netherlands Academy of Arts and Sciences.

The pursuit of prestigious prizes has never been part of my life as a scientist: had it been I would never have chosen to work independently. The award of the Amsterdam Prize warmed and contented me and I expected no more, but in August 1996 a fax from the Volvo Foundation invited me to call them about some important news; it was that their Jury had selected me to receive the 1996 Volvo Environment Prize. The citation singled out the ECD and its applications as my contribution to environmental science that had brought me the Prize, but to my delight, they also mentioned Gaia. We flew to Brussels in October, where I delivered my lecture and received the prize from Princess Désirée, Baroness Silfverschiöld of Sweden. I was deeply moved to be so recognized, and especially since I worked outside the main body of science. What made the Volvo Prize ceremony so memorable for me was the number of scientist friends who took the time and expense to come to Brussels on that day.

In December 1995 our now deeply respected fax machine presented a message from the Nonino Foundation asking if I would accept the decision of their jury to award me the Nonino Prize, and if so would I come with Sandy to Percoto in Italy where the ceremony would take place. We flew to Venice in January 1996 and Antonella Nonino welcomed us and took us in her car to Percoto where we stayed with the Nonino family for four days before the ceremonies. It is a great privilege to live with a family in a distant country, and there is no better way of getting to know and understand another culture. As we shared meals with the Nonino family and talked with them late into the evening, we learnt a great deal more about Italy than years of visits had provided. The Nonino Prize, a literary and philosophical award, was for my first book, *Gaia: A New Look at Life on Earth*. The Foundation awarded the prize at a wonderful ceremony held at the Nonino Grappa distillery. Their grappa was a blithe spirit of quality equal to, or better than, the best of single malt whiskies, and made by a family enterprise. Other winners of the prize included the cultural historian, Edward Said, the Italian author, Gian Luigi Beccaria and the horticultural scientist, Furio Bianco. At the banquet afterwards we met past winners and such luminaries as the conductor Claudio Abbado.

The most extraordinary events of my seventh decade took place in that distant land, Japan, and somehow they typify the extravagant joy that came after three score years and ten. Those who have travelled this far with me will be aware of my lack of respect for time and I am starting my account of Japan with our last visit there in 1997. I have to do this to avoid what would otherwise be an anticlimax.

The culminating event of our Japanese period came modestly. In May 1997 the fax machine at Coombe Mill gurgitated a sheet of paper from the Asahi Glass Foundation. They were frequent correspondents, and often sought nominations for their prestigious Blue Planet Prize. I walked over to Sandy, holding the fax in my hand, as she was discussing the day's meal with Margaret Sargent. Not wishing to disturb them, I started to read the fax when a sentence leapt at me from the page: 'Let us know if you are willing to accept the prize and are free to come to Tokyo in November for the ceremonies.' I was overjoyed and blurted out to Sandy, 'It has happened again, another prize!' The previous year, in similar circumstances, our fax had delivered the news of my award of the Volvo Prize for the Environment.

It was wholly unexpected and left us in a happy daze trying to come to terms with our good fortune. The Asahi Glass Foundation established the Blue Planet Prize in commemoration of the 1991 Rio Conference on the Global Environment. They award two Prizes annually, one to the organization and one to the individual that did most, in the opinion of their jury, to further the aims of the Rio Conference. I was moved and honoured to have my work on the ECD and on Gaia singled out as worthy of the Prize, and in October 1997 we flew from Heathrow in two adjacent seats in the first-class cabin of a British Airways 747 on our way to Tokyo. The twelve-hour flight, mostly over what was once the Soviet Union, would have been hard for me to endure in the economy section of the plane. In our section, with seats that reclined completely to form a bed, it was a pleasant interlude. We arrived at Narita at about midday local time, and were met by the Foundation's representative, Mr Nobuaki Kunii, and taken to a fine suite in Tokyo's Imperial Hotel.

The organization chosen to receive the 1997 Prize was the environmental charity Conservation International, whose representative was Dr Russell A Mittermeier. We each received the Prize at an impeccably staged ceremony in the Imperial Hotel, and for me it included a congratulatory letter from my past Prime Minister, Margaret Thatcher, read out in the preamble to the award. The British Ambassador to Japan, Sir David Wright, then gave his panegyric, and to my delight read a congratulatory letter from our present Prime Minister, Tony Blair. Dr Jiro Furumoto, Chairman of the Foundation, handed us the Prize—a glass sphere with an emblem engraved on it to represent humankind. It was as well that we had rehearsed it in the morning, for it was so heavy that we feared to drop it and see it roll onto the feet of their Royal Highnesses, the Prince and Princess Akishino. All went well and we were introduced to their Highnesses at the reception afterwards. My granddaughter, Mary Flynn, and so many of our Japanese friends of earlier visits were there to join with us in celebrating that wonderful occasion. It was a fitting conclusion to four visits to Japan initiated by that singular and honourable man, Hideo Itokawa. We dearly wished that he could have come to the ceremonies but, sadly, he had suffered a stroke a year earlier.

After the Prize ceremonies, we spent several more days in Japan. Our friend Yumi Akimoto, President and CEO of Mitsubishi Materials Corporation, had organized a meeting on Gaia science, and we spent a productive day with Japanese scientists. The following day, Yumi and Sadako took us to see a traditional Kabuki play, and it moved us deeply. Sandy and I were delighted to go and enjoy our friends' company, but I wondered, before we arrived at the theatre, if it would be one of those quiet cultural affairs where one politely watches an incomprehensible display of costumes. We should have known our hosts better: the Kabuki consisted of a series of entrancing and captivating parables, acted out so well that our lack of Japanese was no handicap. The play gave us a feeling for Japanese history and made us realize how much we in England have lost in the dubious deconstruction of our past.

We went on to see our friends Yasuaki and Keiko Maeda at the Osaka Prefecture University in Sakai, and there renewed our acquaintance with Dr Kozo Ishida of the Horiba Company, before leaving from Kansai airport on the long Trans-Siberian journey home.

An earlier visit to Japan was in 1993, when the Japanese Atomic Industrial Forum invited me to present a paper at their meeting in

Yokohama. I was glad to have a chance to express in public my strong support for nuclear energy. I expect that some time in the next century, when the adverse effects of climate change begin to bite, people will look back in anger at those who now so foolishly continue to pollute by burning fossil fuel instead of accepting the beneficence of nuclear power. I often think of the Green Movement as some global over-anxious mother figure who is so concerned about small risks that she ignores the real dangers that loom. As in the biblical fable, we strain at the gnats of Chernobyl, and swallow the camel of massive pollution by our carbon-burning civilization. It was after the meeting that we first met Dr Yumi Akimoto, who, I was delighted to find, shared my views not only on nuclear power but on Gaia as well. He has expressed them in his book, *Towards an Elastic 21ˢᵗ Century*. We went with him to his home in Kamakura, where he and his wife, Sadako, made us most welcome. I learnt from Yumi that he had been a naval cadet on an island in Hiroshima Bay when the first nuclear weapon exploded in anger. He saw the mushroom cloud and had a real sense of what a nuclear war means, but in no way did the experience diminish his support for nuclear power. He shared with me his view that the best way to dispose of the huge stockpiles of weapon-grade plutonium and uranium would be to burn them in power stations. After our morning of discussion, Yumi and Sadako took us to the shrine at Kamakura followed by a wonderful traditional Japanese meal.

The Akimotos and the Japanese scientist Shigeru Moriyama came to our Gaia meeting in Oxford in 1994. And in 1995 we enjoyed at Coombe Mill visits from Yumi and Sadako Akimoto and from Professor Yasuaki Maeda and his wife Keiko. The Maedas invited us back to Japan in 1996. After arriving at Tokyo Narita airport, they took us to the Imperial Hotel opposite the Royal Palace, where they accommodated us in a wholly delightful suite. We now looked on Japan as some kind of magic kingdom, where always we are greeted as honoured guests.

We all know how Japanese products excel in their attention to detail. Before Japan became the industrial giant it now is, we suffered consumer electronics that seemed to fail as often as they worked. Now, thanks to Japanese diligence, we expect our televisions and high-fi equipment to work unceasingly without breakdown. Less well known is the fact that the same painstaking attention to detail pervades Japanese life. Nowhere ever have we enjoyed such unstinted care and attention as from our friends in Japan. One Saturday not long after our arrival, Yumi had arranged a meeting of scientists interested in Gaia. Even though it was a small select gathering in the hotel, there was simultaneous translation of all we said. Inside our air-conditioned meeting, all was calm and thoughtful, while outside a typhoon raged. After lunch, we briefly felt the fierce wind and horizontally driving rain before entering the cars organized by Yumi to take us to a traditional Japanese guesthouse, owned by his company, for dinner. I have grown to love and feel at home in the calm atmosphere of a Japanese banquet. Kneeling for me comes naturally, and my *yukata* sits comfortably on me after the restriction of Western jacket and tie, and, for me, Japanese food is the best of all.

Next day our hosts took us to Hakone, on the Isu peninsula south of Tokyo. Isu is a resort region rather like our own Lake District in Cumbria, and we went first to the vast crater of a not-so extinct volcano, now a pleasure lake on which sail replica galleons. We boarded one and sailed across to lunch at a hotel on the opposite shore. After lunch, we went by limousine to the Gora Kadan Inn. The Inn is a felicitous combination of Italian style and Japanese tradition, and its owner a delightful young Japanese woman who had inherited it from her father. In the spacious suite of rooms she had chosen for us were our personal attendants for the visit. They performed the necessary task of dressing and preparing us in formal Japanese garments for the banquet soon to be enjoyed, and then took us to a private banqueting room where we joined Sadako, Yumi and Hideo Kobayashi, Yumi's personal assistant, and our host the innkeeper. There were ten courses of Japanese food, exquisite in both style of preparation and taste, and as expected of a perfect meal we were satiated only by the final course. It was a happy occasion, with much laughter, and one we shall never forget. The next morning we said our farewells to our host and to the ladies who had so well cared for us. We went by car to the Hakone Open Air Museum, a beautifully landscaped park at the foot of Mount Fujiyama, in which were tastefully displayed contemporary sculptures by the most distinguished eastern and western artists. We travelled by car from the museum to Nagoya and took the Shinkansen to Osaka. It was good to see Yasuaki Maeda's welcoming face on the platform. He took us to the Osaka Imperial Hotel and to another suite of huge dimensions, in which were two WCs, the latest high-tech versions, and daunting to use. Beside the seat was an illuminated panel of Japanese characters and, when I cautiously pressed one of these, a gentle fountain of warm water began to wash my backside. Another button released a stream of warm dry air. I never dared to try the other six characters.

After breakfast next day we were delighted to find our friend Ralph Cicerone, now Chancellor of the University of California at Irvine, waiting in the hotel lobby, together with Keiko Maeda and two young men from the university. We went with them to the university at Sakai, and there gave our public lectures on environmental affairs, and talked with scientists there. In the afternoon, we went to Kyoto and to the offices of the firm Horiba, famous for its analytical instruments; here I lectured on the ECD. Dr Kozo Ishida took us to a small but exquisite restaurant in the old section of Kyoto. Here we enjoyed an unforgettable meal and an evening of happy conversation. The talk, most unusually for businessmen, covered everything except business. The courtesy and consideration of our Horiba hosts touched us; in a lifetime of business meals, this was a rare exception to the usual incessant shoptalk. Lectures delivered, next day we started a round of sightseeing. Yasuaki and Keiko were wonderfully generous in their efforts to show us the many treasures of Kyoto. They took us to Nara, and we spent much of the day visiting the shrines and temples; unlike the urban and industrial Japan that we knew, Nara was unusually open, and there were green park areas, many trees, and even deer wandering at will.

We often had to pinch ourselves to make sure we were in a real, not some dream, world. What we had imagined as a typical scientist's trip to a lab in another country turned out to be a week among the historical treasures of Japan. We climbed the steps of the White Castle of Himeji and walked the paths of the gardens. One day we took the train to Hiroshima, where we were to stay the night. No one in western civilization can visit Hiroshima without some sense of shame: here at one site was commemorated the greatest triumph of 20th-century science and its most profound misapplication. The sensitivity the Japanese display in their park and Peace Museum deeply moved us. In so many nations, it would have been either a call for vengeance or a whinge of victimhood. Here the simple message was: in war, we all do dreadful things. The next morning we boarded a boat and set off to the island of Miyajima and its maritime shrine. Back in Hiroshima in the evening, we were surprised, and delighted, to be the guests of the Gaia Fan Club. In Japan, they are not frightened of the word Gaia, and use it in the title of a popular natural history programme on television, *The Gaia Symphony*. It was a pleasure to meet and talk with the producer, Jin Tatsumura.

On the last night of our visit to Japan, Professor Maeda and his wife, Keiko, invited us to have supper in his lab. Keiko prepared the meal with the help of the students, and it was splendid Japanese home cooking, with vast pans cooking gently on the lab hot plates and venting their most unscientific fragrance. There could have been no better way of welcoming us into the life of a Japanese university. Our lack of Japanese mattered less here, for half the students were from other Asian countries, and many spoke only their own native language with a smattering of Japanese. They asked many questions during the meal, and Dr Bando of the university acted as translator of both science and language. Their search for knowledge was impressive and there was a complete absence of cynicism; hardly had I swallowed one noodle before they posed the next question. I have never liked lecturing—it gives me no pleasure whatever—and an hour's lecture takes me weeks to prepare. By contrast, I thoroughly like talking with young men and women and trying to answer their questions, and in so doing I often find important gaps in my own knowledge. There was a family feeling in this university group, one of mutual affection and respect, and if this is representative of Japan, one needs look no further for its success. As always with Japan, our departure from Kansai Airport was a sad occasion. Surrounded by our friends it seemed almost a monstrous discourtesy to board the plane.

These wonderful visits to Japan started in the summer of 1991, when a fax came from Fred Myers, an American friend who lives in Tokyo and whom I had met at the United Nations University in Tokyo in the 1980s. Fred conveyed an invitation from a distinguished Japanese gentleman who was interested in Gaia. Would I like to visit Japan and lecture on Gaia in 1992? I was due at the time for more urethral surgery, and not in the mood for long-distance air travel. My reply was not encouraging, and I added that Sandy and I always travelled together and we had no wish to be parted. Another and more specific fax arrived from Fred, saying that his Japanese friend was Hideo Itokowa, head of the Systems Research Institute of Japan, and that if we came there would be two return tickets for us and a lecture fee of at least £10,000. Had we known Hideo Itokowa as well as we do now, I believe we would have travelled to Japan by any means, no matter how uncomfortable. But money does speak and the conditions offered were irresistible.

In September 1992 we started our journey to Japan by flying to Philadelphia for the semi-annual visit to Hewlett Packard, and from there to Chicago and Tokyo on a long fourteen-hour flight on United Airlines. We left Chicago's spacious airport early in the afternoon and arrived in Tokyo at dusk on the next day. We had reclined our seats to the horizontal position and slept for much of the journey across the Pacific. After passing through customs at Narita Airport, we saw Fred Myers waiting, and with him were Hideo Itokawa and two young Japanese friends. There were also the media, with television cameras and journalists to interview us. We were warmly welcomed and, with our bags, taken in a limousine to the New Otani Hotel in the centre of Tokyo, a journey that took nearly two hours. At the hotel, a suite of rooms awaited us, more luxurious than any we had previously known. After an hour to settle in, our hosts invited us to a meal in the hotel's Chinese restaurant. We are immune to jet lag, that misery that comes from travelling by air across time zones, but knew that to be fresh the next day, it would be wise because of our long journey, to stay awake until our usual bedtime of 10 pm. At about 8 o'clock our escorts, Jiro Hata and Hiroshi Yajima, knocked at our door and invited us to accompany them to the private dining room. By now, although dazed, we realized that we were experiencing a royal welcome. These young men were providing care with a degree of attention that made us feel truly wanted, and it was to be like this throughout the whole of the two-week visit. They were there always, ready to carry, to pay and to meet our needs. I began to understand why the rich and the royals never carry money. They do not need to.

Dinner was in a room with a large round table and seated around were our host, Hideo Itokowa, and his friend, Takeshi Kanai. Next to them was a young woman violinist and her husband, and the timber industry's chairman, Motomasa Shimada, and our young friends, Jiro Hata and Hiroshi Yajima. The meal somehow combined the intimacy of a family occasion with the delights of Asian cuisine. It lasted about two hours, by which time we were ready for bed, and knew that this was going to be the most memorable of visits.

There was nothing planned next day until 10 am, when there were two newspaper interviews, and they advised us to sleep late and catch up for any lost sleep on the journey. Hideo invited us to join him and a friend in the hotel dining room for lunch. Our young friends took us there, and to our surprise we found that the huge dining room of the New Otani Hotel was deserted. There were a few people standing outside, all men, but the room itself was empty, and it seemed odd. Sandy and I were taken in and seated at a table with room for about ten. Our two escorts moved to another table some distance away. Soon Hideo joined us and said his friend would be arriving shortly. A well-dressed man wearing one of the most attractive ties I have ever seen came in, and sat next to Hideo, and opposite Sandy and me. Hideo introduced his friend to us and told us that he was the Japanese Finance Minister, Tsutomu Hata, later to be Prime Minister of Japan. We were flabbergasted. I tried to imagine a Japanese couple unable to speak English seated in a similar room with the Chancellor of the Exchequer facing them. The smooth, almost casual way that we had been elevated to the highest levels in Japan overwhelmed us. Hideo was nothing if not a talented showman, and his grin as he watched across the table made me wonder what would be coming next. After the presentation of gifts—an inscribed collection of Japanese stamps—we were served lunch and started our meal.

The main thrust of the conversation with Tsutomu Hata was about the American super-conducting super-collider experiment. This was a colossal science undertaking due in the next few years in Texas. The Finance Minister wanted my opinion on its scientific merit, because Japan might have to pay several billion dollars towards its cost. I have long believed, and have often expressed the opinion that the value of a scientific project is not commensurate with its cost. Perhaps there is an unrecognized law of economics 'The lower the cost the greater the payoff '. I came to this view because few of the large steps in science have cost much. Consider Newton, who did his thinking in his spare time, outside his employment as a government advisor. Consider Darwin, who developed his theory while employed as a naturalist on the *Beagle*. Consider Einstein, working as a clerk at the patent office at Bern and developing his ideas in his spare time. None of these great men needed a hugely expensive experiment. Their brains and a pen and paper to record the steps of their thoughts met, for the most part, their needs. I also remembered Professor CF Powell of Bristol University. His research was also into particle physics, and he received a Nobel Prize for the discovery of the pion. He did not do it by seeking funds for a large atom collider; he did it by sending a pile of photographic plates to the upper air, lifted by some surplus meteorological balloons. Nature provided the source of high-speed particles, the cosmic rays from space. I also thought of my own voyage on the *Shackleton*: how little that research cost, yet its results still reverberate around the scientific community. So here was I, called to account in a high place to justify my opinion. With these thoughts in mind, I answered Tsutomu Hata's question by saying that a better use for the billions might be to fund a series of smaller scientific projects, especially those of environmental importance. I have no idea whether this personal counsel carried weight in the decision by Japan to withdraw from that very expensive project. There was already a particle collider at CERN in Switzerland. I wondered whether one of these monuments of big science was not enough.

When we left Coombe Mill for Japan, Sandy and I did not know about Hideo Itokowa's standing in Japan. We did know that he had been the Japanese equivalent of our own beloved designer and inventor, Barnes Wallis. Hideo had designed the Zero fighter aircraft used during the Second World War, and after the war he turned his talents to space engineering, to violin design and to founding the Systems Research Institute of Japan. But in England, I can think of no scientist or inventor who could invite the Chancellor of the Exchequer to a private lunch with a visiting foreign scientist. We wondered what was next in store for us. After lunch we all travelled by taxi to the main railway station where Ann, Hideo's wife, met us with drinks of iced tea. She was an engaging, young middle-aged Japanese woman. Her laughter and the warmth of her welcome told us how much we would enjoy ourselves. Hideo had told us that Ann did not speak English but did understand it, and we communicated with her by speech and body language well enough. Soon we were all on the train to Ueda-shi. This was before they built the high-speed Shinkansen line for the 1998 Winter Olympics in Nagano, and the journey was to take several hours. As the train travelled, we realized for the first time what an urban country Japan is. We seemed to pass a never-ending succession of factories, houses, and tiny green plots of rice. Not until we reached the central mountains did we see the natural landscape appear.

When we left the train there was a sizeable group to meet us, and across the platform hung banners in English and Japanese saying 'Welcome to Dr James Lovelock'. They were treating us like royalty or sports stars, and then they took us by car to Hideo's 'country cottage'. It was a traditional Japanese farmhouse, built of wood and located just outside the small town of Ueda. It was an old building that they had moved from a site elsewhere in Japan. Hideo took us to our room, which had a futon and en suite facilities, and then we were able to look at each other and wonder about this extraordinary day.

The furnishing was sparse by western standards: the central room had a sunken area with a large low dining table in its middle. This was the important part of the house and where everything went on, just as in the spacious kitchen of an English farmhouse. We joined the family meal by sitting on the cushions placed on the rim of a rectangular depression in the floor. Hideo explained that in wintertime there would be a fire beneath the table for warmth. In all of our time here, and for the greater part of our two-week stay in Japan, we ate and lived in the Japanese way, and enjoyed it immensely.

Next day we took a short walk along the country lanes that went from the house to the hills. As we turned the first corner, there stood before us a huge violin, standing twelve feet high, beside the road. A quarter of a mile further uphill we came to an open-air theatre and concert hall, with its terraced wooden seats, and nearby was an enclosed concert hall, presumably for the cooler times of year. The idea that Japanese country life included a theatre and a concert hall within walking distance was a wonder to us. We walked on past small, about one-acre-sized, fields with whole families working in them. Much of the area seemed to be devoted to fruit growing—apples and the delicious *kyoho* grapes. It was perhaps the Japanese equivalent of Snape Maltings in East Anglia or Tanglewood in the United States. Having absorbed the influence of the countryside, we returned and prepared for an excursion to an active volcano. Jiro Hata and Hiroshi Yajima accompanied us to the volcano, which on this occasion was quiescent with the water-filled crater no more than a calm lake. Steaming vents and fumaroles exhaling their sulphury smells reminded us of the fire beneath. Hideo's friends were Takeshi Kanai, a local farmer who was also a software developer and an architect, and Motomasa Shimada, a prominent person in the timber industry and politically active in Nagano. They were a joyful company, making every day as if it were the best of family holidays; visits to exciting places, heavenly treats in Japanese inns and eating-places, and their warm and welcome company. In no place abroad had I ever felt so much at home. Without Sandy, though, I would have been over-whelmed with the kindness and the joy of it. Life as a hermit at Coombe Mill, and the long years of Helen's decline had not equipped me for the intensity of this welcome. Sandy is at home in any social scene and seems effortlessly to become a part of it. Alone, I would have felt awkward; together, we felt as if we were members of Hideo's extended family.

I gave three public lectures during this visit, sharing the platform with Hideo. I would speak the first few paragraphs of my speech in English and then Hideo would translate it into colloquial Japanese. It made an hour's speech last two hours, but the audience, to judge by their laughter and enthusiasm, did not mind. A bilingual friend told me after one of these lectures that Hideo gave a strictly accurate, although free, translation of my words. They were the most informal occasions: once Hideo stopped speaking, grinned, and asked the audience to excuse him because his bladder was full. He left for the lavatory behind the stage and returned after a few minutes. Among the places to which our tireless escorts, Hata and Yajima, escorted us were the Ise Shrine, and to Toba to see the pearl fishers; and for contrast we visited the industrial city, Yokkaichi. Few tourists to Japan go to Yokkaichi, as unlikely a tourist destination as would be Runcorn, in England, or Wilmington, in the USA. Yokkaichi is a chemical industrial town and was notorious in the 1950s for its pollution. In the 1990s, it was an example of how a city with an economy based on the chemical industry should be. In keeping with the protocol of our journey through his nation, Hideo had arranged for us to meet the mayor and members of his council and the business community. At a small informal banquet they welcomed us and let us hear the leaders of the Yokkaichi community tell us proudly of their climb to excellence. Once again, while I felt at home in Japan, there was this lingering doubt that someone more distinguished should have been in my place.

Near the end of our stay, Hideo and Ann took us to the resort town of Atami Springs, not far from Tokyo. Here we stayed the night, and after an evening meal, a group of us walked through the streets in our *yukatas* and sandals to a special entertainment that Ann and Hideo had chosen. The outside seemed like a small shop, and the entertainer and her husband welcomed us in. We went through into a medium-sized room, which had a raised platform, about a foot high, at one end. Initially our small group of about ten made up the audience, but several *geishas* joined us later. Our hostess stepped onto the platform, faced the audience, and began her show. At first, she warmed up her audience and made them merry; then she began her special repertoire of tricks. They were some extraordinary feats involving the muscles of her vagina. First she inserted a large cork, through which was threaded a length of strong cord, and she challenged the audience to produce a champion who could draw it out. No one who tried could and, after more demonstrations like this, she moved on to her pièce de résistance. She inserted a live goldfish and, with a flourish and a heave of her powerful vaginal muscles, expelled it into a bowl of water on the other side of the room. She did this several times and missed only once. Hideo told us that it had taken her years of patient practice to perfect her skill. In the West, such an exhibition might have been criticized as unseemly, but in Japan, it rated as impermanent art. Sandy and I both felt privileged to see this unusual entertainment and, as we left, the entertainer introduced herself and her proud husband. I could not help but think later, back in England, that the Tate Gallery might have done better to stage its recent Turner Prize exhibitions in Soho, as entertainment as well as art.

Our last joint lecture was due in Tokyo. Hideo and I put on our best effort for Gaia before an impressive audience, and our performance was embellished by a recital played on an Itokawa violin. So ended by far the most fulfilling and extraordinary visit of a lifetime. We felt as if a prince had taken us to his fairy castle and made our dreams real for two whole weeks, but the next morning the Itokawa motorcade took us back to Narita Airport. It was truly a family farewell, and a sad one to judge by the tears that flowed, and we boarded our BA flight back to London feeling that it would transport us from an elevated plane to which we could never return. Our flight home in the comfort of the plane enhanced this feeling. As we flew over the icy forests and mountains of Siberia, they seemed to radiate thoughts of Gulags, torture, and privation. The remembered joy of our visit to Japan, and the comfort as we flew were an almost unbearable contrast to what was once below us.

The last we saw of Hideo and Ann was in November 1997. We travelled from Tokyo to Ueda City with Fred Myers to pay our respects to a dear friend, Hideo, now comatose from a stroke. In the clinical Western ambience of the small hospital, it was unbearably sad to see his small figure curled in a bed like a child. That fine mind, trapped in a damaged brain, could no longer express the laughter, fun, and deep thought that we had known. Hideo died in February 1999.

The 1990s have been the most fulfilling years of my life: the sustained joy of my second marriage, recognition by the international scientific community through the award of three major environmental prizes, one literary prize, the Nonino, eight honorary degrees and, most of all, a visit to Buckingham Palace to receive the honour of CBE from the Queen. I used to think that my work as an independent went unnoticed; that I was like an amateur runner who broke records running round his village green but was never invited to do so in the stadium. I was wrong. For those who would like to do their science as lone individuals, even from their own home, I think I can say it is worthwhile, and it really does work.

As we enter the 21st century, Sandy and I have a sense that we have paid and received our dues. We feel that the rest of our years together should be free of the tasks that we have disliked, but felt the need to do for duty's sake. Prominent among these for me is lecturing and attending meetings and, for us both, answering letters comes next. Instead, we plan to walk the 630-mile path around the southwest coast of England, from Poole in Dorset, via Land's End in Cornwall, to Minehead in Somerset. It involves a total climb of over 91,000 feet, more than three times the height of Mount Everest. This is no epic quest: for mankind it is a pointless and useless endeavour; for us it is a thrilling challenge and a joy to plan. We pore over the Ordnance Survey's Landranger maps that show in the most intricate detail every step of the path we will take. We do practice walks on the most difficult section, the north coasts of Devon and Cornwall, which are only twenty or so miles from Coombe Mill. Soon we shall be taking our long walk. We wonder what the next decade has in store for us.

13

Epilogue

'Why do you want to go to church?' asked Cousin Lily. 'Because I want to hear the bells,' I said. This happened one Sunday morning in April 1926, when I was at my cousin's cottage at Hagbourne in Berkshire. 'Well, off you go,' said Lily, 'and mind you keep still.' The footpath went straight by a field of young wheat, bright in the morning sunlight, and the air was sparkling fresh and full of birdsong. Then, suddenly, across the fields came that evocative sound of bells ringing their changes. Nearby, still worse indoors it is poor music, but heard coming from afar on a sunny Sunday morning, it is magical. I now know why John Betjeman chose to name his book, *Summoned by Bells*; I certainly was.

The track wandered on and under an iron railway bridge that carried the single-track line to Oxford, and there ahead was the village church. All I can remember is going in, sitting at a pew, and listening to the bells. Soon the pews filled and the service began. I do not remember how, as a small boy, I sat and stood through the long morning service, but I do recall the warm welcome afterwards. Who was I and where had I come from? Like the sunshine of the day, the smiles and approval of the congregation left me with a warm glow and let me wander back, as boys do, to Sunday dinner at Lily's cottage.

Things that happen in the period before puberty seem to set the course of one's life. This small event, in spite of my true calling, science, left me with affection for the Anglican Church, which remained until the 1970s when modernizers and the evangelists began to change it. To me, their campaign confirmed Aldous Huxley's prediction in *Brave New World*. They wanted a church led by an arch community songster, not an archbishop. They have all but succeeded in replacing the wondrous words of the Book of Common Prayer and the old Bible with something that fits their own limited understanding. What hubris, what vandalism.

Not long afterwards, back in Brixton, I repeated this Sunday morning trek to church. This time to a strange Byzantine-looking Roman Catholic Church at Tulse Hill, a few hundred yards from where we lived. The experience here was very different. No sooner was I in the pew than a verger came up, took me by the collar to the door, and said, 'Go away and don't come back, you don't belong here.' Catholics in those days were a somewhat beleaguered minority and knew each other; I suspect that the verger knew that I was not part of it and feared that I might be there to make mischief. My mother and my grandparents were strongly anti-Catholic; it was a tribal feeling common amongst working-class Londoners then. I suppose it goes back to the treason of Guy Fawkes and all that. My peer group of schoolboys linked Catholics with cruelty, torture, and the Inquisition. Guy Fawkes Day, the burning of the effigy, was to us the most important day of the year after Christmas. Luther's ancient schism had been tribalized, and the endless civil war of Catholic Ireland confirmed it.

Round about the age of seven I was, for a brief time, aware of sex and was strongly attracted to a girl in the first class of my primary school called Molly Percival, who was, I think, Catholic. I wonder if she is still around. This experience was brief, but it must have stayed in my unconscious thoughts for later, in adolescence, I found Catholic girls unusually attractive. This kind of vague religiosity did not fit in with my family's staunch agnosticism. The merciless slaughter of the First World War deeply affected my mother, as it did many English women. She saw a whole generation of young men pitilessly forced into the murderous abattoir of the trenches, and she was not about to have her son grow up in an environment where he would ripen ready to die in the next European war. During WWI, my mother's job had been that of secretary to the Clerk of Middlesex County Council, and part of her duties was to attend the hearings of conscientious objectors. She soon noted that only the Quakers were treated with any respect. This experience led her to enrol me at the Society of Friends Sunday school, which was just opposite to where we lived in Brixton. The Meeting House was a spacious, semi-detached Victorian house, situated in a pleasant garden and run by the Street family, some of whom had been active as conscientious objectors during WWI. The

Streets unhesitatingly accepted my mother's reasoning and were glad to take me on.

As a small boy, I doubt if I would have put up with the Sunday school of any other church for more than a few weeks. However, the Quakers were something quite different from other churches. Austere they may have been in their adult meetings, but with us children they seemed to compensate by offering enthralling entertainment. I shall not forget the wonderful stories, only rarely religious, that John Street told us, and which kept us rapt, and quiet. Nor shall I forget the open, unfettered discussions that we enjoyed on the lawn in summertime; as much about cosmology as religion, discussions that started me on the course towards a lifelong agnosticism.

Among the many devices the Streets used to keep their young flock entertained were film shows on Saturday afternoons. I do not mean the incredibly dull magic-lantern projections that most churches offered the inmates of their Sunday schools: dim amateur photographs of Jerusalem taken by the vicar on his holiday there. We had sixteen-millimetre films that were entirely secular, such as Felix the Cat and other cartoons, and we loved them and laughed until it hurt. These were the days of the old liberal philosophy of the Enlightenment, and no one I met as a boy questioned the idea of a benign humanism. The good of mankind was what truly mattered, and this was my religious apprenticeship at the Brixton Meeting House. God, if he existed, was no threatening figure, merely something somewhat vague overseeing the Universe. There was, of course, that personal God, who spoke to the Friends themselves—the still small voice within. Conscience, not the thunder from above, was what really mattered to them. It was easy with such a beginning to move into a comfortable agnosticism as science began to fill the empty files of my mind.

I lost touch with the Brixton Meeting House when we moved to Orpington in 1933. My mother, freed from the chores of sustaining a failing art shop, now had time to join the Quakers in Orpington. After a while, she became a Friend herself. For some of the time I went with her, but the serious although worthy air of the Kent meeting was somehow like a soft drink after the sparkling wine of the Street family in Brixton. So, until 1939, when I went to Manchester, I moved into my father's world, a communion with nature. I spent my Sundays walking or bicycling on the small roads and footpaths of the glorious countryside of Kent. The house that Darwin had lived in at Farnborough was only a mile or so from my home in Orpington, and often I walked past it on my rambles. I never thought of it then, but in 1997 when I talked with the eminent biologist, William Hamilton, he told me that his childhood had been enlivened by walks from his home in Sevenoaks, Kent, and we discovered that we had trodden the same paths. I wondered if Darwin had included them in his walks, and were we both treading his footsteps in our different ways.

I am a scientist and an agnostic but I am too much an animal to want to live exclusively in the intellectual world of modern science. So many people I respected for their intelligence and wisdom were religious that I could not help feeling curious about their faith. Over the years, I have occasionally attended religious services: these included Quaker meetings, services in all kinds of Christian churches, in synagogues, and in the temples of Asian religions. Good sermons have moved me, so have the glorious words of the Prayer Book, but never have I acquired faith. At times, I dearly wished to receive a 'religious experience', but always my world, even at its most beautiful, has been down to Earth. By middle age I came to recognize that heaven and hell were here and now and all around me. Once on my way to breakfast at a prominent Las Vegas hotel I walked past the gamblers who had sat and played their cards all night and such a grey misery marred their faces that I felt privileged to have seen Hell without being trapped in it. On mountains especially, there have been moments in Heaven and a longer spell has filled the last twelve years.

We long to love, to be loved, and to belong to some human group. Science may soon offer a complete explanation of these longings, but I suspect that we will still hanker after the transcendental. When romantic love transports me, I get no comfort from the knowledge that my passion is consequent upon the circulation in my blood of a simple steroid, testosterone. A pure almost spiritual joy comes from a discovery of science, or from a well-turned theory, but its quality differs from the passionate arousal of a love letter or a commitment to a tribal cause. The pleasures of science are in the mind, but poetry and music move our hearts as well. No matter how hard we try to make science popular, we will not wholly succeed: it is not merely strange and unnatural, it can never be other than provisional. Its truth and respectability depend on its honest assertion that it can never be certain about anything. This may be why great music does not bless science with praise. We turn to science fiction, such as that of the television series *Star Trek*, for science in a palatable form. It presents something that derives from science, but which is certain and can appeal like a faith.

GK Chesterton's comment that 'Those that give up their faith in God do not believe in nothing, they believe in anything' is much quoted by those who speak for the Christian religion. It sounds good, but does not pass serious test. It is true of cultist beliefs, but ignores the atheists, who are just as strong in their faith in nothing as are Christians in their faith in God. Moreover, atheists are sure that their faith comes from the true fount of knowledge, science. I am neither atheist nor have a religious faith; I put trust, not faith, in science.

Perhaps science is unpopular and popular science is shoddy because the public needs certainty. They expect certainty also from their leaders, and they expect it from their churches. Consider political leaders. Whatever doubts we had about John Kennedy as a man, there is no question that his charisma moved us, and all of us felt keenly his death. I regard Charles de Gaulle as a spiteful man who denied my country the chance to join Europe at its formation, and as an equal partner; he forced us to wait until we were no more than a feeble supplicant. But I acknowledge his eminence as a strong and much needed leader of the French. If only we had had, at the time he rejected us, a leader of comparable quality; instead, we had Anthony Eden and then Harold Wilson.

When I speak of science, I am not thinking of technology. I am thinking of the vast accumulation of knowledge and understanding about life and the universe. It is our most precious possession, but except to its devotees, most of it is no more exciting than a library of books in a foreign language. Science and technology are not synonymous, but science inspires creative feats of technology that move us, just as do works of art: the seemly perfection of a bridge span, the grace of an aeroplane like Concorde, or the views of the planets from space. We see these with a thrill like that delivered by the sight of a cathedral or a painting by Vermeer.

As in a fictional murder mystery, the facts, revealed by the patient, honest, and cumulative investigation of Nature, tell us about our origins. They provide a convincing account of our evolution, that of the Earth, and of the cosmos. By comparison, as a source of factual knowledge, the texts of the religions are, at best, inspired poetry and, at worst, the befuddled imaginings of primitive peoples. Science has rightly taken away from the religions their authority to serve as a source of knowledge on life and the universe, but there is more to religion than its pseudo-science. It provides moral guidance and offers certainty.

As a scientist I know that I can never be certain about anything but I acknowledge that almost all of us desire certainty, and we seem to seek a certainty that is transcendental. Modern science can never give us this. It is too cold and too rational, and often seems to go against common sense. We are not evolved to act rationally; we operate most effectively by unconscious action and by intuition. Even in science when we make a discovery, most often we find that the kernel of it stole in by intuition, as an intruder in the night. The rational part comes later as the explanation. It is our nature to need something certain to follow and to lay down our lives for, something to inspire us to build cathedrals, where we can praise it in glorious music or art. Science so far has failed miserably to inspire in this way.

Lewis Wolpert recognized in his book, *The Unnatural Nature of Science,* just how unnatural science is. The detached, specialist, and unemotional science that brought the triumphs of particle physics and of molecular, neo-Darwinist biology is far from the strong internal drives that move us, and this is why it seems unnatural. Crick and Watson must have felt awe as the structure of the double helix of DNA emerged in their minds, but the science itself came from a long line of painstakingly professional investigation, an investigation where the too human wishes to guess, to take short cuts, were all suppressed by the overarching discipline of science. Our feelings and our urges may have a scientific explanation, but science has little influence in our hearts where these emotions operate.

We are still evolving animals, tribal carnivores. Detached thought and imagination are superficial; what drives us are feelings of hunger, love, hate, fear, and the messages of our senses most often have priority. It may not be as bad as Bertrand Russell's comment, 'The average man would rather face death or torture than think', but feelings come first. Because we are tribal animals, we respect hierarchy and follow leaders. We have an instinctive, perhaps genetic, need for a tribal leader: someone to fear, worship, and adore, to follow without question, and if need be to die for. Small wonder that the tribal chief and God formed a resonance and that religion is usually a part of tribal conflict. We seem to need to codify our political, religious, and even scientific beliefs in a legend. The legend soon becomes for us the truth about our leader, and the tribe. What makes the legend of science special is its capacity to self-correct: all other legends slowly lose touch with reality until violent change overthrows them.

I see us as so limited in understanding, so full of hubris about the wisdom of our discoveries, that we can never imagine the enormity of what we do not know. Among the few scientists who saw this was JBS Haldane, who wrote, 'My suspicion is that the Universe is not only queerer than we suppose, but queerer than we can suppose.' Consider a dog or a cat. These animals are conscious and in their way know the world. In some details, such as the world of smell, they know it better than we do; but we know far more about life and the universe than they will ever know. Now try to imagine an animal much more intelligent and wiser than we are. How would such an animal view our attempts at cosmology and theology? Although we may praise God as we pass the ammunition, we do not hesitate to demand that the scientist play his part in making better guns and shells. The power of science to win wars has helped it to displace religion but, strangely, science recognizes no tribal or national frontiers. It talks in a single language to all peoples of the Earth and is our trusted oracle. Yet, science is cold and bereft of feeling, and is not yet something that we can worship; by embracing science we have lost the comfort that religious faith brings. But, this could be a false view: it could be that modern science has yet to evolve a capacity to comfort as well as inform. The weakness of present-day science is in its love affair with reductionism, but it was not always like this. James Hutton, who lived in the 18th century, and is rightly called the father of geology, was the first to see that the Earth was far older than human history, and he glimpsed the possibility that it was like a living organism and should be studied by physiology. James Hutton's science was both reductionist and holistic and, in spite of Descartes, the top-down and bottom-up views coexisted in the minds of many scientists then.

I hope that the coming century will bring back balance to science. The frigid and unemotional face of science is that of reductionism, the taking apart of everything to find out how it works. It reached its nadir in biological vivisection, so prevalent until recent years. Vivisection, I feel, is something that we should do only when the need is paramount, and then done with that respect for life shown by a good countryman when reluctantly he cuts down a tree. Animal experiments, as we do them now on a massive routine scale, are not only amoral, they are a foolishly inefficient way of doing things. If I want to understand how the computer sitting before me works, the most idiotic thing for me to do would be to take it to pieces and analyse chemically the composition of its parts. That is reduction. Better by far to interrogate it through its keyboard and read the answers on its screen: that is the holistic approach. The same is true of an animal. Just imagine an intelligent robot that wished to know how you worked. You would prefer that it questioned you and recorded your answers, not cut you into pieces for analysis. Of course, we still need reductionist science, but we must not let it dominate.

The philosopher, Mary Midgley, has recently reminded us that Gaia has influence well beyond science. She said:

> The reason why the notion of this enclosing whole concerns us is that it corrects a large and disastrous blind spot in our contemporary world view. It reminds us that we are not separate, independent autonomous entities. Since the Enlightenment, the deepest moral efforts of our culture have gone to establishing our freedom as individuals. The campaign has produced great results but like all moral campaigns it is one sided and has serious costs when the wider context is forgotten.

One of these costs is our alienation from the physical world. She went on to say:

> We have carefully excluded everything non-human from our value system and reduced that system to terms of individual self interest. We are mystified—as surely no other set of people would be—about how to recognise the claims of the larger whole that surrounds us—the material world of which we are a part. Our moral and physical vocabulary, carefully tailored to the social contract leaves no language in which to recognise the environmental crisis.

Mary Midgley did not exclude science from her vision of our alienation from the material world. We now know enough about living organisms and the Earth System to see that we cannot explain them by reductionist science alone. The deepest error of modern biology is the entrenched belief that organisms interact only with other organisms and merely adapt to their material environment. This is as wrong as believing that the people of a village interact with their neighbours but merely adapt to the material conditions of their cottages. In real life, both organisms and people change their environment as well as adapting to it. What matters are the consequences: if the change is for the better then those who made it will prosper; if it is for the worse then the changers risk extinction. Reductionist science grew from the clockwork logic of Descartes. It can only partially explain anything alive. Living things also use the circular logic of systems, where cause and effect merge, and where there is the miracle of emergence.

Strangely, a statesman led me to think similar thoughts to those of Mary Midgley. That noble and brave man, Václav Havel, stirred me to see that science could evolve from its self-imposed reductionist imprisonment. His courage against adversity gave his words authority. When Havel was awarded the Freedom Medal of the United States he took as the title of his acceptance speech, 'We are not alone nor for ourselves alone'. He reminded us that science had replaced religion as the source of knowledge but that modern science offers no moral guidance. He went on to say that recent holistic science did offer something to fill this moral void. He cited the anthropic principle as explaining why we are here, and Gaia as something to which we could be accountable. If we could respect and revere our planet it would be to our, as well as the Earth's, benefit. Perhaps those who have faith might see this as God's will also.

I do not think that President Havel was proposing an alternative Earth-based religion. I take his suggestion as offering something quite different. I think he offered a way of life for agnostics.

Gaia has ethical implications that come from its two strong rules. The first rule states that stability and resilience in ecosystems and on the Earth requires the presence of the environment that sets firm bounds or constraints. The second rule states that those who live well with their environment favour the selection of their progeny. Imagine sermons based on these rules. Consider, first, the guiding hand of constraint. I can see the nods of approval from the congregation. Their own experience of the need for a firm hand in the evolution of their families and in society concurs with the evolutionary experience of the Earth itself. The second rule, the need to take care of the environment, brings to mind a sermon on the abominable transgression of terraforming—the conversion by technology of another planet into a human habitat. What is so bad about terraforming is its objective to make a second home for us when we have destroyed our own planet by the greedy misapplication of science and technology. It is madness to think of converting with bulldozers and agribusiness the desert planet Mars into some pale semblance of the Earth, when we should be improving our way of living with the Earth. The second rule also warns of the consequences of unbridled humanism. Early in the history of civilization, we realized that overreaching self-worship turns self-esteem into narcissism. It has taken almost until now to recognize that the exclusive love for our tribe or nation turns patriotism into xenophobic nationalism. We are just glimpsing the possibility that the worship of humankind can also become a bleak philosophy, which excludes all other living things, our partners in life upon the Earth. The bee is not complete without its hive; all living things need the material Earth. Together with the Earth, we are one in Gaia.

Our planet is one of exquisite beauty: it is made of the breath, the blood, and the bones of our ancestors. We need to recall our ancient sense of the Earth as an organism and revere it again. Gaia has been the guardian of life for all of its existence; and we reject her care at our peril. If we put our trust in Gaia, it can be a strong and joyful commitment, like that of a good marriage where the partners put their trust in each other. The fact that, like us, she is mortal makes that trust even more precious. Gaia should never become a religion, for then it would need a church and a hierarchy. Religions are all too human and fallible and in danger of sinking under the weight of their dogma; a Gaian religion would not be exempt. Gaia is part of science and is therefore always provisional, but the Earth, which is its embodiment, is something real for us to respect and revere. It is something much larger than we are and, unlike imaginary goddesses, can truly reward or punish us. What she does offer is an evolving world view for agnostics and this would require an interactive trust in Gaia, not blind faith; a trust that accepts that, like us, Gaia has a finite life span and is provisional. Gaia is not an alternative to religion but a complement. The great religions have already given us their prescriptions for living with each other in their parables. Gaia's parables, like Daisyworld, are for the Earth. Daisyworld illustrates the mortality of Gaia and that, for every change we make to our environment, there are consequences.

Now that my eightieth birthday has passed, I share some of the feelings that must afflict someone young that has just heard that he is HIV-positive. Our probable life span is about ten years—we may have as little as three but twenty is possible. What we both know is that the decline is under way, and it is odd but comforting to know that Gaia, were she sentient, would share our feeling that time was shortening. Like many females, Gaia is reluctant to reveal her age, but we know that it must be close to four billion years. We think that she has at most a billion years to go. The ineluctable increase of the Sun's heat as it moves to its feverish dotage sets a time limit for all life on Earth. If we change the scale by dividing Gaia's age by fifty million it gives eighty as the answer. In human terms, Gaia, like me, is eighty years old.

It may seem perverse, since I have no belief in a hereafter, that I do not share Philip Larkin's sadness about approaching death, so poignantly expressed in his poem 'Aubade'. Neither do I share Ludovic Kennedy's view from his eightieth year, where he sees himself in a departure lounge awaiting a flight to nowhere. He professes atheism, and perhaps this is why passing time bothers him. I regard the notion of personal life after death as wholly improbable, but I am not an atheist. The scientific evidence is now strong enough for me to take a chance and put my trust in Gaia. It is comforting to think that I am a part of her, and to know that my destiny is to merge with the chemistry of our living planet.

Index

Adrigole   205, 219, 224–5, 308, 311, 316, 336
aerial disinfection   74
air hygiene   84, 91, 101
Akimoto, Yumi and Sadako   xv, 396–398
Allaby, Michael   321
Ambrose Barlow Catholic Society   50, 65
Andreae, MO (Andi)   xiii, xxii, 260, 270
Andrewes, Sir Christopher   71, 76, 85–7, 105, 296
Asahi Glass Foundation   395

ball lightning   89–90
Barber, Edwin   273
Baylor University College of Medicine   145
Berry, RJ   383, 392
Birkbeck College   40, 47, 304
Bishop, Marcus   126
Bishop, Michael   361–2, 363
Bolin, Bert   xii
Boston   116, 119–25, 256, 257, 329, 330, 332, 333

Bourdillon, RB   69, 71, 72, 74, 77, 81, 82, 84
Bower, Frank   216, 223
Bowerchalke   1, 36, 86, 130, 131, 134, 136–7, 140, 145, 156, 172, 173, 174, 204, 205, 206, 207, 208, 217, 218, 281, 287, 295, 306, 314, 315, 383
Brand, Stewart   xv, 267
Brazzos Limited   153, 252, 283
Brixton   9, 12–13, 15, 16, 18, 19, 20–2, 24, 25, 27, 28, 30, 32, 35, 39, 119, 355
   Brixton Hill Galleries   9
   Friends Meeting House   46, 411
   Library   15, 21–2, 29
   Prison   16, 355
   Street family   55, 410
Buffington, Bill and Rosemary   185
burns   83, 183

Cathedral of St John the Divine   316, 345, 373, 374
Chamberlain, Douglas   345–8

Charlson, Robert   xii, 260, 269
chlorofluorocarbons
    (CFC's)   191, 206, 220,
    226, 231, 233, 235, 330
Cicerone, Ralph   217, 219,
    399
cloud algal connection
  cloud condensation nuclei
    (CCN)   xxiii, 184, 271
  dimethyl sulphide (DMS)
    206, 208, 260, 270, 311,
    380
  discussion with Robert
    Charlson   269
  spora and Gaia   274
Co-Evolution Quarterly   267
Common Cold Research Unit
    (Harvard Hospital)   85–8,
    99, 105
common cold   81–2
conscientious objector   46, 53,
    67, 69, 388
Coombe Mill   314–16, 318–20,
    321–3, 339, 340, 341, 343,
    344, 348, 384
Corner, Eric   300
Cornforth, Sir John   137, 160
cryobiology   109, 112, 126
  dimethyl sulphoxide
    (DMSO)   126
  freezing and reanimation of
    animals   125, 126, 127
  glycerol   107, 108, 109, 111,
    126
  preservation of living cells
    124
Culverhouse, Betty
    Hyslop   382, 385

Daisyworld   xiv, 264–7, 270,
    292, 343, 418
Dale Barns   56

Dale, Sir Henry   66, 71, 78
D'Arcy Hart, Phillip   137
Dartmoor National Park
    324–5
Dawkins, Richard   xii, 264,
    265, 266
de Duve, Christian   256, 272
DeBakey, Michael   333, 352
Delahunty, Mary (McGowan)
    51, 57, 58, 63–5
Denton, Sir Eric   XV, 298,
    299, 300, 337, 338
diathermy   108, 114, 125,
    188
Dimmick, Keene   140
Doolittle, W Ford   xii, 264
Dumbell, Keith   86, 99, 128
Dupont Corporation   216,
    220, 300

Ehalt, Dieter   259
environmental pollutants
  lead   26
  mercury   26, 79
  PAN   234–7
  smog   24–5, 27, 203, 204,
    205, 234, 235, 251
Evans, Ron   139
Evans, Sir David   73
evaporite deposits   109

Federal Aviation Administration
    (FAA)   xiii, 219
Fellgett, Peter   xi, 206, 323
flying saucers   88–9
Foulger, Brian   177, 229, 383
Frazer, Lorna   xxi, 127

Gaia
  charity   xvi, 267, 318, 322
  criticisms   3, 111–12, 264–5,
    271

definition   2–3, 5
ethics   278–9, 392, 417–8
first ideas about   241, 245, 254
mathematical model, *see* Daisyworld   264, 266
mechanisms   184, 278–9
naming   3, 255
Oxford meetings   xv, 275–6
phenomenon of emergence   265, 278
rock weathering, biochemical   268
Society   277
theory   xi, 6, 251, 259, 277–9, 282, 310, 388
Garrels, Robert   xii, xiv, xxii, 268, 281
gas chromatography   128–9, 131–3, 139, 140
geophysiology   272
George, Philip   277
Gill, Eric   20, 64
Golding, William   3, 10, xi, xv, 255, 335
Goldsmith, Edward   xv, 267
Goldsmith, Sir James   267, 392
Gordon Conferences   216, 259, 274
Grafton Underwood   81–2
Grassland Research Institute   101–103
Gray, Sir John   300, 338
Green College Centre   273–4
Green College, Oxford   273–5
Green Movement   199, 311, 397
Grenville-Grey, Wilfrid   371, 373, 380
Guerrero, Ricardo   xiv, xxii, 262, 381

haematology
  coagulation   100
  lipoproteins   124
  red blood cells   108, 111, 137, 142
Hahn, JH   230
Haldane, JBS   23, 415
Hamilton, WD   xvi, 266, 278, 412
Hanson, Sir John   273
Harding, Stephan   xvi, 266, 279, 281
Harington, Sir Charles   80, 83, 105, 126, 127, 133, 134, 136, 141, 145, 158, 159, 245
Harvard Medical School   115, 116, 120, 122–4
Hata, Tsutomu   402, 403
Havel, Václav   279, 417
hedgerows   101, 102, 103
Henderson-Sellers, Ann   xiii, 271, 379
Hewlett Packard   180–81, 184, 186, 224, 282, 285, 293–4, 320, 339, 345, 401
Hiroshima   397, 399
Hitchcock, Dian   xi, 169, 246–7, 248, 253
Hobby, George   242, 246
Holland, HD   xii, 271, 276
Holsworthy Doctors   340
homeostasis   2, 111, 112, 261, 276
Horowitz, Norman   xi, 90, 254, 255
hospitals   80, 347, 350, 354, 358, 386
  Barnstaple   359–64
  King's College   349, 350, 355, 358, 359, 361, 363, 368

hospitals (*cont.*)
  Musgrove Park   362, 365, 368
Houston, Texas   147–50, 155, 156, 283, 393
Hutchinson, GE   256, 257, 263

Icarus   250
inventions   5, 131, 186, 190
  argon detector   129, 132, 133, 139–40
  electron capture detector (ECD)   129, 143, 161, 164, 170, 176, 180, 185, 191–3, 196, 198–9, 200, 201, 223, 225, 230, 292, 328
  ion anemometer   91, 195
  leak detector   5
  photoionisation detector   132–134
  transmodulator   289–90
  wax pencil   80
Ireland   205, 218, 224, 303–15, 410
Ishida, Kozo   396, 399
Itokawa
  Ann   xiii, 403–6
  Hideo   401, 402, 403–6

James, Tony   128, 130, 133, 137, 139, 140, 193, 195
Jarrell, Dick and Kiffy   123
Jet Propulsion Laboratory (JPL)   xxiii, 145, 177, 241, 246
Josias, Conrad   152
Jünge, Christian   xii, 211, 230, 231

Kaplan, Lou   xi, 252
Klinger, Lee   xiv, 255

Kloster, Knut   xvii, xviii, 274
Kumar, Satish   323, 343
Kump, Lee   xiv

Lane, John   323, 343
Leakey
  Felix   12, 22, 32
  Hugo   10, 30, 32, 267
  Papa   22
Leete, John   10, 32–3
Leith Hill   24, 27
Lenton, Tim   xvi, xxii, 266, 276, 278, 279
Lidwell, Owen   xxi, 70–71, 74, 76, 77, 81, 83, 84, 101
Lindisfarne Fellowship   xv, 345
Lipsky, Sandy   169, 196, 248, 285–6, 290
Liss, Peter   xi, xii, xiii, 9, 219, 236, 299
Lodge, James   xii, 205, 260, 329–30
London School of Hygiene and Tropical Medicine   84–5
Lotka, Alfred   257
Lovelock
  Andrew   109, 117, 118, 120, 344, 346, 348
  Christine (Curthoys)   xxi, 84, 92, 117, 135, 149, 204, 312, 382, 386
  Helen (Hyslop)   1, 4, 35, 69, 73, 86, 106, 109, 121, 124, 127, 130, 134, 135, 136, 315, 316, 319, 341, 343, 344, 348, 382, 384, 385, 386, 389, 390, 392
  Jane (Flynn)   xxi, 85, 92, 117, 149, 305, 382
  John   xiv, 10, 126, 323, 341, 382

Sandy xvii–xix, 274, 310, 329, 344, 372, 374, 375, 376, 377, 378, 379, 380, 381–4, 387, 389, 404, 406, 407
Tom xxi, 10, 16, 28, 31, 35, 182, 187, 303
Lowbury, Edward 86, 99

Machta, Lester xiii, 175, 260, 283, 314, 328
Maeda, Yasuaki and Keiko 396
Manchester University 33, 56, 67, 174
Manchester 61, 62, 63, 64, 66, 67, 68
March 7
Ann (Mason) 10, 34
Florrie (Leete) 10, 32
Frank 10, 34
Grandfather Ephraim William 8, 10, 12
Grandmother Alice Emily 10, 11, 34, 35
Kit (Leakey) 10, 12, 22, 30, 32
Nell (Lovelock) 7, 11, 15, 25, 31, 35, 63, 65, 134–6, 174, 303, 411
Margulis, Lynn xi–xiv, xxii, 222, 254, 256–7, 259, 260, 265, 301, 331, 332, 339, 345, 369
Marine Biological Association (MBA) xxiii, 91, 298, 302–3, 337, 381
Mars 150, 288
detection of life xvii, 90, 153, 242
Viking mission xvii, 242, 250–1, 283
Voyager mission 248, 250

Marshall, Howard 152–3
Martin, Archer 128–9, 131, 133, 137, 140, 193, 284, 287, 295
May, Sir Robert 297
Mazur, Peter 126
McCarthy, Ray 216, 223, 330
McIntosh, FC 73, 79
Medical Research Council see NIMR xxiii, 65, 69, 134, 141, 192, 213, 221, 300, 361, 389
Merryman, Henry 126
methane 161, 166, 176, 199, 211, 231, 236, 251, 252, 253, 259, 260
microwave oven 188
Midgley, Mary xv, 416–17
Molina, Mario 217, 220, 294
Montefiore, Bishop Hugh xvi, 55, 318
Moriyama, Shigeru xv, 397
Morton, James Parks 316, 373
Morton, Oliver xvi, 277
Murray, Bull, and Spencer Ltd 40, 42, 47
Murray, Humphrey Desmond 40, 41, 62
Myers, Fred xiv, 400, 401, 406
Myers, Norman 256

Nash, Thomas 130, 138
Nathan, Lord 392
National Aeronautical and Space Administration (NASA) xxiii, 144, 169, 282–3
National Bureau of Standards 227, 228
National Institute for Medical Research (NIMR) xxi, xxiii, 30, 66, 69, 106, 333

Hampstead 30, 66, 69, 71, 74, 75, 80, 82, 84, 85, 135, 191, 284, 306, 333, 372

National Oceanic and Atmospheric Administration (NOAA) xiii, xxiii, 175–6, 283, 327–8

Natural Environment Research Council (NERC) xxiii, 206, 299

New Age 264, 267, 274, 276, 277, 339, 342–3

Newton, Edward 43

Norton Croft 10, 12, 13

O'Boyle, Paddy 363, 364, 365, 367

Orpington, Kent 28, 56, 61, 411, 412

Orwell, George 4, 16, 51, 303

Osaka Prefecture University, Sakai 396

O'Sullivan, Michael and Teresa 224–5, 308

oxygen x, 167, 173, 176, 244, 251, 252, 253, 256, 262, 277, 288

ozone
stratospheric 217, 219, 220, 221, 223, 269, 294

patents 72, 80, 139, 186, 197, 283, 290

Pearce, Fred xvi, 275

Pearson, Jos and David 273

Percy's at Coombeshead 304

Peters, Jim and Chris 180, 182

Polge, Chris 107, 108, 112, 159

Porritt, Jonathon xv, 275, 339

Portland, Henry, Lord 388, 389, 392

Powys-Libbe, Jenny 339, 340, 343, 349, 350

Princeton University 254

Prizes
Amsterdam 192, 393, 394
Blue Planet 192, 319, 395
Nonino 394, 406
Norbert Gerbier 270
Volvo 192, 394–5

Quakers (Society of Friends) 46, 54, 55, 57, 67, 410–11

Rapley, Chris xiii

Rasmussen, RA 229, 232, 233, 234, 236, 237

Raymond, Frank 76, 81, 101, 102, 103

Reading University xiii, 205, 220, 393

Rees, RJW 137, 138

rock weathering (biochemical) xiv, 268

Rockefeller Travelling Fellowship in Medicine 115

Rothschild, Victor, Lord xiii, 159, 160, 161, 163, 166, 167, 168, 171, 172, 174, 176, 249, 298

Rowe, Charles 131

Rowland, Sherwood 217, 219, 220, 229, 260

Royal Society of Chemistry 21

Royal Society 66, 81, 90, 108, 124, 125, 126, 127, 145, 159, 219, 249, 250, 295, 296, 297, 298, 299, 389, 391

Sagan, Carl   xi, 248, 250, 253, 256, 257, 373, 375
Santo Domingo   231, 232, 236, 237–8
Sargent, Margaret   323, 360, 384, 385, 395
Saunders, Peter   266
Schellnhuber, John   xiv, 277
Schumacher College   266, 323, 343, 388
Schwartzman, David   xiv, 268
Schweisfurth-Stiftung   xiii
scrub typhus   76–8
Security Services   169–79
Seiler, Wolfgang   211, 230
Shearer, Walter   xiv, 361, 362
Shell Corporation   161–8
Ships   14, 92–8, 208–9, 210–3
   Carmania   156, 160
   HMS Vengeance   xxi, 91–2
   HMS Victorious   90
   Queen Mary   94, 117–19
   Royal Sovereign   14–5
   RV Challenger   299
   RV Meteor   231, 237
   RV Shackleton   xxi, 206–11, 225–7, 229, 230, 231, 232, 233
   Sir Frederick Russell   299
Silent Spring   144, 163, 199
Simmonds, Peter   137, 148, 177, 224
Smith, Audrey   xxi, 107–8, 111, 113, 125
Smith, Frank   92, 93, 94, 98, 99
Smith, John Maynard   xvi, 3, 275
spermatozoa   108, 113, 159
St Mark's Road   325, 387, 393
Strand School   16, 19, 28, 30, 42, 43, 135, 355

super-critical fluid chromatography   128–9, 131

Tellus   xii, 265
Thatcher, Margaret   xvi, 168, 389–92
Thomas, Gordon   169, 246
Thompson, Keith   85
Thompson, William Irwin   xiii, 345, 382
Tickell, Sir Crispin   xv, 273, 274, 277, 302, 319, 390, 391, 392
Todd, Alexander, Lord   xiii, 48, 51, 64, 66, 67, 70, 159, 228, 255
trace gases   282
   dimethyl sulphide (DMS)   xiii, xxiii, 206, 208, 260, 270, 311, 380
   methyl chloride   218, 219
   methyl iodide   206, 210, 218, 311, 328
Tuck, Adrian   217, 219, 255

U.S. National Academy of Sciences   115, 226, 254
United Nations University   xiv, xxiii, 184, 345, 361, 362, 374, 400
University of Houston   145, 147, 149, 393

Van den Ende, M   75–7
Volk, Tyler   xiv, 268

WG Pye of Cambridge   139, 181, 282
Walker, James   263
Warner, Ann   300
Warren, Steven   xiii, 270

Watson, Andrew   xii, xiii, 206,
    264, 265, 268, 299
Weaver, Harry and Ellen   186
Westbroek, Peter   xiv, 265
Whitfield, Michael   xiv, 268,
    298, 300
Windscale   143
Wolpert, Lewis   414

Yale University   169, 196, 248,
    263, 286

Zlatkis
    Albert   145, 147, 148, 153,
        180, 186, 248
    Esther   147